Nelson's Annual Preacher's Sourcebook

2010 EDITION

DAVID WHEELER AND
KENT SPANN, EDITORS

THOMAS NELSON
Since 1798

NASHVILLE   DALLAS   MEXICO CITY   RIO DE JANEIRO   BEIJING

Published in Nashville, Tennessee, by Thomas Nelson. Thomas Nelson is a trademark of Thomas Nelson, Inc.

Thomas Nelson, Inc., titles may be purchased in bulk for educational, business, fund-raising, or sales promotional use. For information, please email SpecialMarkets@Thomas Nelson.com.

Unless otherwise indicated, Scripture quotations marked NKJV are taken from THE NEW KING JAMES VERSION. © 1982 by Thomas Nelson, Inc. Used by permission. All rights reserved.

Scripture quotations noted KJV are taken from the Holy Bible, King James Version.

Scripture quotations marked NIV are taken from the HOLY BIBLE: NEW INTERNA-TIONAL VERSION®. © 1973, 1978, 1984 by International Bible Society. Used by permission of Zondervan Publishing House. All rights reserved.

Scripture quotations marked NASB are taken from the NEW AMERICAN STANDARD BIBLE®. © The Lockman Foundation 1960, 1962, 1963, 1968, 1971, 1972, 1973, 1975, 1977, 1995. Used by permission.

Scripture quotations marked NRSV are taken from the NEW REVISED STANDARD VERSION of the Bible. © 1989 by the Division of Christian Education of the National Council of the Churches of Christ in the U.S.A. All rights reserved.

Scripture quotations marked NLT are taken from the *Holy Bible,* New Living Transla-tion. © 1996. Used by permission of Tyndale House Publishers, Inc., Wheaton, Illinois 60189. All rights reserved.

Scripture quotations marked GNT are taken from THE GOOD NEWS TRANSLATION. © 1976, 1992 by The American Bible Society. Used by permission. All rights reserved.

Scripture quotations marked HCSB are taken from the *Holman Christian Standard Bible* (HCSB). © 1999, 2000, 2002, 2003 by Holman Bible Publishers, Nashville, Tennessee. All rights reserved.

Scripture quotations marked MSG are taken from *The Message* by Eugene H. Peterson. © 1993, 1994, 1995, 1996, 2000. Used by permission of NavPress Publishing Group. All rights reserved.

Typesetting by ProtoType Graphics, Mount Juliet, Tennessee.

Wheeler, David and Spann, Kent (ed.)
  Nelson's annual preacher's sourcebook, 2010 edition.

ISBN 10: 1-4185-4150-8
ISBN 13: 978-1-4185-4150-7

Printed in the United States of America

2 3 4 5 6 7 8 — 12 11 10 09

Table of Contents

Special Occasion Sermons

Funeral Sermons

Special Services

Foreword

Stop!

Take a deep breath!

It's hard to believe that we are almost an entire decade into the new millennium. We heralds of grace were so uneasy when it all began, weren't we? We stewed so over the ominous Y2K and lived through the horrors of 9–11. But we did it! We who preached all survived! What also survived was our sense of calling to the ministry, and the certainty that God is still in charge of history. He rises above the rush of our hurried years across the threshold of yesterday. I believe we were more important than we knew. Preaching and worship still depend upon us who desire to be the faithful men and women who read the times, number their days, and apply their hearts to wisdom.

To be sure, the changes in culture give the spiritually needy a new way of speaking, and a new way of listening. And we who preach the gospel are ever aware, however dour we may feel about the times, we must engage the world where it is, not where we wish it was. Hence *Nelson's Annual Preacher's Sourcebook.* Aware that the times we live in leave us too edgy to guess where our course to the future lies, this book has been carefully assembled. Even though a close-at-hand future, it is an age of change and may frighten us too, but it shouldn't paralyze us. Every age is an age of change. It is said that as the first pair heard the gates of Eden clang shut behind them, Adam turned to Eve and said, "My dear, we are living in an age of transition."

How do we speak to a world that seems increasingly disinterested in our words and world view? Preaching has always taken its task seriously. The world still needs to be called to repentance, just as it did when the Baptizer appeared in the thickets of Jordan crying, "Get it right, right now, for the kingdom of Heaven is at hand." So what is new since that day? Not much. Jesus was about to enter an unappreciative world, when John came preaching. He is still entering daily into an unappreciative world.

But he has us, doesn't he? We may not feel that we are the cleverest of preachers, but we are committed to his agenda of redemption. We go on because we know the power of the Spirit can still blaze with fire and roar with wind. We also know for certain that God continually uses the foolishness of preaching to confound the wiseacres of this world. We have seen with our eyes the failure of the social sciences in their attempt to change a world into utopia. We have also seen with our eyes what happens when the renovating Spirit touches dead hope and energizes dreamless souls with the power of change. So we know we can never abandon the trust committed to us by God.

But helping God reclaim His fallen world is harder than we imagine. We all want to be roaring lions of authority, and yet we who hunger to communicate God's Word should do a little reading before we do our roaring. Maybe then light will fill our sermons where before only heat existed. Still, we all need a little help here and there. Our minds want to traffic in bright, engaging sermons, but producing them at the rate of at least one a week gets a little demanding. And when we think we have written and preached the right one, we are sometimes disappointed. Why? Because we all have those down days of empty homilies we dreamed would be better than they were. We wanted the Spirit, but he seemed miles away in Orlando. Could we who want to proclaim a great gospel, have been so dull only last Sunday? Why could we not rivet our needy flock to our sermon?

The *Nelson's Annual Preacher's Sourcebook* holds within it a wealth of ideas and sermon starters, illustrations, and articles on homiletics. Of course it is possible to read this book and still preach a gospel dud once in a while. But if you take this volume seriously, it ought to improve your preaching by some heavenly percentage.

At least this is the hope of us who have toiled to produce this volume. We who have worked on it are all preachers. And we have all had ugly Sundays when we felt we were miserable failures at the art of proclamation. Still, here in this little book is the glory of our art, and we are all together in our common hunger for excellence. We, who have put together this little volume of homiletical first aid, confess that we too have had our bad Sundays, but we want to do it better in 2010 than we did in 2009.

So here is our best effort! Read it, study it, argue with it, and doubt it! Just don't ignore it. For this volume comes as counsel between brothers, to the glorious end that we all wish for our world: the enlargement of the kingdom of God.

Calvin Miller
Birmingham, Alabama

Introduction

William Ralph Inge, Dean of St. Paul's of London, said, "When our first parents were driven out of Paradise, Adam is believed to have remarked to Eve: 'My dear, we live in an age of *transition.*'" How true!

This is a transition time for *Nelson's Annual Preacher's Sourcebook.* Since its launch in 2002 it has been ably guided by Robert J. Morgan. He was its creator. He was its lifeblood. He made it what it is today. After eight years at the helm, he decided it was time to pass the mantle, to make the transition. The mantle landed on the shoulders of Dr. David Wheeler and Dr. Kent Spann. We can only pray that we will be worthy of wearing the mantle. Robert, you have set a high standard for us.

For those of you who have used the *Sourcebook* for years, you will see much of the same but also some new. You will still get the trademark three sermons for each Sunday of the year. You will still read inspiring stories of great men of the faith from the past. You will also find the much needed funeral sermon to help you during times of death in your church. The special service registry is a staple item.

There are some new elements this year that we hope will encourage you. One is the section entitled "Sharpening Your Preaching Skills." The focus of this section is developing skills to help you be a better preacher. This year we are honored to have Dr. Calvin Miller contributing to this section. Another new chapter is "Shepherding the Shepherd," which focuses on you being the shepherd of God's flock. Whether you are full-time or bi-vocational, pastoring takes a toll on the man of God. This chapter is designed to encourage you, as well as keep you focused on the main components of ministry. Dr. Rich Halcombe's article will challenge you to love your spouse; while Dr. Mark Fuller's article will call you to a life of purity. Finally, you find a new segment called "Shepherding God's People." This segment will provide pastoral helps as you pastor your flock. Dr. Mark Becton, Senior Pastor at Grove Avenue Baptist Church, is our featured writer. His article "Ministering in a Time of Death" provides valuable insights into how to care for our people during this season of life.

One of the new features that will be extremely helpful to the pastor and his worship leader are fully developed worship services corresponding with the Sunday morning message. Dr. Vernon Whaley of

Liberty University has constructed services that include some traditional and contemporary material. As an additional help the source for the material is listed with each service. There is also a new section called "Special Services." There you will find services for special occasions such as a baby dedication or a Christmas Eve service.

This year's sermons are a collection of old and new, the best from previous years mixed in with new material. The sermons are organized in series so you can create a flow in your preaching. Preaching in a series helps the preacher in his sermon preparation; it also helps God's people get a better grasp of a subject. Of course, any sermon can be pulled out of its series and preached individually. There are two new exciting series this year. Tony Perkins, President of the Family Research Council, and Dr. Kenyn Cureton, Vice President for Church Ministries with the Family Research Council in Washington, DC, have written an inspiring series on the family. If ever there was a time we needed to preach on the family, it is now. Dr. Jerry Sutton has written a four-part series on the doctrine of the church that will remind your people of the importance of the church in God's plan for the ages.

It is our sincere desire that this volume encourage you in the trenches of ministry. There is no more important work than preaching and pastoring. If this volume has been helpful to you, we would love to hear from you. You can contact Kent Spann at spann@highlandgrovecity.org; David Wheeler at dwheeler2@liberty.edu.

As always, there are many people we wish to thank. First, we want to thank God for giving us the opportunity to fulfill a life-long dream of writing. Right behind are our wives, Cindy Spann and Debbi Wheeler. Cindy read and edited all the new material . . . she is the master of red ink! Big thanks go out to the folks of Highland Baptist Church and Liberty Baptist Theological Seminary. They have prayed and encouraged us in this project. A huge debt of gratitude goes to our parents, who have loved us to where we are today. Finally we want to thank Michael Stephens, our Thomas Nelson editor, for entrusting us with this monumental task.

Kent's dad went home to be with the Lord in 2008. He didn't get to hear about this project, but he would have been so excited and very proud. This volume is for Dad Spann!

Contributors

Rev. Jason Barber
Senior Pastor of the North Main Baptist Church in Danville, Virginia
www.northmainbc.net

Dr. Mark Becton
Senior Pastor of Grove Avenue Baptist Church in Richmond, Virginia. Grove Avenue Baptist Church has the longest running live television broadcast in the nation. Webcasts and manuscripts of his messages can be found at www.wordsofvictory.net

Dr. Timothy K. Beougher
Billy Graham Professor of Evangelism and Associate Dean of the Billy Graham School of Missions, Evangelism and Church Growth, The Southern Baptist Theological Seminary, Louisville, Kentucky

Paul Borthwick
*Senior Consultant of Development Associates International (DAI), teacher
of missions at Gordon College, Wenhan, Massachusetts, and former Minister of Missions, Grace Chapel, Lexington, MA*

Dr. Stuart Briscoe
*Minister at Large, Elmbrook Church, Brookfield, Wisconsin, as well as a
prolific author*

Dr. John A. Broadus (1827–1897)
Southern Baptist seminary president and preacher

Dr. Kenyn M. Cureton
*A pastor for nearly 20 years and a pioneer leader in the values voter
movement, Dr. Kenyn Cureton also served as Vice President for Convention
Relations for the Executive Committee of the Southern Baptist Convention.
Cureton currently serves as Vice President for Church Ministries with the
Family Research Council in Washington, DC*

Trading Spaces: Understanding Your Husband's Needs (June 13)
Rewired: How to Communicate with Your Mate (June 27)
Maximum Patriotic Impact (July 4)

Dr. Al Detter

Senior Pastor, Grace Baptist Church, Erie, Pennsylvania

Wisdom's Protection Plan (January 17)
How to Treat Your Neighbor (February 7)

Dr. Ed Dobson

Vice President for Spiritual Formation at Cornerstone University in Grand Rapids, Michigan

Integrity in Doctrine (April 18)
Developing Mega-Faith (June 20)
Of Whom Shall I Be Afraid (July 4)
The Upside-down Kingdom of Jesus (August 22)

Dr. Jimmy Draper

Former President of LifeWay Christian Resources, Nashville, Tennessee

The Call from Without (March 7)

Dr. Michael Duduit

Founding publisher and Editor, Preaching Magazine, Franklin, Tennessee. He is also founding dean of the new Graduate School of Ministry and Professor of Christian Ministry at Anderson University in Anderson, South Carolina

A Model for Ministry (January 31)
Loving God with Your Mind (February 14)

Rev. Michael Easley

Former President of Moody Bible Institute in Chicago, Illinois, and Pastor and Teacher, Immanuel Bible Church, Springfield, Virginia

The Forgotten Secret of Happiness (July 25)
Strategic Planning (September 5)

Dr. Roy Fish

Retired Professor of Evangelism, Southwestern Baptist Theological Seminary, Ft. Worth, Texas

Blood on Our Hands (March 14)

Rev. Billie Friel
Pastor, First Baptist Church, Mt. Juliet, Tennessee

> Why Do People Stray? (June 13)

Rev. Mark Fuller
Senior pastor of the Grove City Church of the Nazarene in Grove City, Ohio

> Shepherding the Shepherd—Pink Elephants and Purity
> The Importance of Authority (May 16)
> When Authority Fails (May 23)
> Authority and the Body of Christ (May 30)
> Dealing Practically with Rebellion (June 6)

Dr. David George
Pastor, Lake Arlington Baptist Church, Arlington, Texas

> Faith in the Face of a Giant (July 11)

Rev. Peter Grainger
Pastor, Charlotte Baptist Chapel, Edinburgh, Scotland

> The Fear of the Lord (January 10)
> Come Now, and Let Us Reason (May 2)
> Who Rules? (May 9)
> No Gains Without Pains (November 21)
> The Light of the World (December 5)
> Passing On the Timeless Message (December 26)

Dr. Richard G. Halcombe, Jr.
Serves as the Director of Missions for Southern Baptist churches in central Ohio. We cooperate to network, resource and plant churches. I enjoy being married to Tina, who works as a hospice nurse, along with writing for various publications

> Shepherding the Shepherd—Loving Your Spouse

Dr. Jack Hayford
Senior Pastor, The Church on the Way, Van Nuys, California

> The Wholeness of Worship (February 7)
> Symbols of the Holy Spirit (November 7)

Rev. David Hirschman
Chair of Liberty Baptist Theological Seminary's Online Education Program

On Target (February 7)
The Greatest Love Story (February 14)
The Priority of God (February 21)
What Do You Want to Be Known For? (February 28)
Measuring Our Effectiveness (March 7)
Spiritual Progress (March 14)

Pastor J. David Hoke
Former senior pastor of New Horizons Community Church, Voorhees, New Jersey

Dealing with Satan's Strategy: Part 1 (October 31)
Dealing with Satan's Strategy: Part 2 (October 31)

Rev. Mark Hollis
Former minister of 15 years and current freelance writer in Nashville, Tennessee. Master of Arts in Pastoral Counseling

Avoiding the Big Blowups (January 10)
Remain in Me! (August 8)

Rev. Steve Hopkins
Leader of Bible Teaching and Leadership for the State Convention of Baptists in Ohio. He pastored for twenty-two years

Shepherding the Shepherd—Leader Development
Leading by God's Plan (August 1)
Leading by Revelation or Resolution (August 8)
Leading: The Cost Has Been Counted (August 15)
Leading: Finishing Well (August 22)

Rev. David Jackman
President, Proclamation Trust; Director, Cornhill Training Course, London, England

The Path of Wisdom (January 31)

Dr. David Jeremiah
Senior Pastor of Shadow Mountain Community Church, El Cajon, California, and founder of Turning Point Radio and Television Ministries

Dr. Calvin Miller

Professor of Preaching and Pastor Ministries, Beeson Divinity School, Birmingham, Alabama. Artist and author of over forty books

Foreword
Sharpening Your Preaching Skills—Retelling the Old, Old Story
Rahab: The Christmas Prostitute (December 12)

Dr. Robert Morgan

Pastor of the Donelson Fellowship in Nashville, Tennessee. He is also an author and speaker

Heroes of the Faith—E. M. Bounds
Why Prudence Isn't a Bad Word (January 3)
The God of Fresh Starts (January 3)
Gregarious Giving (January 24)
Staying Moral in an Immoral Age (February 21)
Knowing What to Say and When to Say It (February 28)
It Was Necessary (March 28)
Living Your Faith in the Work Place (May 2)
Making the Most of Your Nervous Breakdown (May 2)
A Mood-altering Prayer (July 25)
A Hurt Only God Can Heal (August 1)
God's Prayer Requests (October 24)
A Neglected Corner (November 7)
From Old, Even from Everlasting (November 28)
A Humble Holiday (December 12)

Dr. Stephen Olford (1918–2004)

Founder of the Stephen Olford Center for Biblical Preaching, Memphis, Tennessee

The State of Barrenness (February 28)

Dr. Larry Osborne

Senior Pastor, North Coast Church, Vista, California

Faith: The Spiritual Tool We Can't Live Without (May 6)
Spirit Filled (November 7)

Tony Perkins

President of Family Research Council

Rev. Richard Sharpe Jr.

Director of Small Church Ministries and President of Christian Home Crusade

I Pledge Allegiance to Jesus Christ (September 12)

Dr. Kent Spann

Pastor of the Highland Baptist Church in Grove City, Ohio, and co-editor of Nelson's Annual Preacher's Sourcebook 2010 Edition

Sharpening Your Preaching Skills—Expository Preaching Plain and Simple

Sharpening Your Preaching Skills—Planning Your Preaching

Special Occasion Sermons—Living Well (Funeral)

Shepherding God's People—Compassionate Hospital Visitation

It's the Gospel Truth! (April 4)

The Ultimate Sacrifice (May 30)

Praying for Us as Citizens (June 20)

Praying for the President (June 27)

Praying for the President (July 4)

Remembering the Unforgettable (October 24)

The Greatest Gift of All (December 19)

What Do We Do Now That Christmas Is Over? (December 26)

Rev. Charles Haddon Spurgeon (1834–1892)

Pastor, Metropolitan Tabernacle, London

Feeble Faith Meets Strong Savior (July 18)

Grace and Glory (August 29)

When Satan Attacks You (October 31)

Dr. Jerry Sutton

Associate Professor of Christian Proclamation and Pastoral Theology at Liberty Baptist Theological Seminary in Lynchburg, Virginia. He has ministered as Senior Pastor for 31 years and is the author of three books

The Church Is . . . Christ's Body (September 26)

The Church Is . . . Christ's Bride (October 3)

The Church Is . . . Christ's Building (October 10)

The Church Is . . . Christ's Beloved (October 17)

W. H. Griffith-Thomas (1861–1924)
Anglican minister, Bible teacher, and author

Chock Full of Christ (July 11)

Dr. R. A. Torrey (1856–1928)
American evangelist, pastor, educator, and writer

Eternal Life: What It Is and How to Get It (April 11)
Why I Am Glad I'm a Christian (November 14)

Dr. Vernon Whaley
Director of the Liberty University Center for Worship and Chairman of the Department of Worship and Music Studies in Lynchburg, Virginia

Worship services

Dr. David Wheeler
Associate Professor of Evangelism, Liberty University and Liberty Baptist Theological Seminary, Lynchburg, Virginia

A Time to Trust (January 3)

Rev. Drew Wilkerson
Pastor, Jersey Shore Church of God, Jersey Shore, Pennsylvania

Unbroken Cords of Friendship (August 22)
Pray! (September 26)

Dr. Melvin Worthington
Pastor, Former Executive Secretary, National Association of Free Will Baptists

How Can I Find God's Will for Me (January 24)
Jonah's Journey (April 25)
Thanksgiving Truths (November 21)

2010 Holidays

JANUARY

1st (Friday)	New Year's Day
17th (Sunday)	Sanctity of Life Day
18th (Monday)	Martin Luther King, Jr., Day

FEBRUARY

14th (Sunday)	Valentine's Day
15th (Monday)	President's Day
17th (Wednesday)	Ash Wednesday

MARCH

14th (Sunday)	Daylight Savings Time starts
17th (Wednesday)	St. Patrick's Day
20th (Saturday)	First Day of Spring
28th (Sunday)	Palm Sunday
30th (Tuesday)	First Day of Passover

APRIL

1st (Thursday)	April Fool's Day
2nd (Friday)	Good Friday
4th (Sunday)	Easter
6th (Tuesday)	Last Day of Passover
15th (Thursday)	Tax Day
21st (Wednesday)	Administrative Professionals' Day
22nd (Thursday)	Earth Day

MAY

6th (Thursday)	National Day of Prayer
9th (Sunday)	Mother's Day
15th (Saturday)	Armed Forces Day
23rd (Sunday)	Pentecost
31st (Monday)	Memorial Day

JUNE

14th (Monday)	Flag Day
20th (Sunday)	Father's Day
21st (Monday)	First Day of Summer

JULY

4th (Sunday)	Independence Day/July 4th
25th (Sunday)	Parents' Day

SEPTEMBER

6th (Monday)	Labor Day
12th (Sunday)	Grandparents' Day
17th (Friday)	Citizenship Day
18th (Saturday)	Yom Kippur
23rd (Thursday)	First Day of Autumn

OCTOBER

1st–31st	Pastors' Appreciation Month
11th (Monday)	Columbus Day
31st (Sunday)	Halloween

NOVEMBER

1st (Monday)	All Saints' Day
2nd (Tuesday)	Election Day
7th (Sunday)	Daylight Savings Time Ends
11th (Thursday)	Veterans' Day
25th (Thursday)	Thanksgiving
28th (Sunday)	First Sunday of Advent

DECEMBER

5th (Sunday)	Second Sunday of Advent
12th (Sunday)	Third Sunday of Advent
19th (Sunday)	Fourth Sunday of Advent
21st (Tuesday)	First Day of Winter
24th (Friday)	Christmas Eve
25th (Saturday)	Christmas
31st (Friday)	New Year's Eve

January 2010

Sunday

Date	Main Sermon	Second Sermon	Third Sermon
3	New Year's Sermon A Time to Trust By Dr. David Wheeler Joshua 6:6–11, 14–16, 20	Wise Up Why Prudence Isn't a Bad Word By Robert Morgan Proverbs 1:4	The God of Fresh Starts By Robert Morgan Psalm 139
10	Give Till It Feels Good The Joy of Giving By Dr. Timothy K. Beougher Philippians 4:14–23	Wise Up The Fear of the Lord By Rev. Peter Grainger Proverbs 1:1–7; 3:1–8	Avoiding the Big Blowups By Rev. Mark Hollis James 1:19–21
17	Sanctity of Life Sunday Choose Life Dr. Kenyon Cureton Deuteronomy 30:19	Wise Up Wisdom's Protection Plan By Dr. Al Detter Proverbs 2:11–22	Give Till It Feels Good How Should We Then Give? By Dr. Timothy K. Beougher 2 Corinthians 8:1–13
24	What's Right with the Church By Dr. Timothy K. Beougher Acts 9:31	Wise Up How Can I Find God's Will for Me By Dr. Melvin Worthington Proverbs 3:5–6	Give Till It Feels Good Gregarious Giving By Robert Morgan 2 Corinthians 8:13—9:5
31	A Model for Ministry By Michael Duduit 1 Thessalonians 2:1–12	Wise Up The Path of Wisdom By Rev. David Jackman Proverbs 3:13–26	Give Till It Feels Good Money Can Hurt You By Dr. Timothy K. Beougher James 5:1–6

February 2010

Sunday

Date	Main Sermon	Second Sermon	Third Sermon
7	The Wholeness of Worship By Jack W. Hayford Isaiah 6:1–8	Wise Up How to Treat Your Neighbor By Dr. Al Detter Proverbs 3:27–30	On Target By Dave Hirschman 1 Thessalonians 5:1–5
14	Valentine's Day Loving God with Your Mind By Michael Duduit Luke 2:19; Matthew 22:35–37	Wise Up Making Wise Decisions By Kevin Riggs Various Proverbs	The Greatest Love Story By Dave Hirschman John 3:16
21	Why True Love Waits By Joshua D. Rowe Various Scriptures	Wise Up Staying Moral in an Immoral Age By Robert Morgan Proverbs 7	The Priority of God By Dave Hirschman Romans 14:1–12
28	The State of Barrenness By Dr. Stephen Olford Jeremiah 11:3; 17:5; 48:10	Wise Up Knowing What to Say and When to Say It By Robert Morgan Proverbs 10:19–21	What Do You Want to Be Known For? By Dave Hirschman 1 Thessalonians 1:3–8; Hebrews 11

March 2010

Sunday

Date	Main Sermon	Second Sermon	Third Sermon
7	On Mission with God The Call from Without By Dr. Jimmy Draper Acts 16:6–10	The Revelation of Christ The Majesty of the Unveiled Christ By Dr. Denis Lyle Revelation 1:9–16	Measuring Our Effective- ness By Dave Hirschman 1 Thessalonians 2:11–14
14	Daylight Savings starts On Mission with God Blood on Our Hands By Dr. Roy Fish Ezekiel 33:7–9	The Revelation of Christ The Mastery of the Unveiled Christ By Dr. Denis Lyle Revelation 1:17–19	Spiritual Progress By Dave Hirschman Hebrews 5:11—6:1
21	On Mission with God Confidence for Soul- Winning By Dr. Darrell Robinson John 20:19–23	The Revelation of Christ The Ministry of the Unveiled Christ By Dr. Denis Lyle Revelation 1:17–19	Love Like There's No Tomorrow By Jason H. Barber John 13:1–5; Philippians 2:5–8
28	**Palm Sunday** Three Crosses and Two Choices By Denis Lyle Luke 23:32–43	It Was Necessary By Robert Morgan Luke 24:46–49	A Strange Invitation By Jason Barber Mark 10:17–22

April 2010

Sunday

Date	Main Sermon	Second Sermon	Third Sermon
4	**Easter** It's the Gospel Truth! By Dr. Kent Spann 1 Corinthians 15:1–11	Easter: How Do We Know and Why Does It Matter? By Dr. David Jeremiah Luke 24:25–27	Fear Should Not Be a Factor By Jason H. Barber 2 Timothy 1:7-8a
11	On Mission with God A Look at the Hereafter By D. James Kennedy Matthew 7:13–14	Eternal Life: What It Is and How to Get It By Dr. R. A. Torrey Romans 6:23	Lukewarm Laodiceans By Jason H. Barber Revelation 3:14–22
18	Integrity in Doctrine By Ed Dobson Titus 1:5–9	The Lifestyle of the Righteous and Faithful By Dr. David Jeremiah Ephesians 4:25–32	Powerful Prayer Walking By Jason H. Barber Acts 17:16–23
25	Jonah's Journey By Melvin Worthington Jonah 1–4	Outward, Inward, Upward By Paul Borthwick Matthew 9:35–38	Intentional Intercession By Jason H. Barber Genesis 18:16–33

May 2010

Sunday

Date	Main Sermon	Second Sermon	Third Sermon
2	Come Now, and Let Us Reason By Peter Grainger Isaiah 1:1–31	Living Your Faith in the Work Place By Robert Morgan Colossians 3:22–25	Making the Most of Your Nervous Breakdown By Robert Morgan 1 Kings 19:1–21
9	**Mother's Day** Extreme Home Makeover Divine Design: God's Plan for Marriage By Dr. Kenyn Cureton Genesis 1:26–28; 2:18–24	To Marry or Not to Marry By Dr. Timothy K. Beougher 1 Corinthians 7:1–9	Who Rules? By Peter Grainger Daniel 4
16	Extreme Home Makeover Marriage: Turning the Ordinary into the Extraordinary By Tony Perkins John 2:1–11	Taming the Tongue By Dr. Timothy K. Beougher James 3:7–12	Stay Covered The Importance of Authority By Mark Fuller 1 Samuel 15:22, 23
23	Extreme Home Makeover Trading Spaces: Understanding Your Wife's Needs By Kenyn Cureton Ephesians 5:22–23	Learning to Count By Dr. Timothy K. Beougher Philippians 3:1–10	Stay Covered When Authority Fails By Mark Fuller Genesis 9; Acts 4; 1 Samuel 24
30	**Memorial Day Weekend** The Ultimate Sacrifice By Dr. Kent Spann John 15:13	What the Gospel Means to Me By W. Graham Scroggie Romans 1:16	Stay Covered Authority and the Body of Christ By Mark Fuller 1 Corinthians 12:12–20

June 2010

Sunday

Date	Main Sermon	Second Sermon	Third Sermon
6	Dare to Be a Daniel By Dr. Timothy K. Beougher Various Scriptures	Faith Is the Victory Faith: The Spiritual Tool We Can't Live Without By Dr. Larry Osborne Various Scriptures	Stay Covered Dealing Practically with Rebellion By Mark Fuller Romans 9:11–21; 2 Corinthians 10:4–6
13	Extreme Home Makeover Trading Spaces: Understanding Your Husband's Needs By Dr. Kenyn Cureton Genesis 3:16; Ephesians 5:22–33	Faith Is the Victory Faith Amid Famine By Rev. Todd M. Kinde 1 Kings 17:7–24	Why Do People Stray By Rev. Billie Friel James 5:19–20
20	**Father's Day** Extreme Home Makeover The Prodigal Father: Returning to God's Idea of Fatherhood By Tony Perkins Luke 15:11–32	Faith Is the Victory Developing Mega-Faith By Ed Dobson Mark 7:24–30	How to Pray for the President Praying for Us as Citizens: Part 1 By Dr. Kent Spann 1 Timothy 2:1–4
27	Extreme Home Makeover Rewired: How to Communicate with Your Mate By Dr. Kenyn Cureton Ephesians 4:29	Faith Is the Victory Focus on Faith By Dr. Denis Lyle 1 Thessalonians 3:1–13	How to Pray for the President Praying for the President: Part 2 By Dr. Kent Spann 1 Timothy 2:1–4

July 2010

Sunday

Date	Main Sermon	Second Sermon	Third Sermon
4	**Independence Day Maximum Patriotic Impact** **By Kenyn Cureton** **Matthew 22:15–21**	Faith Is the Victory Of Whom Shall I Be Afraid By Ed Dobson Psalm 27	**How to Pray for the President** Praying for the President: Part 3 By Dr. Kent Spann 1 Timothy 2:1–4
11	How to Be a Star By Dr. Timothy K. Beougher Philippians 2:14–18	**Faith Is the Victory** Faith in the Face of a Giant By David George 1 Samuel 17:1–54	Chock-Full of Christ By W. H. Griffith Thomas Hebrews 1
18	Anchors during Adversity By Dr. Timothy K. Beougher Romans 5:1–11	**Faith Is the Victory** Feeble Faith Meets Strong Savior By Charles Haddon Spurgeon Mark 9:14–29	The Gospel According to You By Dr. David Jeremiah 1 Thessalonians 2:1–12
25	The Forgotten Secret of Happiness By Michael Easley Psalm 32	**Faith Is the Victory** Is Your Faith Genuine? By Dr. Timothy K. Beougher James 2:14–20	A Mood-altering Prayer By Robert Morgan 1 Samuel 1

August 2010

Sunday

Date	Main Sermon	Second Sermon	Third Sermon
1	**God-Focused Leadership** Leading by God's Plan By Steve Hopkins Jeremiah 29:11–14	Conditions of Revival Outline by W. Graham Scroggie Various Scriptures	A Hurt Only God Can Heal By Robert Morgan 1 Samuel 2:1–10
8	**God-Focused Leadership** Leading by Revelation or Resolution? By Steve Hopkins Joshua 1:1–9	**The Way of the Disciple** Remain in Me! By Rev. Mark Hollis John 15:1–8	The World Is a Dangerous Place By Kevin Riggs Psalm 3
15	**God-Focused Leadership** Leading: The Cost Has Been Counted By Steve Hopkins Luke 14:25–31	**The Way of the Disciple** Dead Center By Rev. Todd M. Kinde 1 Peter 3:13—4:2	Boast in the Cross By W. Graham Scroggie Galatians 6:14
22	**God-Focused Leadership** Leading: Finishing Well By Steve Hopkins Joshua 23–24	**The Way of the Disciple** The Upside-down Kingdom of Jesus By Ed Dobson Mark 10:35–45	Unbroken Cords of Friendship By Drew Wilkerson Ecclesiastes 4:9–12
29	How to Live in the Last Days By Woodrow Kroll Matthew 24:32–35	**The Way of the Disciple** The Marks of Discipleship Based on a Sermon by J. J. Luce Matthew 26:69–73; Luke 14:26–27	Grace and Glory By Rev. Charles Haddon Spurgeon Psalm 84:11

September 2010

Sunday

Date	Main Sermon	Second Sermon	Third Sermon
5	Strategic Planning By Rev. Michael Easley Nehemiah 2:9–20	**The Way of the Disciple** A Taxing Decision By Stuart Briscoe Matthew 9:9–13	A Man to Mimic By Dr. David Jeremiah Acts 7:54—8:1
12	Bringing a Friend to Jesus By Dr. Timothy K. Beougher Mark 2:1–17	**The Way of the Disciple** I Pledge Allegiance to Jesus Christ By Rev. Richard Sharpe Matthew 10:32	Daring Determination By Dr. Timothy Beougher Mark 2:1–5
19	**Be an Encourager** The Barnabas Secrets By Stuart Briscoe Acts 11:24	**Be an Encourager** Sons of Encouragement By Stuart Briscoe Acts 4:36	**Be an Encourager** Encouraging Others By Dr. Timothy K. Beougher 1 Thessalonians 3:1–8
26	**The Church Is . . .** The Church Is Christ's Body By Dr. Jerry Sutton Ephesians 1:22–23	Some Laws of Spiritual Work Based on an outline by John A. Broadus John 4:32–38	**Drop to Your Knees** Pray! By Drew Wilkerson 1 John 5:14–15

October 2010

Sunday

Date	Main Sermon	Second Sermon	Third Sermon
3	**The Church Is . . .** The Church Is Christ's Beloved By Dr. Jerry Sutton Ephesians 2:1–7	**Kingdom Workers** Kingdom Workers: Part One By Dr. Timothy K. Beougher 1 Corinthians 3:5–9	**Drop to Your Knees** Epaphras—The Man Who Prayed By Dr. David Jeremiah Colossians 1:7; 4:12
10	**The Church Is . . .** The Church Is Christ's Building By Dr. Jerry Sutton Ephesians 2:11–22	**Kingdom Workers** Kingdom Workers: Part Two By Dr. Timothy K. Beougher 1 Corinthians 3:10–15	**Drop to Your Knees** Praying with a Purpose By Rev. Kevin Riggs Philippians 1:1–11
17	**The Church Is . . .** The Church Is Christ's Bride By Dr. Jerry Sutton Ephesians 5:22–33	**Kingdom Workers** Kingdom Workers: Part Three By Dr. Timothy K. Beougher 1 Corinthians 3:16–23	**Drop to Your Knees** Pray for Us By Rev. Todd M. Kinde 2 Thessalonians 3:1–5
24	**Lord's Supper** Remembering the Un-forgettable By Kent Spann 1 Corinthians 11:23–26	**Kingdom Workers** Kingdom Workers: Part Four By Dr. Timothy K. Beougher 1 Corinthians 4:1–5	**Drop to Your Knees** God's Prayer Requests By Robert Morgan Various Scriptures
31	Halloween **Know Thy Enemy** When Satan Attacks You By Charles Haddon Spurgeon Job 1:1–12	**Know Thy Enemy** Dealing with Satan's Strategy: Part 1 By Pastor J. David Hoke Various Scriptures	**Know Thy Enemy** Dealing with Satan's Strategy: Part 2 By Pastor J. David Hoke Various Scriptures

November 2010

Sunday

Date	Main Sermon	Second Sermon	Third Sermon
7	**Daylight Savings Ends** **Come Holy Spirit** Symbols of the Holy Spirit By Jack W. Hayford Mark 1:1–11	**Come Holy Spirit** Spirit Filled By Dr. Larry Osborne Ephesians 5:15–20	**Come Holy Spirit** A Neglected Corner By Robert Morgan Ephesians 1:13–14; 4:30; 2 Corinthians 1:21–22; 5:5
14	Shaking Off Discouragement By Stuart Briscoe Haggai 2	Relationships in a Model Church By Dr. Timothy Beougher 1 Thessalonians 5:12–15	Why I Am Glad I'm a Christian By Dr. R. A. Torrey 2 Corinthians 9:5
21	Thanksgiving Truths By Dr. Melvin Worthington Psalm 100; 145	Amazing Grace By Kevin Riggs Titus 2:11–15	No Gains Without Pains By Peter Grainger 2 Timothy 2:3–7
28	First Advent From Old, Even from Everlasting By Robert Morgan Micah 5:1–5a	Devotions By Dr. Woodrow Kroll Psalm 19:9–11	The Lord Is My . . . By Joshua Rowe Various Scriptures

December 2010

Sunday

Date	Main Sermon	Second Sermon	Third Sermon
5	**Second Advent** A Root Out of Dry Ground By Rev. Charles McGowan Isaiah 53:1–6	The Light of the World By Peter Grainger Isaiah 9:1–7	Worshiping God by Name By Dr. David Jeremiah Various Scriptures
12	**Third Advent** Rahab: The Christmas Prostitute By Dr. Calvin Miller Joshua 2:1–6, 8–13, 17–21; 6:22–23; Matt. 1:5	A Humble Holiday By Robert Morgan Luke 1:39–54	Celebrating Christmas By Dr. Timothy K. Beougher Luke 2:17–20
19	**Fourth Advent** Who Is He in Yonder Stall? By Morris Proctor Matthew 1:18–25	Why Did He Come? By Dr. Timothy K. Beougher Hebrews 2:14–18	**Christmas Eve Service** The Greatest Gift of All By Dr. Kent Spann 2 Corinthians 9:15
26	What Do We Do Now That Christmas Is Over? By Dr. Kent Spann Matthew 2:1–12	The Wonder of Christmas and New Year's Day By Kevin Riggs Luke 2:52	Passing On the Timeless Message By Peter Grainger 2 Timothy 2:1–2

Preaching Series

Many of the messages are placed in series. Series offer many advantages. First, they assist the preacher in planning and preparation. Second, they build continuity for the audience. Third, they help the worship leader plan the upcoming worship services. Fourth, if you use powerpoints, visual aids, or notes you can create a visual aid for the series instead of one for each individual message.

The user is free to preach individual sermons out of the series, change the order of the sermons, select another time of the year, and change the title of the series.

Wise Up (January 3, 10, 17, 24, 31; February 7, 14, 21, 28)

This nine-sermon series is taken from different Proverbs. Add a few more Proverbs to extend the series.

Give Till It Feels Good (January 10, 17, 24, 31)

This four-sermon series will look at the blessing of giving in contrast to selfishness and materialism.

On Mission with God (March 7, 14, 21; April 11)

This four-sermon series challenges believers to be on mission with God. It focuses on evangelism and the state of the unbeliever.

The Revelation of Christ (March 7, 14, 21)

A three-sermon series by Denis Lyle from Revelation 1 that magnifies the greatness of the Christ of the Revelation.

New Extreme Home Makeover (May 9, 16, 23; June 13, 20, 27)

This six-sermon series by Dr. Kenyn Cureton and Tony Perkins calls for a makeover of the home according to God's plan. It focuses on the key relationships in the marriage and the keys to building a great marriage.

Stay Covered (May 16, 23, 30; June 6)

In this four-sermon series, Mark Fuller shows the importance of understanding and living under our God-given authorities. God has placed these authorities in our lives to protect us from harm.

Faith Is the Victory (June 6, 13, 20, 27; July 4, 11, 18, 25)

An eight-part series by various preachers looking at the characteristics of biblical faith as well as its importance and application in the life of the believer.

How to Pray for the President (June 20, 27; July 4)

In this three-part series, Dr. Kent Spann shares how to pray proactively and specifically for the leader of our nation. This is a great series for a mid-week prayer meeting.

God-Focused Leadership (August 1, 8, 15, 22)

Steve Hopkins puts into sermon form the principles he teaches in his article "Leader Development" in this four-part series. A great series to develop leaders in your church.

The Way of the Disciple (August 8, 15, 22, 29; September 5, 12)

A six-sermon series calling God's people to be real disciples of Jesus Christ. Believers will discover the characteristics and cost of following Christ.

Be an Encourager (September 19)

Stuart Briscoe and Timothy Beougher's messages on encouragement are sure to encourage you and your congregation.

The Church Is . . . (September 26; October 3, 10, 17)

The church is under attack from both without and within. The church is seen by many as irrelevant and obsolete. What is the church? Is it still relevant? Dr. Jerry Sutton shows why the church is so important to Christ and His plan for the ages.

Drop to Your Knees (September 26; October 3, 10, 17, 24)

The only thing the disciples asked the Lord to teach them to do was pray. This five-part series by various preachers challenges believers to pray like never before.

Kingdom Workers (October 3, 10, 17, 24)

There is one title that God has given to every single believer—"Kingdom Worker." There is no observation gallery in the Christian life. Dr. Timothy Beougher examines the biblical teaching on the believer's kingdom work.

Know Thy Enemy (October 31)

This three-part series takes a look at the enemy of the faith and his cunning strategy.

Come Holy Spirit (November 7)

God sent His Spirit at Pentecost. He now dwells in every believer. This simple three-part series reminds God's people of the ministry of the Holy Spirit.

Advent (November 28; December 5, 12, 19)

Advent provides a meaningful way to celebrate the Christmas season. *Advent* means "coming." In the Christian calendar it consists of the four Sundays prior to Christmas. A Google search will yield many valuable resources and sample services that can be used in celebrating the Advent season.

SERMONS AND
WORSHIP SUGGESTIONS
FOR 52 WEEKS

JANUARY 3, 2010

NEW YEAR'S MESSAGE   SUGGESTED SERMON

A Time to Trust

Date preached:

By Dr. David A. Wheeler

Scripture: Joshua 6:6–11; 14–16, 20.

Introduction: Several years ago I was supposed to catch an early morning flight out of Morganton, North Carolina. Upon arriving at the airport, I noticed that the fog was thick and holding low to the ground. Nevertheless, we boarded the flight a few minutes before it was scheduled to leave. We sat on the plane for about thirty minutes until the pilot finally shared the news that every traveler hates to hear, "Ladies and gentlemen, I am sorry to inform you that we cannot make this flight because the fog is too thick. In addition, federal regulations require at least one-quarter of a mile clearance before taking off. Again, I apologize for the inconvenience. Please deplane in an orderly fashion and we will do our best to get you to your final destination as soon as possible."

Passengers immediately began to leave the plane . . . that is, except for me. I remained in my seat for several more minutes and proceeded to have a conversation with God. I reminded Him that I had been away from my family and the office for almost a week and needed to go home immediately, if not sooner! I also recall stating that the pilot and the people in the tower had access to radar. They obviously knew how to use it!

With the flight attendant glancing my way, I remained steadfast until God responded by way of His still small voice. He asked, "David, do you know the pilot? After all, he could be a drug addict. He could have forged his pilot's license. In fact, you have no idea about his character or his flying skills. Still, you are willing to bet your life on his ability to fly through the fog!" It was then that God reminded me about the essence of trust and how we are so quick to dismiss the God of our faith. He said, "Assuming all of this is true, then I find it very difficult to believe that you would trust a man you do not know, to take you somewhere he cannot see, when you will not trust Me to take you where I can see."

Embarrassed and yes, enlightened, I deplaned and waited for the next flight. I will never forget taking off. When the plane finally rose above the clouds it was a magnificent scene. The mountains were glistening from the sunlight and the leaves were changing . . . it looked like a Thomas Kinkade painting! It was then that God spoke to me again. He simply said, "See, David. See what I see!"

In a new year, we must learn to view possibilities through the eyes of God. Just as the Israelites were on the verge of finally obtaining their Promised Land in Joshua 6, many congregations are at the same juncture . . . they must learn to fully *trust God!*

So . . . how did Joshua respond to the enormous challenge?

1. **Joshua learned to trust God's promises (v. 2).** In Joshua 6:2, God tells Joshua emphatically, "See, I have given Jericho into your hand, its king, and the mighty men of valor." We are reminded of two essential issues:

   A. **Truth is the essence of God's nature.** God cannot tell a lie. His nature is truth and faithfulness.

   B. **For proof, look to the past.** This reminds us about a similar promise that God made to Joshua in Joshua 1:2, 3. He states, "Now therefore, arise, and go over this Jordan, you and all this people, to the land which I am giving to them—the children of Israel. Every place that the sole of your foot will tread upon I have given you."

2. **Joshua learned to trust God's Plan (vv. 6–10).**

   A. **His plan is always to our advantage.** While God's plan may seem complicated and odd, rest assured that He always wants the best for His children.

   B. **His plan is never designed to exalt us.** Marching around Jericho was unorthodox at best. After all, no bombs or air assaults, just faithful followers trusting Him to provide.

3. **Joshua had to learn to trust God's Power (v. 11).**

   A. **His power is without limit.** God can do anything! The ark of the Lord represented His presence and power among His people.

   B. **His power is personal.** While the battle is ultimately God's to win, He allows His followers the privilege to participate. This is when we become representative of His provision!

4. Joshua had to learn to trust God's Provision (v. 20).

    A. Obedience comes before provision. The people marched as they were told; they shouted only when they were encouraged. As a result, "The wall fell down flat." Obedience is essential!

    B. God knows how to finish the job. The use of the emphatic word *flat* shows that God rewards faithfulness and is committed to fully meeting the needs of His children.

Conclusion: God has a promised place for every Christian if they are willing to be faithful. The bottom line, what can God do through you and your congregation in a new year, if you are willing to radically trust His leadership and calling?

SUGGESTED ORDER OF WORSHIP

The God of Fresh Starts

Prelude—Instrumentalist
    Great Is the Lord

Call to Prayer for the New Year—Pastor with all men at the front of church

Call to Praise—Congregation
    CH 353 *Victory in Jesus* (v. 1, chorus, v. 2, chorus)
    CH 513 *Thank You, Lord* (2x)

Worship in Prayer—Pastoral Staff

Welcome—Pastoral Staff

Welcome Song—Pastoral Staff (meet and greet during song)
    SPW 100 *Bless the Name of Jesus*—Congregation

Scripture Reading—Worship Leader with the Congregation
    CH 698 Selections from Hebrews, 2 Timothy, 1 John and Psalm 91

Praise and Worship—Congregation
    CH 171 *Come into His Presence* (2x)
    BH *Shout to the Lord* (2x)
    CH 705 *It Is Well with My Soul* (chorus, last verse, chorus)

Prayer of Dedication and Praise—Pastor
CH 599 *Jesus Is Lord of All* (2x chorus)

Worship with Our Gifts—Pastoral Staff

Praise and Worship During Offering
CH *Jesus, Name Above All Names*—(2x)

Message—*God of Fresh Starts* from Psalm 139—Pastor

Hymn of Response/Invitation—Worship Leader and
Congregation
CH 481 *Come, Just As You Are*

Hymn of Benediction—Congregation
CH *Great Is the Lord*

Postlude—Instrumentalists
Great Is the Lord

Additional Sermons and Lesson Ideas

SERIES: WISE UP

Why Prudence Isn't a Bad Word

Date preached:

By Robert Morgan

Scripture: Proverbs 1:4

Introduction: In our microwave, drive-through, 60-second society, we want things quickly. Some churches are now even offering "express services" for busy weekenders—worship services guaranteed not to exceed 40 minutes. Well, there is one book of the Bible, believe it or not, that provides wisdom in quick, bite-sized chunks. Drive-through wisdom. Microwave wisdom, in quick, fast chunks. It is the book of Proverbs. A *proverb* has been described as a heavenly rule for earthly living. It is when the *wit* of one becomes the *wisdom* of many. The ability to distill and condense great truths in simple, quotable statements makes for unique literature, and everyone from Benjamin Franklin (*Poor Richard*) to Yogi Berra has tried his hand at it. In Proverbs 1:4, we're told that one of the results of studying the book of Proverbs will be the acquisition of "prudence." In recent years, *prudence* has conjured images of prim and proper old ladies, or doddery, prunish old men. The related words *prude* and *prudish* have even worse connotations. But the dictionary defines *prudence* as "the ability to govern and discipline oneself by the use of reason; shrewdness in the management of affairs; good judgement in the use of resources." Since this is a quality most of us badly need, I would like to tell you that this word occurs 31 times in the Bible (NKJV), half of them (15 times) in the Book of Proverbs, where we learn:

1. **Prudent people are like cats—they know that some things are best covered up.** "But a prudent man covers shame" (Prov. 12:16). The NRSV says "ignore an insult." Matthew Henry said, "It is kindness to ourselves to make light of injuries and affronts, instead of making the worst of them." Most of us are too sensitive, too touchy, and too easily offended. It's often better to laugh off a criticism and complaint, to have a duck's-back attitude about the rudeness of other people. Prudent people don't take themselves too seriously.

2. **Prudent people give cautious answers.** The NCV says, "They don't tell everything they know" (Prov. 12:23). Jesus often withheld information, giving only partial or concealed answers. He wasn't being dishonest, but prudent. We don't have to say everything we know. Very often the wisest people give the shortest and quietest answers.

3. **Prudent people think ahead.** "[The prudent] look ahead to see what is coming" (Prov. 14:8 NLV). Most of us make spot decisions, without thinking through the implications. We make an impulse purchase, then suffer financial stress later when the bill comes in. We join a team

or club without considering how much of our time will be demanded. One of the earmarks of prudence is to "look before we leap."

4. **Prudent people have a healthy skepticism.** They don't believe everything they hear (Prov. 14:15). Most of us have learned through sad experience not to put too much stock in the promises of politicians during the election season. We need to practice the same cautious listening when it comes to what we're being told by the media and in the colleges and universities. Sometimes the experts and professors are still seeking for wisdom when the janitors and cooks have found it long ago.

5. **Prudent people handle correction well (Prov. 15:5).** When was the last time you felt defensive and offended? Perhaps your husband or wife made a suggestion about your behavior or appearance? Perhaps a co-worker or supervisor offered some unsolicited advice. Wise people listen to criticism, discarding what is invalid and heeding the rest.

6. **Prudent people study.** "The heart of the prudent acquires knowledge" (Prov. 18:15). Prudent people turn off the television and open the bookcase. They take classes and courses. They become personal students of the Scriptures.

7. **Prudent people take precautions (Prov. 22:3; 27:12).** They don't live in fear, but they fasten their seatbelt, establish an emergency fund, monitor their investments, do maintenance on their homes and cars, and guard against "the evil day."

Conclusion: According to Proverbs 1:1–4, we develop prudence by studying the Proverbs. Since there are 31 chapters, it almost seems that God intended for us to read one chapter a day. Since this is the first week of the month, why not ask the Lord to develop within you a more prudent mind and heart? Begin today with Proverbs 1, and read a chapter from this book each day, reading carefully, perhaps comparing one translation with another, and underlining the verses that most impress you. Memorize and meditate on the Proverbs of Solomon. And by the time February rolls around, you'll be a wiser and more prudent person.

The God of Fresh Starts

Date preached:

By Robert Morgan

Scripture: Psalm 139

Introduction: Psalm 139:16 says, "All the days ordained for me were written in your book before one of them ever came to be." At the beginning of another set of 365 days, we can find our bearing by considering:

1. God knows (vv. 1–4).
2. God dwells (vv. 5–12).
3. God creates (vv. 13–16).

4. God loves (vv. 17, 18).
5. God judges (vv. 19–22).
6. God sanctifies (vv. 23, 24).

Conclusion: Make this your prayer for the New Year: Search me, O God, and know my heart; try me, and know my anxieties. See if there is any wicked way in me, and lead me in the way everlasting.

JANUARY 10, 2010

SERIES: GIVE TILL IT FEELS GOOD   SUGGESTED SERMON

The Joy of Giving

Date preached:

By Dr. Timothy Beougher

Scripture: Philippians 4:14–23, especially 14–20

Introduction: When we buy something we usually get a receipt showing the date, product, and amount of purchase. Some receipts we discard, but others we keep for various reasons. A receipt is a record of a transaction that has taken place. The book of Philippians is a receipt acknowledging the generous gift the Philippians had sent the apostle Paul. Epaphroditus had made a six-week journey from Philippi to Rome to deliver this gift, and Paul had sent this letter back, saying in essence, "Received in Full." In doing so, he emphasized that the important thing in giving is not what the gift does for the recipient, but what it does for the giver. This passage describes four things that happen as we give. In giving, we . . .

1. **Become partners with others in ministry (vv. 14–16).** Paul emphasized that he had the ability to live in contentment in any and all circumstances through Christ's empowerment, but he didn't want the Philippians to think he was ungrateful for what they had done. He told them they had done well to share with him. The word "well" means "beautiful," and he later commended them in 2 Corinthians 8:1–5. There he indicated the Philippians had given out of difficult circumstances and extreme poverty, yet with overflowing joy and a desire to share in Paul's ministry. Whenever we support a ministry, we become part of it, partners in it. All over the world, people are hearing the good news of the gospel of Christ because we have given to the Lord's work.

2. **Offer a sacrifice pleasing to God (vv. 17–18).** Everything we do for the Lord counts (1 Cor. 15:58). Here we're told that the Philippians' gift was a fragrant aroma, an acceptable sacrifice, well-pleasing to God. It isn't so much the amount as the attitude that counts (as in the widow's mite in Luke 7). Paul credited the Philippians with the proper attitude behind their gift—a genuine offering presented to God to promote the spread of the gospel.

3. **Position ourselves for God's giving to us (v. 19).** This promise about God supplying all our needs is given to those who themselves are givers. Some have called this the greatest promise in the Bible, but it is not a universal promise we can claim apart from its context. Verses 14–18 give us the premise to the promise. Notice the parallel passage in 2 Corinthians 9:6–8: If we sow bountifully, God is able to make all grace abound to us, that always having all sufficiency in everything, we may have an abundance for every good deed. There are two extremes in religious circles concerning money: (1) God wants everybody to be a millionaire, the health/wealth gospel; and (2) Having money is evil. According to the Bible, having money is not evil, but making the pursuit of money the all-consuming passion of our lives leads to all kinds of evil. This passage strikes a healthy balance. It does not cover our *greeds* but our *needs*.

4. **Help change the world! (vv. 20–23).** Verse 20 is a doxology: "Now to our God and Father be glory forever and ever. Amen." As Paul reflected on God's gracious provisions, he burst into praise. All praise and glory is due the One who cares for us, who meets all our needs. In his closing greetings in verses 21–23, he indicated that the gospel had penetrated the highest strata of the Roman Empire. And—take note—the Philippians, through their giving, had a part in that! They were seemingly a small, insignificant church, yet through their giving they had impacted Caesar's household!

Conclusion: We give not to win His grace but because His grace has won us.

SUGGESTED ORDER OF WORSHIP

Theme: We Worship Jesus . . .

Prelude—Instrumentalists
   CH 42 *All Hail the Power of Jesus' Name*

As Savior and Lord . . .
Call to Praise—Congregation
   CH 42 *All Hail the Power of Jesus' Name*
   CH 102 *All Hail King Jesus*

Prayer of Praise—Pastoral Staff

Welcome—Pastoral Staff

Hymn of Welcome—(meet and greet during song)—
Congregation
MSPW2 *Lord, I Lift Your Name on High* (2x)

As Shelter and Refuge . . .

Praise and Worship—Congregation
SPW 39 *In His Time* (2x)
MSPW 22 *Crown Him King of Kings* (2x)

Worship by Hearing the Word—Pastor, Psalm 139:1–18; 23, 24
CH 583 *You Are My All in All* (2x)
CH 79 *My Jesus, I Love Thee* (vv. 1 and 4)

Prayer of Praise—Worship Leader (keyboard play next song
during prayer)
CH 591 *Have Thine Own Way, Lord*

. . . As Tower of Strength!
Offertory Prayer—Pastor

Offertory Praise—Congregation
SPW 74 *Isn't He?*

Sermon—Pastor

Hymn of Invitation—Congregation
CH 481 *Come Just as You Are*

Hymn of Benediction—Congregation
CH 213–214 *We Bring the Sacrifice/He Has Made Me Glad*

Postlude—Instrumentalists

Additional Sermons and Lesson Ideas

SERIES: WISE UP

The Fear of the Lord

By Rev. Peter Grainger

Date preached:

Scripture: Proverbs 1:1–7; 3:1–8, especially 1:7

Introduction: The opening paragraph of the Book of Proverbs summarizes the message of the whole book: "The fear of the LORD is the beginning of knowledge, but fools despise wisdom and instruction" (Prov. 1:7). There are two contrasting ways to live:

1. **The way of the wise.** The wise person, the one who is really in the know, lives his or her life in relationship with God. We should note that we can believe in God yet still be a fool.

    A. **We should fear the Lord in a relational sense (Prov. 1:1–7).** Both the word "fear" and the special name for God, "the LORD," demonstrate that living wisely means living your life in relationship with God. The word "fear" has both negative and positive aspects. Negatively it means "dread" or "terror"; positively it means "awe" or "reverence." So the wise person lives in the fear of the Lord—drawn by the beauty of the radiance of the Lord's presence yet not overstepping the bounds into a familiarity in which the same light can also damage or even destroy a mere mortal.

    B. **We should fear the Lord in a universal sense (Prov. 3:19–20).** This fear of the Lord extends to every part of life, not just to some religious dimension or activity. Why? Because the Lord is the Creator and Governor of all things which reflect and display His purpose and design. So Proverbs 3 tells us, "The LORD by wisdom founded the earth; by understanding He established the heavens; by His knowledge the depths were broken up, and clouds drop down the dew" (vv. 19–20). So the wise person who lives in the fear of the Lord lives in harmony with the world God has created. Our very lives belong to God; we must live in obedience to God and in dependence on God.

2. **The way of the fool (Prov. 3:1–8).** The way of the fool is already obvious, for it is diametrically opposed to the way of the wise. It is to live in rebellion or opposition to God: passively, by trying to ignore Him, and actively, by directly disobeying Him. We must recognize two things:

    A. **Humans have all chosen the fool's way (Ps. 14:1–3).** Human history is full of foolish rebellion against God, beginning with our first parents who chose to disobey the Creator's instructions and eat the forbidden fruit. They believed the serpent, that in eating it they would become all *wise* like God (Gen. 3). The promise was a lie, and the harmony of God's perfect creation was disrupted as sin and death entered the world. The relationship with God for which human beings were made was broken. Despite this, ever since then all human beings have followed the same path, for by nature we are rebels against God's authority.

B. **Humans are without excuse for choosing the fool's way (Rom. 1:18–23).** From this passage, we see that being religious does not make us wise; we can be religious fools. We were created to be worshipers. The problem is that we want a religion where we are in control, a god who will legitimatize how we want to live, and a god whom we can manipulate to do what we want. So we make and worship idols and dethrone the true God from His rightful place in our lives and in our societies.

Conclusion: So, there are only these two ways to live: the way of the wise and the way of the fool. We have all chosen the wrong option, resulting in the tragic consequences of pain and death; this is the bad news. The New Testament gives us the good news, the "gospel" which means "good news." Rather than leaving us to suffer the consequences of our foolish rebellion which we fully deserve, God stepped into our fallen world in human flesh in the person of His Son, Jesus. For the first time in human history since Adam fell, a human being (Jesus) perfectly lived the way of the wise, in perfect harmony with the Creator's design, in perfect obedience to the Father's will. Now, beyond the evidence of God's character seen in creation and in His will as revealed to Israel, God spoke finally and decisively through His Son, Jesus: His last and best Word. When Jesus died on the Cross, He paid the price for our rebellion and made a way by which we can be reconciled to God— provided that we lay down our arms and submit to His authority. I beg you to make this decision today, the wisest decision you will ever make.

Avoiding the Big Blowups

Date preached:

By Rev. Mark Hollis

Scripture: James 1:19–21

Introduction: James offers five steps toward overcoming anger.

1. Be slow to speak (v. 19). Weigh your words carefully (Prov. 17:28 and 29:20).
2. Be quick to listen (v. 19). Avoid erupting into anger. Assume the posture of a listener (Prov. 18:13).
3. Be slow to anger (vv. 19, 20). No amount of yelling at my children will turn them into the righteous young people I long for them to be.
4. Get rid of all moral filth and evil (v. 21). When distracted by sin we cannot dedicate ourselves to controlling our anger.
5. Humbly accept the Word of God (v. 21). Submit to the Word as the final authority and guide for your life.

Conclusion: What if I do blow up? Admit it, ask for God's help, confess to the people you hurt, and continue.

JANUARY 17, 2010

SUGGESTED SERMON

Choose Life: Sanctity of Human Life Sunday

Date preached:

By Dr. Kenyn M. Cureton

Scripture: Deuteronomy 30:19, "Choose life that you may live."

Introduction: Like a 9/11 attack, over 3,000 innocent people are murdered every day. One unsuspecting human life will be destroyed every 20 seconds. That adds up to 1.3 million Americans a year. Fully 50 million innocent people have been murdered in these United States over the last 37 years. January 22, 1973, is a date that will live in infamy, for on that date the U.S. Supreme Court made it legal[1] for our nation to murder its unborn by what doctors call an abortion.[2] Abortion is a moral outrage and is the American Holocaust. Consider three main points as we strive to "Choose life."

I. **Deceptive Arguments by the Abortionists**

A. **The fetus is not a baby.** There are some who say, "The fetus is not really a baby." Yet the biological facts are absolutely conclusive that the fetus is a living human being. Many in the scientific community agree, but fall short of granting them personhood. But *fetus* is just Latin for "baby." Like Nazi Germany with the Jews, the effort is to depersonalize and dehumanize them, semantically destroy them before you physically destroy them.

B. **What about rape and incest?** Abortions due to rape and incest, and even those to save the life of the mother, all three account for less than 4 percent of all abortions—4 percent.[3] These three account for about 96 percent of the pro-abortionist's rhetoric. If a choice must be made between the unborn child and the mother,

---

[1]Roe v. Wade, 410 U.S.; 113, 163–164 (1973).
[2]"Abortion in the United States: Statistics and Trends," National Right to Life, Internet, http://nrlc.org/abortion/facts/abortionstats.html.
[3]See the stats provided by the Alan Guttmacher Institute: http://www.agi-usa.org/presentations/abort_slides.pdf.

then indeed the mother's life may be chosen because of first domain. There is a great deal of emotion attached to victims of rape and incest. Should a baby conceived by rape or incest not live?

C. **What about handicaps and birth defects?** Add up all the abortions in the case of rape, incest, saving the life of the mother, and the cases of deformity and handicaps, that's only about 7 percent of all abortions.[4] What about the other 93 percent? Fully two-thirds of the women who abort their babies are over twenty years old, white, and middle class. More than 40 percent of abortions are performed on patients multiple times. But 76 percent of women who abort their babies are unmarried, and 53 percent have no other children.[5]

D. **Doesn't a woman have the right to choose?** No, not according to the law. In most states, it is illegal for a woman to be a prostitute or get intoxicated with alcohol and drive. In civilized society, a woman does not have the right to do as she pleases with her body. Yet the human embryo, the fetus, is technically not her body. The human embryo has separate and unique genetic information and biological material, a different set of chromosomes, a different set of genes, and half the time a different gender. This is a guest, a baby, living inside the host, the mother.

2. **Declared Absolutes of Scripture**

A. **Unborn human life in the Old Testament.** See Psalm 139:13–16. These verses tell us that God forms that child in a mother's womb, and that child is the subject and object of God's love and concern. This is a person made in the image of God. Look at Jeremiah 1:5.

B. **Unborn human life in the New Testament.** In Luke 1:39–45, Mary, who was pregnant with Jesus, went to visit her relative Elizabeth, who was pregnant with John the Baptist. The Greek word *brephos* for baby can mean, "unborn child, embryo, fetus, a newborn child, an infant, a babe." No distinction is made

---

[4]See http://www.nrlc.org/abortion/facts/abortionstats2.html. Statistics can be found at: http://www.agi-usa.org/presentations/abort_slides.pdf.
[5]See the stats provided by the Alan Guttmacher Institute: http://www.agi-usa.org/presentations/abort_slides.pdf.

in the Greek New Testament between an unborn baby and a newborn—only one term is used.

C. **Unborn human life must be protected.** See Proverbs 24:11, 12. Speak up for the unborn because abortion is wrong! It is premeditated murder! It violates the Sixth Commandment in Exodus 20:13.[6] Proverbs 6:17 says God hates the shedding of innocent blood! His ears are filled with the cries of the innocent being slain in this nation, and there will be a day of reckoning! The unborn must be protected.

3. **Definite Actions for Those Who Choose Life**

A. **Be informed.** Keep up with the threats to human life by our government by visiting www.frc.org and signing up for the *Washington Update.*

B. **Be compassionate.** Christians should be as compassionate before the pregnancy and after the pregnancy as we are passionate during the pregnancy. Support Pregnancy Care Centers.

C. **Be active.** Get involved and make an impact. Participate in the democratic process. Visit www.ivotevalues.org. Find out where the candidates stand on the issue of abortion. Be that voice for those who have no voice.

D. **Be prayerful.** Pray that God will change the direction of a nation that is drowning in a sea of innocent blood. Pray that even as slavery ended and the Jewish Holocaust ended, the American Holocaust might end and by the grace of God the murder of the unborn might end.[7] Amen!

---

[6]When God set forth the final five of the Ten Commandments to protect people's rights and preserve order in society, the first one is a prohibition is against taking someone's life. In fact, the high value God places on human life is the justification for capital punishment. See Genesis 9:6, which says, "Whoever sheds the blood of man, by man shall his blood be shed for in the image of God has God made man." When you murder another person, you have committed a great evil. Why? Because God created man in His image, and your malicious attack against another human being is considered an indirect attack on God Himself. And that crime is worthy of the death penalty. Romans 13 in the NT talks about the fact that God has ordained government to carry out that penalty-the authority "does not bear the sword for nothing—He is God's servant, an agent of wrath to bring punishment on the wrongdoer." Human life is precious in God's sight, the object of his great love. Anyone who takes a life wrongfully is the object of God's wrath. See also Ex. 21:12–17, 22, 23, 29.

[7]A Full Text Sermon may be found at http://www.frc.org/get.cfm?i=WX08A03.

SUGGESTED ORDER OF WORSHIP

Theme: I Choose Life . . .

Prelude—Instrumental
Shine, Jesus Shine

Call to Worship—Pastor
Deuteronomy 30:15–20*

Call to Praise—Congregation, Choir, and Orchestra
CH 42–43 *All Hail the Power* (vv. 1 and 3)

Prayer of Praise—Pastoral Staff

Welcome—Pastoral Staff

Hymn of Welcome—Congregation
CH 5 *I Sing Praises*

Praise and Worship—Congregation
How Majestic Is His Name (from *Bless His Name Medley*)
Blessed Be the Name (from *Bless His Name Medley*)
In the Name of the Lord (from *Bless His Name Medley*)
Lord, I Lift Your Name on High (from *Bless His Name Medley*)
Bless the Lord, O My Soul (from *Bless His Name Medley*)

Prayer of Praise—Pastoral Staff

Prayer Response—Congregation
CH 638 *I Need Thee Ev'ry Hour*

---

*15 "See, I have set before you today life and good, death and evil, **16** in that I command you today to love the LORD your God, to walk in His ways, and to keep His commandments, His statutes, and His judgments, that you may live and multiply; and the LORD your God will bless you in the land which you go to possess. **17** But if your heart turns away so that you do not hear, and are drawn away, and worship other gods and serve them, **18** I announce to you today that you shall surely perish; you shall not prolong your days in the land which you cross over the Jordan to go in and possess. **19** I call heaven and earth as witnesses today against you, that I have set before you life and death, blessing and cursing; therefore choose life, that both you and your descendants may live; **20** that you may love the LORD your God, that you may obey His voice, and that you may cling to Him, for He is your life and the length of your days; and that you may dwell in the land which the LORD swore to your fathers, to Abraham, Isaac, and Jacob, to give them" (NKJV).

SUGGESTED ORDER OF WORSHIP—*Continued*

Offertory Prayer—Pastor

Offertory Praise—Praise Team
God's Own Lamb

Video—Bella–thought about Adoption from WingClips.com
(http://www.wingclips.com/cart.php?target=product&
product_id=16704&substring=Abortion)

Sermon—Pastor
Choose Life

Hymn of Invitation—Congregation
CH 481 *Come Just as You Are*

Benediction Hymn—Congregation
CH 5 *I Sing Praises*

Postlude—Instrumentalists
CH 5 *I Sing Praises*

Additional Sermons and Lesson Ideas

SERIES: WISE UP

Wisdom's Protection Plan

By Dr. Al Detter

Date preached:

Scripture: Proverbs 2:11–22, especially v. 11

Introduction: I'm going to paint two pictures today. The first is a cruise ship in the Caribbean. You're on the open sea. The weather is great. So is the food and entertainment. There's the occasional rough water, the occasional storm, the occasional virus affecting a third of the passengers, but it's basically a fun ride with no real significant threats to safety. The second picture is a cargo ship approaching a harbor noted for hidden reefs and dangerous rocks. There are valuables on the ship along with some good friends. You are navigating safely to harbor but you can't be ignorant of the dangers or it could be deadly. The illusion in the kind of life most of us live is that life is like a cruise ship of fun. We can do pretty much as we wish and not get hurt. The truth is that life is really more like a cargo ship in constant danger. Wisdom reveals the rocks that would otherwise threaten us in the darkness, but it's up to us to steer clear of them. Without wisdom, we won't even see them. In the sea of life there are many dangerous rocks. In this text, we see that wisdom will guard us from two major destructive rocks.

1. **Rock #1: Bad friends and their sinful behavior (Prov. 2:12–15).** Without discretion and understanding, we won't see this rock. We won't understand who is good for us and who isn't. The function of wisdom is to deliver us from this rock (v. 12). There are people in life who walk in the way of evil (v. 12a). It's not that these people necessarily do the worst of sins, but that they live outside the prescribed path of God for human beings as outlined in His Word. They speak words that ought not to be spoken (v. 12b). Sometimes their language is rotten and vile. Sometimes it is cutting and demeaning. Their words are harmful. When you have wisdom, you realize these aren't your friends. Neither are people who don't live according to Scripture (v. 13). They do what they want to do regardless of what the Bible says. When sin no longer bothers a person, it's a sure sign they're on the wrong path (v. 15). They are devious. If you have wisdom, you can see the wrong way. Watch out for false wisdom. False wisdom says that you will be a good influence on bad friends. It doesn't work that way. That's why the apostle Paul says in 1 Corinthians 15:33, "Do not be deceived: 'Evil company corrupts good habits.'"

2. **Rock #2: Immoral relationships (Prov. 2:16–19).** Immorality is the second huge rock. Without wisdom, the likelihood is high that people are going to crash into it. We live in a sea of dangerous immoral rocks. The function of wisdom is to deliver us from immoral relationships

(v. 16). We are cautioned about "the immoral woman" in verse 16. The proper sexual expression is only between two people of the opposite sex who are married to each other. All other sexual activity is strange or immoral. We see a total lack of wisdom in Hollywood. The immoral woman of verse 16 is described as a seductive (v. 16b) and covenant-breaking person (v. 17). She comes on to the man with flattering speech to break the Seventh Commandment. She was formerly married but left her husband. She had a relationship with God but reneged on that as well. She promises a good time but in verses 18, 19, we see that her appeal is deadly. Her house bows down to death (v. 18; cf. Prov. 7:27). The road of sexual permissiveness is a one-way street to death (v. 19).

Conclusion: The role of discretion and understanding is to put a warning light by the major destructive rocks of life. Wisdom marks them out and says, "Steer clear of these rocks. Hit them and you can sink your vessel." If you are smart enough to see the warning light and steer clear of the rocks, verses 20, 21 say that you will enjoy the blessings of God in your life.

SERIES: GIVE TILL IT FEELS GOOD

Why Should I Give God Ten Percent?   *Date preached:*
By Robert Morgan

Scripture: 2 Corinthians 8:1–9

Introduction: Tithing is a practice followed by many of the heroes of Scripture, but why should we give God ten percent of our hard-earned money?

    1. The motivation of example (vv. 1–7). Paul used the motivating exam-
       ple of the Macedonian churches.
    2. The motivation of love (v. 8).
    3. The motivation of grace (v. 9).

Conclusion: So let each one give as he purposes in his heart, not grudgingly or of necessity; for God loves a cheerful giver (2 Cor. 9:7 NKJV).

JANUARY 24, 2010

SUGGESTED SERMON

What's Right with the Church *Date preached:*

By Dr. Timothy Beougher

Scripture: Acts 9:31, "Then the churches throughout all Judea, Galilee, and Samaria had peace and were edified. And walking in the fear of the Lord and in the comfort of the Holy Spirit, they were multiplied" (NKJV).

Introduction: How often we hear news coverage of scandals or crimes in the church! More often, we hear people complain or give reasons not to attend church. In any case, a tremendous focus is placed upon problems in the church. This morning I want to look at a different picture, a picture of a church that was doing it right. Throughout history, Christians have looked to the church in the Book of Acts as a model of what Christ wants in His body. Our verse for the morning sets forth five evidences of a healthy church.

1. **Climate of Peace.** Notice that the verse begins with the word *then*. The context of this verse is the conversion of Saul and the resulting decrease of external persecution on the church. However, peace involves much more than the absence of persecution. A church can have peace outwardly and not inwardly. Peace involves absence of conflict, both outwardly and inwardly, and the presence of harmony. A church filled with division will not see multiplication. The climate of peace naturally produces an atmosphere of unity. Are you helping to unify your congregation, or do you create divisions?

2. **Consistent Spiritual Growth.** Notice the verse says, "and were edified." *Edify* here literally means "to build a house," referring to us, the household of God! It's a reference to spiritual growth. A healthy church is one blossoming with spiritual growth in its members. We grow spiritually through spiritual food and spiritual exercise. Our spiritual food is the regular intake of God's Word, and our spiritual exercise is our ministry and service. If you are going to grow spiritually, it will cost you time and effort (see Col. 2:6, 7).

3. **Compelling Spiritual Vitality.** Acts 9:31 tells us the New Testament church was "walking . . . in the comfort of the Holy Spirit." This

church was alive! A clear spiritual dynamic was at work! Distinct characteristics identify a dynamic church. The church must live by faith (Heb. 11:6; 2 Cor. 5:7). The church must commit to holiness (Eph. 4:30). The church must depend on prayer (Eph. 6:18). Without these components, our church would be dead! Are we making progress in these areas?

4. **Consistent Numerical Growth.** The New Testament church was multiplied. A healthy church will experience consistent numerical growth. Not numbers for numbers' sake, but because numbers represent people and people matter to God! We need to reach people for Christ! A healthy church is a church where lives are changed by the gospel, a church that sees consistent numerical growth. Now there are settings where a church is reaching people and not growing numerically. In areas of rapidly declining population, a church may reach many for Christ and not see a numerical increase. For most churches, however, this is simply not the case.

5. **Consuming God Focus.** A key phrase in our verse is "walking in the fear of the Lord." Walking involves a way of life. The fear of the Lord portrays an idea of being afraid to offend God in any way. A healthy church seeks God's will above all else. A church that pleases God is a church where the people honor Christ in their daily conduct, in their thoughts (Phil. 4:8), deeds (2 Cor. 7:1), and words (Eph. 4:29).

Conclusion: In the face of all the problems in the church, we can become part of the solution. We need to follow the model of the New Testament church, cultivating the lifestyle of peace, spiritual growth and vitality, numerical growth, and godliness. Will you commit yourself to help build that type of church here? It has been said there are three kinds of people: those who make it happen, those who watch it happen, and those who wonder what happened. Will you commit to be a part of that first group, those who make it happen?

STATS, STORIES, AND MORE

More from Dr. Timothy Beougher
An article in Dr. Thom Rainer's newsletter, "The Rainer Report," of March, 2003, was titled "Ten Reasons Many Churches Do Not Grow." Under reason number two, "Conflict in the Church," Rainer wrote: "I wish I could say that conflict in the American church has abated, but that just does not seem to be the case. The reasons behind the conflicts are as innumerable as one could imagine: Leadership style, facility differences, power and control, worship style, programming, times of services, and the list goes on and on. It seems that for many the church has become the place to have 'my needs and desires met,' rather than seeking to serve God and others through the local congregation."

Have you ever noticed that the words *unite* and *untie* use the same five letters? The difference is where you put the letter "i."

There are two mottos that churches can adopt: (1) "We've never done it that way before!" or (2) "We can do all things through Christ who strengthens us" (Phil. 4:13 NKJV).

Vance Havner said, "If the Holy Spirit were to leave all the churches in America, 95 percent of them could continue on with no interruption of activity."

The House of Many Lamps
There is a legend of a village in Southern Europe that boasted of a church called "The House of Many Lamps." When it was built in the sixteenth century, the architect provided for no light except for a receptacle at every seat for the placing of a lamp. Each Sunday night, as the people gathered, they would bring their lanterns and slip them into the bracket at their seat. When someone stayed away, his place would be dark; and if very many stayed away, the darkness became greater for the whole. The regular presence of each person lit up the church.

SUGGESTED ORDER OF WORSHIP

How Can I Find God's Will for Me?
Proverbs 3:1–9

Prelude—Instrumentalist
   CH 213, 214—*We Bring the Sacrifice/He Made Me Glad*

Prayer of Worship—Worship Pastor

Worship and Praise—Congregation
   MSPW2 *Holy Spirit Rain Down*

SUGGESTED ORDER OF WORSHIP—*Continued*

Baptismal Celebration—Pastoral Staff

Prayer—Pastoral Staff

Welcome—Pastoral Staff

Hymn of Welcome—Congregation
CH 213 *We Bring the Sacrifice*

Worship and Praise—Congregation
CH 36 *He Is Exalted* (F)
CH 47 *Jesus, Lord to Me* (F/G)
CH 34 *He Is Lord* (G/Ab)

Scripture Reading*—Proverbs 3:1–9 (NKJV)

Hymn of Surrender & Worship—Congregation
CH *Take My Life and Let It Be*

Sermon—Pastor
Wise Up

Hymn of Response/Invitation—Congregation
CH—*In My Life, Be Glorified* (3 verses)

Hymn of Benediction—Congregation
CH 36 *He Is Exalted*

Postlude—Instrumental

Scripture Reading from Proverbs 3:1–9

Worship Leader:
1 My son, do not forget my law, But let your heart keep my commands;

Congregation:
2 For length of days and long life And peace they will add to you.

Worship Leader:
3 Let not mercy and truth forsake you; Bind them around your neck, Write them on the tablet of your heart,

Congregation:
4 And so find favor and high esteem In the sight of God and man.

Worship Leader:

5 Trust in the Lord with all your heart, And lean not on your own understanding;

Congregation:

6 In all your ways acknowledge Him, And He shall direct your paths.

Worship Leader:

7 Do not be wise in your own eyes; Fear the Lord and depart from evil.

Congregation:

8 It will be health to your flesh, And strength to your bones.

Worship Leader:

9 Honor the LORD with your possessions, And with the firstfruits of all your increase; 10 So your barns will be filled with plenty! May the Lord add His blessings to the reading of His Word. Amen.

Additional Sermons and Lesson Ideas

SERIES: WISE UP

How Can I Find God's Will for Me?

Date preached:

By Dr. Melvin Worthington

Scripture: Proverbs 3:5, 6

Introduction: When Eskimos travel through northern Alaska, they are often in danger, for there are no natural landmarks and few permanent roads. In a snowstorm, even familiar trails are hard to follow, and the possibility of freezing to death is a constant threat. So the trails are marked with tripods, each bearing reflective tape. By following the tripods, the travelers can find their way. As we read the Bible, we continually come across the truth that God erects tripods for His children. This is not only assumed but illustrated over and over. We need divine guidance. Human schemes are wretched substitutes for divine guidance. Life is made up of choices, and very often we have no idea what choice to make. But wise Christians learn to spot God's tripods.

1. **The prerequisites for divine guidance.** The first prerequisite is confidence in the Sovereign: "Trust in the Lord with all your heart." The second prerequisite is caution regarding one's self: "And lean not on your own understanding." The third prerequisite is consideration: "In all your ways acknowledge Him." Our actions must be examined in light of God's will for our lives, consulting Him, recognizing that His plan for us is best (Jer. 29:11).

2. **The promise of divine guidance.** "And He shall direct your ways." Proverbs 3:6b assures us that God guides His children in their daily lives. The Christian should never wonder or worry if God will guide. His guidance is *personal.* He wants to direct us—straight and plain— safely to our journey's end. God's guidance is *practical.* The Lord is vitally interested in directing us in every area, under all circumstances. God's guidance is *perfect*—infallible, reliable, and trustworthy. Divine guidance is *patient.* He leads His children step by step (Ps. 23:2).

3. **The principles for divine guidance.** *Submission to the Sovereign* is a key principle in guidance (Rom. 12:1; Jonah 1:1, 2). The Lord is not looking for better methods or bigger men or women. He is looking for surrendered hearts. Another principle of divine guidance is *searching the Scriptures* (Ps. 119:105). God speaks to His children through His Word. *Supplication in the Spirit* (James 1:5) is necessary to obtain divine guidance. Daily, disciplined, diligent prayer is never a waste of time, and very often the Lord gives us insights while we are in the very act of praying. We also need *suggestions from our soul mates*—the advice of our close friends and family members (Prov. 15:22). A final principle is *satisfaction in the soul* (Is. 26:3), an inner conviction or "gut instinct," a sense of peace from God about a possible course of

action. In his booklet, *Getting to Know the Will of God,* Dr. Alan Redpath tells about trying to decide whether he should enter the ministry or stay in his present profession as a chartered accountant of the staff of Imperial Chemical Industries, Ltd. He made a list on paper of all the reasons for staying in business, and each morning during his devotions, he asked the Lord to show him particular Bible verses that would counter or affirm the reasons listed. "Lord," he prayed, "I am not here to evade you. I am here because I want to know your will." What happened? "Day by day I turned to my Bible. Almost every day a verse seemed to speak to me and I began to write that verse against one of the arguments. At the end of a year, every argument in favor of staying in business had been wiped out. It took over a year, but I was not in a hurry. I was willing to wait; I wanted it to be in God's time. Too much was at stake to dash into the thing. I wanted to intelligently find the will of God. And I found it as I sought the Lord through my daily reading and meditation."

Conclusion: The great question is not "Will God guide me?" but "Am I willing to be led?" Are you willing to do whatever He asks? Whenever? Wherever? His plans are perfect, His paths are pleasant, and His presence is promised for every step of the way. George Truett once said, "To know the will of God is the greatest knowledge. To do the will of God is the greatest achievement."

SERIES: GIVE TILL IT FEELS GOOD

Gregarious Giving

By Robert Morgan

Date preached:

Scripture: 2 Corinthians 8:13—9:5

Introduction: This passage falls into three sections, each one giving us a different guiding principle for the way the apostle Paul directed his own stewardship campaign.

1. **The principle of equity (8:13–15).** Paul felt there was something wrong among his churches when some Christians were overly wealthy while others were starving. He believed those with greater resources had an obligation to help those suffering from want. In other words, God provides some people with more money that they might be of greater help. There should be equality of sacrifice.
2. **The principle of honesty (8:16–24).** Here Paul reassured the Corinthians about his handling of the monies raised. He wanted to avoid any criticism about the way the funds were handled.
3. **The principle of charity (9:1–5).** We're prone to ask ourselves, "How little can I get by with? What is the least amount I can reasonably promise to give?" But the Lord does not want gifts "grudgingly given."

Conclusion: God wants eager, enthusiastic, generous gifts—and givers.

JANUARY 31, 2010

A Model for Ministry

Date preached:

By Michael Duduit

Scripture: 1 Thessalonians 2:1–12, especially verse 4, "As we have been approved by God to be entrusted with the gospel, even so we speak, not as pleasing men, but God who tests our hearts."

Introduction: A young pastor was conducting the funeral of a war veteran. The dead man's military friends, wanting a part in the service, asked him to escort them to the casket, stand with them for a moment of remembrance, then lead them out through the side door. The pastor did precisely that, but not being familiar with the funeral home, he picked the wrong door. They marched with military precision into a janitorial closet! That story says two things about leadership. First, if you're going to lead, you'd better know where you're going. Second, if you're going to follow, you'd better follow someone who knows where he's going. Thousands of books, articles, and conferences focus on leadership, yet we have few outstanding leaders. We need examples of integrity. This passage gives us such a model. Paul, Silas, and Timothy came to Thessalonica to establish a church, but the religious officials drove them from town. Even so, Paul demonstrated a model of leadership in which the fledgling church there could have confidence.

1. **Christian leaders prioritize on God.** Paul's opponents impugned his motives, but they weren't successful because his ultimate priority was God's approval, not the approval of man. Authentic leadership places its focus on God: His approval, purpose, and will above all else. How do we recognize such leaders?

   A. **Their motives come from God (v. 3).** Paul faced three accusations. First, that he was teaching incorrectly: "Our exhortation did not come from error." Paul reminded them that his teaching and leadership came from God's truth. Too often we ask, "Will it work?" rather than "Is it true?" A second charge was "or uncleanness." This was probably an accusation of sexual immorality. In a pagan culture like Thessalonica, such a charge was not uncommon. If Paul could be discredited here, Christianity could be disdained. Paul denied the accusation, and later, in chapter 4, underscored the issue of sexual purity. It's vital for leaders to be pure and faithful. A third accusation involved manipulation or trickery: "Nor was it in deceit." This word was used of catching a fish with bait. But Paul renounced handling the Word of God deceitfully (2 Cor. 4:2). He was above reproach.

B. **Their model comes from God (v. 4).** Christian leaders serve so as to meet God's test. Sometimes we're duped by so-called leaders, but God cannot be fooled. Paul wasn't trying to please men but God, who tests the heart. Who are you trying to please? That's an important question because it determines how high we set our standards. Suppose I said I could jump twelve feet in the air. If I used my own measuring standard in which an inch equals a foot, I might make it! We tend to set our own standards, and the moral judgments of our culture are easy to achieve, but they won't stand the test of eternity.

2. **Christian leaders convey God's love (vv. 7–9).** Leadership is more than talents and techniques; it is caring for those we're leading. Notice the images in verses 7 and 11: "We were gentle . . . as a nursing mother . . . as a father." In verse 9, Paul says he supported himself on behalf of the church. If we're going to be leaders in God's service, it can't be done from a distance. We must lower our defenses and love people for Christ's sake.

3. **Christian leaders focus on God's kingdom.** Good leaders don't get sidetracked. In his biography of Ronald Reagan, Edmund Morris observes that Reagan decided to have two or three primary objectives in office. Lots of issues could have waylaid him, but he focused on those major goals. As a result, he accomplished much of what he set out to do. Paul kept his eyes on the prize, maintaining a focus on God's Kingdom in all he did.

A. **Leaders have "kingdom focus" in their lifestyle (v. 10).** Paul and company were (1) devout in their behavior toward God; (2) just in their behavior toward the Thessalonians; (3) blameless in their behavior toward themselves.

B. **Leaders have a "kingdom focus" in their message (vv. 11, 12).** Christians encourage others to experience Christ, helping them live "worthy of God."

Conclusion: Management guru Peter Drucker remembers when he was thirteen. A teacher asked his class, "What do you want to be remembered for?" When none of the boys answered, the teacher said, "I didn't expect you to be able to answer that now. But if you can't answer it by the time you're fifty, you'll have wasted your life." Knowing how you want to end up makes the difference in how you get there. What do you want to be remembered for?

STATS, STORIES, AND MORE

More from Michael Duduit
It's not that we don't recognize the value of leadership. Just imagine what might have happened in World War II if England had not had a leader like Winston Churchill. We might still be singing "God Save the Queen" if the American colonies had not had a leader like George Washington. How many companies and organizations have become great successes because of talented, visionary leaders? Likewise, how many efforts have failed for the lack of a good leader?

Someone Once Said . . .

🖎 Personal leadership is not a singular experience. It is, rather, the ongoing process of keeping your vision and values before you and aligning your life to be congruent with those most important things. —Stephen Covey

🖎 Great leaders are almost always great simplifiers, who can cut through argument, debate, and doubt to offer a solution everybody can understand. —Colin Powell

🖎 The key to being a good manager is keeping the people who hate me away from those who are still undecided. —Casey Stengel

The Greatest General
A man died and met Saint Peter at the gates of heaven. Recognizing the saint's knowledge and wisdom, he wanted to ask him a question. "Simon Peter," he said, "I have been interested in military history for many years. Tell me, who was the greatest general of all times?"

Peter quickly responded, "Oh, that is a simple question. It's that man right over there."

The man looked where Peter was pointing and answered, "You must be mistaken. I knew that man on earth, and he was just a common laborer."

"That's right," Peter remarked, "but he would have been the greatest general of all time—if he had been a general."

—Mark Twain, quoted by John Maxwell

The Joy of Giving

Prelude—Instrumentalist
Shine, Jesus Shine

Call to Worship—Reading Team

Praise Hymn—Congregation
CH 10 *Majesty* (1x)/*Come, Thou Almighty King* (2 verses)/
Majesty (1)

Welcome—Pastoral Staff

Welcome Song—Congregation (optional meet and greet during
song)
Shine, Jesus Shine (2x)

Prayer of Praise—Pastoral Staff

Praise and Worship—Congregation
God Is So Good (3x)
Give Thanks (2x)
Find Us Faithful (2x)

Offertory Prayer—Pastor

Offertory Praise
CH *Great Is Thy Faithfulness* (vv. 1 and 2, chorus, v. 3,
chorus)

Morning Message—Pastor
The Joy of Giving

Hymn of Response/Invitation
CH 591 *Have Thine Own Way, Lord*

Benediction Hymn
CH *I Love You, Lord*

Postlude—Instrumentalists
Joy Unspeakable and Full of Glory

SUGGESTED ORDER OF WORSHIP—*Continued*

All Readers: Stand up!

Reader One: And praise the Lord your God!

Reader Two: Who is from everlasting to everlasting!

All Readers: Blessed be your glorious name!

Reader Three: And may it be exalted above all blessing and praise.

All Readers: You alone are the Lord!

Reader One: You made the heaven!

Reader Two: Even the highest heavens!

Reader Three: And all their starry hosts!

Reader Four: The earth and all that is on it!

Reader Two: The seas and all that is in them.

Reader Three: You give life to everything,

Reader One: And the multitudes of heaven worship you.

All Readers: Stand up!

Reader One: And praise the Lord your God!

All Readers: Blessed be your glorious name!

Reader Three: And may it be exalted above all blessing and praise.

All Readers: You alone are the Lord!

All Readers: (Soft) Amen!

All Readers: (Loud) Amen!

All Readers: (Louder) Amen!

All Readers: (Very Loud!) Amen, Praise the Lord! Hallelujah!

From Nehemiah 9:5b, 6

Additional Sermons and Lesson Ideas

SERIES: WISE UP

The Path of Wisdom

Date preached:

By Rev. David Jackman

Scripture: Proverbs 3:13–26, especially verse 13

Introduction: Is God really interested in everyday life, or is He only involved in the bits that seem to be Christian? Is God involved in your everyday life? If He is, the implications are colossal. As Christians, our tendency is to retreat from the everyday world into our contained Christian groups, which can readily become a sort of Christian ghetto. It cripples our ability to build bridges to unbelievers. The wisdom literature of the Old Testament forces us to reflect upon life in God's world in the light of God's Word. The great themes of Proverbs are covered in chapter 3:

1. **Wisdom is what you've always wanted (vv. 13–18).** Verse 13 begins "Happy is the man who finds wisdom, and the man who gains understanding." The verses that follow are a hymn in honor of wisdom. Wisdom is typically personified as a woman because the writer wants to make the abstract principle of wisdom personal. Finding wisdom and getting understanding is the best investment you'll ever make in life. That's the thrust in these verses. The language in verses 14 and 15 is taken from the marketplace with words such as "profits, silver, gain, gold, precious, rubies." The writer tells us these things cannot compare with wisdom. The possession of wisdom is the greatest treasure you can acquire. Verses 16–18 describe the rewards of wisdom with words like "length of days, riches, honor, pleasantness, peace, happy." These verses aren't intended to promise certain treasures to those who take hold of it, but they teach us a different currency, that wisdom is of greater value than all these possible blessings. Verse 18 refers to the "tree of life," a reference to the Garden of Eden, saying that wisdom is "a tree of life to those who take hold of her." What was lost at the Fall of man into sin can be, to some extent, regained on earth through the wisdom of God and will lead us on a path to eternal life where all things will be restored.

2. **Wisdom is how God has always acted (vv. 19, 20).** "The Lord by wisdom founded the earth; by understanding He established the heavens; by His knowledge the depths were broken up, and clouds drop down the dew." If we understand how something works and why, we're much more likely to use it and benefit from it. Think of all the training manuals you've used for five minutes and then tossed on the shelf. Proverbs tells us the training manual for wisdom is creation. It points to creation as the handbook of wisdom. Biblical wisdom grounds its worldview in the fact that the universe is God's

creation. He is the one God over the whole world. Because it was fashioned after the wisdom of God, the world we live in isn't a random or meaningless phenomenon. The incredible complexities of this world point us to the wisdom of the Creator. This should motivate us to understand His wisdom more through His revealed Word. The wisdom God has shown us through creation and revelation guarantee us meaning in life. The wise person sets aside time and effort to discern and understand the structure of creation so as to be able to live appropriately within it.

3. **Wisdom is why we can always live confidently (vv. 21–26).** The thrust of these last few verses is that if we live according to God's wisdom, we will have confidence in every area of life. It imparts discretion (v. 21), gives life to the soul (v. 22), brings adornment to the neck (v. 22), allows us to walk securely (v. 23), liberates us from fear (v. 24), and protects from fear of terror (v. 25). The Lord Himself is our confidence and will keep us from error (v. 26). The faithful, covenant Lord should be the basis and the grounds for our confidence.

Conclusion: Wisdom is walking with God characterized not only by good management of our resources, but over and above that, characterized by the Lord's personal care over His people. The Lord is our confidence. There's a quiet poise and integrity to the life of someone with wisdom and understanding. Wisdom is to live in a right relationship with God the Creator, within the moral order of His world, as it's revealed in His Word.

SERIES: GIVE TILL IT FEELS GOOD

Money Can Hurt You
By Dr. Timothy Beougher

Date preached:

Scripture: James 5:1–6, especially verse 5.

Introduction: Jesus talked more about money than any other topic, often warning of its danger. James tells us that money can hurt us when:

1. **We value it wrongly (vv. 1–13).** James doesn't condemn money, but the love of money because it is *temporal* and we are to focus on the *eternal* (Matt. 6:19–20; Luke 12:15–21; 1 Tim. 6:17).

2. **We obtain it wrongly (v. 4).** Scripture commands against gaining money deceitfully (see Deut. 24:14, 15). Do we lie about taxes or keep the extra $10 the cashier accidentally gave us as change? This type of *temporal gain* will always earn us *spiritual pain.*

3. **We use it wrongly (vv. 5, 6).** Those who hoard riches and neglect the needy are pictured as fattened cattle headed for slaughter, unaware of their fate! Enjoy God's provision (Ps. 34:8), but beware if your luxury is to the neglect or oppression of others (Eccl. 5:13)!

Conclusion: Be a good steward of God's provision to you!

FEBRUARY 7, 2010

SUGGESTED SERMON

The Wholeness of Worship

Date preached:

By Jack W. Hayford

Scripture: Isaiah 6:1–8, "In the year that King Uzziah died, I saw the Lord sitting on a throne, high and lifted up, and the train of His robe filled the temple. Above it stood seraphim . . . And one cried to another and said: 'Holy, holy, holy is the LORD of hosts; The whole earth is full of His glory!' . . . So I said: 'Woe is me, for I am undone! Because I am a man of unclean lips, and I dwell in the midst of a people of unclean lips; for my eyes have seen the King, the LORD of hosts.' Then one of the seraphim flew to me, having in his hand a live coal that he had taken with the tongs from the altar. And he touched my mouth with it, and said: 'Behold, this has touched your lips; your iniquity is taken away, and your sin purged.' Also I heard the voice of the Lord, saying: 'Whom shall I send, and who will go for Us?' Then I said, 'Here am I! Send me.'"

Introduction: The best times for worship are sometimes in the middle of crises or disappointments. Here, amid the crisis of King Uzziah's death, Isaiah learns something about the impact of worship and holiness on our hearts.

I. **Unholiness is revealed by worship.** Isaiah's vision of God's throne gave him a horrible sense of his own unworthiness and sinfulness, and it does the same for us. The Lord's presence makes us aware of our sin. We feel "undone" and "unclean" like Isaiah. But the Lord meets us at our point of need by purifying us. God sent an angel with a hot coal to touch Isaiah's perceived point of unworthiness—his lips. Had he felt his hands were unclean, the Lord would have touched Isaiah's hands. The fire of the coal brought regeneration to the place of impurity Isaiah was most sensitive to. The "fire" of worship:

A. **Refines.** It burns out the residue of what's unworthy.

B. **Consumes.** It takes the bondage out of our lives and burns it up.

C. **Melts.** Our hearts are made soft.

D. **Warms.** Our cold hearts are thawed.

E. **Ignites.** When we've turned off, He turns us back on. What is the point of your greatest weakness? If we will come to God, in the midst of His holiness, His purifying fire will touch us at that point.

2. **Holiness is activated by worship.** Every time we hear praise going on around the throne of God, we hear, "Holy, holy, holy!" The focus is on God's holiness. We tend to think of holiness as the purity we are trying to achieve, and that God will reject us if we don't. Even among people who genuinely love the Lord, there are those who draw back because they feel unholy, unworthy. There's a natural inclination to avoid worship because of feelings of unworthiness. But the Lord wants us to worship Him because it is there we will find wholeness. There is a root relationship between the words *whole, healthy, wholeness,* and *holy.* When we talk about holiness, we are talking about wholeness. Holiness is God's entirety entering my incompleteness. The only way for that to happen is to come into His presence.

3. **Wholeness is restored by worship.** The word "worth" comes from *axios,* which originally described a coin of full weight. In the ancient world, the coins were made of valuable metals which wore thin rapidly, causing the coin to lose some of its value. That's how Isaiah felt. But God calls us to worship in His presence in order that a transfer of His being into us may take place. Then the worth that has been worn off the coin of our lives—His nature within us— begins to be restored through worship. Worship is the situation in which wholeness is restored. Because of God's worth poured into us, we become worthy.

4. **Mission is found in worship.** The mission of our lives is also found in worship. After the angel purified Isaiah's lips, the Lord gave him a mission. You can only find your direction and intended purpose in the context of worship.

Conclusion: Just as we inherit certain characteristics from our biological parents, so, as we worship, the image and nature of our heavenly Father begins to manifest in our lives. My likeness to my heavenly Father comes from being in His presence. The fact that God is holy relates to our healing and restoration, not our shame and condemnation. His life is already in us, and we will be holy because He is our Father, and He is holy. That's a promise (1 Pet. 1:16).

STATS, STORIES, AND MORE

Someone Once Said . . .

- As I read the Bible, I seem to find holiness to be His supreme attribute. —Billy Graham

- It does not seem proper to speak of one attribute of God as being more central and fundamental than another; but if this were permissible, the scriptural emphasis on the holiness of God would seem to justify its selection. —Louis Berkhof, in *Systematic Theology*

- Lower our sense of holiness, and our sense of sin is lowered. —Dan DeHaan

- Divine holiness . . . stands apart, unique, unapproachable, incomprehensible, and unattainable. —A. W. Tozer

Holy, Holy, Holy!

Philadelphia pastor James Montgomery Boice once spoke to a discipleship group on the attributes of God. He began by asking them to list God's qualities in order of importance. They put love first, followed by wisdom, power, mercy, omniscience, and truth. At the end of the list they put holiness. "That did surprise me," Boice later wrote, "because the Bible refers to God's holiness more than any other attribute." The Bible doesn't generally refer to God as *Loving, Loving, Loving!* Or *Wise, Wise, Wise!* Or *Omniscient, Omniscient, Omniscient!* But over and over we read the cry of the angels, *Holy, Holy, Holy!*

Go Forth!

Jonathan Goforth became a powerful evangelist throughout Asia, a rarity for a Westerner, and his crowds sometimes numbered 25,000. His Chinese home was open to inquirers—one day alone over 2,000 showed up. Multitudes throughout the Orient came to Christ through Jonathan and his wife, Rosaline. During his missionary career, fifty Chinese converts went out as ministers or evangelists. What led Goforth overseas? Dr. George Mackay, veteran missionary to Formosa (Taiwan), had been traveling across America for two years trying to recruit young men for Asian evangelism. One night as Jonathan, a college student at the time, listened, "I heard the voice of the Lord saying: 'Whom shall I send, and who will go for us?' and I answered: 'Here am I, send me.' From that hour I became a foreign missionary."

The Wholeness of Worship

Prelude—Instrumentalists
Days of Elijah

Call to Praise—Congregation
O Worship the King (vv. 1 and 2)
I Sing Praises to Your Name (2x)
O Worship the King (v. 4)

Prayer of Praise—Pastoral Staff

Welcome—Pastoral Staff

Welcome Song—Congregation (optional meet and greet)
What a Mighty God We Serve

Praise and Worship—Congregation[1]
We've Come to Bless Your Name[1]
Great and Mighty Is the Lord (2x)[1]
Great and Mighty Is He (2x)[1]
Mighty Is Our God[1]
We've Come to Bless Your Name[1]

Scripture Reading—Pastoral Staff or Music Personnel
Philippians 2:12–18; 3:7–10

Song of Response—Congregation
I Love You, Lord (2x)

Prayer of Praise—Pastoral Staff

Song for Worship—Congregation
I Surrender All (2x)

Offertory Prayer—Pastoral Staff

Offertory Praise—Congregation
The Heart of Worship

---

[1]Medley for Choir or Congregation from *God for Us,* Integrity Music, Mobile, Alabama.

Sermon—Pastor
The Wholeness of Worship

Hymn of Response/Invitation—Congregation
Just As I Am

Benediction Hymn—Congregation
What a Mighty God We Serve

Postlude

Additional Sermons and Lesson Ideas

SERIES: WISE UP

How to Treat Your Neighbor

By Dr. Al Detter

Date preached:

Scripture: Proverbs 3:27–30

Introduction: Many of you may be familiar with the second great commandment, "Love your neighbor as yourself" (Matt. 22:39). In Jesus' view, how we treat our neighbors is second only in importance to our love relationship with God. The word *neighbor* in Proverbs means anyone from our casual acquaintances to our very best friends. The word in Proverbs is used even for our enemies. So how should we treat others, our neighbors?

1. **Help your neighbors when they have a need (Prov. 3:27, 28).** Did you ever stop to figure out how God meets needs? God doesn't send chariots from heaven with money and clothes and food. He meets the needs people have through other people. These two verses indicate two kinds of neighbors we should bless:
    A. **Be generous with the neighbor whose need we owe (v. 27).** This verse is talking about relationships in which we owe a debt of some kind, "Do not withhold good from those to whom it is due." The literal sense is the idea of paying a financial debt we owe, but this verse goes much deeper. By virtue of some relationships, you owe the other person something. If you are married, you *owe* good to each other. Children owe their parents obedience and honor; parents owe children time, love, and discipline. The list goes on. Are you paying your "debts" to others out of the gifts, time, resources, and talents God has equipped you with?
    B. **Be generous with the neighbor whose need we know (v. 28).** What do we do about the needs of people who aren't very close to us, even people we don't know at all? Once we know of a need and realize we have resources that can help, we become obligated. There's a flip side to the coin. Perhaps someone asks for help that you know, maybe someone in the church. In our individualistic mindset fed to us by our culture, we think they should have worked harder, that there's no reason for us to bail them out, so we either avoid them or flat out refuse. We are not to ignore or refuse the need when we have the resources to meet the need. We are to step up immediately and minister a blessing.
2. **Guard against mistreating your neighbors in any fashion (Prov. 3:29, 30).** We live in a day of troubled relationships. There will be times that relationships will be strained. It happens in every marriage, in every friendship, in every partnership. Solomon gives us some good advice. Don't make unnecessary trouble with your neighbor.

A. **Avoid harmful intentions and actions against other people (v. 29).** The most important part of this verse is the period. There are some people in life we just aren't naturally drawn to. There are some we may not like. There are some who have wounded and injured us. It doesn't matter. There is never a reason to plan harm against someone else. Period! God says, "Vengeance is Mine. I will repay" (Heb. 10:30).

B. **Be sure there is an offense before you confront (v. 30).** There is a time and a place to confront someone. When you need to confront someone and don't, things will only get worse. But we are not to be contentious in our manner of life—confronting and challenging and faultfinding about everything that offends us. The word for "contend" in verse 30 is a strong word. It literally means "to come to hard blows." It came to mean "to quarrel, to argue noisily, to fight because one is angry." It describes a reaction we have in response to an actual or perceived injustice against us.

Conclusion: Two great hindrances to our blessing others were in our text today—selfishness (vv. 27, 28) and aggression (vv. 29, 30). We need the wisdom of God if we are going to treat people right. Your neighbor is the person in your marriage. It's the parent or child at home. It's the person you know in this church. It's the ticket agent in the airport. It's the person who has wronged you. Are you willing to take an honest look at how you are treating your neighbors?

On Target (Believers and Churches)
By Dave Hirschman

Date preached:

Scripture: 1 Thessalonians 5:1–5

Introduction: What does it mean to be on target? How important is it to be on target? To a hunter or airplane pilot, being on target is extremely important, but what about in the church? Paul wrote to the believers at Thessalonica, instructing them in how to live and be on target in anticipation of the coming Day of the Lord.

1. **On target believers and churches exhibit an attitude (v. 5).** As believers our attitude should reflect the Light, project the Light, and protect the Light.
2. **On Target believers and churches expect attacks (vv. 6–8).** When you expect attacks you are aware, you are alert, and you are prepared!
3. **On target believers and churches engage in activity (vv. 9–11).** You are active in your relationships: your relationship with the Lord, with each other, and with the lost.
4. **On target believers and churches enjoy assurance (vv. 23, 24).**

Conclusion: Be an on-target follower of Jesus!

FEBRUARY 14, 2010

Loving God with Your Mind

Date preached:

By Michael Duduit

Scripture: Luke 2:19 with Matthew 22:35–37, "But Mary kept all these things and pondered them in her heart."

Introduction: Thinking is a very God-ordained activity. Jesus said we should love the Lord our God with all our . . . minds. So this morning, at the onset of this great season, let's get a grip on our perspectives by looking at the Lord's great commandment as recorded in Matthew 22:35–37. Elsewhere in Scripture Jesus quoted the "Shema" as it appears in Deuteronomy 6:5. But here He altered it slightly to say we should love God with our minds. Maybe the particular Pharisee to whom He was speaking was proud of his mental agility, and he needed to understand that his mind was meant for devotion to God. What, then, does it mean to love God with your mind? The word translated "mind" was a common Greek term *dianoia* conveying several ideas:

1. **Loving God with your mind involves your intellect.** A common meaning of this word involves human thought or intellect. The ability to reason is a gift of God, and using that gift is an act of worship, as we see through Mary's example. If God deserves our best—our greatest love, our deepest commitment, our highest service—that is no less true of our minds. Sometimes we're tempted to produce less than the best our minds can deliver. For example, there's the young person in school who feels pressure not to be the brain in class. Some kids say it's not cool to be academic achievers. Then there are those who expect God to directly reveal everything, and they don't use their minds to adequately process His Word. Others fear intellectual pursuits because they're afraid they might learn something damaging to their faith. Real education, however, doesn't harm a person's faith because all truth is God's truth. What can damage young people are the secular, materialistic presuppositions of many university faculties. It's possible to use our minds to try to create thrones for ourselves, bowing before the altar of ego. That's why it's essential to let Scripture be our guide. The Bible is

our judge, not the other way around. God calls us to use our intellect to His glory.

2. **Loving God with your mind involves your attitudes.** Another common use of *dianoia* involved a "way of thought" or "disposition"—a person's attitudes and perspectives about life. Hugh Downs observed, "A happy person is not a person in a certain set of circumstances, but rather a person with a certain set of attitudes." Much of what we accomplish in life is determined by our attitudes. When we come to faith in Christ, we receive a new mind, new thoughts, new attitudes. In fact, the Greek word for repentance, *metanoia*, literally means "a change of mind." As Christians, we think differently about life and have a new attitude because Christ lives in us. Our attitudes are reflected in things we say and do. Can you imagine saying, "Sure he's flunking all his classes, but he has such a good attitude about school!" That makes as much sense as Linus telling Charlie Brown, "I love humanity. It's people I can't stand!" What is on the inside—the kind of person we truly are—will inevitably surface in our words and actions. Are you loving God with your attitudes? Do you have an attitude of loving concern toward others?

3. **Loving God with your mind involves your will.** Several ancient writers used the word *dianoia* to describe the will. Loving God with your mind means placing your will under His control. It doesn't mean you won't have to make any decisions, but it does mean you'll seek to make decisions that honor God. No decision has greater consequences than how we'll respond to Christ's call. Surrendering your life to His lordship means accepting His authority over your life. We accept His rule and agree to submit ourselves in obedience to His will.

Conclusion: In Matthew 27:22, Pilate asked, "What shall I do with Jesus who is called Christ?" That may be the most important question posed in the entire Bible, and it is a question which can only be answered with a decision. If you've never given your life to Christ, you can make that decision right now and propel your life forward in a new direction.

STATS, STORIES, AND MORE

◦ The human brain weighs only three pounds, yet it is the most complex structure in the body. The brain encases more than 100 billion cells and is capable of sending signals to thousands of other cells at speeds of more than 200 mph. Over its lifetime the brain will establish trillions of connections within the body. All that power—and we still manage to forget where we put our car keys! The human brain really is an incredible machine. It goes far beyond any man-made computers in terms of its complexity and capability. Your brain serves as the command and control center of your body, enabling your various organs to function while simultaneously helping you operate at an intellectual level, retaining facts, learning to reason, and thinking. The mind is one of God's most incredible creations. That's why I've always been fascinated with this statement by Jesus, that we are to love God with all our minds.

—Michael Duduit

◦ A wildlife organization offered a bounty of $5,000 for each wolf captured alive. Sam and Jed decided they'd start hunting for wolves, and they began spending their days scouring the forests and mountains. One night they were exhausted and fell asleep right in the woods dreaming of all the money they were going to make. Suddenly Sam awoke to see that they were surrounded by fifty hungry wolves. He jabbed his friend in the side and said, "Wake up, Jed. We're rich!" That was a positive attitude!

—Michael Duduit

Someone Once Said . . .

◦ Every temptation comes to us via our thoughts.　　—Erwin Lutzer

◦ The mind of man is the battleground on which every moral and spiritual battle is fought.　　—J. Oswald Sanders

◦ Our defeat or victory begins with what we think, and if we guard our thoughts we shall not have much trouble anywhere else along the line.　　—Vance Havner

◦ Self-control is primarily mind-control.　　—John Stott

◦ Every kidnapping was once a thought. Every extramarital affair was first a fantasy.　　—Leslie Flynn

Loving God with Your Mind

Prelude—Congregation
Shine, Jesus Shine

Prelude to Praise—Congregation
CH 353 *Victory in Jesus* (3 verses and choruses)
CH 513 *Thank You, Lord* (1x)

Prayer of Praise—Pastoral Staff

Welcome—Pastoral Staff

Welcome Hymn—Congregation (optional meet and greet time)
CH 209 *This Is the Day*

Scripture Praise—Pastoral Staff
Psalm 150

Worship and Praise—Congregation[1]
Blessed Be the Name (2 verses)
CH 42 *All Hail the Power* (2 verses)
CH 102 *All Hail King Jesus* (2x)
CH 34 *He Is Lord* (1x)

Prayer of Praise and Worship—Pastoral Staff

Celebrating with Our Gifts—Pastoral Staff

Congregational singing during offering time—As a prayer
CH 9 *Glorify Thy Name* (2x)
CH 591 *Have Thine Own Way, Lord* (1x with tag)
CH 79 *My Jesus, I Love Thee* (vv. 1 and 3)

Morning Message—Pastor
Loving God with Your Mind

Hymn of Commitment/Invitation—Congregation
CH 481 *Come Just As You Are*

Benediction Song
Give Thanks

Postlude

---

[1]This medley for congregation is available from Prism Music, Nashville, Tennessee, and in the choir book *Glory, Honor, and Praise!*

Additional Sermons and Lesson Ideas

SERIES: WISE UP

Making Wise Decisions
By Kevin Riggs

Date preached:

Scripture: Various Proverbs

Introduction: Some decisions we make are more important than others, but all need to be made with care. The Book of Proverbs gives us four principles for wise decisions.

1. **Place your trust completely in God (Prov. 3:5, 6).** The closer I am to God the more apt I am to make wise choices (Prov. 16:3).
2. **Plan ahead and think things through (Prov. 6:6–8; 10:5; 31:21).** See the examples of the wise ant, the wise son, and the wise housewife.
3. **Gather All the Facts (Prov. 13:16).**
4. **Seek Godly Counsel (Prov. 12:15; 15:22).**

Conclusion: Are you facing a tough decision? Once you have applied these four principles you can move forward with confidence, keeping two promises in mind: God will never lead you contrary to His Word, and He will not allow you to make a wrong decision if you have been sensitive to His leadership at every point.

The Greatest Love Story
By Dave Hirschman

Date preached:

Scripture: John 3:16

Introduction: In the early seventies, a movie, *Love Story,* touched everyone's heart. It was a story of tender, self-sacrificing love of a young couple. The Bible is a book of love stories: the love of Jacob for Rachel, of Boaz for Ruth, and of Joseph for Mary. But the greatest story is not one of these; rather, it is the story of God's love for ordinary people!

1. **It is the story of an unreasonable love.**
   "For *God* so loved the world . . ." Unreasonable because God's love is not requested or respected and is seldom reflected. When things go wrong in the world (war in Iraq, trouble in Iran, terrorism, homelessness, AIDS, drugs), most people blame God. The world's response to trouble is to seek diplomatic, economic, and social solutions. God's love is not respected (valued) because it is viewed as old fashioned, Victorian, rigid, restrictive. God's love is seldom reflected in a world that worships success, popularity, and power. Yet, God still freely loves the world—what an unreasonable love!

2. **It is the story of an unreserved love.**
   ". . . that He gave His only Son . . ." Unreserved in that what God gave, He gave freely. Without hesitation, no debates, conferences, or deliberations, what He gave was the only one—unique, incomparable, unmatched, and without equal. And what He gave was His Son! What an unreserved love!

3. **It is the story of an unrestricted love.**
   ". . . that whoever believes in Him . . ." Unrestricted in that there are no qualifications to measure up to, achievements to master, or requirements to maintain. What an unrestricted love!

4. **It is the story of an unrestrained love.**
   ". . . should not perish, but have everlasting life." Unrestrained in that God's love for you has no limits—nothing it cannot do (Heb. 7:25)—and knows no bounds—no place where it is hindered or ineffective, and will never end (Heb. 13:5). What an unrestrained love!

5. **Sadly, it is also a story of an unrealized love.**
   "For God did not send His Son into the world to condemn the world, but that the world through Him might be saved. He who believes in Him is not condemned; but he who does not believe is condemned already, because he has not believed in the name of the only begotten Son of God" (vv. 17, 18).

   There are many who have yet to respond or even hear of God's love.

Conclusion: Those who know God's love must take it to those who have yet to hear.

FEBRUARY 21, 2010

Why True Love Waits

Date preached:

By Joshua D. Rowe

Scripture: Various

Introduction: True love waits. Is that true? It sounds boring. Sexual abstinence isn't a popular concept. We don't want to wait on anything in our culture. But I want you to understand that waiting is awesome. Waiting for your husband or wife is not passive; it's very active. It's a challenge, an adventure, and a commitment to a God who deserves everything, and to your future spouse who deserves your purity.

1. **True Love.** Before we dive into our topic of sexual abstinence, I want you to understand one very important thing. You will never have the strength to hold up a commitment to purity until you are totally committed to Jesus Christ as your Lord and Savior. The greatest commandment in Scripture is to "love the LORD your God with all your heart, with all your soul, with all your mind, and with all your strength." Without this commitment, you will never be able to commit yourself to true purity. If you have not made this commitment, I invite you to do so today.

2. **True Love Waits.** Scripture clearly teaches that we shouldn't commit sexual sin, but these passages don't make sense until we understand why sex is an important and wonderful gift from God. That's what I want to focus on. Why wait? Because sex, the way God intended it, is too wonderful to pass up.

   A. **The lies of Satan and society.** What do your friends at school think about sex? Do they joke about it? Brag about it? Is casual sex normal? Most teenagers view sex as a goal to attain quickly, not a gift to understand biblically. Some adults tell us we need to wait until we are mature enough or until we understand all the consequences of sex. Some kids are more mature than others, I know. Most of you are aware of the consequences of sex. The real problem is that most of your generation does not have a biblical view of sex.

B. **The truth of Scripture.** I know most of you are expecting me to say, "The Bible says sex is bad," or, "You need to just suck it up and wait no matter how hard it may be." But I'm here to tell you that sex is an incredible gift from God, and waiting to have sex is a worthwhile adventure.

(1) **The goodness of sexual love.** Let's look at Scripture. When God created the world, He said that the light was good (Gen. 1:4); He said the land was good (Gen. 1:10); He said the vegetation was good (Gen. 1:12); He said the solar system was good (Gen. 1:18); He said all ocean creatures and birds were good (Gen. 1:21); He said land animals were good (Gen. 1:25); He said that man was good, along with everything He had made (Gen. 1:31)! God only saw one thing out of all creation that was not good, "It is not good that man should be alone." God saw that man could not emotionally or sexually express himself in a marriage relationship, and it wasn't good. See! God doesn't want you to wait your whole life while you burn with desire. He wants you to have one sexual partner, one spouse to share yourself with. Notice that in all these verses Satan never created anything! All Satan does is twist things. He takes the perfect model of the sexuality God gave us and twists and perverts it. God gave us this gift of sexual love to be shared in marriage, but Satan lies to us through the media, through friends, and through our own selfishness to twist sex into a self-gratifying sin. We must focus on how wonderful sex really can be if we follow God's model.

(2) **The goal of sexual love.** Genesis 2:24, 25 tells us, "Therefore a man shall leave his father and mother and be joined to his wife, and they shall become one flesh. And they were both naked, the man and his wife, and were not ashamed" (NKJV). I'm willing to bet that many of you here today are ashamed. Perhaps you've had sex, or sinned through pornography or fantasy, or maybe you have just been too physical with another person; whatever it is, you feel or have felt ashamed.

    Imagine being in a marriage relationship, where there is no shame. You can express every physical desire and have a deep, loving, wonderful relationship. You can share your hearts, your goals, your strengths, your weaknesses, your futures, and your bodies together and without shame! God doesn't want to torture you by telling you to wait, but He wants to bless you by keeping you pure for this incredible gift. Sexual sin is like eating too many hamburgers when you are promised a steak dinner. Why do that? Don't spoil your appetite! Don't make yourself ashamed!

C. **The adventure of waiting.** So, what do you do in the meantime? There's freedom in waiting. As we read before, sex makes you one flesh with someone else. My advice is to enjoy life now like you won't be able to later so that later you can enjoy life like you can't now. You may never have as much spare time as you do now to enjoy your social life, your hobbies, or your family. In life, we must focus on the gifts God has given us at any particular moment. Now, you have freedom and fun. Later you will be sexually active in marriage. Enjoy each as they come to you. Don't allow Satan to twist the blessings God has given you.

Conclusion: Perhaps you realize that you don't have a true love relationship with Jesus Christ. I invite you to make a commitment today to follow Him. For all of you who do have that relationship, I invite you to make a commitment to remain sexually abstinent until your wedding night.

Closing Prayer: Pray these words in your heart with me, "Lord, I present my body as a living sacrifice, holy, acceptable to You, which is my act of worship to You. I will not be conformed to this world, but I will be transformed by the renewing of my mind, so that I might prove what is that good and acceptable and perfect will of God" (see Rom. 12:1, 2 NKJV).

SUGGESTED ORDER OF WORSHIP

Theme: He Is Worthy . . .

Prelude—Intrumentalists
Come into His Presence with Thanksgiving in Your Heart

Call to Praise—Praise Team or Congregation
Open the Eyes of My Heart

Of Our Worship . . .

Prayer of Praise—Pastoral Staff

Welcome—Pastoral Staff

Hymn of Welcome—Congregation (optional meet and greet)
Bind Us Together

Praise and Worship—Congregation
Blessed Be the Name of the Lord (2x)
Worthy of Worship (stanzas 1, 2, 3)
I Worship You (1x)

Of Our Service . . .

Worship and Scripture Presentation—Drama Team and Congregation
Lead Me, Lord
I'll Go Where You Want Me to Go

Prayer of Praise—Pastoral Staff

Worship Response—Congregation
Spirit of the Living God

. . . Of Our Devotion

Offertory Prayer—Pastoral Staff

Offertory Praise—Praise Team and Congregation
CH 583 *My All in All*

Sermon—Pastor
Why True Love Waits

Hymn of Invitation—Congregation
Softly and Tenderly

Benediction Hymn—Congregation

Postlude

Additional Sermons and Lesson Ideas

SERIES: WISE UP

Staying Moral in an Immoral Age

Date preached:

By Robert Morgan

Scripture: Proverbs 7

Introduction: Sex outside of marriage is a violation of the character and the Laws of God. We don't know if this young man was engaging in premarital or extramarital sex, but Ephesians 5 says, "Among you there must not be even a hint of sexual immorality" (NIV). Sex itself isn't bad; it's a gift of God. But premarital sex, extramarital sex, postmarital sex, and homosexual behavior are perversions of God's plan. The entertainment industry is on a vast evangelistic mission to convince us otherwise, but the devil can never alter the character or standards of a holy God. So, as the writer of Proverbs 7 stood in his window and peered through the lattice, he witnessed a scene with three storylines.

1. **Seduction.** This young man was seduced, presented with temptation so attractive he seemed unable to resist it. Verse 7 calls him a youth, so we would suppose he was full of hormonal energy. Verse 13 says that a woman met him, embraced him, and passionately kissed him. Having ignited this masculine energy, she said, "Let's go to my place." With persuasive words, she seduced him. The devil is in the same business today. He plies his trade by plastering our television shows, movies, and magazines with stimulating sexual images. He does it with men and women who dress immodestly. He does it by getting us involved with a platonic friendship at work. And he does it with the Internet.

2. **Destruction.** The youth paid a high price for his evening of pleasure (vv. 22ff). We don't know what happened to him. Perhaps he caught a sexually transmitted disease. Perhaps the husband found out and it led to a fight. More likely, the writer was saying that this young man's immorality took him down a road that led him away from God, from holiness, and from eternal life. See Galatians 6:7, 8.

3. **Instruction.** The whole purpose of Proverbs 7 is to instruct, warn, and help us avoid the tragic mistake this youth made. A careful reading of the chapter gives three weapons for staying moral in an immoral age.

   A. **Store up God's commandments within you (vv. 1–5).** See Psalm 119:11 and Matthew 4:1–11. When we fill our minds with the Word, we have ammunition to fend off the devil's attacks.

   B. **Whenever possible, avoid the temptation.** Verse 7 says the youth lacked judgment. How do we know? Because of verse 8: "Passing along the street near her corner; and he took the path to her house." He wasn't just an innocent victim. He was looking to be seduced. He was walking in that direction. What change do you need to make in your lifestyle that will lessen temptation? How can you walk down another street, away from the seducer's neighborhood?

C. **Make up your mind to stay pure.** Verses 24, 25, "Listen . . . pay attention . . . Do not let your heart turn aside to her ways." Determine not to sin in these ways. Set your standards in advance, before you face the temptation.

Conclusion: Compare this young man to two others in the Bible. When faced with a similar temptation, Joseph turned and fled, leaving his cloak in the woman's hands. He realized it is better to lose one's coat than one's character (see Gen. 39:1–13). The second young man is Jesus Himself. He was tempted in all ways as we are, yet without sin. You and I don't have the strength ourselves to remain victorious. But when Christ, who never sinned, lives within us, He can live His life through us. In Jesus Christ, we can be more than conquerors.

The Priority of God
By Dave Hirschman

Date preached:

Scripture: Romans 14:1–12

Introduction: Priority is determined by the importance we place on something. What priority does God have in our lives? God cannot be *a* priority in our lives, He demands to be *the* priority!

1. **If God will be *the* priority in your life, then you can expect that He is determined to influence every area of your life (vv. 7, 8).** Under His influence, His design, His desire, and His direction become most important in your life.

2. **If God will be the priority in your life, then you can expect that He will demand the submission of all other areas (v. 9).** Submission accepts everything else as secondary, God's continuing evaluation, and God remaining as the priority.

3. **If God will be the priority in your life, then you can expect that He will diminish the importance of every other area (v. 10).** When priorities and perspectives change, true value is discovered, prized, and pursued.

4. **If God will be the priority in your life, then you can expect that He will become the only thing that you cannot do without (v. 11).**

FEBRUARY 28, 2010

The State of Barrenness

Date preached:

By Dr. Stephen Olford

Scripture: Jeremiah 11:3; 17:5; 48:10, especially 11:3, "Cursed is the man who does not obey the words of this covenant."

Introduction: After twenty-one consecutive years in the pastorate in two metropolitan churches in London and New York, and having traveled vastly in religious circles, I'm aware that we can be in the most spiritual circumstances and yet know barrenness in our lives—a dryness and an aridness. God punctuates this amazing prophecy of Jeremiah with some of the most solemn warnings we'll find anywhere in Scripture. I have chosen three of them that have searched and re-searched my heart.

1. **Barrenness is the consequence of disobedience to the Word of God (Jer. 11:3).** Contextually, this is an interesting verse. Undoubtedly it has reference to King Josiah in his eighteenth year after having rediscovered the Book of the Law. After reading it and searching his own heart, Josiah felt convicted and sought to bring about a renewal—a revival among his people. Josiah arranged to have the Scriptures read openly. If you read the story carefully, you'll discover that God's people didn't rise to the occasion. Because of their disobedience and refusal to bow to the authority of God's Word, the prophet Jeremiah came with this warning. A similar situation is found in 1 Samuel 15:10–23. It concerns King Saul, who was commanded to smite the Amalekites. He chose his own terms of obedience and saved Agag the king and the best of the cattle. The prophet Samuel walked into that situation and heard the bleating of the sheep and the lowing of the cattle. Samuel promptly rebuked King Saul with these solemn words: "You have rejected the word of the LORD, and the LORD has rejected you" (1 Sam. 15:26). There is no substitute for total obedience.

2. **Barrenness is the consequence of not trusting the power of God (Jer. 17:5).** Here are dramatic and devastating words addressed to

God's people, who of all the nations of the earth had seen the mighty demonstrations of God's power. Yet they had turned from Jehovah God and sought alliances with Egypt and Assyria. God's prophet had to come and say, "Cursed be the man who trusts in man and makes flesh his strength" (Jer. 17:5). One illustration of this principle is Moses in his early days. Moses thought that "by his hand" he could deliver Israel (see Acts 7:25). He smote an Egyptian, ran into the desert, and for forty years God had to show him that he couldn't trust in his own hand. Only after those forty years of utter brokenness could God take a man who was afraid to even open his mouth and use him to deliver His people from slavery in Egypt. I want to remind every one of us that all power is inherent in God. All power ultimately belongs to Him.

3. **Barrenness is the consequence of deceitfulness in doing the work of God (Jer. 48:10).** These are such vehement words that the higher critics and others have sought to remove it from the prophecy of Jeremiah and say that it's not part of Scripture, but that is completely unwarranted. We not only believe in the inerrancy of God's Word, but we also know that this teaching often occurs elsewhere in the Bible. One of these is in the New Testament: the case of Ananias and Sapphira (Acts 5:1–11). There is nothing God hates more than deceitfulness in the work of the Lord. Ananias and Sapphira were members of the Jerusalem church, and they had seen Barnabas come with all his wealth and lay it all at the apostles' feet. Ananias and Sapphira decided that they too wanted to make a good impression on the leaders of the church, so they sold some land and gave part of the proceeds to the apostles while pretending to give it all. They conferred together to lie. They presented their gift to the apostles, but the discerning Peter by the power of the Holy Spirit saw right through the fraud and phoniness of it all and said, "Why has Satan filled your heart to lie to the Holy Spirit?" (Acts 5:3). Immediately, Ananias and then Sapphira were smitten by the judgment of God. This illustrates the truth that God will not look with favor upon deceitfulness in the work of the Lord.

Conlcusion: Let's bring our hearts into submission to God's Word; let's bring our lives into submission to God's Spirit; let's bring our entire actions into submission to God's work.

STATS, STORIES, AND MORE

More from Dr. Olford

My very dear friend, Dr. Alan Redpath, has a motto that has hung in every one of his studies during his pastoral years: "Beware of the barrenness of a busy life." George Goodman, that great Brethren Bible teacher, used to say, "Beware lest service sap spirituality."

If you were to ask me what the single most important word in the Christian vocabulary is—from the moment of your commitment to Christ initially in salvation to that moment of final redemption when Jesus comes back again, from Genesis to Revelation—I would say *obedience.* There is no substitute for absolute obedience. I heard Dr. William Fitch once say at the Mid-America Keswick Conference in Chicago, "Any point of defective obedience constitutes *total* disobedience."

All across America today in evangelical circles among preachers, there's an attitude of "do it yourself theology." This means that your own brains will take you through, your own culture will take you through; your string of degrees will take you through, although God has condemned all these notions (Gal. 3:1–3)! That is no indictment upon hard work and hard study and hard application of truth, but our life is a miraculous life. I cannot by any means convert myself or by any means live by the power of an indwelling Christ in and of myself—since it's only Christ and Christ only who can do this in me. Having begun totally dependent on Christ, I must live my Christian life that way too.

SUGGESTED ORDER OF WORSHIP

The State of Barrenness

Prelude

Call to Praise—Congregation
Days of Elijah

Prayer of Praise—Pastoral Staff

Welcome—Pastoral Staff

Hymn of Welcome (meet and greet during song)
SPW 87 *Praise the Name of Jesus* (1x)

Praise and Worship
SPW 87 *Praise the Name of Jesus* (2x)
SPW 88 *His Name Is Life* (D) (2x)

There's Something About That Name (2x)
His Name Is Wonderful (1x)

Scripture and Praise
Hebrews 1—Pastoral Staff
CH 365 *Alleluia* (3 verses)—Congregation

Prayer of Praise—Pastoral Staff
CH 47 *Jesus, Lord to Me*—Congregation

Offertory Prayer

Offertory Praise—Praise Team and Soloist
Broken and Spilled Out

Sermon—Pastor
The State of Barrenness

Hymn of Invitation/Response—Congregation
Trust and Obey

Benediction Hymn—Congregation
'Tis So Sweet to Trust in Jesus

Postlude

Additional Sermons and Lesson Ideas

SERIES: WISE UP

Knowing What to Say and When to Say It
By Robert Morgan

Date preached:

Scripture: Proverbs 10:19–21, especially verse 21

Introduction: Many of our problems in life occur because we say the wrong thing, or we say it at the wrong time, or we say it in the wrong way. A thirty-second tirade can damage a thirty-year career, a thirty-year marriage, or thirty years of reputation. As he wrote Proverbs, Solomon was cognizant of the power of the tongue, and when you read his thoughts on this subject in Proverbs, you find God's wisdom in small doses telling us to:

1. **Shut up.** Some verses tell us in plain English to be cautious about what we say, to never miss an opportunity to keep our mouths shut (see Prov. 17:9, 14, and 27; also see Prov. 11:12; 12:16; 19:11; 20:3; 26:20–22). Certain things are necessary for life—food, water, and protection; but some things are not life-necessities—it isn't necessary to state our opinion on every subject, to have the last word in every argument, to demand our way in every discussion, to defend ourselves from every criticism, or to draw a line on every issue. Sometimes we just need to keep our thoughts and words to ourselves.

2. **Build up.** But it isn't enough just to shut up. God hasn't called us to take vows of silence like medieval monks. He gave us the remarkable capacity for human language, for He wants us to build others up (see Prov. 10:11 and 19; also see 12:18; 15:4 and 23; 16:23–24). When Lou Gehrig was starting his baseball career, he went into a slump and grew so discouraged he thought of quitting. A friend named Paul Krichell heard Lou was slumping, and he took a train to Hartford and invited Lou to join him for a steak dinner at the Bond Hotel. Lou poured out his frustrations, and Paul could see the player's confidence was shot. He spent the evening telling Lou that all hitters go through slumps, that the best ones—even Ty Cobb—don't get hits six or seven out of every ten tries. But eventually good hitters start hitting again; and, said Paul, you're a good hitter. After dinner, Gehrig walked with Paul to the train station and thanked him for coming. The next day, Lou started blasting the ball again, and over the next eleven games he came through with twenty-two hits, including six home runs—and his career took off. "I decided not to quit after all," he said.[1] Sometimes we need to take a train, track down someone, buy them a steak, and encourage them with wise counsel.

---

[1] Jonathan Eig, *Luckiest Man: The Life and Death of Lou Gehrig* (New York: Simon & Schuster, 2005), pp. 48–49.

3. **Speak up.** Other times we need to speak up (see Prov. 31:8–9). In 1955, when Rosa Parks was a seamstress in Montgomery, Alabama, the city buses were segregated. One day, Rosa got on the bus, went back to the black section, and took the first available seat. A few stops later, the bus filled up and a white man got on. The bus driver demanded she give him her seat, and she spoke four words that changed history: "No, I will not." With those words, she almost single-handedly launched the Civil Rights movement in America.

Conclusion: If a lightning bolt struck a transformer near your house, it could send a powerful surge of electricity through the lines and into your house, frying your computer. So we have circuit breakers and surge protectors that interrupt the flow of electricity before any damage is done. These verses in Proverbs are the circuit breakers and surge protectors for the soul. The air around us is often static with anger, and our social atmospheres change as often as the weather. We need to install some of today's verses as spiritual circuit breakers, committing them to memory and to conscious thought. We must become more and more like Jesus, for no one ever spoke as He did. The great secret of the book of Proverbs is that in describing the wise person it offers us a pen-portrait that was perfectly fulfilled in our Lord Jesus. Receive Him as your Lord and Savior, and grow up into Him in all things. And let the words of your mouth and the meditations of your heart be pleasing in His sight.

What Do You Want to Be Known For?

Date preached:

By Dave Hirschman

Scripture: 1 Thessalonians 1:3–8; Hebrews 11

Introduction: Living in the Washington, D.C. area provides access to many things. D.C. is known for history, government, international influence (embassies), universities, and traffic! Many places are distinct because of what they are known for. As a church, what are you known for? What do you want to be known for?

There are a number of options, but what is the best one? An OT verse repeated three times in the NT (Hab. 2:4; Rom. 1:17; Gal. 3:11; Heb. 10:38); compare to 1 Thessalonians 1:3–8. Faith is believing God and taking Him at His word!

1. **Faith is confident in what it knows (Heb. 11:1).** A pilot climbs into the cockpit of a plane confident that air flowing over the wing will produce lift and cause the plane to fly; an Olympic athlete, having trained for years, is confident that given the chance, he/she can win a medal; a surgeon looks down on the operating table, confident his specialized ability can help correct the patient's condition. The impossibility of blind faith—faith is always in something or someone known! Who and what do you know?

Hopefully you know God's provision for you—how He has provided for you (examples)—perhaps financially. Hopefully you know how God has preserved you through difficulties; and hopefully you know how God has proved Himself through you. If this is true, then you can be confident in what you know.

2. **Faith acts on what it knows (Heb. 11:6).** People of faith want to see what they know is true! Consider tithing, praying, peace, trouble. Faith is intended to be used; faith invites us to believe the impossible, and faith inspires victorious living.

3. **Faith experiences what it knows and acts on (Heb. 11:7–40).** When we act upon that in which we are confident, we become even more confident in Christ (1 Thess. 1:5); our lives are transformed (1 Thess. 1:6); we become examples to others (1 Thess. 1:7); and our faith can impact the world (1 Thess. 1:8).

Conclusion: What will you be known for?

MARCH 7, 2010

SERIES: ON MISSION WITH GOD SUGGESTED SERMON

The Call from Without

Date preached:

By Jimmy Draper

Scripture: Acts 16:6–10

Introduction: The cries of a lost world resound with a deafening, thunderous roar. Never has there been so much devastation in the hearts of individuals as there is today. Never have so many enjoyed so much of the things of this world; yet, the despair and hopelessness in the human heart is greater than ever before. The lostness of mankind clamors for our attention today.

I. **We must hear the call (vv. 6–9).** Those with vision will hear. The call comes, but it is only heard by those with listening ears and willing hearts.

A. **The preparation for the call (vv. 6–8).** Paul was moving in the will of God. He was committed to doing God's will. In Acts 13:46, he announced that he had turned to preach to the Gentiles. He never wavered in that assignment. His confidence in that task is seen in Acts 28:28 (KJV), "Be it known therefore unto you, that the salvation of God is sent unto the Gentiles, and that they will hear it."

Paul knew God's will for his life, and, without vacillation, he moved ever forward in that will. He was doing what God had instructed him to do.

The Holy Spirit had forbidden him to go to Asia and to Bithynia. It is important for us to allow God to close doors, as well as open doors. It is vital to note that need is not the only criterion to determine a place of ministry.

Asia and Bithynia were areas of great need. Too many times we initiate programs and ministries based upon need only, rather than following the leadership of the Holy Spirit.

One person's vision may not be another person's vision. God has a vision for you, but you must be faithful. It is unlikely that God will give you a new vision if you are not aggressively following

His will now. Obedience is the preparation required to hear the call, to see the vision.

Remember when God spoke to young Samuel (1 Sam. 3)? His response to that call was, "Speak; for thy servant heareth" (1 Sam. 3:10). The use of the word *servant* reflected obedience. It was as if he said, "Yes, Lord. Now what's the command?" That type of obedience is essential if we are to hear God's call.

Further, Paul was in prayer when the vision came. He was seeking direction and making himself available to God. He was willing to obey without knowing the course or the cost of that obedience.

The one who hears the call, who sees the vision, must first hear God's call and make himself available. It is the committed and faithful follower whom God gives a vision. Paul was obedient and prayerful, thus prepared to hear God's call.

B. **The presentation of the call (v. 9).** The Macedonian simply cried, "Come over into Macedonia, and help us" (Acts 16:9). The Macedonian man did not know what his country needed; he just knew help was required. He had a great need. Something was missing. There was a great void in his life. That void is present in every person's life.

Within the heart of each individual in the world is a longing that only Christ can satisfy. "Whosoever drinketh of this water shall thirst again: But whosoever drinketh of the water that I shall give him shall never thirst; but the water that I shall give him shall be in him a well of water springing up into everlasting life" (John 4:13, 14).

"I am the bread of life: he that cometh to me shall never hunger; and he that believeth on me shall never thirst" (John 6:35).

"Come unto me, all ye that labor and are heavy laden, and I will give you rest. . . . ye shall find rest unto your souls" (Matt. 11:28, 29).

Oh, hear the cry of the lost today! The cry of the man in Macedonia was the cry of Europe for Christ. Today, lost humankind calls for help from every continent and nation.

It is reported that when the French Revolution began, a person observed, "This is a riot!" Another answered, "No, this is a revolution!" The world today is crying for help out of the hopelessness of world revolution.

A population revolution is taking place. Over 5 billion people are in the world today, and this number will explode to 8 billion by the turn of the century. Twenty-seven percent of the United States population lives in the suburbs, yet only 15 percent of evangelism takes place in the suburbs. More than 160 cities in the world today have a population in excess of 1 million. By the turn of the century, 85 percent of Americans will live in cities. Rural areas are facing declining population; farms are disappearing; and even the cities are in transition.

There is revolution among the peoples of the world that is issuing forth in violence and hostility. While the walls of communism have crumbled, other walls are being erected; violence is now the pattern for international relationships. This violent revolution is shaking every nation.

There is a family revolution. We are seeing the disintegration of the American family. One out of two marriages ends in divorce, and the rate is predicted to rise far beyond that figure. More than 50 percent of American adults are single. Almost 70 percent of American women work. More than 50 percent of our children will live with only one parent at some time during their growing-up years. Loneliness is an American trademark now. Twenty million adults now live alone!

My phone rang one morning at two o'clock. A local police officer said they had arrested a woman, who insisted on speaking to me. She had attended our church but was not a member. She had gone to a bar and been picked up by a man. They both got drunk, and he left her stranded and abused in a parking lot. She cried out of her loneliness about being abandoned by her husband and being driven by the emptiness of her heart. Her cry was, "Come over and help me!"

There is a religious revolution taking place. Dead and dying churches are becoming the norm. Ritual and programs have become ends in themselves. The greatest mission field in America today may well be within the church! Business as usual won't cut it. Evangelism is not debatable.

We are in an economic revolution. Worldwide recession and inflation are running wild. The instability and turmoil of the economy of this world is frightening. Our own nation is plunging deeper and deeper into economic bankruptcy and collapse.

There is an emotional revolution in the world today. Stress and trauma, depression and discouragement, and disappointment and despair are very much a part of the lives of people today. Only Jesus can fill the longing of this world.

Oh, hear the call of this lost world! Leadership is the key. There is a worldwide lack of people, truly called of God, who are willing to suffer scorn, poverty, and the shame of the cross for the sake of Christ and the lost people of the world.

Oh, hear the call of this lost world! Neil Simon, who wrote *The Odd Couple* and *Barefoot in the Park,* was asked on *The Dick Cavett Show* whether making a lot of money concerned him. The studio went silent when Simon said, "No. What does concern me is the fear of dying."

"Come over and help us," the world cries today. We must hear the call.

2. **We must heed the call (v. 10).** Paul was not praying about whether to go, but where to go! "Immediately we endeavored to go" (Acts 16:10).

Once we hear God's call, we must heed it! The call was to preach the good news to the lost. "Preach the gospel" is one word in the Greek language of the New Testament, *evangelion.* It literally means to evangelize. Paul clearly understood that the call was to evangelize the lost.

The gospel is revealed to us in the Bible. The Bible speaks not only of the content of what is preached, but also of the act, process, and execution of the proclamation. Content and process of preaching are one. We must not separate them. The preaching of this gospel is charged with power (Rom. 1:16)!

What is the gospel? God has acted for the salvation of the world in the incarnation, death, and resurrection of Jesus Christ. Jesus Christ became sin for us, dying in our place, paying the penalty for our sins on the cross. He rose bodily and victoriously from the grave, ascended to heaven, and will one day return for His own to establish His kingdom eternally on this earth. Each individual must turn from his or her sins and, by faith, trust Him as Lord and Savior. That is the gospel.

We must heed the call to preach the gospel. The great missionary Robert Speer once said, "You say you have faith? Well, then, either give it out or give it up." Faith is personal, but it is never private.

The great English preacher Charles Spurgeon was once asked,

"Do you believe the heathen who have never heard the gospel are really lost?" Spurgeon replied, "Do you believe the ones who have heard the gospel and never shared it are really saved?"

Heed the call! Paul went to Macedonia, and people were converted everywhere—Lydia and her household, a demon-possessed girl, the jailer and his household—all in the sixteenth chapter of Acts!

God's blessings always attend our obedience. To heed the call is simply a matter of obedience in following Him into a lost world to preach the gospel.

Will we heed the call? We have the message—will we declare it? Will we faithfully obey God so He can give us the vision and the call? We must hear the call. We must heed the call.

SUGGESTED ORDER OF WORSHIP

The Joy of the Lord Is My Strength[1]
(with Baptismal Celebration)

Prelude—Instrumentalists
CH 214 *He Has Made Me Glad*

Prayer of Worship—Pastoral Staff

Song of Commitment—Congregation
Without Him (verse, chorus 2x)

Baptismal Celebration—Pastoral Staff

Prayer—Pastoral Staff

Welcome—Pastoral Staff

Hymn of Welcome—Congregation (meet and greet during song)
He Has Made Me Glad

Worship and Praise—Congregation
CH 308 *There Is a Redeemer* (3 verses and choruses)
Something Beautiful (1x)
We Will Glorify (2x)

---

[1]Reproduced with permission of the North American Mission Board, Alpharetta, Georgia. All rights reserved.

SUGGESTED ORDER OF WORSHIP—*Continued*

Scripture Praise—Psalm 91:1–7, 9–12, 14, 15[2]

Offertory Prayer—Pastoral Staff

Offertory Hymn—Congregation
   CH 583 *All in All*

Sermon—Pastor

Hymn of Invitation—Congregation
   CH 481 *Come Just as You Are*

Benediction—Pastoral Staff

Postlude

---

[2]Psalm 91:1–7, 9–12, 14, 15 (NIV)

1 He who dwells in the shelter of the Most High will rest in the shadow of the Almighty.

2 I will say of the Lord, "He is my refuge and my fortress, my God, in whom I trust."

3 Surely he will save you from the fowler's snare and from the deadly pestilence.

4 He will cover you with his feathers, and under his wings you will find refuge; his faithfulness will be your shield and rampart.

5 You will not fear the terror of night, nor the arrow that flies by day,

6 nor the pestilence that stalks in the darkness, nor the plague that destroys at midday.

7 A thousand may fall at your side, ten thousand at your right hand, but it will not come near you.

9 If you make the Most High your dwelling—even the Lord, who is my refuge—

10 then no harm will befall you, no disaster will come near your tent.

11 For he will command his angels concerning you to guard you in all your ways;

12 they will lift you up in their hands, so that you will not strike your foot against a stone.

14 "Because he loves me," says the Lord, "I will rescue him; I will protect him, for he acknowledges my name.

15 He will call upon me, and I will answer him; I will be with him in trouble, I will deliver him and honor him."

Additional Sermons and Lesson Ideas

SERIES: THE REVELATION OF CHRIST

The Majesty of the Unveiled Christ

By Dr. Denis Lyle

Date preached:

Scripture: Revelation 1:9–16, especially verse 13

Introduction: Have you ever faced a problem so big or a devastation so great that you began to question God? John lived in the midst of persecution so great that Christians were being tortured and killed daily, yet all his attention was refocused when he received a vision of the unveiled Christ. It had been over sixty years since John had seen the Lord Jesus, but he immediately recognized Him as "the Son of Man" (see Dan. 7:13, 14). Who did John see? Remember that while this is symbolic language, it still portrays actual and eternal truth.

1. **He is the commanding Christ (v. 13).** The clothing of Christ describes the authority of the King! In ancient times, this was the recognized apparel of authority, dignity, and royalty. In Old Testament times, a long robe was the clothing of spiritual leaders of high rank, whether it be the high priest (Ex. 25:1), a king (1 Sam. 24:5), a prince (Ezek. 26:16), or a judge (Ezek. 9:1). Jesus is all of these. Do you see how John saw Christ? If your life seems out of control, remember that Jesus is the King of kings, fully in charge of whatever is going on in your life.

2. **He is the consecrated Christ (v. 14).** The imagery of snow describes the purity of the King. Do you know what freshly fallen snow is like? Have you ever considered the fact that the Lord Jesus is the only Man who never had a guilty conscience? He is the only person who never had to confess a sin.

3. **He is the comprehending Christ (v. 14).** Christ's fiery eyes refer to the sagacity of the King. He has vision that penetrates. We would say today He has X-ray vision. Jesus cannot be deceived. He sees every minister, notes every member, observes every ministry, and views every motive with X-ray vision.

4. **He is the condemning Christ (v. 15).** From His fiery eyes John looks down to see Jesus' red-hot feet, glowing like burnished metal in a fiery furnace. This refers to the severity of the King. His feet glowed to indicate the fire of the Final Judge. There will be no escape from the wrath of God when Christ's burning feet touch the earth. John now moves from sight to sound.

5. **He is the communicating Christ (v. 15).** The voice sounding like many waters refers to the integrity of the King. This was the same voice that had calmed the storm, that taught His disciples, and that called everything into existence. Jesus' voice is still as powerful and

loud as the roar heard at the base of a waterfall. At a time when so many voices are being raised against Christ, we can be assured that one day they will all be silenced. The coming Christ won't endure beatings and crucifixion again; He will come as the King of kings and Lord of lords to judge, rule, and reign.

6. **He is the controlling Christ (v. 16).** The seven stars He holds refer to the sovereignty of the King. The stars are the angels or messengers of the churches. The risen Lord holds in His very hand this moment His church, His people, and His servants. This church is not my church, your church, or our church; this church is His church.

7. **He is the conquering Christ (v. 16).** Christ holds a deadly two-edged sword; this refers to the ferocity of the King. One of these days the Lord Jesus is coming to do battle with the nations of the world; His weapon will be the Word of God (Eph. 6:17). When confronting great problems, what weapons are you using? Money, medication, manipulation, meanness, or memory? If Christ will use God's Word one day to conquer the world, why do you think it is insufficient for you today?

8. **He is the compelling Christ (v. 16).** Finally, John sees Christ's face shining with the glory of God; this refers to the glory of the King. Once that face was marred and spat upon, but here it shines in resplendent glory: unveiled, unmasked, and unadulterated!

Conclusion: John had become so preoccupied with Christ that although his circumstances had not changed, his despondency had lifted. What vision of Christ are you missing because you are so preoccupied with yourself, your problems, or your circumstances? In the midst of your despondency, turn around. Focus on Christ. Why? When you are preoccupied with the Savior, there is no time to fret over your problems.

Measuring Our Effectiveness

Date preached:

By Dave Hirschman

Scripture: 1 Thessalonians 2:11–14

Introduction: Every church and every Jesus follower should want to be effective in their life and ministry. Recent years have produced methods designed to make our churches effective and formulas to measure that effectiveness. However, how do we measure effectiveness? Many churches measure their effectiveness by "man centered" criteria (attendance, budget, ministries); but these can vary in every church. What is a reliable measurement for all churches regardless of variables? How do we measure effectiveness in terms of people?

1. **People can be effective only as they know the truth (v. 13a).** Items held as truth have been proven wrong over time. God's Word is the

only truth that is divinely inspired, can change eternity, will last forever, and the only truth that we have to offer.

2. **People become more effective as they are changed by the truth (v. 13b).** God's Word produces change, increase, and Christlikeness.

3. **People are truly effective when they live the truth (v. 14).** Those who live the truth are focused, are sure, and endure with joy.

Conclusion: If we are introducing people to the truth, and helping them to be changed by the truth, so that they are living the truth focused, assured and enduring with joy—then we are effective! Do you know the truth? Are you being changed by the truth? Are you living the truth?

MARCH 14, 2010

SERIES: ON MISSION WITH GOD   SUGGESTED SERMON

Blood on Our Hands[1]

Date preached:

By Dr. Roy Fish

Scripture: Ezekiel 33:7–9

The very title of this message contains a terribly frightening prospect for a minister of the gospel: *"Blood* on Our Hands." It contains the kind of implication from which, if we followed our instinct, we would tuck our tails and run: "Blood on *Our* Hands." Serious thought of the possibility of such a reality is almost enough to overwhelm even the strongest of us: "Blood on Our *Hands."*

Out of the imagery of the Old Testament comes the idea for the message. All major cities in the Old Testament world had a watchman stationed atop a tall tower on the wall, where a maximum range of visibility would be his. If an enemy army approached the city, the watchman's duty was to warn the city of an impending attack. If the watchman failed in his duty of warning, and the city was overrun and its citizenry massacred, the watchman would be held responsible. The blood of those who had perished would be on his hands. With this symbolism in mind, God said to the prophet Ezekiel: "Son of man, I have appointed you a watchman for the house of Israel . . . When I say to the wicked, 'O wicked man, you shall surely die,' and you do not speak to warn the wicked from his way, that wicked man shall die in his iniquity, but his blood I will require from your hand. But if you on your part warn a wicked man . . . you have delivered your life" (Ezek. 33:7–9 NASB).

1. **The relevance of blood on our hands.** Because of the location of the text and the seriousness of its inference, the tendency today is to lay the issue of blood on our hands on a man-made shelf of Old Testament irrelevancy. With the attitude of "what happened before Christ came does not pertain to us," much of contemporary Christianity would reject this principle as outmoded—a thing of the past. This may be a legitimate claim except for the fact that the apostle

---

[1]Reproduced with permission of the North American Mission Board, Alpharetta, Georgia. All rights reserved.

Paul, inspired by the Holy Spirit, contends that the principle of bloodguilt for negligence is still binding in this Christian age. When he left the city of Ephesus, he boldly stated, "I am pure from the blood of all men. For I have not shunned to declare unto you all the counsel of God" (Acts 20:26, 27 KJV). The apostle might have left the city of Ephesus with blood on his hands. But rather, "I am not guilty of blood in Ephesus," he cries. "My hands are clean." According to the New Testament, a failure to discharge a God-given responsibility to speak out means the blood of eternal souls is on our hands. The bloodguilt principle found in the Old Testament is repeated in the New Testament. Its recurrence enforces its ratification in your life and mine.

2. **The reality of blood on our hands.** Relevance suggests reality, and there is no more frightening reality in the life of any Christian than the reality of being held responsible for the souls of others. That we, by our negligence, can be guilty of a kind of spiritual homicide— that our hands can be stained with blood because of indifference toward those who are lost—what an awesome truth! The reality of blood on our hands rebukes anything short of total commitment to the task of sharing the exciting news of Jesus. The reality of bloodguilt is a reproof to anything short of a life controlled by the Holy Spirit, being in the right place at the right time, playing a part in God's redemptive activity. The reality of bloodguilt is a censure on careless living, sin-obstructed testimonies, and Spirit-grieving habits. It is a constant rebuttal to the kind of cowering fear that causes Christians to shut up when they ought to speak up.

   But the heart of this message has to do with how the blood may be removed.

3. **The removal of blood on our hands.** Blood on our hands is a frightening reality. But the blood can be removed. Every preacher of the gospel should seriously consider how. **First, blood can be removed by the cultivation of converts into witnesses.** A slighting of any part of the plan of our Lord can involve us in the bloodguilt of others. There is a part of His plan that generally has suffered sad neglect. This neglected part of His plan is the cultivation of converts into personal witnesses for Christ.

   In the fourth chapter of Ephesians, the apostle Paul states clearly that the primary task of the pastor is to mature Christians for the work of the ministry, for the building up of Christ's body. Pastors are to train their people in the work of soul-winning. Jesus said we are not only to make disciples, but we are also to train those who become disciples to make disciples (Matt. 28:20). Most of us have regarded the training aspect of the Matthew commission as optional. But the question pastors face is not only, "How many people have I won?" It is also, "How many people have I trained to win others?" It is an indictment against our negligence of the commission of our Lord that only a small percentage of pastors are employing any effective method of training personal witnesses. Thank God if you are actively engaged in winning the lost. But I remind you that if we do not train converts to reach the lost, we are responsible for those who may have been reached through our multiplied ministry.

Second, blood can be removed by consistent concern for lost people. I choose the word "consistent" for a particular reason. Most of us are noticeably *inconsistent* in our concern. Sometimes we are on fire; other times, we are smoking embers. But one mistake in the area of concern is that many times we let *our* level of concern determine whether or not we will witness. If we feel concerned, we share with others. If we don't feel a concern, we fail to share. But our efforts in reaching the lost must not be regulated by our feeling of concern. Rather, our efforts are to be regulated by our Lord's feeling of concern for the lost. He is always concerned about them. It is the burden of *His* heart that should drive us to reach lost people. Not our compassion for sinners but His compassion for sinners must be our motivating factor in witnessing for Him. For this reason, not a love for souls but a love for Christ is the basic condition of effective personal evangelism. If we love Him, His interest will be our consuming interest, and His basic interest toward those who are lost is a redemptive interest.

Third, blood can be removed by a constant commitment to our task. Have you ever considered what failure in consistent witnessing can mean? One missed opportunity can mean one more Christless life and one more Christless grave, which could have been otherwise. On the other hand, consistency in remaining available as a witness delivers us from bloodguilt.

I am far from being what I ought to be as a witness for our Lord. Late one evening, I was exhausted from a teaching session of three hours. I had told the Lord earlier in the day that I was available to Him if He wanted to use me to touch someone's life. It was after midnight when, on an elevator, I ran into Tony. My desire was to get to my room as quickly as possible and get to bed. But the Lord reminded me of my commitment to Him to be available. On the elevator, I sensed the Lord saying to me, "My child, did you really mean it when you told me you were at my disposal? Are you available to me for this situation?"

I responded, "Lord, I am tired. It's almost one o'clock in the morning, and I want to go to bed. And to be honest, Lord, I couldn't care less. But, grudgingly, I make myself available to you."

Tony was reading a newspaper. Before I stepped off the elevator, I took a Billy Graham tract out of my pocket and said to Tony as I stepped off the elevator, "Excuse me, sir, but here is some good news you won't read in today's newspaper."

I shoved the pamphlet into his hand. He took it, turned it over, and saw the name Billy Graham. I didn't know, but the Holy Spirit knew that Tony Maringo, born in Turkey, fluent in eleven languages, worker in the United Nations with Dag Hammarskjold, had once attended a Billy Graham crusade. At that crusade, God had spoken to his heart about becoming a Christian. He left that crusade service lost, but hungry to know more. When he saw Mr. Graham's name on that pamphlet, the hunger in his heart was revived, and in the early morning, on the fourth floor of that hotel, Tony invited Christ into his heart. I received a phone call from a pastor on Long Island shortly after that, telling me that Tony had come forward in a revival service in his church, confessing Christ as his Savior.

Being consistent in our availability and witness! This is the way to keep blood off of our hands.

Theme: Jesus Is Still the Answer . . .

Prelude

Call to Praise—Congregation
To God Be the Glory (vv. 1 and 2)

For Our Every Need . . .
Prayer of Praise—Pastoral Staff

Welcome—Pastoral Staff

Hymn of Welcome—Congregation (meet and greet)
My Life Is in You, Lord

Praise and Worship—Congregation
Lord, I Lift Your Name on High (2x)
Bless the Lord, O My Soul (2x)

Video Testimony (Keyboard continue to play under testimony)
Here I Am to Worship (Chris Tomlin) (2x)
Be Glorified (3x)
I Surrender All (v. 1, chorus, v. 2, chorus)

Each and Every Day . . .
Prayer of Praise—Pastoral Staff (play next hymn)

Song of Dedication—Congregation
CH 583 *You Are My All in All* (2x)

. . . Through All Eternity!!
Offertory Prayer

Offertory Praise—Solo or Congregation
The Wonder of It All

Sermon—Pastor

Hymn of Invitation—Congregation
   CH 79 *My Jesus, I Love Thee* (vv. 1 and 4)

Benediction Hymn—Congregation
   Blessed Assurance, Jesus Is Mine

Postlude

Additional Sermons and Lesson Ideas

SERIES: THE REVELATION OF CHRIST

The Mastery of the Unveiled Christ
Date preached:

By Dr. Denis Lyle

Scripture: Revelation 1:17–19

Introduction: What is your reaction when you are faced with Christ's Glory? John was as we should be when we are faced with Christ:

1. **Prostrate before him in sinfulness (v. 17).** He lay before the resplendent Redeemer: undone, unmasked, and unraveled! The holiness of Christ exposed his own impurity just as it did to Isaiah (see Is. 6:5).
2. **Prostrate before him in stillness (v. 17).** John collapsed at Christ's feet as a dead man. We often express ourselves to God so much that we forget to be still in His presence (Ps. 46:10).
3. **Prostrate before him in submissiveness (vv. 17–19).** Have you ever surrendered your life to Christ so sincerely that you've fallen at the feet of the Savior as though dead? Once John saw the majesty of Christ and fell before Him, Christ called him into service (v. 19)—to help write the Word of God!

Conclusion: Do you long to do something of eternal significance? When have you fallen prostrate at the feet of the Lord Jesus? Does He have complete mastery over you?

Spiritual Progress
Date preached:

By Dave Hirschman

Scripture: Hebrews 5:11—6:1

Introduction: Everyone wants to make progress in life. When we think of progress, we can easily identify with financial progress, marital/parental progress, and progress in one's career and schooling, but what about spiritual progress? Spiritual progress requires leaving where we are (Hebrews 6:1).

1. **There is the expectation of spiritual progress in the life of a Jesus-follower (Heb. 6:1).** Before we can move on, we must be certain of: things that should be known, things that anchor your life, and things that position for growth.
2. **The expectation of spiritual progress is not always fulfilled (Heb. 5:11–14).** Believers don't progress because some are deceived, some are distracted, and some are disobedient.
3. **A true follower of Jesus progresses spiritually (Heb. 5:13, 14).** This happens by cooperating with God, learning spiritual truth, and by becoming mature.

Conclusion: Do you want to make spiritual progress?

MARCH 21, 2010

SERIES: ON MISSION WITH GOD   SUGGESTED SERMON

Confidence for Soul-Winning[1]

By Darrell W. Robinson

Date preached:

Scripture: John 20:19–23

Introduction: What happened to the disciples? They had heard Jesus say, "If any man would come after me, let him deny himself and take up his cross daily and follow me" (Luke 9:23 RSV). Now they were hiding in fear behind locked doors.

Fear erects a barrier that dominates the mind, depresses motives, and discourages the mission of Jesus' followers. Fear turns attention inward toward self. Fear defeats soul-winning.

Can we get rid of the fear that hinders evangelism? Yes, indeed! The presence of Jesus removes fear for those who trust and obey Him. Jesus suddenly appeared in their midst and said, "Peace be with you" (John 20:19 RSV). Then, "he showed them his hands and his side. Then the disciples were glad when they saw the Lord" (John 20:20 RSV).

Knowing Jesus' love and loving Jesus overcomes fear. "There is no fear in love, but perfect love casts out fear" (1 John 4:18 RSV).

1. **The person of Jesus gives confidence for soul-winning.**

    A. **Peace comes from the abiding presence of Jesus (John 20:21).**

    (1) **Jesus said, "Peace be unto you" in verse 19.** He said it to resolve their fear of His sudden appearance and their anxiety for personal safety.

    (2) **Later he gave assurance, as His followers were sent out on mission to be His witnesses.** Jesus affirmed His presence with the disciples in Matthew 28:20 (KJV), "And, lo, I am with you alway, even unto the end of the world."

    Summary: Jesus promised to give His peace as we obey Him in soul-winning.

    B. **Peace comes from the authoritative presence of the person of Jesus (John 20:21).**

---

[1]Reproduced with permission of the North American Mission Board, Alpharetta, Georgia. All rights reserved.

(1) He was sent by God, the Father, as the eternal Son to redeem the lost world: "As My Father has sent Me . . ."

(2) He has sent His followers as an extension of His mission to redeem the lost world: ". . . Even so I send you."

Summary: The followers of Jesus are sent under divine authority to reach lost people with the gospel of Christ.

2. **The plan of Jesus gives confidence for soul-winning.** Jesus' plan is recorded in the Great Commission (Matt. 28:19, 20). This same commission is found in different forms in the four Gospels and in Acts. Repetition is the key to establishing direction and building enthusiasm for soul-winning.

It is Jesus' plan: "So I send you" (John 20:21 RSV).

A. **To involve every christian:** Total participation of the membership is required to reach every person with the gospel.

(1) **Christians do not witness because they are not sent for by lost people.**
   - The lost are in spiritual darkness and do not see their need (see 2 Cor. 4:3, 4).
   - The lost are in spiritual deadness and have no power to change, apart from the work of God and the work of the Holy Spirit (Eph. 2:1).

(2) **Christians do go to witness because they are sent by the Lord (Matt. 28:19, 20; Mark 16:15; Luke 24:47–49; Acts 1:8).**

B. **To include every person:** Total penetration of every geographic area with the gospel, not overlooking any person, is Jesus' plan.

3. **The power of Jesus gives confidence for soul-winning (John 20:22, 23).** God uses three things to reach people for Himself:

A. **The work of the spirit (John 20:22).** "He breathed on them, and said to them, 'Receive the Holy Spirit.'" The Holy Spirit came and filled the church at Pentecost later. God breathed into the body of the first Adam the breath of life and he became a living soul (Gen. 2:7). God breathed His Spirit into the body of Christ, the last Adam. The church became the dynamic body of Christ. The Holy Spirit empowers the believer for effective witness (Acts 1:8).

B. **The word of salvation (John 20:23).** No person has the power to forgive any other man's sins. The power to remit or retain sins is in the word of salvation. God forgives as people respond in repentance and faith. This verse is parallel to Jesus' word to Peter about the keys of the kingdom of heaven (Matt. 16:19). The word of forgiveness is entrusted to believers.

(1) **The believer witnesses to convey forgiveness to repentant hearts.** Their sins are remitted.

(2) **The believer warns sinners that they are forfeiting the forgiveness of God.** Their sins are retained.

C. **The witness of the saved.** It is the privilege and responsibility of every believer to bear the good news of God's forgiveness through Christ to every lost person.

Conclusion: Jesus came "to seek and to save that which was lost" (Luke 19:10 KJV). If our hearts beat as beats the heart of Jesus, we will seek and reach the lost with the gospel of salvation.

SUGGESTED ORDER OF WORSHIP

Theme: Give Unto the Lord . . .

Prelude

Welcome—Pastor

Hymn of Welcome—Congregation (meet and greet)
What a Mighty God (2x)
Great and Mighty (2x)

Give Him Glory . . .

Worship Through Reading the Scripture—Pastoral Staff
Col. 1:15–22[1]

---

[1]Colossians 1:15–22:

[15]He is the image of the invisible God, the firstborn over all creation. [16]For by him all things were created: things in heaven and on earth, visible and invisible, whether thrones or powers or rulers or authorities; all things were created by him and for him. [17]He is before all things, and in him all things hold together. [18]And he is the head of the body, the church; he is the beginning and the firstborn from among the dead, so that in everything he might have the supremacy. [19]For God was pleased to have all his fullness dwell in him, [20]and through him to reconcile to himself all things, whether things on earth or things in heaven, by making peace through his blood, shed on the cross. [21]Once you were alienated from God and were enemies in your minds because of your evil behavior. [22]But now he has reconciled you by Christ's physical body through death to present you holy in his sight, without blemish and free from accusation.

SUGGESTED ORDER OF WORSHIP—*Continued*

Praise and Worship—Congregation
Come into His Presence
We Have Come into His House
We Are Standing on Holy Ground
O the Glory of His Presence

Give Him Honor . . .
Prayer of Praise—Pastoral Staff
Knowing You (chorus, verse, chorus)—Congregation

. . . Give Him Strength!
Offertory Prayer—Pastoral Staff

Offertory Praise—Praise Team and Congregation
As the Deer

Sermon—Pastor

Hymn of Invitation—Congregation
I Surrender All

Benediction Hymn—Congregation
Great and Mighty

Postlude

Additional Sermons and Lesson Ideas

SERIES: THE REVELATION OF CHRIST

The Ministry of the Unveiled Christ
By Dr. Denis Lyle

Date preached:

Scripture: Revelation 1:17–19

Introduction: As John lay prostrate before the feet of Christ, the Lord did something that was typical of Him. He reached down and touched John.

1. **He conveys His sympathy (v. 17).** Christ told John not to fear. As you read through the Gospels, Christ often touched people to heal and restore them. No wonder the risen Lord reaches out and touches John. Do you need to sense His touch or hear His voice saying, "Fear not"?
2. **He reveals His identity (vv. 17, 18).** Christ said " I am," which reveals His deity (Ex. 3:14). "The first and the last" reveals His eternality. The words "I am He who lives" reveal His victory, so there's truly nothing to fear!
3. **He affirms His authority (v. 18).** The keys Christ possesses signify His sovereign authority to open and close the grave. Christ decides who dies and when.

Conclusion: Feel the hand of God comforting you despite your circumstances, and hear the voice of God affirming His authority over you. Fear not!

Love Like There's No Tomorrow
By Jason H. Barber

Date preached:

SCRIPTURE: John 13:1–5, 12; Philippians 2:5–8

INTRODUCTION: How can we think like Jesus in order to serve like Jesus?

1. **The Attitude of Jesus—think like Christ:**
   A. He was leaving (vv. 1, 3b). Knowing that we are one day leaving puts this existence in a proper perspective (Gen. 45:20).
   B. He loved them completely (v. 1; John 3:16; 1 Cor. 13).
   C. He lived above His circumstances (v. 2). The presence of evil did not hinder His demonstration of love (Luke 23:34).
   D. He had nothing to lose (v. 3). He was secure in His identity and aware that all things belong to Him (Eph. 1:22; Heb. 2:8).
2. **The Actions of Jesus (John 13:4, 5; Phil. 2).**
   A. He arose from the table as He did his throne in heaven.
   B. He laid aside His garments as He had divine attributes.
   C. He poured water in a basin as He would pour out His life.
   D. He washed their Feet just as He renews our thinking.
   E. He returned to His seat just as He returned to his throne.

Conclusion: "For even the Son of Man did not come to be served, but to serve, and to give His life a ransom for many" (Mark 10:45).

MARCH 28, 2010

Three Crosses and Two Choices

By Denis Lyle

Date preached:

Scripture: Luke 23:32–43, especially verse 43

Introduction: All of us have sin *in* us, but we are divided when it comes to sin *on* us. Some have the penalty of sin resting on them; others have, by grace, shifted it over to Christ. The great question is this: Is your sin *on you* or *on Christ* who paid its penalty? On the hill of Calvary, there were three crosses and three men. One man died *in* sin, one man died *to* sin, one man died *for* sin. Over the first cross, we envision the word:

1. **Rejection.** Sometimes we forget that there were two thieves. It has been said, "One thief was saved that no sinner might despair; one thief was damned that no sinner might presume." These two men had the same opportunity, they heard and saw the same things, yet one died and went to heaven, and the other died and went to hell. Over this first cross we have the word *rejection*. He was a man who:

   A. **Despised the presence of Jesus Christ (vv. 34–38).** The first thief should have *heard Jesus' prayer:* "Father, forgive them; for they do not know what they do" (v. 34). This man should have *read Jesus' title:* perhaps the first gospel tract that was ever written hung over the head of Christ, "JESUS OF NAZARETH, THE KING OF THE JEWS" (v. 38; John 19:19). Instead, he despised the presence of Christ. Is that what you have done? Has the Lord laid you low in order that you might think of Him? Has God allowed peculiar trials to cross your path? Even in trials, Jesus extends to us His salvation; don't despise His presence!

   B. **Despised the person of Jesus Christ (v. 39).** This thief was no different from those who bypassed the cross and taunted Jesus (Mark 15:29). Imagine, a man on the brink of eternity, on the very precipice of hell, mocking the Savior's person! Yet has your action or attitude been any different from this man? Perhaps the only time you take the Savior's name on your lips is not in prayer, but in mockery.

C. **Despised the power of Jesus Christ (v. 39).** Again, on the brink of eternity, the same thief challenges the power of God, saying in effect, "If you are the Anointed One, demonstrate your power!" I wonder, is this one of the problems you have in becoming a Christian. Are you unsure whether Christ has the power to save you forever? Over the first cross is "rejection," but over the third cross we envision the word:

2. **Reception.** This man believed on Christ's name in faith, so Jesus saved him (vv. 42–43; see John 1:12). At first he insulted the Lord Jesus, but then:

A. **He began to look at the Savior (vv. 34–38).** He looked at the face of the Son of God, that face so marred. He saw holiness and peace there! He saw Deity stamped on that noble brow. He saw the crown of thorns, the spiky emblem of the curse. He read the title the Romans nailed to the cross. Perhaps he began to remember the teaching of his boyhood days, the words of the prophet Isaiah (Is. 53:5). Have you looked to Jesus in faith (see John 3:14–15)?

B. **He began to listen to the Savior and His mockers (vv. 34–39).** The second thief listened as Jesus forgave His enemies (v. 34), and it seems that he heard the gospel from Jesus' mockers (vv. 34–39; Matt. 27:40–42)! He believed in the innocence of Jesus (v. 41), in the ability of Jesus (v. 42), and in the royalty of Jesus (v. 42). This man was not sitting in a comfortable seat, listening to God's plan of salvation, surrounded by Christians. He did not have a single page of the New Testament. He was racked with fearful pain, yet he believed because he *looked at* and *listened to* Christ in faith. Finally, over the center cross, we envision the word:

3. **Redemption.** One man died *in* sin, one man died *to* sin, but Jesus died *for* sin, purchasing our freedom, becoming our redemption:

A. **The basis of redemption—*through His blood* (Eph. 1:7).** Only the precious blood of Christ could purchase us out of the slave market of sin.

B. The blessing of redemption—*the forgiveness of sins* (Eph. 1:7).
Are your sins forgiven and blotted out by Jesus (Is. 43:25)?

Conclusion: Over the first cross is the word *rejection*. Is that you, still rejecting the Savior? Over the second, the center cross, is the word *redemption*. Jesus made our redemption possible, through faith in His blood (Rom. 3:25). As we commemorate the sacrifice of His body through the Lord's Supper, let's check ourselves to be sure that, like the thief on the third cross, we have *received* Jesus.

> Was it for crimes that I have done
> He groaned upon the tree
> Amazing pity, grace unknown
> And love beyond degree.

SUGGESTED ORDER OF WORSHIP

Shout to the Lord![1]

Prelude

Welcome and Announcements—Pastoral Staff

Hymn of Welcome—Congregation (meet and greet)
    CH 214 *He Has Made Me Glad*

Prayer of Worship—Worship Pastor (keyboard play next song during prayer)

Song of Worship—Congregation
    Shout to the Lord (2x)
Testimony (1 girl—2-minute video)
    For His Salvation

Worship and Praise—Congregation
    I Sing Praises (2x)
    O How He Loves You and Me (2x)

---

[1]Theme: Shout to the Lord . . . His Salvation . . . His Healing . . . His Faithfulness.

Scripture Praise—Pastoral Staff
Hebrews 1:1–3, 10–12[2]
CH 583 *You Are My All in All* (2x)

Offertory Prayer—Pastoral Staff

Testimony—(1 guy; 2 minute video)
For His Healing

Song of Praise—Congregation
Holy Spirit Rain Down

Testimony (1 girl—2 minute video)
His Faithfulness

Song of Praise—Solo
When It's All Been Said and Done

Sermon—Pastor

Hymn of Invitation—Congregation
CH 481 *Come Just As You Are*

Song of Benediction—CH 214 *He Has Made Me Glad*—
Congregation

Postlude

---

[2]Hebrews 1:1–3, 10–12

1 In the past God spoke to our forefathers through the prophets at many times and in various ways, **2** but in these last days he has spoken to us by his Son, whom he appointed heir of all things, and through whom he made the universe. **3** The Son is the radiance of God's glory and the exact representation of his being, sustaining all things by his powerful word. **10** "In the beginning, O Lord, you laid the foundations of the earth, and the heavens are the work of your hands. **11** They will perish, but you remain; they will all wear out like a garment. **12** You will roll them up like a robe; like a garment they will be changed. But you remain the same, and your years will never end."

Additional Sermons and Lesson Ideas

It Was Necessary

Date preached:

By Robert Morgan

Scripture: Luke 24:46–49

Introduction: Crucifixion was the most horrible kind of execution ever conceived. After His resurrection, Jesus spoke of:

1. **The Necessity (v. 46).** It was necessary for Christ to suffer.
2. **The Need (v. 47).** Repentance and remission (forgiveness) should be preached.
3. **The news (vv. 48, 49).** We are witnesses, endued with power from on high to share this message with others.

Conclusion: Every human being either needs the gospel, or needs to be sharing the gospel with others.

A Strange Invitation

Date preached:

By Jason H. Barber

Scripture: Mark 10:17–22

Introduction: You are here today at someone else's invitation. Outside of the Alamo, Col. Travis extended a strange invitation, "Come and die for freedom's cause." Long ago, Jesus extended an invitation to a man that surely seemed strange to him.
This man was:

1. **Rich (vv. 21, 22).** Relative to the world, most Americans are wealthy.
2. **Religious (vv. 17, 19, 20).** He believed he was good.
3. **A Ruler (Luke 18:18).** He was a person of influence.
4. **Running (v. 17).** While he may have everything in this life, he is concerned about his afterlife.

Concerning eternal life, Jesus invites him to:

1. **Discard his god—money.** Jesus has addressed his self-righteousness, now He addresses his idolatry.
2. **Die to self.** Taking up the cross is a death sentence.
3. **Be His disciple.** To follow Jesus is to walk in His steps.

Conclusion: This man walked away in hopes that he could keep his life. Tradition says that Moses Rose fled the Alamo in hopes of saving his life, but he never made it out of Texas alive. Today, Jesus invites you to exchange your life for His (cf. Matt. 16:25).

APRIL 4, 2010

EASTER SUNDAY SUGGESTED SERMON

It's the Gospel Truth!

Date preached:

By Dr. Kent Spann

Scripture: 1 Corinthians 15:1–11

Introduction: Ask people what day they think changed the world, and you will get all sorts of answers. An older person might say December 7, 1941, when Japan bombed Pearl Harbor. A radio broadcaster claimed that September 11, 2001, was the day that changed our world.

What was the day that changed our world? The day that *really* changed the world was the day that Jesus was raised from the dead, when Jesus came out of the tomb.

There were no news reporters, no lights, and no cameras. Tom Brokaw didn't flash on the screen. There were no interviews on *Larry King Live*. Life didn't come to a screeching halt. Governments were not called into emergency session. There were no shockwaves that reverberated around the world as they did on September 11. No, Resurrection Day was not an international event like September 11, but my friends, it changed the world forever.

Yet unlike September 11 or other historic days, many do not believe in the veracity of the Resurrection Day. The idea of the Resurrection of Jesus Christ has been relegated to the world of mythology right up there with Homer's *Iliad* and *The Odyssey*. Santa Claus, the Easter Bunny, and the Resurrection of Jesus Christ are just fairy tales.

Skepticism about the Resurrection of Jesus Christ is nothing new. There were scoffers in Paul's day just like today. In 1 Corinthians 15:1–11, Paul boldly declares that the Resurrection is the gospel truth! He tells us how we know it is the gospel truth.

1. **We know the Resurrection is true because the gospel declares it (15:1, 2).** Paul uses the word *gospel* two times in these verses. What is the gospel? The word *gospel* means literally "good news." What does the gospel declare? Paul succinctly states what the gospel is in verses 3 and 4. The gospel in a nutshell is this: ***Jesus died, was buried, and was raised from the dead on the third day.***

A. This is the gospel that people have believed and accepted down through the ages, *"Which you received."* It is the same gospel that Paul preached when he first came to Corinth during his second missionary journey (Acts 18). There in Corinth he preached the gospel and people responded (18:7, 8). A church was established called the Corinthian church.

Paul makes it clear that years later he has not changed his message one iota. He had not found anything that changed his mind about the gospel and the Resurrection of Jesus Christ.

That is the testimony of the church. For two thousand years the church, the true church, has faithfully declared the gospel of Christ.

We have nothing new to offer to the 21st century. We just have the same old message that Jesus died and rose from the grave.

B. This is the gospel that people have staked their lives on, *"Which you have taken your stand."* The apostles lost their lives defending the truth of the Resurrection. The early believers staked their lives on it, even when faced with the threats of Nero. People still continue to stake their lives on it today.

C. This is the gospel that people have staked their salvation on, *"By this gospel you are saved."* People have put their hope for eternal life in the Resurrection of Jesus Christ. The gospel doesn't hold out any hope other than salvation by faith in Jesus Christ's death and resurrection.

The unchanging message of the church is the gospel. This is the message that the church is founded upon. It is the cornerstone of the church. The church is not organized around a personality, a social cause, a need, etc. It is organized around the gospel. The church exists because of the gospel. If there were no gospel, then there would be no church. It is the one and only message the church has to offer to the world. We have no other message than the gospel.

The testimony of the church is that Christ has been raised from the dead. The church has always affirmed the Resurrection. The church has gone through the battles and debates about the Resurrection, but it always returns to the truth of the gospel.

2. **We know the Resurrection is true because the Scriptures foretold it (15:3, 4).** Did you notice the little phrase *according to Scriptures* repeated over and over again. All this stuff about Jesus dying and being resurrected was not something made up. It was all *according to Scriptures.* The Scriptures which Paul referred to are the Old Testament Scriptures. One of the great evidences for Christianity, and for that matter the Resurrection, is the Scriptures themselves. The Scriptures written hundreds and even thousands of years before Christ's birth foretold all that would happen.

   A. **The Scriptures foretold that Christ would die for our sins on a cross (Ps. 22:16–18; Is. 53:4–9).**

   B. **The Scriptures foretold that Christ would be raised from the dead (Ps. 16:10; Is. 53:11).**

3. **We know the Resurrection is true because eyewitnesses testified to it (15:5–8).** Paul calls *eyewitnesses* to the witness stand.

   A. **Peter or Cephas.** Peter was the first apostolic witness to Jesus according to Luke 24:34.

   B. **The Apostles.** This refers to the apostles. It doesn't mean there were actually twelve, because we know that Judas was dead. The apostles were still referred to as the Twelve.

   C. **The Five Hundred.** The skeptics have scoffed at the testimony of the disciples. They say the disciples were in a state of shock. They couldn't let Him go. They were delirious and must have been hallucinating. Ok, let's give them that argument, but what about five hundred other people who saw Him *at the same time,* and most of whom were still alive for questioning?

   D. **James, the half-brother of Jesus.** This was James, the former skeptic and unbeliever (John 7:5), but now a believer. What converted him? The resurrection of Jesus Christ.

   E. **Saul, now Paul.** Paul was a powerful witness because he was formerly a hostile fanatic Jesus-hater who had come to the other side. What changed him? The Resurrected Christ.

4. **We know the Resurrection is true because lives are changed by it (15:9–11).** There is one final evidence no one can deny and that is the lives changed by the Resurrection of Jesus Christ.

A. Paul's life was changed by the Resurrection.

B. The Corinthians' lives were changed by the Resurrection.

C. Countless lives have been and continue to be changed by the Resurrection. History is still writing the book on the lives changed by the Resurrection. Murderers, homosexuals, prostitutes, community leaders, politicians, arrogant athletes, etc., all are being changed by the gospel of Jesus Christ.

D. My life was changed by the Resurrection. Preacher should briefly share his/her own conversion testimony.

Conclusion: The evidence is overwhelming for the Resurrection of Jesus Christ. Professor Thomas Arnold, chair of Modern History at Oxford University in England, writes of the Resurrection:

> *The evidence for our Lord's life and death and resurrection may be, and often has been, shown to be satisfactory; it is good according to the common rules for distinguishing good evidence from bad. Thousands and tens of thousands of persons have gone through it piece by piece, as carefully as every judge summing upon a most important case. I have myself done it many times over, not to persuade others but to satisfy myself. I have been used for many years to study the histories of other times, and to examine and weigh the evidence of those who have written about them, and I know of no one fact in the history of mankind which is proved by better and fuller evidence . . . Than the great sign which God hath given us that Christ died and rose again from the dead.*[1]

Charles Hodge, a theologian, says, in reference to the Resurrection: *It is the best authenticated event in ancient history.*[2]
THE RESURRECTION OF JESUS CHRIST IS THE GOSPEL TRUTH!

---

[1]*Resurrection Truth: 1 Corinthians 15*, John MacArthur, 25.
[2]Ibid., 25.

EASTER:
How Do We Know and Why Does It Matter[1]
Luke 24:25–27

Prelude—Instrumental Group
CH 357 *Christ Arose*

Call to Worship—Congregation
CH 368 *He Lives* (v. 1, chorus, v. 2, chorus)
CH 372 *Our God Reigns* (1x in Ab)

Scripture Reading—Congregation and Worship Leader
He Is Risen, Indeed!

Worship and Praise
CH 365 *Alleluia! Alleluia!* (as written with transitions)
CH 366 *I Live* (1x in G, 1x in Ab)
CH 367 *Christ the Lord Is Risen Today* (vv. 1 and 4)

Worship in Prayer—Pastoral Staff

Welcome—Pastoral Staff

Welcome Hymn—Pastoral Staff (meet and greet)
CH 362 *Celebrate Jesus* (2x in F)

Worship and Praise—Congregation
SPW 123 *Because He Lives* (chorus, v. 1, chorus, v. 3, chorus in F)
MSPW2 *The Wonderful Cross* (m13 to end in D)

Offertory Prayer—Pastoral Staff

Offertory Praise—Choir, Solo, or Congregation
It's Still the Cross

Easter Message—Pastor
How Do We Know and Why Does It Matter?

---

[1]Luke 24:5, 6; 1 Cor. 15:54–57; John 11:25 NKJV, © 2009 Vernon M. Whaley.

SUGGESTED ORDER OF WORSHIP—*Continued*

Hymn of Response/Invitation—Congregation
CH 487 *Room at the Cross*

Benediction Hymn—Congregation
CH 195 *Bless the Name of Jesus* (2x in C)

Postlude—Instrumental Group
CH 357 *Christ Arose*

Responsive Reading: He Is Risen, Indeed!

Worship Leader: Why do you seek the living among the dead? He is not here, but is risen! Remember how He spoke to you when He was still in Galilee?

Congregation: He is Risen Indeed!

Worship Leader: The Lord has risen.

Congregation: He is Risen Indeed!

Worship Leader: So when this corruptible has put on incorruption, and this mortal has put on immortality, then shall be brought to pass the saying that is written: "Death is swallowed up in victory."

Congregation: "O Death, where is your sting? O Hell, where is your victory?"

Worship Leader: The sting of death is sin, and the strength of sin is the law.

Congregation: Thanks be to God, who gives us the victory through Jesus Christ.

Worship Leader: Jesus said to her, "I am the resurrection and the life. He who believes in Me, though he may die, he shall live."

Additional Sermons and Lesson Ideas

EASTER:

How Do We Know and Why Does It Matter

By Dr. David Jeremiah

Date preached:

Scripture: Luke 24:25–27

Introduction: In this great Easter text, Jesus chided the disciples for being slow of heart to believe. He also explained the importance of His Resurrection and the Old Testament witness about Himself.

1. **How do we know the Resurrection really happened?**
   A. The Soldiers—Matthew 27:62–66
   B. The Seal—Matthew 27:66
   C. The Stone—Matthew 27:59–60; 28:2
   D. The Sepulcher—Matthew 28:5–6
   E. The Shroud—John 20:3–8
   F. The Scars—John 20:26–28
   G. The Sightings—1 Corinthians 15:3–8
   H. The Survival of the Church
   I. The Sunday Worship
2. **Why is the Resurrection important today?**
   A. The resurrection of Jesus Christ is about Our past (saved from our sins).
   B. The resurrection of Jesus Christ is about our present (saved to serve Him).
   C. The resurrection of Jesus Christ is about our future (saved to be with Him forever).

Conclusion: Have you considered inviting Him into your life to take control?

Fear Should Not Be a Factor for You

By Jason H. Barber

Date preached:

Scripture: 2 Timothy 1:7, 8a

Introduction: The primary reason Christians do not witness is because of fear. But, we should not be ashamed of the gospel, because:

1. **God has given us power.** If we were won by the power of God (Eph. 2:8), and we walk by the power of God (Gal. 5:25; Eph. 3:16b), then we should rely upon the power of God to witness (Acts 1:8; cf. 1 Cor. 2:4, 5).
2. **God has given us love.** God demonstrated His love for us while we were still sinners in that His Son died for us (Rom. 5:8). The same love God manifested at the cross has been generously given to us

(Rom. 5:5b). The first evidence of the Spirit is love (Gal. 5:22a). "There is no fear in love, but perfect love casts out fear" (1 John 4:18a).

3. **God has given us a sound/properly-prioritized mind.** The lies of the Devil should not scare us into silence (cf. Mark 8:38).

Conclusion: Therefore, fear should not be a factor for you (v. 8a).

APRIL 11, 2010

A Look at the Hereafter

Date preached:

By D. James Kennedy

Scripture: Matthew 7:13, 14, especially verse 14, "Narrow is the gate and difficult is the way which leads to life, and there are few who find it."

Introduction: Years ago, I heard someone pejoratively described as a man that was "so heavenly minded that he was no earthly good." Well, today, for every person who is so heavenly minded he's no earthly good, there are 10,000 people who are so worldly minded they're of no heavenly good. We live in a secular age. The word "secular" comes from the Latin *saecularis,* which means, "time perceived without any concept of eternity." It is like a smoked glass dome placed over the secular city so that one can see neither up to God nor out to eternity. It wasn't always that way. In earlier days, there were thousands of volumes of prose and poetry written about heaven. But, of course, in those days, sex was taboo. Today, you can't turn on the television without seeing some program about sex. But death and eternity have become the taboos of our age.

1. **Unbelievers face death.** When Professor T. H. Huxley, the father of agnosticism, came to the end of life, the nurse attending him said that as he lay dying, the great skeptic suddenly looked up at some sight invisible to mortal eyes, and staring a while, whispered at last, "So it is true." And he died. I wonder how many young people in college who are being taught about agnosticism are taught that? According to Svetlana Stalin, when her father, Joseph Stalin, was dying, he was lying with his eyes closed. At the very last moment, he suddenly opened his eyes and looked at the people in the room. It was a look of unutterable horror and anguish. Then he lifted his left hand, as though pointing to something, and dropped it and died. I wonder how many budding Communists are told how Stalin left the world.

2. **Christians face death.** The departure of Christians is far different, and our destination is many light years away. Dwight L. Moody said

as he was dying, "This is my coronation day! It is glorious!" The great Puritan, John Owen, having come to the end of life, dictated from his deathbed a final letter to a friend, saying: "I am yet in the land of the dying, but I hope soon to be in the land of the living." So it is, that those of us who trust in Christ will be more alive at our death than we have ever been before, for we go to a far better place than we have ever known before; a place the Bible calls heaven; the city that comes down from God (Rev. 21:1–4).

3. **Two destinations.** The Bible makes it clear there are two different destinations after death—heaven and hell. Hell is a place of eternal death, eternal torment, eternal punishment. Many people act as if somehow modern skepticism has evaporated hell. But it has not changed at all, as many in the last moment of the cold, clammy sweat of their death agonies have discovered to their unutterable horror. Jesus called it "Gehenna," the valley of Hinnom which was outside Jerusalem. It was a dump where all manner of garbage burned continually and the smoke of its burning went up everlastingly (Mark 9:44; Rev. 22:15; 1 Cor. 6:9b, 10). I say to you, with heavy heart, that there are some here in this sanctuary who will never see the inside of Paradise. They have deceived themselves into supposing all is well, yet they know in their hearts they've never truly repented of their sins or surrendered themselves to Christ. Perhaps they're waiting for "someday." But remember what Christ said to the man in Luke 12:20: "Fool! This night your soul will be required of you." God offers you freely the gift of eternal life, paid for at infinite cost by Jesus Christ. It is a straight and narrow way. The portal to Paradise is as narrow as the Cross. There on the blackened hill of Golgotha, Jesus Christ took our sin upon Himself.

Conclusion: Many people spend more time preparing for a two-week vacation than for where they will spend eternity! Do you know you have eternal life? Do you know you're on your way to heaven? The Scripture says, "These things I have written to you who believe in the name of the Son of God, that you may know that you have eternal life." Oh, Jesus, I come. I come.

STATS, STORIES, AND MORE

- Half of all adults (51 percent) believe that if a person is generally good or does enough good things for others during his life, he will earn a place in heaven. —George Barna in 2001 Survey

- I remember one time being in a building and when ready to leave, I opened a door thinking that it was an exit, only to discover that I had stepped into a tiny broom closet! Of course I stepped out instantly and closed the door. I probably was in there only one or two seconds at most. Now, wouldn't it be extraordinarily odd if I were to spend the rest of my life talking about that little closet? Since it is without doubt that we will spend 99.99+ percent of our lives in heaven, or wherever it is we are going, then why do we spend all our time talking about this "little closet" which will be but a moment's fleeting passing in the prospect of eternity? —D. James Kennedy

- Two men struck gold in the wilderness during the great Klondike Gold Rush. Each day they could hardly wait to get out of their bunks to continue their search for gold. They found more and more each day. They were so busy they didn't notice that summer had passed and that fall was upon them. They didn't notice the chill in the air because they were so eager to get more and more of the glittering yellow gold. One morning they awoke to find themselves in the midst of a howling snowstorm that lasted four days. When it was over, they discovered they were snowbound. The winter months had come, and within a few weeks, their food supply was exhausted. Several years later, the prospectors' cabin was discovered. All that remained of them were their skeletons. On a rough-hewn table, next to bags of gold, was found a note describing what had happened to them, of how they had not noticed that winter was coming, and they were caught unprepared. —D. James Kennedy

Theme: Eternal Life—What It Is and How to Get It
By Dr. R. A. Torrey

Scripture: Romans 6:23

Call to Prayer and Worship—Pastor
(All Men Asked to Come to Front of Church for Group Prayer for Service)

Prelude—Instrumentalist
Shout to the Lord

Call to Worship—Congregation
SPW 9 *Firm Foundation* (2x F)
CH 408 *How Firm a Foundation* (2 verses G)

Prayer of Worship—Pastoral Staff

Jesus . . . Our Sovereign Lord

Welcome—Pastoral Staff

Welcome Hymn (meet and greet)
CH 601 *Yes, Lord, Yes* (2x in Eb)

Testimony of Praise (2-minute testimony live or on video)

Jesus . . . Our Savior

Praise and Worship—Congregation
CH 308 *There Is a Redeemer* (verse 1, chorus, chorus in D)
SPW 6 *Because We Believe* (3x in D)
CH 139 *Great Is Thy Faithfulness* (v. 1, chorus, v. 3, chorus (D), chorus (Eb))

Offertory Prayer—Pastoral Staff

Offertory Praise—Praise Team or Ensemble
We Serve a Mighty God

Jesus . . . Our Sustainer

Message—Pastor
Eternal Life: What It Is and How to Get It

Hymn of Response/Invitation—Congregation
CH 481 *Come Just as You Are*

Benediction Hymn/Postlude—Congregation
SPW 100 *Bless the Name of Jesus*

Additional Sermons and Lesson Ideas

Eternal Life: What It Is and How to Get It
By Dr. R. A. Torrey

Date preached:

Scripture: Romans 6:23

Introduction: How wonderful to go to bed at night with the assurance of eternal life.

   1. **What eternal life is:**
     A. Eternal life is real life (1 Tim. 6:12, 19).
     B. Eternal life is abundant life (John 10:10).
     C. Eternal life is joyous life (1 Pet. 1:8).
     D. Eternal life is a life of true knowledge (John 17:3).
     E. Eternal life is endless Life (John 10:28).
   2. **Who can have it? Anybody can (Rev. 22:17).**
   3. **How to get it:**
     A. It is a gift.
     B. It is in Jesus Christ. When you have Christ, you have eternal life (1 John 5:12).

Conclusion: Eternal life is God's gift to you through Jesus Christ. Will you receive it?

Lukewarm Laodiceans
By Jason H. Barber

Date preached:

Scripture: Revelation 3:14–22

   1. **The problem**
     A lukewarm church is:
     A. A compromising church (vv. 15, 16). The water supply to the city could easily be cutoff, leaving them helpless and vulnerable. Like the city, the church learned the art of appeasement and compromise.
     B. A comfortable church (*I am rich*).
     C. A conceited church (*I have become wealthy*).
     D. A complacent church (*I have need of nothing*).
     E. A clueless church (*and do not know that you are*).
   2. **The Prescription:**
     A. He advised them to buy (Is. 55:1) some things:
       1) Proud of their wealth, they needed gold (Faith) (1 Pet. 1:7).
       2) Proud of their woolen garments, they needed white garments (righteousness).
       3) Proud of their eye salve, they needed sight (discernment).
     B. He advised them to be some things:
       1) Be zealous.
       2) Be repentant.

APRIL 18, 2010

SUGGESTED SERMON

Integrity in Doctrine

Date preached:

By Ed Dobson

Scripture: Titus 1:5–9, especially verse 9, "Holding fast the faithful word as he has been taught, that he may be able, by sound doctrine, both to exhort and convict those who contradict."

Introduction: This passage has to do with the qualifications for church leaders, and the overall requirement is blamelessness. Elders must be blameless in family life (v. 6), personal character (vv. 7, 8) and doctrine (v. 9).

1. **Leaders must be committed to sound doctrine—***Holding fast the faithful word.* The same verb was used in Luke 16:13 where Jesus said we cannot be *devoted* to two masters. An elder must be exclusively devoted to the faithful word. The Greek for "faithful word" is πιστoo λόγου (*pistoo logoo*), the faithful word or trustworthy saying. This phrase is unique to the writings of Paul and specifically to the Pastoral Epistles. (See 1 Tim. 1:15; 3:1; 4:9; 2 Tim. 2:11; Titus 3:7–8.) Paul and the apostles had provided authority for the early church, but they were growing old. In future years where could the church turn for authority? Paul was saying, "When I'm no longer here, you still have the authority—it is the authority of the word of God. Hold it firmly."

2. **Leaders must be committed to public proclamation of sound doctrine—***as he has been taught, that he may be able, by sound doctrine, both to exhort and convict.* The public proclamation of the word of God is a central focus of the church. This is one of the major themes of the Pastoral Epistles (see 1 Tim. 3:2; 4:13; 5:17; 2 Tim. 2:1, 2, 15, 25; 4:1, 2).

3. **Leaders must make practical application of sound doctrine—***Both to exhort and convict those who contradict.*

   A. **The leader must exhort and encourage by sound teaching.** The word "encourage" is the word παρακαλεω (*para-ka-lĕ-ō*). The preposition *para* means "alongside of something"; the stem means "to call." Teaching and preaching is not merely the dissemination of theological truth or the passing out of information. We are to communicate God's truth so as to call people alongside of the truth of God. How does God's Word apply to our lives?

B. The leader must convict by sound doctrine. We are to refute those who oppose the truth. The word "refute" means to bring to light, to expose, to set forth, or to convince and convict. We must teach God's Word clearly enough to expose error and to allow the Holy Spirit to convince and convict those who oppose it.

Conclusion: Let me suggest, by way of application, that there are three dimensions or categories to our doctrine:

- There is absolute truth—the truth that draws a line between believers and non-believers. These are essential doctrines necessary for salvation, such as the person of Christ, the power of His shed blood for the remission of sins, His bodily resurrection, etc. We adhere to these truths because we accept the authority of inspired Scripture.
- There are convictions, which do not have to be accepted in order to go to heaven. These are our beliefs about things such as details about baptism, the gifts of the Spirit, or the return of Christ.
- There are preferences. Different Christians and different churches enjoy different styles of worship or types of music, for example.

There are three dangers in the area of absolutes, convictions, and preferences. Number one is to take everything you believe and elevate it to an absolute. A second danger is to so focus on one of the convictions to the exclusion of all the others. Danger number three is saying, "We just believe in Jesus. Doctrine is really not all that important. After all, doctrine divides and love unites." May I suggest that *lack* of doctrine divides. When everyone believes whatever they want without a commitment to doctrine, then you have division. As pastor of this church I have a personal commitment to doctrine, to publicly proclaiming it, and to applying it to my life and, hopefully, to the lives of our attendees. I'm also committed to our heritage here of absolutes, convictions, and preferences. That is who we are. It is incumbent upon leadership to keep these things in balance while at the same time loving those outside our congregation who are brothers and sisters in Jesus who differ with us in our convictions and in our preferences.

STATS, STORIES, AND MORE

Between Two Worlds

- John R. W. Stott wrote a book several years ago about preaching entitled *Between Two Worlds.* His thesis was that preaching or teaching involves two worlds, the world of biblical truth and the world of human reality. Preaching or teaching the Bible is the process of building a bridge from the world of biblical truth into the world of human experience so that we apply the truth of God to daily life. —Ed Dobson

Someone Once Said . . .

- Great saints have always been dogmatic. —A. W. Tozer

- There can be no spiritual health without doctrinal knowledge. —J. I. Packer

- We cannot have the benefits of Christianity if we shed its doctrines. —D. Martyn Lloyd-Jones

- The truth is, no preacher ever had any strong power that was not the preaching of doctrine. —Phillips Brooks

- The time will come when they will not endure sound doctrine. —2 Timothy 4:3

- Contend earnestly for the faith. —Jude 3

- Theology means "the science of God," and I think any man who wants to think about God at all would like to have the clearest and most accurate ideas about Him that are available. —C. S. Lewis

- Some pastors preach "longhorn sermons," a point here, a point there, and a lot of bull in between. —Anonymous

Statistics from George Barna on America's Theology

- 60 percent of all adults agree that "the Bible is totally accurate in all of its teachings" (2001).

- Nearly three out of five adults (58 percent) say that the devil, or Satan, is not a living being but is a symbol of evil (2001).

- Half of all adults (51 percent) believe that if a person is generally good, or does enough good things for others in life, that person will earn a place in heaven (2001).

- More than two out of every five adults (43 percent) believe that when Jesus Christ lived on earth He committed sins. Conversely, 41 percent of Americans believe that Jesus lived a sinless life on earth (2001).

Theme: Only Through the Blood of Jesus . . .

Prelude—Instrumentalist
When I Survey

Redeemed by the Blood . . .

Call to Worship—Congregation
CH 15 *No Other Name* (2x in D)
MSPW2 *That Wonderful Cross* (as printed in D)

Prayer of Worship—Pastoral Staff

Welcome—Pastoral Staff

Welcome Hymn (meet and greet)—Congregation
CH *Lord, I Lift Your Name on High* (2x in G)
CH 195 *Bless the Name of Jesus* (2x in F)
CH *O Come, Let Us Adore Him* (1x in F, 1x in G)

Cleansed by the Blood . . .

Testimony of Praise (2-minute salvation testimony live or on video)

Praise and Worship—Congregation
CH *O the Blood of Jesus*
CH *Nothing but the Blood*
CH *Power in the Blood*

. . . Covered by the Blood!

Song of Praise—Solo or Congregation
CH *Blessed Redeemer*

Message—Pastor

Hymn of Response/Invitation—Congregation
CH 488 *Just as I Am*

Benediction Hymn
CH *I Love You, Lord* (2x)

Postlude

Additional Sermons and Lesson Ideas

The Lifestyle of the Righteous and Faithful
By Dr. David Jeremiah

Date preached:

Scripture: Ephesians 4:25–32

Introduction: This section of Ephesians is a litmus test for all of us who say we are believers. Our walk with God is pictured outwardly by the things we do. In these verses, Paul spells out five areas where Christians are to be distinctive from the world.

    1. **Our Morality (v. 25).**
    2. **Our Moods (vv. 26, 27).**
    3. **Our Money (v. 28).**
    4. **Our Mouths (vv. 29, 30).**
    5. **Our Manners (vv. 31, 32).**
        A. Put off meanness (v. 31).
        B. Put on kindness (v. 32).

Conclusion: Can you imagine the impact we would have on our city if we lived like that? Every day when you wake up, say, "Holy Spirit, take control of my life. Make me the kind of person You want me to be." Then watch God work in your life to make you someone with the lifestyle of the righteous and faithful.

Powerful Prayer Walking
By Jason H. Barber

Date preached:

Scripture: Acts 17:16–23

Introduction: If evangelism is the ground war, prayer is the air assault that prepares the way. Paul models for us how one should pray over an area before presenting the gospel in that area.

    1. **Pass through the area (v. 23).** *Passing through* as Paul did means to extensively and thoroughly travel through and around an area (Rom. 5:12b; Heb. 4:14a).
    2. **Pay attention to spiritual & religious indicators (v. 16, *"While he waited, he saw"*).** Paul was observing the spiritual and religious climate of Athens (Matt. 6:22, 23).
    3. **Ponder about that which you've seen (v. 23, *"Considering"*).** Paul not only took note of what he saw, he considered the implications of their religious expressions (Heb. 13:7).

4. **Pray with passion (v. 16).** Paul's spirit was *provoked within him*. Let their spiritual condition be the burden you present before God in prayer (2 Pet. 2:8).

5. **When possible, present the gospel (vv. 17, 22).** Whether in the local synagogue or the prestigious Areopagus, Paul was ready to explain the gospel when provided the opportunity (1 Pet. 3:15).

APRIL 25, 2010

SUGGESTED SERMON

Jonah's Journey

Date preached:

By Melvin Worthington

Scripture: Jonah 1–4, especially 1:1–3, "Now the word of the LORD came to Jonah the son of Amittai, saying, "Arise, go to Nineveh, that great city, and cry out against it; for their wickedness has come up before Me." But Jonah arose to flee to Tarshish from the presence of the LORD."

Introduction: The Book of Jonah differs from other minor prophets. It is a narrative, biographical rather than prophetic. It's the story of a servant, a storm, and a sovereign God. Jonah is God-called but disobedient; the storm is God-appointed and God-controlled, and God's powerful attributes are evident throughout the story. Jonah himself is a strange paradox: a prophet of God, and yet fleeing from God; thrown into the sea, yet alive; a preacher of repentance, yet needing repentance. He is pictured as sanctified in spots, self-willed, godly, courageous, prayerful, obedient after chastisement, bigoted, concerned with his own reputation, zealous for the Lord. As if this was not enough, Jonah is a great missionary book, and Jonah himself a great evangelist.

1. **The Rebellious Prophet (ch. 1)**

    A. **The word heard (vv. 1, 2).** God spoke to Jonah and instructed him to go to the wicked city of Nineveh and cry against it because of its wickedness. This word from God was a definite word, a disturbing word, a distinct word, and a disobeyed word.

    B. **The will hardened (v. 3).** Jonah *understood* God's word and yet he was *uncomfortable* with God's word and *unwilling* to obey God's word. He acted as people often do who don't like God's commands—he rebelled and ran away, thus removing himself as far as possible from being under the influence of God.

    C. **The wrath hurled (vv. 4–16).** The truths embedded in these verses include the *directed storm* (v. 4), the *discovered sin* (vv. 5–13), and the *devoted sailors* (vv. 14–16).

D. **The whale handy (v. 17).** The sailors cast Jonah into the sea and a huge fish swallowed him. Jonah was in the belly of the fish three days and three nights. Truths found in this verse include the *prepared fish*, the *providential fact*, the *prophetic figure*, and the *prophet's fate*.

2. **The Repentant Prophet (ch. 2)**

A. **The servant speaks (vv. 1–9).** These verses record Jonah's *supplication* (v. 1), *suffering* (v. 2), *statement* (vv. 3–6), *submission* (vv. 7, 8), and *singing* (v. 9). Jonah's prayer reveals a note of triumph. He prayed out of the belly of the fish but with an absolute confidence in God and in His deliverance. He had disobeyed God and God had disciplined him, and now he abandoned his disobedience and vowed to be obedient—obey God's Word.

3. **The Sovereign speaks (v. 10).** This verse reminds us of the *faithfulness* of Jehovah, the *freedom* of Jonah, and the *focus* on Jehovah and Jonah. God caused the fish to vomit Jonah up on dry land. God hears and heeds the prayers of His people.

4. **The Re-commissioned Prophet (ch. 3).**

A. **The willing prophet (vv. 1–4).** *The Renewed Commission (vv. 1, 2).* God is a God of second chances. Illustrations abound that confirm this—Peter, Thomas, John Mark, and Samson. God disciplines Jonah for his rebellion, Jonah repents, and the word of the Lord comes a second time. This time Jonah is ready to obey God's word. He recognized that this second chance was undeserved, unexpected, unparalleled, unique, and unequivocal. God did not change the task but changed His man. *The Ready Compliance (vv. 3, 4).* Jonah is as ready to obey now as he was to disobey in the beginning.

B. **The wicked people (vv. 5–9).** The people of Nineveh responded to the message of Jonah. They *believed* (v. 5). It affected their *behavior* (v. 5). The repentance *began* with the leaders and extended to the people (vv. 6, 7). They *beseeched* God for mercy (vv. 8, 9).

C. **The wondrous pardon (v. 10).** God saw their conduct and spared the city. Divine judgment was averted.

5. **The Raging Prophet (ch. 4).** Jonah was filled with rage when God spared the city.

   A. **The grieved prophet (vv. 1–5).** His *grief* (v. 1) in light of God's action reveals his shortsightedness, selfishness, stubbornness, and superficiality. His *grip* (v. 2) indicated that he knew this would be God's response to the repentance of the people of Nineveh and he didn't want God to withhold judgment. His *groaning* (v. 3). Jonah wanted to die. His *grace* (v. 4). God responded to Jonah's attitude and actions with gentle, gracious grace. His *grudge* (v. 5). He went out of the city and made a booth and sat in its shadow waiting to see what God would do.

   B. **The gracious provision (vv. 6–11).** God dealt with Jonah by using the *plant* (v. 6), the *pest* (v. 7), the *passion* (v. 8), and the *principle* (vv. 9–11).

Conclusion: The love of God in our hearts will constrain us to that full commitment which God sought from Jonah and which he received so joyfully from Paul. To be an effective servant of the Lord one must, like Jonah, die to the lusts, the attractions, allurements, and rewards which man has to offer and be content with the compensation which God gives. We must be worldwide witness. We must hear God's call to a solemn, sacred stewardship of life and possessions.

STATS, STORIES, AND MORE

Is Jonah Historical?

"It is a mistake (based in part on the difficulty some readers have in coming to terms with the miraculous character of the story line) to assume that the events and actions of the book are not historical in nature. While the story line is unusual, it is presented as normal history. Further, Jesus used the story of Jonah as an analogy of His own impending death and resurrection (Matt. 12:39–41). Jesus' analogy depends on the recognition of two historical realities: (1) the historical experience of Jonah in the belly of the great fish, and (2) the historical experience of the repentance of the people of Nineveh based on the preaching of Jonah (Luke 11:29–32). Indeed, the phrase 'the sign of the prophet Jonah' must have been a recurring phrase in the teaching of Christ, for it is found on more than one occasion in Matthew's account of Christ's ministry (Matt. 16:4). Thus any view of the Book of Jonah that does not assume it describes historical events is obliged to explain away the clear words of Jesus to the contrary."

—From *Nelson's New Illustrated Bible Commentary*,
edited by Earl Radmacher, Ronald B. Allen,
and H. Wayne House

Obedience

A missionary translator was endeavoring to find a word for "obedience" in the native language. This was a virtue seldom practiced among the people into whose language he wanted to translate the New Testament. As he returned home from the village one day, he whistled for his dog and it came running at full speed. An old man, seeing this, said, admiringly in the native tongue, "Your dog is all ear." Immediately the missionary knew he had his word for obedience.   —from *Encyclopedia of 7700 Illustrations* by Paul Lee Tan

Jonah's Journey

Prelude—Instrumental

Prayer of Worship—Pastoral Staff

Welcome—Pastor

Hymn of Welcome (meet and greet)—Congregation
What a Mighty God (2x)
Great and Mighty (2x)

Praise and Worship—Congregation
CH 87 *Fairest Lord Jesus* (1st and 2nd verse)
CH 88 *More Precious Than Silver* (2x in F)
CH 191 *Father, I Adore You* (2x in F)
SPW 220 *You Are My All in All* (1x in F/1x in G)

Offertory Prayer—Pastoral Staff

Offertory Praise—*CH 15 No Other Name*—Congregation

Message—*The Journey*

Hymn of Invitation/Response—Congregation
CH 505 *He Touched Me*

Postlude—Instrumental

Additional Sermons and Lesson Ideas

Outward, Inward, Upward
By Paul Borthwick

Date preached:

Scripture: Matthew 9:35–38, especially verse 38

Introduction: Traveling in other countries is often an overwhelming experience. The city of Delhi, India, for example, has a larger population than all of New England. Mexico City's population is around twenty million. Manila has over ten million people. Many of these over-populated areas have "squatter villages" near city dumps where inhabitants scavenge food. How do we respond to these desperate situations? And the needs are not only global, they are local and very personal. Every day, people around us are in crisis. What can we do to help? Jesus gives us the answer in today's text.

1. **Our outward response (v. 36).** "But when [Jesus] saw the multitudes, He was moved with compassion for them, because they were weary and scattered, like sheep having no shepherd." The word *compassion* means to "suffer alongside." God's eyes are eyes of compassion. As we watch the nightly news each evening, it's easy to become apathetic, seeing the same stories and accepting them without thinking of the people involved. Do we realize that even terrorists are sinners who need Christ? Jesus saw tax collectors and prostitutes as needy people. What about that person with whom you work—the one who drives you crazy? The one who blocked your promotion or attacked your integrity? Can you see the need behind that person's action, the hurt behind his or her words? We must look outwardly with compassion, reflecting the concern God has for people.

2. **Our inward response (v. 38).** If the word *compassion* describes the vision we should have outwardly, the word "laborer" describes the commitment we should have inwardly. The Bible describes us as workers, laborers, servants, stewards, soldiers, and ambassadors. All these words convey our position: We are at the disposal of our Master. When the Old Testament heroine, Esther, went to the king to lobby on behalf of her captive people, she was willing to die because her life was not her own (Esth. 4:16). Paul said, "Let a man so consider us, as stewards . . . of Christ" (1 Cor. 4:1). This is the attitude we should have. Unfortunately, many of us have a "back-pocket Jesus," an "open-in-case-of-emergency Jesus," or an "ATM Jesus." We go to Him when we have a need rather than realizing we were bought with a price. We must view ourselves as people at the disposal of our Master, Jesus Christ. What role does He want you to play in His global and local work?

3. **Our upward response (v. 38).** In light of the need of people in verse 36 and the need for workers in verse 38, Jesus tells us to pray. Prayer

reminds us we have a Master and it is His harvest. Many believers constantly lie to one another about prayer. I wonder how many times "I'll pray for you" is spoken and immediately forgotten. As we remember our position as laborers, we should remember whom we serve, the Lord of the harvest. We all are called to pray, but many of us are strangely apathetic about prayer. Maybe we are afraid that if we pray for the Lord to send laborers, we'll end up being called ourselves! We are an integral part of God's global purpose. Perhaps the lack of workers in our church and the low numbers of young people going into vocational Christian service is the result of our failure to obey Jesus' command here in verse 38—to pray for laborers to be raised up.

Conclusion: In a city dump in the Philippines is a "squatter village" called "Smokey Mountain" with needy people everywhere; but in the middle of the dump stands a new building with a banner over it, saying: "Welcome to Smokey Mountain." It is the Smokey Mountain headquarters of Youth With A Mission. These youth teach about health, give inoculations, and run literacy programs. If you were to ask them why they're located in the middle of a dump, they'd say, "The Lord of the Harvest sent us. We wanted to be obedient. We know God loves these people, though circumstances are forcing them to live in a dump." This is a symbol of our church—a beam of hope in the middle of a hopeless world. It's also a symbol of you and me, ambassadors for Christ in the midst of the moral dump of this city. Let's be His laborers, viewing people compassionately, submitting and praying to Christ as Master, and allowing Him to use us for His global purpose.

Intentional Intercession

By Jason H. Barber

Date preached:

Scripture: Genesis 18:16–33

Introduction: The current ministry of Jesus is that of Intercessor (Rom. 8:34; Heb. 7:24, 25). Our text reveals what is required of one who intentionally intercedes for the salvation of others.

1. **A revelation from God (vv. 7–9).** Their prayer is preceded by a revelation from God. God informs Abraham of His plan (cf. Amos 3:7).
2. **A pure life (vv. 20, 21).** Abraham's life is contrasted with the lifestyles of those who lived in the cities of the plain. No impure incense could be offered on the altar of incense in the Holy Place (Ex. 30:9).
3. **Understanding our position (vv. 22, 23).** Abraham was positioned between the living and the dead. Abraham *drew near*—he stood between the Lord and the people of the plain. In the Holy Place, the altar of incense stood between the High Priest and the Holy of Holies (Ex. 30:6).

4. Passionate and persistent praying (vv. 23–33). God directs the prayer of Abraham who pleads for the safety of his family. In the Holy Place the incense was to burn continuously (Ex. 30:7, 8).

Conclusion: When we intercede on behalf of others, we are joining Jesus in His current ministry.

MAY 2, 2010

SUGGESTED SERMON

Come Now, and Let Us Reason   *Date preached:*

By Rev. Peter Grainger

Scripture: Isaiah 1:1–31, especially verse 2, "Hear, O heavens, and give ear, O earth! For the Lord has spoken."

Introduction: When we have visitors in Edinburgh, we take them atop Blackford Hill for a panoramic view of Edinburgh, a wholly different perspective from the one on Princes Street. A prophet like Isaiah is, in a sense, someone who sees things from a different perspective because his vantage-point is higher. Isaiah had "eagles' eyes" (Is. 40:31), and his book tells what he saw. His message is focused on a tiny nation in the Middle East through whom the Lord had promised to bless the earth. Israel was in danger, but the Lord had not given up on her. Striking parallels exist between Isaiah's day and ours. We see a world in turmoil; and God's people, who hold the key to His purposes, are in disarray. Isaiah's opening chapter contains three themes that recur throughout his long ministry.

1. **An Alarming Accusation (vv. 1–17).** The scene is a courtroom. The universe is called to attend, the Judge is the Lord, and His people are in the dock. The charges are very serious, a deadly cocktail of outright rebellion and outward religion.

    A. **Outright rebellion (vv. 2–10).** God says with amazement that even oxen and donkeys recognize their master's voice, but His children have rejected His authority. Rebellion often flourishes during prosperity, and Isaiah began his ministry during the reign of Uzziah, a period of peace and prosperity. Yet it had been used by the rich to exploit the poor. Justice was bought and sold to the highest bidder, gaps in society widened, and bloodshed was common. The people had prostituted themselves (vv. 21–23). The crucial question for those of us who are Christians is: Do we live under the authority of the Lord and of His Son? We rebel against His authority by refusing to submit every area of life to His Lordship. It's only a matter of time, unless something is done about it, that sons become rebels and rebels become harlots.

    B. Outward religion (vv. 11–17). Despite their rebellion, the Israelites didn't abandon religion, but the Lord could no longer bear rituals (vv. 11–14) which were prescribed in the Law of Moses to give outward expression to inner obedience. The Lord would sooner they suspended their religion than indulge in hypocrisy (Rev. 3:15). Notice how seriously the Lord regards sin in His people. But that is not, thank God, the sum of Isaiah's message. In the middle of this chapter, and running like a silver thread through the book, is a message of hope.

2. **An Incredible Invitation (vv. 18–20).** Verse 18 is one of the great texts of the Bible, especially when read in context, because of its tone and its terms.

    A. Its tone. Its tone is one of reason rather than demand. The righteous Judge is also the loving Father. In fact, His tone all along has been one of sorrow over His children's sin (vv. 5–6). The Son of God would later express the same anguish (Luke 13:34). What an amazing thing that God reasons with us when we stray. How incredible that the Lord Jesus knocks at the door of His lukewarm church (Rev. 3:20).

    B. Its terms. Stepping from His bench, the Judge offers the accused full pardon. Both wool and snow are white by nature; the Lord is offering to give His people a new heart and nature. Neither the sacrifices of animals nor the multitude of rituals can ever pay the debt owed. The Judge had to descend from His throne, become a human being, and suffer in our stead (see Is. 53). But there is a condition. A change of direction—repentance—is required (vv. 19, 20). In subsequent chapters, the Israelites refused to repent. Was that, then, the end of the Lord's plan for them? No. The chapter finishes with a third theme:

3. **A Painful Purification (vv. 21–31).** Though they were like Sodom, Judah's fate would be different. The Lord, Isaiah said, will come in judgment, but for purification, not annihilation. Those who persist in doing evil would be judged through a process whereby Israel would be purged of its sin and refined, for God wants His people to declare His character and draw others to Himself (vv. 26–28).

Conclusion: It was all fulfilled when Christ came to His own, though they did not receive Him. The consequence was judgment, and only a remnant was preserved. But God's great plan, conceived in eternity and executed in time, was fulfilled as Gentiles were grafted into God's people. Christians are "a chosen generation, a royal priesthood, a holy nation, His own special people" (1 Pet. 2:9). God is seeking to reason with us, the choice is ours, and the time is now: "Come now, and let us reason together."

STATS, STORIES, AND MORE

Amnesty
The word *amnesty* comes from the word from which we get *amnesia.* It means to forget. When God washes away our sins, they are forgotten. We're left whiter than snow, purer than wool.

Whiter Than Snow
Evangelist E. Howard Cadle (1884–1942) was converted from a debauched life through the power of Isaiah 1:18. He was the black sheep of four children in a Christian family who started drinking at age twelve. He became addicted to alcohol, gambling, and sexual adultery, becoming known as the "Slot Machine King" in much of the Midwest because of his gambling enterprises. He attempted to murder a man, only narrowly escaping the penitentiary. Broken in finances and health, he finally "hit bottom" and returned home and collapsed into his mother's arms, saying, "Mother, I'm tired of sin. I've broken your heart, betrayed my wife, broken my marriage vows—I'd like to be saved, but I've sinned too much." His mother replied, "Son, I've prayed for 12 years to hear you say what you've just said." Getting out her Bible, she turned to Isaiah 1:18, and on that morning, March 14, 1914, E. Howard Cadle was converted. He later became a powerful and popular evangelist and radio preacher.

SUGGESTED ORDER OF WORSHIP

Living Your Faith in the Work Place

Prelude—Instrumental Group
Evermore

Call to Worship—Congregation
CH 195 *Bless the Name of Jesus* (2x in C)
SPW 1 *We Bring a Sacrifice* (1x in D; 1x in Eb)
SPW 3 *What a Mighty God* (2x in Eb)
SPW 4 *Great and Mighty* (1x in Eb)

SUGGESTED ORDER OF WORSHIP—*Continued*

Worship in Prayer—Pastoral Staff

Welcome—Pastoral Staff

Welcome Hymn (meet and greet)—Pastoral Staff
(CH 86) *Jesus, Name Above All Names* (1x Eb, 1x F)

Worship and Praise—Congregation
(CH 87) *Fairest Lord Jesus* (v. 1, v. 3, transition)
(CH 88) *More Precious than Silver* (1x in F)
(CH 79) *My Jesus, I Love Thee* (1x in F, mod, 1x in G)
(Use text from BH for last stanza)

Offertory Prayer—Pastoral Staff

Offertory Praise—Congregation
(CH 186) *In My Life Lord, Be Glorified*
vs. 1 *In My Life*
vs. 2 *In My Heart*
vs. 3 *In Our Home*
vs. 4 *In Our Church*

A Case for Faith Video from Wingclips (http://www.wingclips.
com/cart.php?target=product&product_id=16464&
substring=Faith)

Message—Pastor
Living Your Faith in the Workplace

Hymn of Response/Invitation—Congregation
CH 481 *Come, Just As You Are*

Benediction Hymn—Congregation
CH 195 *Bless the Name of Jesus* (2x in C)

Postlude—Instrumental Group
CH 86 *Jesus, Name Above All Names*

Additional Sermons and Lesson Ideas

Living Your Faith in the Work Place

Date preached:

By Robert Morgan

Scripture: Colossians 3:22–25

Introduction: God created work to give us a sense of dignity, to teach us responsibility, and to give our lives accomplishment. What difference will your faith make on the job site? Paul mentions four distinguishing marks of those who live out their faith at work.

1. **Submission (v. 22).** Obedience and submission in the work place is how you show "reverence" to your Lord.
2. **Diligence (v. 23).** When you look at your job as "working for men" you can get angry, depressed, dissatisfied, apathetic. When you look at it as "working for the Lord" you will be grateful and diligent.
3. **Excellence (v. 24).** Our reward is not our paycheck, but what the Lord will give us, and He has the best retirement plan around.
4. **Honesty (v. 25).** If you realize you are really working for God, then you will know that when you are dishonest, you are cheating God as well as men.

Conclusion: The Christian's ultimate employer is the Lord. We work for Him with all our heart, and from Him comes our reward.

Making the Most of Your Nervous Breakdown

Date preached:

By Robert Morgan

Scripture: 1 Kings 19:1–21, especially verses 1–3a

Introduction: *The Wall Street Journal* ran a front page story on the subject of nervous breakdowns, saying, "The nervous breakdown, the mysterious affliction that has been a staple of American life and literature for more than a century, has been wiped out by the combined forces of psychiatry, pharmacology, and managed care. But people keep breaking down anyway." By studying his experience we can learn how God deals with us when we're overwrought and overstrained. The Lord wrote a sevenfold prescription for Elijah. The same therapy will work for us.

1. **Sleep and nourishment (vv. 4–8).** Elijah was exhausted, for he had combated paganism for three years, waged a vigorous war on Mt. Carmel against the prophets of Baal, prayed with exceeding earnestness, and had run a virtual marathon back to Jezreel. Verses 4–8 tell of how God provided sleep, bread, and water for Elijah under the broom tree.

2. **Angelic help (vv. 5–7).** The Lord sent an angel to care for Elijah (Heb. 1:14).

3. **Ventilation (vv. 9, 10).** God allowed Elijah to repeatedly ventilate his frustrations.

4. **God's still, small voice (vv. 11–13).** The ultimate answer to life's downturns is rediscovering God's infallible Word. Elijah needed a gentle word of reassurance, a gentle whisper.

5. **A renewal of purpose (vv. 14–17).** The Lord gave Elijah a set of new assignments. Nothing helps us overcome discouragement like rediscovering our purpose in life and setting to work at what God has called us to do.

6. **Reassurance (v. 18).** Things are never as bad as they appear where God is concerned.

7. **A friend (vv. 19–21).** The Lord provided the solitary Elijah with a friend, Elisha, to share the load. A healthy life keeps its friendships in good repair.

Conclusion: Are you overwhelmed, stressed, discouraged, depressed? God wants to renew your strength and to restore your soul. The way He revived Elijah is the pattern He wants to use to revive your spirit, too.

MAY 9, 2010

SERIES: EXTREME HOME MAKEOVER   SUGGESTED SERMON

Divine Design: God's Plan for Marriage

Date preached:

By Dr. Kenyn Cureton

Scriptures: Genesis 1:26–28; 2:18–24

Introduction: Home Makeover Mania is sweeping the nation! TV shows have teams of experts come in and remodel and redecorate rooms or whole houses. There is *Extreme Makeover Home Edition, Trading Spaces, Clean House, Curb Appeal, Design on a Dime, Divine Designs,* and that last one is the title of the message: Divine Design.

Question: Can you imagine building or remodeling a home without a plan? Saying, "Let's just wing it?" No sensible person would think of starting without a well-thought-out plan or blueprint from an architect. Yet many couples try to build their marriages without consulting the Master Architect's design for that divine institution we call marriage. The result? Two people hammering away under the same roof, trying to build a model marriage based on two different sets of incomplete and imperfect plans and designs. It is often a mess!

I. **Get direction from the original design.**

A. **The process.** We need to put away our amateur ideas of how to build a good marriage and start our extreme make-over with the divine design found in God's Word. Marriage makeovers are not simple. Anybody who has remodeled a home knows that it:

(1) Takes longer than you planned;

(2) Costs more than you figured;

(3) Causes more mess than you anticipated;

(4) Requires greater determination than you expected. Remodeling a marriage is no different. The only hope for having a successful marriage is to remodel it according to God's design and ask the Master Architect to help us do it.

B. **The review.** God said in Genesis 2:18a that it was "not good for the man to be alone." There was something missing, so He made the woman. In Genesis 2:18b, God described her as a "helper suitable for him." Adam needed a companion, but no suitable helper was found (vv. 19, 20). That word *helper* means "to assist another." The word for *suitable* means "corresponding to him, in harmony with him, and completing him." God made the woman so that man might be complete. So God gave marriage in order to meet many of our deepest spiritual, emotional, physical, and psychological needs.

Having placed a desire in Adam's heart, God took out one of Adam's ribs to make this "suitable helper" (vv. 21, 22a). Then notice that God brought her to the man (v. 22b). Unless the Lord gives the gift of celibacy, He has a specific someone in mind for us. And the most important thing we can do is be the right person and pray for God's insight to know when He brings you the right person. Adam, recovering from surgery, looks up and there is the missing part. He scans this perfect Ten and says: "This is now bone of my bones and flesh of my flesh" (v. 23). Based on the Hebrew, he said, "Wow! That's more like it!" The Divine Design is the pathway to joy!

2. **Follow the steps in the owner's manual.** In verse 24, we find the steps to achieving God's design for marriage:

A. **Severance.** "A man shall leave his father and his mother." The Hebrew word for *leave* means "loosening something or being free from someone." And a lot of marriage problems are the result when this principle is not followed. Now I'm not talking about abandoning your parents, or forsaking your parents. Nor does this mean that you can ignore your obligation to honor your father and mother. It does mean that a husband and wife must put each other first.

B. **Permanence.** The King James Version says, "And shall cleave unto his wife." The Hebrew for *cleave* means "to cling, to glue, to bond, to permanently fix." Marriage is to be a permanent bond. Jesus said, "What God has joined together, let not man separate" (Matt. 19:5). Paul said, "Love never fails" (1 Cor. 13:8). Honor God's word by working through difficulties, staying in your marriage and giving God a chance to work. God can restore your relationship and even the feelings you have lost (see Joel 2:25).

C. **Unity.** "They will become one flesh." Remember in Genesis 2:18 that God said, "I will make a suitable helper for Adam." In Hebrew, the term *helper* literally means "second self." Now God never intended for you as husband and wife to become carbon copies of one another, but He does want you both to be transformed into the image of Christ and move toward oneness. Adam and Eve were originally one, and now they could become one again in a new and better way. So can we in a marriage relationship with God as our helper.

Conclusion: Marriage as God designed it is the union of one man and one woman for life and Jesus Christ as Lord of that home. But you can't have a Christian home without Christ and two Christians any more than you can have an apple pie without apples. If you want a Christian home, it must begin by both husband and wife giving their hearts to Christ and submitting to Him as Lord.

SUGGESTED ORDER OF WORSHIP

Mother's Day—God's Plan for Marriage

Prelude—Instrumentalist
Shout to the Lord

Call to Prayer—Pastoral Staff

Songs of Worship—Congregation
CH 102/103 *All Hail King Jesus* (1x in Eb; 1x in F)
CH 104 (with intro) *O Worship the King* (v. 1 in G, v. 5 in Ab)

Prayer of Worship—Pastoral Staff

Welcome and Recognition of Mothers—Pastoral Staff
Oldest Mother in the Service
Youngest Mother in the Service
Mother with the Most Children

Prayer of Commitment for Mothers

SUGGESTED ORDER OF WORSHIP—*Continued*

Praise and Worship—Congregation
Foundation Medley (from *God in Us*—Integrity Music)
The Solid Rock (choir) (1x in Eb)
MSPW 1 *Ancient of Days* (2x in C)
Firm Foundation (2x in F)

Offertory Prayer—Pastoral Prayer

Offertory Praise—Ladies Ensemble—*The Church Triumphant*

Message—God's Plan for Marriage—Pastor

Hymn of Invitation—Congregation
CH *Take My Life and Let It Be*

Benediction Hymn—Congregation
—MPW 54 *As for Me and My House*

Postlude—Instrumentalist

Additional Sermons and Lesson Ideas

To Marry or Not to Marry
By Dr. Timothy Beougher

Date preached:

Scripture: 1 Corinthians 7:1–9

Introduction: While this message may be of particular help to those of you who are still single, Paul's words are very important to understand for all of us, as we have single children, friends, coworkers, etc., who may ask us for wisdom. Scripture is our source of wisdom, so let us study this topic together:

    1. **Consider the context of this passage (v. 1a).**
    2. **Realize that singleness is not second class (v. 1b).**
    3. **Understand that marriage is the common course (v. 2).**
    4. **Recognize the obligations of marriage (vv. 2–5).**
        A. Mutual Monogamy (v. 2).
        B. Mutual Responsibility (v. 3).
        C. Mutual Respect (vv. 4, 5).
    5. **Follow God's gifting and direction (vv. 6–9).**

Conclusion: Marriage is the norm, but God has called certain special people to a fuller devotion to His ministry, and has enabled them to carry out this calling.

Who Rules?
By Rev. Peter Grainger

Date preached:

Scripture: Daniel 4

Introduction: Nebuchadnezzar thought he was the supreme ruler, but this chapter tells of his encounter with the King of kings.

    1. **Nebuchadnezzar rules.** Nebuchadnezzar ruled the kingdom, but his pride became too strong (vv. 28–32). Like us, he was guilty of:
        A. Ignoring God (cf. Luke 12:16–21). Although Daniel warned him (v. 27), he allowed his pride to destroy his reign.
        B. Marginalizing God (cf. Mark 10:17–31). Nebuchadnezzar gloried in his own majesty (v. 30) rather than the Lord's.
    2. **The Lord rules.** Daniel prophesied that the king must learn that the Lord rules (v. 26). Nebuchadnezzar had to learn the hard way.
        A. The Fiery Furnace (Dan. 3)
        B. The Disturbing Dream (Dan. 4:19–27)
        C. The Painful Process (Dan. 4:28–33)

Conclusion: Nebuchadnezzar learned that the Lord rules. It resulted in his conversion (vv. 34–37). How are you dealing with successes and difficulties? May we recognize the Lord rules and attribute to Him the majesty due His name!

MAY 16, 2010

SERIES: EXTREME HOME MAKEOVER   SUGGESTED SERMON

Marriage: Turning the Ordinary into the Extraordinary

Date preached:

By Tony Perkins

Scripture: John 2:1–11

Introduction: A wedding feast was the location of Jesus' first public miracle. Why? Could it be because marriage is the one earthly relationship that illustrates His relationship to the church? Could it be because marriage and family are the cornerstone of a society? Jesus could have performed His first miracle in the synagogue or in the marketplace or in the halls of government, but He chose to start at a wedding, which reminds us of the beginning when God created man and woman and brought them together in Eden.

Here are three keys to turning the ordinary marriage into the extraordinary:

1. **You must invite Jesus.** Your relationship with your spouse reflects your relationship with Christ (Eph. 5:22–29). He must have preeminence in your marriage. How does that work out practically in how you relate to one another?

   A. **First *S* is *submission*.** Submission is the proper way for a wife to relate to her husband's need for respect (Eph. 5:22–24).

   B. **Second *S* is *selfless-love*.** Selfless love is the proper way for a husband to relate to his wife's need for security (Eph. 5:25–30).

2. **You must recognize your need.** Your relationship with your spouse is critical to your Christian walk (1 Pet. 3:7). Here are seven practical steps for improvement:

   A. **Trust.** In order to trust, both need to maintain absolute honesty and transparency to provide a basis for mutual confidence.

   B. **Communicate.** Keep lines of communication open. There must be a constant readiness to talk things out. This includes the willingness to say, "I am sorry," and "I forgive you." We've had a policy in our almost 23 years of marriage of never letting the sun go down upon our wrath. So we've never gone to sleep angry. Of course we've gone without sleep for a few days at a time.

C. **Overlook.** Show grace by overlooking minor faults and idiosyncrasies. Love covers a multitude of sins. Don't demand perfection in others when you are unable to produce it in yourself.

D. **Unite.** Work together for unity in decision making, child raising, and especially in spending, saving, and giving finances. Avoid overspending, installment buying and the desire to keep up with the Joneses. Debt creates tension and division.

E. **Work.** Remember that love is a commandment, not an uncontrollable emotion. Love is not all honey and no bees. Love is hard work. Love means all that is included in 1 Corinthians 13. For instance, love is courteous. Love will keep you from criticizing or contradicting your spouse in front of others. Love will keep you from quarreling in front of your children, which could undermine their security. In these and a hundred other ways, love creates a happy atmosphere in the home and rules out strife and separations.

F. **Renew.** Tell your spouse that if you had it to do over, you would do it again and there is no one else you would rather spend your life with. Communicate your love, even if you don't feel like it. Men, tell your wife you love her. I heard of one couple that had been married for 40 years and the husband had never told his wife that he loved her. She brought it up one day in a disagreement and he responded by saying, "I told you I loved you when we got married, and if it ever changes I'll let you know."

G. **Ask.** Don't be afraid to ask for help. Go on a marriage enrichment retreat. Get Christian-based counseling when there is a need. But above all, go to God for help in prayer and pray together.

3. **Yield glory to God.** Your relationship with your spouse should minister life to the world. Jesus calls us the salt of the earth (Matt. 5:13).

A. **Salt cleanses and heals.** Salt has an antiseptic quality to it. Your marriage should be a launch pad for ministry to others for help and healing.

B. **Salt preserves.** Salt is a natural preservative. Your marriage should be a witness to God's design for marriage, and therefore a preservative against all alternatives such as cohabitation or homosexuality.

C. **Salt seasons.** Salt brings out the flavor. Your marriage should be a winsome witness to your children, to your family, and to a watching world.

   Question: Are others inspired by your marriage?

Conclusion: There was a story published on Valentine's Day about a couple named Paul and Mary Onesi from Niagara Falls, who were celebrating their 80th wedding anniversary.[1] One of their grand-children's response to a question by the reporter showed the real impact of the couple's commitment. There had been no divorces among the couple's six children or 28 grandchildren, and the reporter inquired as to why. The response from a granddaughter: "In our family, no one ever wanted to get divorced because no one wanted to tell them." Your marriage can make a lasting impact on the lives of your children and your children's children. With the Lord's help, you and your spouse can turn the ordinary into the extraordinary!

---

[1]Carolyn Thompson, "Nation's longest-married couple never celebrated Valentine's Day," Associated Press, 14 February 1998.

STATS, STORIES, AND MORE

More from Tony Perkins

Doctor's Visit: A woman accompanied her husband to the doctor's office for a checkup. Afterwards, the doctor took the wife aside and said, "Unless you do the following things, your husband will surely die. Every morning make sure he gets a good healthy breakfast. Have him come home for lunch each day so you can feed him a well-balanced meal. Make sure you feed him a good, hot dinner every night. Don't overburden him with any household chores. Also, keep the house spotless and clean so he doesn't get exposed to any unnecessary germs." On the way home, the husband asked his wife what the doctor said. She replied, "You're gonna die!"

Schibley Incident: I read an article a couple of years ago about an incident in Orlando, Florida. An 83-year-old man died after he lay injured in his yard for three days, ordering his wife not to call doctors. Glen Schibley was found dead with his wife by his side. He had been working in his yard when he fell and was unable to get up.

Mr. Schibley told his 79-year-old wife, Harriet, not to call authorities because of previous bad experiences with doctors. So she brought her husband food, water and medicine, and covered him with a tarp during rainstorms. She slept beside him at least once. During those three days, the temperature once dropped to 55 degrees and almost 2½ inches of rain fell in Orlando.

"I don't know what was on Harriet's mind. She loved the man deeply," neighbor Tim Elfman said. "If he said don't call anybody, I guess she figured he would get up." The two were found when their son-in-law came by to check up on them. Mrs. Schibley was transported to Florida Hospital East, where she was listed in fair condition.

Neighbors could not see the pair because of a fence around the junk-strewn yard. "They wanted to be left alone, and we left them alone," neighbor Sherman Brunell said. "Maybe we shouldn't have left them alone."

Turning the Ordinary into the Extraordinary

Prelude—Instrumentalist
Shout to the Lord

Prayer of Worship—Pastoral Staff

Hymn of Worship—Congregation
WH 585 *Brethren, We Have Met to Worship* (2x in G)
CH 5 *I Sing Praises* (1x in G; 1x in Ab)

Welcome—Pastoral Staff

Welcome Song—Congregation (meet and greet)
CH 715 *He Is Jehovah* (3x)
CH 716 *Jehovah Jireh* (2x)

Worship and Praise—Congregation
CH 170 *Give Thanks* (2x)
CH 171 *Come into His Presence*
CH 311 *Hallelujah, What a Savior*
CH 705 *It Is Well with My Soul*

Offertory Prayer—Pastoral Staff

Offertory Praise—Solo, Praise Team, or Choir
MSPW2 *He Knows My Name*

Message—Pastor
Taming the Tongue

Hymn of Response/Invitation—Congregation
CH 481 *Come Just As You Are*

Benediction Hymn—Congregation
CH 5 *I Sing Praises* (1x in G, 1x in Ab)

Postlude—Instrumental
Shout to the Lord (chorus 2x)

Additional Sermons and Lesson Ideas

Taming the Tongue
By Dr. Timothy Beougher

Date preached:

Scripture: James 3:7–12

Introduction: This passage deals with one of our greatest problems.

1. **The uncontrollable character of the tongue (vv. 7, 8).** The tongue makes a mockery of our professed wisdom and self-control.
2. **The revealing nature of the tongue (vv. 9, 10).** Whether lifting up or cutting down others, the tongue reveals what is in our heart.
3. **The spiritual cure for the tongue.**
   - Admit the problem (James 1:26; Is. 6:5).
   - Focus on your heart (Matt. 12:34; 2 Cor. 5:17; Ps. 51:10).
   - Ask God for help (Prov. 4:23; Ps. 19:4; 141:3).
   - Talk less (James 1:19; Prov. 10:19; 29:20).
   - Cultivate positive speech (Col. 4:6; Eph. 4:29).

Conclusion: A young lady once said to John Wesley, "I think I know what my talent is. It's to speak my mind." He replied, "I don't think God would mind if you bury that talent."

SERIES: STAY COVERED (Authority—God's Covering for My Life)
The Importance of Authority, Part 1
By Mark Fuller

Date preached:

Scripture: 1 Samuel 15:22, 23

Introduction: In the same way that a warm blanket can protect your life from exposure to the harsh cold of winter, God's authority is a warm blanket protecting you from the harsh, life-threatening influences of Satan's attacks. How we understand and respond to authority has profound implications in every area of life . . . at home, at work, at school, at church . . . in marriage, as a parent, as a child, as an employee, or an employer, as a student, as a teacher, and as a citizen. We are faced with the issue of authority in every aspect of life.
I will never discover God's purpose for my life until I place myself under His delegated authority.

Two principles that govern the universe:
1. God's authority—Romans 11:36.
2. Satanic rebellion—Revelation 12:4; Isaiah 14:12–15.
   - I am operating under Satanic rebellion whenever I take for myself what belongs to God (Gen. 2:16, 17).

- God puts me under authority so that I will learn obedience (Gen. 3:6).
- When I disobey God's delegated authority, I am in fact rebelling against God.

Two decisions that govern my life:
(Speaker wraps up in quilt, open right flap to reveal the word "trust")
1. Trust in God's authority (Acts 4:12; John 3:16).
   (Open left flap to reveal the word "obey")
2. Obey God's authority (1 Sam. 15:13–23, especially verse 22).
   God values my obedience more than my sacrifice.
   It is possible for me to be right and still be in rebellion (Acts 23:1–5).

Conclusion: Simple disagreement does not warrant disobeying delegated authority.

As long as delegated authority is not requiring something unethical, unbiblical, or immoral, I have a divine privilege and responsibility to submit to that authority. When I do, I am covered.

If I disobey delegated authority, I am moving out from under God's protection and am putting myself at risk to Satan's deception along with everyone under my authority.

MAY 23, 2010

SERIES: EXTREME HOME MAKEOVER   SUGGESTED SERMON

Trading Spaces: Understanding
Your Wife's Needs
Date preached:

By Dr. Kenyn M. Cureton

Scripture: Ephesians 5:22–33

Introduction: Paul was a great teacher, so he knew the power of an object lesson. He compares the marriage relationship with Christ and the church. As Christ is to the church so the husband is to be to the wife. That analogy is the key to understanding a husband's role and a wife's needs.

1. **A wife needs her husband to be a leader.** Christ is the head of the church and the husband is the head of the wife (vv. 22–24). He is to be the leader in the home. And as the leader, he is primarily responsible for the spiritual, emotional, and financial health and welfare of the home. Husbands have tried to pass off their duty as the leader to their wives, to the schools, to the churches, to the scouts, etc. But Joshua said, "As for me and for my house, we will serve the Lord" (Josh. 24:15). Joshua stepped up and shouldered the responsibility for the spiritual well-being of his family.

   Unfortunately in so many homes today, men are passive at best and at worst they're hindering the family and each member in it from being what they could be under God. Seriously, a man who won't lead is a man outside the will of God, and a man outside the will of God is no good to himself or to his wife, his family, or to anyone around him. So men, step up. Your wife needs you to take the lead in the home.

2. **A wife needs her husband to be a lover.** Look at the instruction to the husband in verse 25. The one thing that ought to characterize the husband's role as the leader in the home is love. A wife not only needs her husband to be a leader, she also needs him to be a lover. Love is a hard word to nail down, because we use it so loosely: "Oh, I love that new dress." Or "I love my new phone."

A. Types of love. Four Greek words for love: *storge, eros, phileo,* and *agape.*

- **Familial love:** The Greek word *storge* is not used in the New Testament, but it meant love among family members. The love of a father for his child. The love of a child for his mother, etc.
- **Erotic love:** The Greek word *eros* speaks primarily of physical love or sexual love.
- **Friendship love:** The Greek word *phileo* speaks of brotherly love, the love you would have for a close friend, someone you really like. Reciprocal love.
- **Sacrificial love:** The Greek word *agape* speaks of God's kind of love. The love that seeks another's highest good. It is servant-oriented love. It is sacrificial love. Paul uses the word *agape* here to describe the love a husband is to have for his wife.

B. God's kind of Love. God says *agape* your wife. Love her expecting nothing in return. Love her whether the attraction is still there or not. Love her when she is unlovely. That's what Jesus did with us: "While we were still sinners, Christ died for us" (Rom. 5:8).

(1) Primary example Is Christ. The analogy that Paul gives cannot be improved upon. We are to love our wives "as Christ loved the church and gave Himself up for her." How did Jesus love? He loved the church by serving, giving and sacrificing. He loved the church by laying aside the privileges that were His as God as it says in Philippians 2:7, 8, which is the ultimate expression of love. So Paul is saying: Husband, love your wife, serve your wife, sacrifice for your wife, put her needs ahead of your own. When Jesus hung on that cross and bore our sins, He was putting our needs ahead of His own. And husbands, that is our model. Jesus is the primary example.

(2) Primary teaching is 1 Corinthians 13. Paul sets forth the content and character of God's kind of love in what we call the "Love Chapter" (1 Cor. 13). God wants husbands to take the initiative and show this level of love toward your wives. It is agape love. In other words, it is a love that puts your wife's needs, dreams, and desires ahead of your own, even if it means extreme sacrifice. And as Paul says, this kind of love "always protects, always trusts, always hopes, always perseveres. Love never fails!" (vv. 7, 8). That's the kind of love your wife needs.

Conclusion: My love for Christ is a direct response to His love for me. In the same way, husband, as you love your wife, as you cherish her, as you serve her and put her needs above your own, she will receive and return your love and bloom and blossom into the role that God has called her to. And when that happens, you marriage will begin to be what God wants it to be and more than you ever dreamed it could be.

STATS, STORIES, AND MORE

More from Dr. Kenyn M. Cureton
That's a Mom: Several years ago Jeff Foxworthy came up with "You might be a redneck if . . ." Well, here's the Mother's Day version. You know you are a mom if . . .

- You believe that Happy Meals, PBJ, Spaghetti-Os, and Popsicles are the 4 major food groups.
- You are beginning to have romantic dreams about that purple dinosaur—Super-D-Duper.
- You're so desperate for adult conversation that you spill your guts to the telemarketer and HE hangs up on you.
- You count the sprinkles on each kid's cupcake to make sure they're equal.
- You have time to shave only one leg at a time.
- Your definition of living "la vida loca" is staying awake long enough to watch the weather during the 11 o'clock news.
- Spit is your number-one cleaning agent.
- Two words that strike mortal fear into your heart: Projectile. Vomiting.
- You can't find your cordless phone, so you ask a friend to call you, and you run around the house madly, following the sound until you locate the phone in the laundry basket.
- In your bathroom, there are toothpaste globs in the sink, water on the floor, an eternally empty toilet paper dispenser, and a perpetually unflushed commode.
- Your feet stick to the kitchen floor . . . and you don't care anymore.
- Your typical 18-hour day runs like this: dragging out of bed, dressing, brushing, buckling, feeding—them, not you. Driving, dropping, paying bills, clipping coupons, shopping, loading, unloading, vacuuming, dusting, sweeping, flushing, wiping, picking up, washing, drying, ironing, folding, changing sheets, changing diapers, cooking, serving, rinsing, washing, helping with homework, bathing, putting to bed, singing, praying. PLUS: coloring, swinging, playing baseball, basketball, football, and soccer, riding bikes,

pushing trucks, cuddling dolls, blowing bubbles, flying kites, filling plastic pools, jumping rope. Plus: mowing, trimming, raking, planting, gardening, and painting. Plus: refereeing fights, doctoring cuts, scheduling appointments, and accommodating your husband. You have no time to eat, sleep, drink, or go to the bathroom, and yet you somehow manage to gain 10 pounds . . . That's a mom! And God bless every one of you!

Treat Her Like a Real Woman
There's a story told about a Texas community where the Emergency Broadcasting System sirens went off, people gathered in the town square, and the announcement was made that the world was about to end. People were in a panic, trying to find a place to hide. One young woman jumped up and screamed: "I can't take this. I'm not going to die like an animal. If I'm going to die, let me die feeling like a real woman . . . Is there a real man here who's man enough to make me feel like a real woman?" Immediately, a strapping hunk of a man waded through the frenzied crowd, and flashed a handsome smile. He strode up to her, tore off his shirt, his massive chest heaving and huge muscles rippling in the sun, and he stood before her with shirt in hand and said: "Here, iron this!" Wrong! Men, she was not designed to serve you as if she were a slave, but she was designed to follow your lead.

Marriage Barometer
We are going to introduce you men to a high-tech device called a marriage barometer. The first thing it will tell you is the condition of your marriage on a scale of 1–10 with 1 being awful and 10 being heaven. Now remember the average barometer reads between 3 and 4. Second thing this marriage barometer will tell you is precisely the exact steps you need to take to move your marriage condition toward 10—heaven. Now you won't have to pick up the marriage barometer on the way out, but you will want to take her home, because she's sitting right next to you! Men, if you have the courage, here's your homework assignment this afternoon. Sit down with your marriage barometer and ask her to rate your marriage, and listen very carefully and lovingly to what she has to say. Let her share with you specifically and precisely how you can better meet her needs. Bottom line: If momma ain't happy, ain't nobody happy. I mean isn't that in Proverbs or somewhere? Gotta be in the original Hebrew, Amen? Consult your marriage barometer!

Understanding Your Wife's Needs

Prelude—Instrumental
Days of Elijah

Call to Worship—Pastoral Prayer

Praise and Worship—Congregation
MSPW *Open the Eyes of My Heart* (2x in E)
CH 3 *Holy, Holy, Holy* (vv. 1 and 4 in E)

Welcome—Pastoral Staff

Song of Welcome (meet and greet)—Congregation
SPW 1 *We Bring a Sacrifice of Praise* (1x in C, 1x in Db)
CH 214 *I Will Enter His Gates* (1x in Db, 1x in Eb)

Worship and Praise—Congregation
MSPW 1 *Ancient of Days* (2x in D)
MSPW 52 *Sanctuary* (1x in D, 1x in E)
MSPW2 *We Sing Worthy* (1x in E, 1x in F, 1x in G)
SPW 123 *Because He Lives* (1x in G, 1x in Ab)

Song of Commitment—Solo, Praise Team, or Choir

Offertory Prayer—Pastoral Staff

Offertory Praise—Congregation
MSPW2 *Holy Spirit Rain*

Message—Pastor

Hymn of Response/Invitation—Congregation
CH 481 *Come Just As You Are*

Hymn of Benediction

Postlude—Instrumental
SPW 1 *We Bring a Sacrifice of Praise*

Additional Sermons and Lesson Ideas

Learning to Count
By Dr. Timothy Beougher

Date preached:

Scripture: Philippians 3:1–11

Introduction: A study in Chicago schools found that many children couldn't perform simple arithmetic without a calculator. Christians also need to learn to count. The word "count" in our text means to evaluate or to consider.

1. **Count it all joy (vv. 1–3).** We must beware the killjoys of the Christian life: false teachers, false teaching, dogs, evil workers, legalists.
2. **Count it all loss (vv. 4–8).** The verb "I counted" indicates Paul made a conscious decision to repudiate his religious heritage and accomplishments.
3. **Count it all gain (vv. 8–11).** Nothing else matters but gaining Jesus Christ, being found in Him.

Conclusion: Look at your own ledger sheet—what are you writing under *gain?* Under *loss?* "Nothing in my hand I bring, simply to Thy cross I cling."

SERIES: STAY COVERED (Authority—God's Covering for My Life)
When Authority Fails, Part 2
By Mark Fuller

Date preached:

Scripture: Genesis 9; 1 Samuel 24; Acts 4

Introduction: Anyone can respect and appreciate the importance of submitting to God's direct authority. After all, He's perfect. He doesn't make mistakes. He always has our best in mind. But the Bible clearly teaches that God has established delegated authority through which He works out His will in our lives. We have names for them such as parents, teachers, pastors, bosses, police, government officials, the IRS, etc. And from God's standpoint, to rebel against His delegated authority is the same as rebellion against Him. Now, we can live with that as long as the delegated authority doesn't mess up, right? But they are human and they deal with the same fallen nature we all have. So they will blow it. They will fail. And it is at this point that our obedience and submission to authority is really put to the test. We mustn't forget the very purpose of authority, to learn obedience. So let's look at three principles from the Bible to help us learn how to obey God especially when authority fails.

1. **Cover those in authority (Gen. 9:20–27).** There is a difference between covering those in authority and condoning sin. We should never "wink" at sin. But neither are we to judge those in authority over us.

That is God's job. To cover those in authority absolves you of the judgment of sin and frees you to be part of God's solution.

2. **Obey God's higher authority (Acts 4:18–20).** When God's delegated authority conflicts with God's direct authority, we must obey God's higher authority. Yet even then we must respond with a submissive spirit.

   A. **Obedience is related to conduct—it is** *relative.* Submission is related to heart attitude: It is *absolute.*

   B. **God alone deserves unqualified obedience.** Delegated authority deserves *qualified* obedience.

   C. **We should submit to delegated authority from God.** We should *disobey* the order that offends god—*Spiritual Authority* by Watchman Nee. I should only disobey delegated authority when it requires me to do something immoral or unbiblical.

3. **Respect God's anointed authority (1 Sam. 24:1–20).** Whenever I take matters into my own hands to usurp an authority that has failed me, I bring the curse of rebellion upon myself.

   Submitting to authority is not being submissive to a person, but rather to the person's God-given position.

Conclusion: If you have lived any length of time, some authority has failed you. Maybe it was a parent, a husband, a pastor, or a boss. What have you done with that hurt? Have you forgiven them? Have you released your right to hold onto that offense? Maybe the reason you're suspicious of those in authority or don't respect authority is because you have never forgiven that authority figure who failed you in the past. Harboring a spirit of unforgiveness short-circuits God's covering in your life. Release that offense today and restore God's covering over your life.

MAY 30, 2010

MEMORIAL DAY SUGGESTED SERMON

The Ultimate Sacrifice

Date preached:

By Dr. Kent Spann

Scripture: John 15:13

This sermon was followed by a time of prayer and then the playing of "Taps."

The true story is that in July 1862, after the Seven Days battle at Harrison's Landing (near Richmond), Virginia, the wounded Commander of the 3rd Brigade, 1st Division, V Army Corps, Army of the Potomac, General Daniel Butterfield reworked, with his bugler Oliver Wilcox Norton, another bugle call, "Scott Tattoo," to create "Taps." He thought that the regular call for Lights Out was too formal. "Taps" was adopted throughout the Army of the Potomac and finally confirmed by orders. Soon other Union units began using "Taps," and even a few Confederate units began using it as well. After the war, "Taps" became an official bugle call. Col. James A. Moss, in his Officer's Manual first published in 1911, gives an account of the initial use of "Taps" at a military funeral:

"During the Peninsular Campaign in 1862, a soldier of Tidball's Battery A of the 2nd Artillery was buried at a time when the battery occupied an advanced position concealed in the woods. It was unsafe to fire the customary three volleys over the grave, on account of the proximity of the enemy, and it occurred to Capt. Tidball that the sounding of Taps would be the most appropriate ceremony that could be substituted."

They honored those who had fallen.

On this day when we remember our fallen comrades, I can think of no greater verse than the very words of Jesus in the Upper Room on the night before His betrayal.

"Greater love has no one than this, than to lay down one's life for his friends" (John 15:13).

Jesus demonstrated that kind of love the very next day. As we have pondered the sacrifice of the men and women of the Armed Forces this morning, so I want us to ponder the sacrifice of Christ.

1. **His sacrificial death was voluntary.** Among those who gave their life in the service of the country, most gave it voluntarily. We have all heard the stories of those who made a decision to give their lives for others in a foxhole.

   The story of Jesus' death has been spun in many and varied ways. In composition there is something known as the Tragedy. A Tragedy is a dramatic composition, often in verse, dealing with a serious or somber theme, typically that of a great person destined through a flaw of character or conflict with some overpowering force, as fate or society, to downfall or destruction.

   Jesus' death was not a tragedy, because *His life was not taken from Him; it was given up by Him.*

   Look at John 10:11–18. Jesus makes four amazing claims in this verse about His death.

   A. No one could take his life (John 19:7–12).

   B. He would lay it down Himself (Matt. 27:50).

   C. He had full authority to lay it down (Matt. 26:53, 54; Acts 2:22–24).

   D. This was all according to the Father's plan.

2. **His sacrificial death was victorious.** Unless you have been on the battlefield, you cannot understand the carnage of war. The movie *Saving Private Ryan* portrayed it about as accurately as it could be done by Hollywood.

   There is no such thing as a glorious war. The battlefield is never glorious. War is vicious and reprehensible. It is full of cruelty.

   Jesus' death was a vicious death. The movie *The Passion of the Christ* by Mel Gibson revealed the horror of the crucifixion. Yet, I am not sure that even Mel Gibson portrayed the totality of the horror.

   "But he didn't begin that way. At first everyone was appalled. He didn't even look human—a ruined face, disfigured past recognition" (Is. 52:14 MSG).

   But why was His death so vicious? Because sin is vicious. Sin is never a beautiful thing. Satan dresses it up but do not be deceived by that image. Sin is horrid and cruel. Sin disfigures and ruins. It destroys what is beautiful and good. Sin maims and mutilates. It produces carnage. Billions have been its victim. See Romans 5:12.

3. **His sacrificial death was vicarious.** Disney's *The Lion King* portrays the primal struggle between good and evil through its main character. Simba, a cub on his way to becoming the lion king, faces trials that help him understand his purpose in life. The most moving scene was when Simba's father, Mufasa, falls to his death after saving Simba. Mufasa gave his life for Simba.

The word *vicarious* means to take the place of another person or thing, to act as the substitute.

Jesus vicariously suffered for us.

"For He made Him who knew no sin *to be* sin for us, that we might become the righteousness of God in Him" (2 Cor. 5:21).

"Who Himself bore our sins in His own body on the tree, that we, having died to sins, might live for righteousness—by whose stripes you were healed" (1 Pet. 2:24).

Jesus died so we can live!

4. **His sacrificial death was victorious.** How was His sacrificial death victorious?

A. He paid the sin debt in full (John 19:30).

B. He rose from the dead three days later (Acts 2:23, 24; Rom. 4:25).

C. He is coming back some day as King of kings and Lord of lords (Heb. 9:27, 28).

Our response: What should be our response to the sacrificial death of Christ this Memorial Day? Jesus tells us. Look at John 15:9–17.

- Obey His commands (9–11).
- Love others (12–14, 17).
- Produce fruit (16).

Theme: Jesus Is a Friend and I Will . . .

Prelude—Instrumentalist
Evermore

Call to Worship and Prayer—Pastor *(Pastor calls all men and women to altar to pray for service)*

Worship and Praise—Congregation
MSPW 2 *Who Can Satisfy?* (chorus, v. 1, chorus, v. 2, chorus)

Love and Serve Him . . .

Welcome—Pastoral Staff

Welcome Song—Congregation (meet and greet)
CH 213 *We Bring a Sacrifice* (2x in D)
MSPW 1 *Ancient of Days* (2x in D)

Worship and Praise Him . . .

Worship and Praise
CH 10 *Majesty* (2x)
WH 4 *How Great Thou Art* (chorus, v. 1, chorus, mod. v. 4, chorus)

Prayer of Praise—Pastoral Staff
MSPW2 104 *There Is None Like You* (2x in G)

. . . Believe and Trust Him!

Offertory Prayer—Pastoral Staff

Offertory Praise—Praise Team or Congregation
SPW *Wonderful, Merciful Savior*

Message—Pastor
The Ultimate Sacrifice

Hymn of Response/Invitation—Congregation
CH 79 *My Jesus, I Love Thee*

Benediction Hymn

Postlude—Instrumentalists

Additional Sermons and Lesson Ideas

What the Gospel Means to Me
By W. Graham Scroggie

Date preached:

Scripture: Romans 1:16

Introduction: Looking toward the capital of the Roman Empire the thing that impressed the apostle Paul was not the authority of Caesar, but the power of the gospel. How his soul was thrilled as he wrote this verse. His testimony was: "I am not ashamed of the gospel."

    1. **The Definition of the Gospel**—*the power of God*
    2. **The Design of the Gospel**—*Unto Salvation.*
    3. **The Scope of the Gospel**—*to Everyone.*
    4. **The Reception of the Gospel**—*Who Believes.*

Conclusion: The efficacy of this message was unchallengeable, for Paul himself was the example and witness of its saving power.

SERIES: STAY COVERED (Authority—God's Covering for My Life)
Authority and the Body of Christ—Part 3
By Mark Fuller

Date preached:

Scripture: 1 Corinthians 12:12–20

Introduction: Take this quiz with me as we learn how God's authority works its way out in the church.

    1. **The best expression of God's authority is found in the relationship between:** (a) rulers and people, (b) parents and children, (c) masters and servants, (d) Christ and His church. *The answer is* (d) Christ and His church. Why is this so? Because Christ and His church is the only relationship that is an organic whole. No healthy head would ever do harm to its own body (1 Cor. 12:12; Eph. 4:15).
    2. **God has ordained the church to be:** (a) an organization, (b) an organism, (c) an institution, (d) a corporation. *The correct answer is* (b) an organism. The church is a living organism. It is the body of Christ (1 Cor. 12:12).
      • The church functions not as a democracy but as a theocracy.
      • The church in Laodicea illustrates a church functioning as a democracy (Rev. 3:17).
      • *Laodicea* means "people's rights." The purpose of the church is not to meet the needs of the people, but to bring glory to Christ.
    3. **In our physical bodies some movements are conscious while others are automatic. For example, the hand picks up a pencil in response**

to a conscious command, but the heart beats automatically, not waiting for any order. In the body of Christ, many of God's people will obey only conscious commands, thus hindering the unity and function of Christ's Church: True or False? The answer is *true*. Sometimes God calls us to intentional obedient acts, but often it is simply the impulse of the Holy Spirit that prompts us to respond in certain ways (1 Cor. 12:18).

Doctors have a word for cells in the body that operate independently . . . *cancer*. It has the same destructive effect on the body of Christ. Cells in the body of Christ do not exist for themselves, but for the good of the Body (Eph. 4:16). The reason many Christians burn out is not because they are doing too much, but because they are not doing what God has called them to do in the body of Christ.

4. **The church is a place for worship and fellowship, but it is not a place to learn Authority: True or False?** The answer of course is *false*. A church built on mutual fellowship without an understanding of authority is like a body trying to function without a head. The result would be confusion and chaos (1 Cor. 12:18).

5. **In the body of Christ, the members that have multiple functions are more valuable than those with singular Functions: True or False?** Again the answer is *false*. Every member, from the weakest to the strongest, from the biggest to the smallest, from the most presentable to the least presentable is a vital part of Christ's body. In fact, to reject or discredit a member of Christ's body is the same as rejecting Christ (1 Cor. 12:25, 26).

6. **The function of each member of the body of Christ constitutes its authority: True or False?** This is absolutely *true*. When someone is gifted, anointed, and appointed for a specific function in the body, we should submit to that functional authority regardless of who we are (1 Cor. 12:21).

7. **When one member of the body refuses to accept the supply of the other members, it creates poverty in that member, as well as in the church: True or False?** The answer is *true*. It is bald-faced pride to presume that anyone could or should possess all the gifts. This attitude creates division and as a result the body of Christ suffers (1 Cor. 12:29, 30).

8. **God uses authority to oppress and stifle the growth of the individual member so that the greater body may benefit: True or False?** This is a *false* statement. The irony in the body of Christ is that when you die to yourself and submit to God's authority, you receive His blessings.

9. **Much of what I receive from god, I receive through the body of Christ: True or False?** I have found this to be absolutely *true*. That is why Satan's tactic is to try and isolate you from the church (1 Cor. 12:21).

10. **Most people want god to speak to them directly, but his preferred way to speak to us is through delegated authority: True or False?** Have you discovered this to be *true?* I have. I often hear people say, "God never speaks to me like he does you." What they really are saying is, "I'm not willing to listen to what God is saying to me through my parents, my pastor, my mentors, and His Word."

Conclusion: There is no more perfect pattern to witness how spiritual authority works than the relationship between Christ, the head, and the church, His body. Find your place in the body of Christ.

JUNE 6, 2010

SUGGESTED SERMON

Dare to Be a Daniel

Date preached:

By Dr. Timothy Beougher

Introduction: Different countries have different cultural norms, and what is appropriate in one culture may be offensive in another culture. For example, you should never touch a person's head in Thailand; the head is considered sacred. In Portugal you should never write anything in red ink; it is very offensive. Chewing gum is illegal in Singapore and can result in a large fine. In our message today Daniel illustrates for us how to live when we "leave home" or encounter new situations. While this message is focused especially on those graduating from high school, it applies to all of us. Anytime something changes in our lives (a new job, a new house, a new school, a new stage of life), we face challenges to our faith. Daniel illustrates how to live when we leave what is familiar to us and encounter new situations.

I. **You will face a test: to walk with God in a "strange" land.** Daniel 1:3–7 introduces us to Daniel and three of his friends who were carried off in captivity to Babylon. They are called "young men," a phrase used to describe teenagers between the ages of twelve and fifteen. These young men had grown up around Jerusalem. There they were constantly reminded about God through His Word and worship at the temple. Instead of being surrounded by a culture that supported walking with God, they found themselves in a pagan nation surrounded by pagan practices and people. Verse 4 introduces us to the king's reprogramming effort; Daniel was enrolled at Babylon State University on a full scholarship. He was in a new location; no one was watching him and his actions. His parents weren't there; his pastor wasn't there. The opportunity for temptation was great. But Daniel remembered that God was there! The Babylonians gave them new names to fit that culture. Do you see the challenge that Daniel faced? He was thrust into a pagan culture in this strange land and was expected to conform. But Daniel was a teenager with convictions. He made a choice: "I'm going to walk with God even in a strange land." Just because your circumstances have changed doesn't mean God has changed.

2. **You must fight the temptation to compromise your convictions.**
Verses 5 and 8 tell us about the food and wine at the king's table,
but Daniel resolved not to defile himself. We are not sure why the
food represented a compromise for Daniel, but it is clear Daniel
drew a line in the sand. As we encounter new situations, we must
fight the temptation to compromise our convictions. Some of you
will be going to schools where you will experience what one pastor
has called "cultural brainwashing." You will be challenged to abandon your beliefs, to become like everybody else. Don't give in!
Determine not to conform (Rom. 12:2). The decisions you make
over the next few years will greatly impact the rest of your life. There
are three key issues:

A. **Truth Issue: What is truth?** The Babylonians sought to educate
Daniel and his friends in their history and culture. Education is
not evil; it's good and important to learn. But as we learn, we
need wisdom to sort out truth from opinion. Daniel and his
friends were being challenged to accept a pagan view of life. The
key is that they mastered the material, but it never mastered
them. The world will try to get you to adopt their view of truth.
You will face the temptation to become intellectually sophisticated. You will be pressured to conform! Don't compromise your
convictions! Do not determine what is right based on cultural
norms. There are absolutes in God's Word. The bottom line is
that it doesn't matter what others say; ultimately, what really
matters is what God says.

B. **Identity Issue: Who am I?** *Daniel* means "God is judge." *Hananiah* means "The Lord is gracious." *Mishael* means "Who is like
God?" *Azariah* means "The Lord helps." They were given new
names: Daniel became *Belteshazzar*, "Bel will protect" (Babylonian god). Hananiah became *Shadrach*, "Command of Aku" (a
Babylonian moon god). Mishael became *Meshach*, "Who is like
Aku?" (Babylonian god). Azariah became *Abed-Nego*, "Servant
of Nebo" (another god). The identity issue is a key issue. By
what name will others know you? Teenagers, college students,
graduate students, adults, you're going to have to make a choice.
Are you willing to be called a Christian in your culture? You
must deal with the temptation to compromise your identity. Take
a stand! Be proud of being a Christian!

C. **Morality Issue: How will I live?** Daniel had to decide whether to obey King Nebuchadnezzar and live like him, or to follow the King of kings and obey Him completely. Will we adopt the world's immorality or live by God's morality? You must fight the temptation of compromising your convictions.

3. **You can triumph by staying pure in a fallen world.** The Babylonians changed these young men's homes, their names, and their education, but they couldn't change their hearts! These young men had decided to follow God no matter what the cost. They didn't give in to the voices: "It's okay—everybody else is doing it." "I'll just keep my faith to myself—after all, faith is a private matter."

"When in Rome, do as the Romans do." They requested a different diet, and God honored them. God honored Daniel and his friends: they became healthier (vv. 15, 16) and wiser (vv. 17–20) than the others. When your heart truly belongs to God, you can be in any location and in any situation and still do the right thing.

Application: First, *commit to walk with God* (see v. 8). Let people know you're a Christian from the moment you set foot on that campus or the first day on your new job. Second, *spend time with the Lord each day in the Word and in prayer*. Either the Bible will keep you from sin or sin will keep you from the Bible. Next, *memorize key verses to deal with temptation* (see Ps. 119:11) and *develop a bond of accountability* (see Eccl. 4:9, 10). Graduates can find a campus fellowship (see Heb. 13:3). It's also necessary to find a good church, so don't sleep in! Finally, *trust God* (Prov. 3:5, 6). In 1873 hymn writer Philip Bliss wrote a gospel song about this story called "Dare to Be a Daniel." We should all heed these words of wisdom:

> Dare to be a Daniel.
> Dare to stand alone!
> Dare to have a purpose firm!
> Dare to make it known.

Graduation Sunday

Prelude—Instrumentalists
   CH 401 *The Church's One Foundation*

Welcome—Worship Leader

Prayer of Worship—Worship Leader

Baptismal Celebration—Pastoral Staff

Prayer of Praise—Pastoral Staff

Processional—Graduating Seniors walk in together
   Pomp and Circumstance, or
   CH 42 *All Hail the Power of Jesus' Name*—Congregation

Recognition of Graduates—Pastor and Director of Student
   Ministry

Graduation Charge—Guest Speaker (10 minutes) or Pastor

Graduation Prayer—Guest Speaker or Pastor

Song of Worship—Congregation
   CH 3 *Holy, Holy, Holy* (3 verses)

Worship and Praise—Congregation
   MSPW2 4 *God of Wonders* (2x)
   MSPW2 *Our Great God* (2x)
   MSPW *I Could Sing of Your Love Forever* (2x)

Offertory Prayer—*Pastoral Staff*

Offertory Praise—Senior Soloist or Small Singing Group of
   Graduating Seniors

Message—Pastor

Hymn of Response/Invitation—Congregation
   CH 186 *In My Life Lord, Be Glorified*

Recessional—Graduating Seniors (optional)
   Pomp and Circumstance

Benediction Hymn—Congregation
   CH 195 *Bless the Name of Jesus* (2x in C)

Postlude

Additional Sermons and Lesson Ideas

SERIES: FAITH IS THE VICTORY

Faith: The Spiritual Tool We Can't Live Without   *Date preached:*
By Dr. Larry Osborne

Scripture: Various

Introduction: While it's the most basic of spiritual tools, faith is probably also the one most misunderstood by both non-Christians and Christians alike.

    1. **What it is.** Faith is trusting God enough to do what He says (Heb. 11:1–40; James 2:14–24; 1 John 2:3–5). Here are some common misconceptions and Scriptures that disprove them:
        A. Faith has no room for doubt (Acts 12:1–19; Dan. 3:16–30).
        B. Faith has no room for fear (1 Cor. 2:1–3; 1 Pet. 3:4).
        C. Faith has power in itself (1 Kin. 18:21–40).
        D. Faith defies logic (John 14:11; 20:31).
    2. **How important it is.** Without faith it's not possible to please God (Heb. 10:28–30; 11:6; Prov. 3:5–8; Rom. 1:17; 2 Cor. 5:7; Gal. 2:20). We must believe that He exists and that He rewards (Heb. 11:6).
    3. **How we can get the faith we need.** Remember the mustard seed principle: it's not about having *more* faith (Luke 17:3–6; Mark 9:24; John 3:16), it's about who your faith is in.

Conclusion: Who is your faith resting in?

SERIES: STAY COVERED (Authority—God's Covering for My Life)

Dealing Practically with Rebellion, Part 4   *Date preached:*
By Mark Fuller

Scripture: Romans 9:11–21; 2 Corinthians 10:4–6

Introduction: Rebellion begins in the heart, the seat of our affections. But then it quickly moves into the mind, and then finally works its way into our behavior and lifestyle. We've already addressed the "heart" of the issue. Let's learn how rebellion affects our thinking and how to win the battle for our minds.

    Rebellion finds its expression through:
        A. *Human Reasoning* (Rom. 9:11–22). The apostle Paul isn't trying to establish a reasonable response to the apparent conflict we see between God's sovereignty and man's free will. Rather, he is challenging us to move beyond our understanding to a place of humble worship before a God whose reasoning far exceeds our

ability to understand. People who have trouble with the "unreasonableness" of God have never submitted to His authority in their hearts.

When I am tempted to reason rather than obey, I need to:

forget who I am and remember who He is.

forget my reasoning and remember His Word (Rom. 11:33, 34).

B. *Human Arguments* (2 Cor. 10:3–5). The walled fortresses and high towers of our minds are intellectual strongholds of willful ignorance, prejudice, superstition, tradition, and idolatry. They are not changed easily. I must take captive every thought and make it obedient to Christ.

When I am tempted by stinkin' thinkin', I need to:

take captive every thought.

obey Christ with every thought.

Replace destructive thought patterns with constructive ones. For example, "I am a failure" to "I can do all things through Christ." God will only renew a mind that is governed by a surrendered will.

"My faith has found a resting place, not in device or creed. I trust the ever-living One, His wounds for me shall plead. I need no other argument, I need no other plea. It is enough that Jesus died, and that He died for me."　　　—Lidie H. Edmunds

Conclusion: In the final analysis, analysis is not final . . . God is. He is a mystery. And His ways are mysterious. The "unreasonableness" of God is not to cause you to worry, but to lead you to worship. God doesn't want to argue with you, He is simply there to be worshiped, loved, and adored.

JUNE 13, 2010

SERIES: EXTREME HOME MAKEOVER   SUGGESTED SERMON

Trading Spaces: Understanding Your Husband's Needs

Date preached:

By Dr. Kenyn M. Cureton

Scripture: Genesis 3:16; Ephesians 5:22–33

Introduction: The problems today with breakdown in the home started in the Garden of Eden. It all goes back to the fall into sin. You remember that Adam was alone, then God made Eve and that made Adam happy. Everything was great until they ate the forbidden fruit, and conflict came into their marriage over the issue of leadership.

1. **The problem with leadership in the home:**

    A. **Women desire to run the home.** God told Eve, not only will you have increased pain in childbirth, there's going to be friction in the home: "your desire will be for your husband and he will rule over you" (Gen. 3:16). The Hebrew word translated here as *desire* can also mean "to urge, to compel, to take control over something or someone." The same word is used in Genesis 4:7 when God talked to Cain: Sin is like a wild animal that desires to overpower you.

    B. **Men desire to be the leader.** God says in that same verse, "But he is going to rule over you" (Gen. 3:16). The original language speaks of authoritarianism.

    C. **The desire to control leads to conflict.** Because of the sinful nature, Eve is going to try to control Adam, and Adam is going to rule over Eve. So the battle of the sexes began with the fall into sin. Simply stated, it is the natural desire of fallen woman to manipulate and dominate her husband, and therefore take his place as the leader in the home.

2. **God's solution to leadership in the home.** Paul compares the relationship between husband and wife to the relationship between Christ and the church (vv. 22–24).

A. **A wife's role is helper.** According to Genesis 2, the wife's role is that of "suitable helper." How can she assist him in becoming all that God intended? She is the key to meeting several vital needs that her husband has:

(1) **Need for companionship.** One of man's deepest needs is companionship (Gen. 2:18). God made Eve to complete Adam. Men need someone they can share their life and love, deepest thoughts, struggles, and dreams with.

(2) **Need for support.** Your husband needs your support—personal and emotional support. Every man needs to know that his wife stands with him (Prov. 31:10–12). A suitable helper encourages her husband and is his most loyal supporter of every aspect of his life.

(3) **Need for admiration.** Every man needs a wife who will admire him. It is interesting that Paul never says, "Wives, love your husbands." He says: "Wives, respect your husbands." He desperately needs to know that you think he's important, has value, and that his life counts for something.

B. **A wife's response is submission.** In Ephesians 5, Paul gives us the proper response of a wife to her husband as the loving leader in the home: submission. The Greek word for *submit* was originally a military term, but basically submission is one equal voluntarily placing himself or herself under another equal, that God may therefore be glorified. So a wife's proper response to her husband's role is submission.

No organism can function without a head. Dr. Adrian Rogers used to say: "Anything with no head is dead, but anything with two heads is a freak." God, in His wisdom ordained the husband to be the head of the wife (v. 25). There must be authority, but does that imply inferiority? Jesus Christ is not inferior to God the Father (1 Cor. 11:3; Phil. 2:5, 6), nor are women inferior to men. Both are equal before God (Gal. 3:28). Submission rightly understood does not restrain so much as it releases. Every believer who is willing to totally submit to the Lord Jesus Christ knows the power and authority of the Lord Jesus Christ.

Titus 2:4, 5 gives us a description of the core responsibilities of a woman. The wife's submission is a way of validating her husband's God-given role as the loving leader in the home. Your submission will actually make him a better husband, because it will force him to take the lead, which is his God-given role. See also Col. 3:18.

Conclusion: For your marriage to have the best chance of working right, both partners have to strive to align your lives with God's pattern. Paul begins this section by saying: "Be filled with the Spirit" (Eph. 5:18). It is not possible to be the loving leader in your home, men, unless you are filled with the Spirit. And it is not possible to submit to your husband, ladies, unless you are filled with the Spirit. But when both of you are filled with the Spirit, he can lead you lovingly, and you can submit to him respectfully, because that is God's desire, and God's design, and so shall your home be as the days of heaven on earth!

STATS, STORIES, AND MORE

More from Dr. Kenyn M. Cureton

Give the Man a Chicken: A farmer's boy was getting ready to marry. And the farmer said to his boy, "John, when you get married you're going to lose all your liberties." And the boy said, "I don't believe that, Dad." And the dad said, "OK, I'll prove it to you, boy." Go out and catch a dozen chickens, tie their legs together, and put them in the wagon. Then go and hitch my two best horses to the wagon and drive into town. Stop at every house, knock on the door, and ask, 'Who's the head of this house?' At every house where the man is the head of the house, give away a horse. At every house where the lady is boss, give away a chicken." The boy said, "All right, but you're going to lose those prize horses of yours." And the father said, "We'll see."

So the boy did like his father asked. He put twelve chickens in the wagon and drove into town with his father's two best horses. He went to eleven houses and had to give away eleven chickens. So he walked up to the last house and knocked on the door. The man and his wife opened the door, and the boy asked, "Who is the head of this house?" The lady said, "My husband is." The boy explained the proposition, then he said, "Mister, I'd like for you to choose the horse you like best." The man went out and looked and said, "I believe I'll take the black horse, because it's the better of the two." The wife said, "I think the bay horse is the best horse." The husband says, "OK, we'll take the bay horse." The boy says, "No you won't, you'll take a chicken."

Men Failing to Lead: It was God's intention for you and you and you to simply work the garden a little, eat grapes from the vine, go fishing, pet the lions, and enjoy perfect fellowship with God. That was to be our life. But dumb-head Adam had to listen to Eve and take a bite of that fruit, and together he and Eve literally ate us out of house and home! I heard about a preacher who came home from a hard day of ministry, and he was in the

STATS, STORIES, AND MORE—*Continued*

kitchen telling his wife about his day while she was cooking supper. And as he was talking, she lifted a piece of food to his mouth, and said, "Take a bite of this." And like an obedient beast, he took a bite. And she said, "See how easy that was." We men haven't learned a thing.

Look at the trouble that resulted when a man submitted to the lead of his wife. Not to her need, but to her lead. Adam listened to Eve and God kicked them out of the Garden of Eden, because he ate the forbidden fruit. Abraham listened to Sarah his wife. God had promised them a child even though they were both past the childbearing years. But Sarah got impatient and told Abraham, "I'm too old to have a baby, so I want you to go have a baby with my young maid Hagar." And Abraham said, "Sounds like the will of God to me!" He went to Hagar, and they had a baby. Abraham and Sarah had a baby just as God had promised.

But think of the problems caused by Abraham listening to his wife rather than waiting on God. The child he fathered with Hagar was Ishmael, and he is the father of the Arabic peoples. The child he fathered with Sarah was Isaac, and he is the father of the Jews. And what started out as a family feud over 4,000 years ago is now a continual international crisis in the Middle East, because they want to annihilate one another! But all this trouble started out because a man listened to his wife's counsel rather than the word of God.

Apocryphal Conversation between Adam and God: God said: "Adam, I know you're lonely, so let me tell you what I'm going to do. I'm going to make you a woman, I mean a perfect 10, and she is going to meet your every need. She's going to get up at 5:00 a.m. every morning, lay out your clothes, have breakfast and the newspaper on the table when you get ready. Kiss you passionately when you leave for work, put love notes in your briefcase, and call you to find out what you want for supper and tell you how much she loves you and can't wait for you to get home. She's going to meet you at the door every evening wearing something exciting. After you slip into something comfortable, she will give you a full body massage, and then usher you to the table for a sumptuous feast. And, Adam, after you have dessert, you get to have her." And Adam was excited so he said, "God, that's great! But that's too good to be true, what's the catch? What will it cost me?" And God said, "It will cost you an arm and a leg." Adam thought about it for a minute and said, "What can I get for a rib?" And God made woman . . .

Man in the Mirror: Remember Snow White? The wicked queen asked, "Mirror, mirror on the wall, who's the fairest one of all?" A man has two significant mirrors in his life: his work and his wife. And looking into these two mirrors he asks important questions about his identity, worth, and meaning. Now of these two mirrors, obviously, ladies, you are the more valuable. So how you feel about him, how you smile at him, and draw along side him, and tell him, "I think you're wonderful. I am proud of you. I'm glad I married you." That will make all the difference in a man's self-worth, and therefore how he relates to you in the home.

SUGGESTED ORDER OF WORSHIP

Prelude—Instrumental Group
God of Wonders

Call to Prayer—Pastoral Staff

Worship and Praise—Congregation
HPW 15 *Come, Christians, Join to Sing* (1x in F, 1x in F#, 1x in G)

Welcome—Pastoral Staff

Song of Welcome (meet and greet)—Congregation
CH 212/213 *We Bring the Sacrifice of Praise* (2x in D)
CH 214 *He Has Made Me Glad* (2x in D)

Worship and Praise—Congregation
MSPW 1 *Ancient of Days* (2x in D)
MSPW 31 *I See the Lord* (2x in D)
CH 3 *Holy, Holy, Holy* (2x in D)
MSPW 51 *Step by Step* (2x in G)

Offertory Prayer—Pastoral Staff

Offertory Praise—Solo or Praise Team
We Fall Down (Don Marsh Arr) (2x in D, 1x in E)

Message—Pastor

Hymn of Response/Invitation—Congregation
CH 481 *Come Just as You Are*

Benediction Hymn—Congregation
CH 431 *Shine Jesus, Shine* (2x in Ab)

Postlude—Instrumental Group
God of Wonders

Additional Sermons and Lesson Ideas

SERIES: FAITH IS THE VICTORY

Faith Amid Famine

Date preached:

By Rev. Todd M. Kinde

Scripture: I Kings 17:7–24, especially v. 24

Introduction: This morning we are going to be learning quite an object lesson through a bin of flour and a jar of oil. I realize that talking about flour, oil, bread, and food can make your mouth water. I hope today we all came into this building hungry—at least spiritually hungry. Do you have a financial problem? Are your relationships hurting? Do you need a fresh encounter with the Lord? Jesus said, "I am the bread of life. He who comes to Me shall never hunger, and he who believes in Me shall never thirst" (John 6:35 NKJV).

1. **A parchedness of faith (1 Kin. 17:7–9).** The Word of the Lord came to Elijah, instructing him to go to the town of Zarephath, where a widow would supply him with food. The drought was an object lesson of the dryness of the nation's relationship with God (cf. Amos 8 and Ps. 42). Now that the brook had run dry, the Lord placed Elijah in Zarephath, a suburb of the capital city where the wicked Jezebel's father was king!

2. **A preview of faith (1 Kin. 17:10–15a).** In Zarephath, Elijah found a certain widow. Elijah asked for a flask of water. He tested her willingness and obedience. When she agreed, Elijah added a request for bread. She told Elijah she had only enough for her and her son to have a last meal before starvation. Most of us would have reacted harshly, but this woman said, "As surely as the Lord your God lives." She knew Yahweh was the Living God, but He was not her God ("*your* God lives"). The gentle hand of God was leading her into progressive faith. Elijah said, "Can I have a drink? Can I have a slice of bread? Make me a pancake." As we respond to God's Word with trusting obedience in each step, so He will lead us to greater understanding of Himself and the blessing of His promise of salvation.

3. **A provision of faith (1 Kin. 17:15b, 16).** It's safe to assume that neither the flour jar nor the oil jug was large. At the end of each day, her jug and jar looked to be just as nearly empty as they did that first evening when she met Elijah. God gave her and Elijah only their daily bread (Matt. 6:11). Faith is progressive, not a one-time commitment. Elijah and the widow did not respond with faith just once and then receive a warehouse full of flour and oil. At the end of each day, they had to acknowledge their complete dependence upon the Lord and trust Him for enough grace for the next day (see Lam. 3:22, 23).

4. **A prayer of faith (1 Kin. 17:17–23).** We don't know how long this way of life continued, but some time later the son of the woman became

ill and died. Then her faith was tested in a new dimension. The woman faced death yet again, saying to Elijah, "What have I to do with you, O man of God? Have you come to me to bring my sin to remembrance, and to kill my son?" (v. 18). Did not God promise life when He gave the promise of food? On the basis of the promise of God's Word, Elijah prayed to the Lord to revive the boy. We should pray with such awareness of the Word of the Lord that our prayers are built on the foundation of God's promises.

5. **A profession of faith (1 Kin. 17:24).** The woman's response was a deeper and more personal profession of faith in the one true living God. She understood that there was more to this than simply the death of her son's body. It had to do with her sinfulness and spiritual death. Her confession is seen in verse 24. She comprehends the truth. God's Word can be trusted beyond doubt. You can trust the Word of the Lord for all your needs in life and death.

Conclusion: We don't live by bread alone but by every word that comes from the mouth of God (Deut. 8:3). Do not seek to satisfy the longing of your soul with bread, but trust the Lord of life who gives living water and the Bread of Life. Cling to the Cross of Christ. Through it you have the forgiveness of sin and the promise of life eternal. May we say, "Now we know that the Word of the Lord is the truth," and make that truth into a living faith.

Why Do People Stray?

Date preached:

By Rev. Billie Friel

Scripture: James 5:19, 20

Introduction: The hardest person to reach, according to surveys, is the person who has drifted away from the Lord and is out of fellowship with God's people.

1. **The reality of straying people (v. 19).** Christians can stumble in many ways (James 3:2). Christians can stray or wander from the truth. We are not perfect.
2. **The reasons people stray (v. 19).** People stray because of sin (1:14, 15), bitterness towards others, falling out of good habits, doubts, or trials that cause them to think God has failed them.
3. **The response of Christians (vv. 19, 20).** A healthy Christian is used by God to turn the straying person back to the truth. In so doing, a person may be saved from premature death and the committing of needless sins.

Conclusion: We participate with God in a noble work with eternal dividends when we are used to bring the straying Christian back to Christ and His people.

JUNE 20, 2010

SERIES: EXTREME HOME MAKEOVER   SUGGESTED SERMON

The Prodigal Father: Returning to God's Idea of Fatherhood   *Date preached:*

By Tony Perkins

Scripture: Luke 15:11–32

Introduction: In our day, the fathers have left their children. According to the U.S. Department of Health and Human Services, over the last four decades there has been a dramatic increase in the number of children growing up in homes without fathers. In 1960, fewer than 10 million children did not live with their fathers. Today, the number is nearly 25 million. More than one-third of these children will not see their fathers at all during the course of a year. Studies show that children who grow up without responsible fathers are significantly more likely to experience poverty, perform poorly in school, engage in criminal activity, and abuse drugs and alcohol.

1. **Characteristics of the Prodigal Son**

    A. **Self-absorbed (v. 12).** He rejected his father's government. He didn't want to live by his rules. He knew better than his father.

    B. **Short-sighted (vv. 13–16).** No delayed gratification. He wanted it all *now!*

    C. **Surrendered (vv. 17–19).** Broken, he was willing to surrender his legal position as son.
    These same characteristics are seen in today's prodigal father. Remember, fathers don't have to physically leave to be absent.

2. **Characteristics of the Prodigal Father**

    A. **Self-absorbed.** Seek their own pleasure.

    B. **Short-sighted.** They live for today.

    C. **Surrender.** They relinquish their role as father, physically and/ or emotionally, allowing others (e.g., mothers) and the culture to raise their children. Feminist Gloria Steinem is credited with saying, "A woman needs a man like a fish needs a bicycle." No, children need a dad like a fish needs water.

Roughly 70% of incarcerated males have had little or no interaction with their fathers. Young girls hardly fare better. Fathers, the best way to prevent your daughters from falling into the arms of someone who will take advantage of them is to frequently hold them in yours.

3. **Characteristics of a Godly Father**
   F—Forgiving (vv. 22–24). The father forgave his son immediately. He did not sulk. He celebrated his son's return. Our children need to see and hear that from their dads.
   A—Available (v. 20). An eight-year-old wrote about love and true love: Love is when Daddy reads me a bedtime story. True love is when he doesn't skip any of the pages.
   T—Teaching (vv. 31, 32). He took the eldest aside and used the return of the youngest as a teachable moment. Do not nag or arbitrarily assert authority (Eph. 6:4). Take advantage of teachable moments that happen every day (Prov. 22:6).
   H—Having integrity (v. 17). The son knew his father could be counted on—a man of integrity.
   E—Expressive (v. 20). The father was incredibly affectionate. He kissed his son and wrapped his arms around him.
   R—Respectful (vv. 12, 31). The father was respectful of both his sons' wishes. He allowed the one to fail in order to learn. He allowed the other to complain but reaffirmed his love. Don't provoke your children to make rash decisions based on your responses, be respectful enough to hear them out (Col 3:21).

Conclusion: What do kids need today? They desperately need fathers who are there to:

- . . . play catch, enjoy tea parties or wrestle because the heart of a child is there and they set out to capture it.
- . . . laugh till their belly hurts and tears fall from their eyes while secretly creating deep friendships and memories that last a lifetime.
- . . . place an out-of-tune preschool concert or a ten-year-old's baseball game on life's agenda because of the infinite worth of those playing.

- . . . love at all times, because love is a gift freely given and not a reward for service well done.
- . . . listen eye to eye and with both ears, even if it means getting on one knee.
- . . . admit when they are wrong and work to make things right.
- . . . hear about those in need and say, "Let's do something to help right now!" and set off an uncontrollable wildfire of generosity and kindness.
- . . . give the credit to others and empower those they touch to succeed in all that they do.
- . . . model love as action, commitment, and truth even when it hurts because they believe God can work miracles in even the hardest heart and in the most difficult of circumstances.
- . . . love the Lord with all their heart, soul, and mind and know that the rest is just details.

The statistics I shared earlier are just that—statistics. You and your children do not have to be statistics. You can start right where you are today and build a strong relationship with your children. Single parents, your children can succeed, but you are going to have to work hard.

What is riding on fatherhood and to a great extent the family? Simply this: Our future. It is time fathers returned home!

STATS, STORIES, AND MORE

More from Tony Perkins

The movie *The Pursuit of Happyness* is a story of a young black man and woman who had a son. They were not married and the woman walked out during tough times, leaving Chris Gardner, played by Will Smith, with the boy. Gardner decides to stick it out with the boy as he tries to build a career for himself. They lived on the streets, in homeless shelters—but they were together. He didn't run from his responsibility as a father. He finally succeeded in his career and became very successful on Wall Street. It's a great story, but the reason a movie was made about it was because it is unusual today.

In *My Father's Face,* author James Robison tells of a federal prison chaplain who decided to improve morale. The clergyman approached a major greeting card company and asked for a donation of 500 Mother's Day cards, one for each inmate. Spotting a good PR story when they see it, the company agreed. Each inmate enthusiastically filled out a card for his mom, and morale picked up. For Father's Day, the chaplain decided to duplicate his previous success. Again, the greeting card company agreed to donate 500 cards. But this time, the project crashed and burned. Not a single inmate—not one—wished to fill out a card for his dad.

General Douglas MacArthur, one of our greatest military leaders, said, "By profession I am a soldier and take pride in that, but I am prouder—infinitely prouder—to be a father. A soldier destroys, a father builds. The one has the potentiality of death; the other embodies creation and life. It is my hope that my son, when I am gone, will remember me not from the battlefield, but in the home, repeating with him our simple daily prayers."

In *The Decline and Fall of the Roman Empire,* completed in 1787, Edward Gibbon lists the following reasons for the fall of Rome:

1. The rapid increase of divorce; the undermining of dignity and sanctity of the home, which is the basis of human society.
2. Higher and higher taxes and the spending of public money for free bread and circuses for the populace. (Most social programs are trying to make up for where the family is falling short.)
3. The mad craze for pleasure; sports becoming every year more exciting and more brutal.
4. The building of gigantic armaments when the real enemy was within: the decadence of the people.
5. The decay of religion—faith fading into mere form—losing touch with life and becoming impotent to guide the people.

According to David Blankenhorn, in his book *Fatherless America*, girls who grow up without fathers are 111 percent more likely to have children as teenagers, 164 percent more likely to have a premarital birth, and 92 percent more likely to dissolve their own marriages.[1]

[1]David Blankenhorn, *Fatherless America: Confronting Our Most Urgent Social Problem* (New York: BasicBooks, 1995).

Father's Day

Prelude—Instrumental Group
CH 431 *Shine Jesus, Shine* (2x in Ab)

Call to Worship—Praise Team
Mercy Came Running

Worship in Prayer—Worship Pastor

Worship and Praise
CH 102/103 *All Hail King Jesus* (1x in Eb, 1x in F)
CH 104 O *Worship the King* (1x in G, 1x in Ab)

Welcome—Pastoral Staff

Welcome Hymn (meet and greet)—Congregation
CH 542 *My Life Is in You, Lord* (2x in G)

Recognition of Fathers—Pastor

Worship and Praise
CH 333 *O the Blood of Jesus* (v1, 2, 4) (2x in D, 1x in Eb)
CH 323 *At the Cross* (Chorus Only) (1x in Eb, 1x in F)
CH 336 *There Is a Fountain* (v1, v3 in Bb)
Shout to the Lord (from *God for Us*—Integrity) (1x in Bb, 1x in C)

Prayer—Worship Pastor

Drama on Father's Day

Offertory Prayer for the Fathers—Pastor

Offertory Praise—Congregation
Days of Elijah

Message—Pastor

Hymn of Invitation—Congregation
CH 487 *Room at the Cross*

Hymn of Benediction—Congregation
CH 431 *Shine Jesus, Shine* (2x in Ab)

Postlude—Instrumental Group
CH 431 *Shine Jesus, Shine* (2x in Ab)

Additional Sermons and Lesson Ideas

SERIES: FAITH IS THE VICTORY

Developing Mega-Faith

Date preached:

By Ed Dobson

Scripture: Matthew 15:21–28; Mark 7:24–30

Introduction: In this story Jesus left the Jewish area of Galilee for the seaport of Tyre, a pagan Gentile area. This was a very un-Jewish and un-rabbinical thing to do, but He knew there was a desperate mother there. Notice the verbs describing her: she heard about Him, came, fell at His feet, and begged His help. Yet Jesus answered her not a word. Her response to His non-response was to keep crying for mercy. Desperate people do desperate things. When you're desperate you don't care what people think, nor do you give up easily. Jesus finally said, in summary, "I've been sent to the lost sheep of Israel. My mission is the Jews. Why take the food of children and give it to dogs?" The word *dog* would be better translated, *little dog* or *puppy*. "It is not right to take the children's bread and toss it to their puppy." Jesus was not being unkind, but making a theological point—His first priority was the Jewish people. "Yes, Lord," the woman replied, "but even the puppies under the table get some crumbs." In other words, "What you're saying is true, but I don't need the full meal. Just a few crumbs will be sufficient." Can you sense this woman's faith? Jesus did. "Woman," He said, "you have great faith!" The Greek word is μεγασ (*megas*), source of the English prefix *mega*. This woman had mega-faith! From this story, notice the characteristics of mega-faith:

1. **Mega-faith does not deny the problem.** It is not the power of positive thinking or a way of looking at life through rose-colored glasses. Mega-faith is realistic, acknowledging the challenges, difficulties, struggles, and sufferings.

2. **Mega-faith goes directly to the source of blessing.** As soon as she heard of Christ, she came and fell at His feet. We sometimes depend too much on our own abilities and resources. But great faith knows that beyond our own resources is the source of all power and blessing—God Himself (see Heb. 4:14–16)!

3. **Mega-faith throws itself at the feet of Jesus.** This was an act of submission, carrying the idea of abandonment to the purpose, plan, and power of God. She didn't come with her own plan and ask Jesus to bless it. She said, "Lord, I give this to You." It's frightening to give up control, but when we yield control to Christ, what freedom comes!

4. **Mega-faith is persistent.** At first, Jesus doesn't answer this woman; and when He finally did answer her, His tone was discouraging. But she kept begging. We should always pray and not faint. Prayer and faith persist, even when God seems to respond not a word.

5. **Mega-faith repeats the word of God.** This woman took what Jesus said, repeated it back to Him, then added a request to it. Great faith is anchored in Scripture.

6. **Mega-faith responds with submission.** "Yes, Lord," the woman said. Those are two very important words in our prayer vocabulary. They acknowledge Him who is in charge, like Jesus in the Garden, ". . . not my will, but Your will be done." Great faith surrenders the outcome to God, Who knows what is best for us.

7. **Mega-faith is always rewarded.** Going home, this woman found her child whole and the demon gone. Great faith is always rewarded with divine intervention which comes either through a miracle or through a specific message from God that enables us on the journey.

Conclusion: Maybe you're thinking, "That's easy for you to preach, but you don't know what I'm facing this morning." The beauty of this story is that it was not the faith of the demon-possessed girl that brought healing, it was the faith of her loving mother. If you can't muster mega-faith, learn to trust in the faith of those around you. God honors their faith on your behalf. Never underestimate the prayers and faith of others in your behalf. God, grant us great faith. Amen!

SERIES: HOW TO PRAY FOR THE PRESIDENT

Praying for Us As Citizens, Part 1
Date preached:

By Dr. Kent Spann

Scripture: 1 Timothy 2:1–4

Introduction: Paul exhorts us in this passage to pray for our government leaders. No leader of our government needs prayer more than the President of the United States. No person needs divine guidance more than the President of the United States.

George Washington, our first President, said, "It is impossible to rightly govern the world without God and the Bible."

But what if that President holds different beliefs and convictions then we do? We need to remember that in this passage Paul is calling for prayer for Nero, a pagan king who persecuted the church.

So how do we pray for our President? It begins with praying for us as citizens.

1. We would honor our President (Ex. 22:28; Eccl. 10:20; 1 Pet. 2:17).
   A. We would not be bitter towards him.
   B. We would not be disrespectful of him.
2. We would submit to our government (Rom. 13:1–5; Titus 3:1; 1 Pet. 2:13, 14).
3. We would seek the welfare of our nation (Jer. 29:5–7).
4. We would live lives of righteousness (Prov. 11:11).

5. We would thank God for our country and its leaders (1 Thess. 5:18; 1 Tim. 2:1).
   A. We live in a country where we have the privilege of voting.
   B. We live in a country where there is a peaceful transition of power.
   C. We live in a country where we are free to worship.

Conclusion: Before we can pray for the President, we need to be sure that we are living God-honoring lives as citizens of the United States.

JUNE 27, 2010

SERIES: EXTREME HOME MAKEOVER   SUGGESTED SERMON

Re-Wired: How to Communicate with Your Mate

Date preached:

By Dr. Kenyn M. Cureton

Scripture: Ephesians 4:29

Introduction: This message is about communication in marriage. Most marriage counselors agree that the single most important element in a long-term marriage relationship is the ability to communicate. It is ironic that we have developed high-tech communication systems to talk to someone in space or across the country, yet very often husbands and wives can't communicate across the dinner table. Not being able to talk through problems and difficulties can be fatal to a marriage relationship.

1. **Definition of Communication.** Communication is the act of sending and receiving a clear message containing information and feelings. It takes two to communicate. The words you use, the way you say them, and your body language all add up to the total message you send.

2. **Five levels of Communication.** In his book, *Why Am I Afraid to Tell You Who I Am?*, John Powell gives five levels of communication.[1] There are five concentric circles with outside circles being less significant and inside being more significant.

   A. **Clichéd Conversation.** Outside circle: "How are you?" "How's it going?" Most of the time, it is surface level. You say "Fine" even if you are really hurting.

   B. **Factual Conversation.** We just report facts, giving the weather report, talking scores, sales, etc. Still no personal self-revelations, just the facts as we perceive them.

---

[1] John Powell, *Why Am I Afraid to Tell You Who I Am? Insights into Personal Growth* (Thomas More Association, 1995).

C. **Philosophical Conversation.** Sharing ideas and judgments, values and beliefs, like talking politics or religion.

D. **Emotional Conversation.** Feelings are intimate and sometimes awkward to share. This is the next deepest level of communication. Most are guarded at this point because of the vulnerability.

E. **Intimate Conversation.** Innermost circle: It is when husband and wife can honestly tell each other who you are, what you think, feel, desire, fear, hope for, etc. Authentic and lasting marriages should be built on this kind of complete intimate communion.

3. **Five Communication Killers**

A. **Presence of Fear.** People are afraid of being rejected or made fun of. So they naturally won't open up. People are afraid to open up because if they expose themselves as they really are, and they are made to feel bad for doing so, they won't open up again.

B. **Lack of Honesty.** We all put a mask on at some point or another and we play a role like an actor . . . for acceptance. The danger with this is you can lose touch with yourself.

C. **Act of Coercion.** Psychologist and author Dr. Henry Brandt says that no nakedness is comparable to emotional nakedness.[2] When our mate points out our deficiencies, we grasp at something to cover up. Tears can be used to coerce, often by women, but some men can do it as well. That can be manipulation, not communication.

D. **Failure to Listen.** The fourth communication killer is the failure to listen. A message sent must be a message received, or communication is killed.

E. **Sound of Silence.** The fifth communication killer is silence or pouting. Have you ever been given the "silent treatment"? We hold it in. Doctors tell us that this type of reaction is a leading cause of ulcers, high blood pressure, and divorce.

---

[2]Quoted by Tim LaHaye, *How to Be Happy Though Married* (Wheaton, IL: Tyndale, 2002), 106.

4. **Five Steps to Good Communication**

   A. **Take time.** Take time for one another. We face all kinds of demands in this fast-paced world that we live in. Spending quality time with your spouse is essential to the health and growth of your relationship. The more you are together and interacting, the better you will learn to communicate.

   B. **Learn to listen.** James 1:19 says, "Be quick to listen and slow to speak." Listening demands concentration. Let your mate know what you heard him/her say by restating what has just been said.

   C. **Understand that your mate's perceptions are different from yours.** You will never see things exactly the same way all the time because you are an individual, but respect the perspective of your mate when there is a difference.

   D. **Speak for yourself.** Communication gets confused when you tell your mate what he/she thinks or feels or what he/she should think and feel. Don't try to judge the other's motives. Express your own feelings. Use "I" messages: "I feel this way when you . . ."

   E. **Speak the truth in love.** Ephesians 4:15 says, "Speak the truth in love." The more truth you speak, the more love you should convey. State your concern in love, and state it only once (Prov. 27:15).

Conclusion: There are two expressions that are essential to maintaining good communication in marriage:

   1. **I'm sorry:** Remember Romans 3:23. How many have sinned? All. Therefore there is no such thing as a perfect marriage. So when (not *if*) you are wrong, say: "I'm sorry."

   2. **I love you:** Tell your mate that you love him/her through your words, actions, tone of voice, willingness to listen. Simple but powerful words: "I love you."

      These two statements "I'm sorry" and "I love you" can help you get re-wired better than anything I know.

STATS, STORIES, AND MORE

More from Dr. Kenyn M. Cureton

Failure to Communicate: A woman went to her attorney to file for divorce. And the attorney said, "Do you have grounds?" She said, "Yes, about two acres." He said, "No, I mean do you have a grudge?" She said, "Yes, you can park two cars in it." He shook his head and said, "Well, does the man beat you up?" She said, "No, I let him sleep in." He was exasperated and said, "Well, what is your problem?" She said, "We just can't communicate."

Definition of Communication: Communication is the act of sending and receiving messages. Two Indians were in New Mexico sending smoke signals to each other. As they were laboring over their campfires there on opposite mesas, trying to create perfect smoke, at that exact moment, the Atomic Energy Commission exploded the first atomic bomb, which produced a huge mushroom cloud and a shockwave that literally knocked them both down. One Indian saw that huge cloud and sent the following smoke signal: "Wow! I wish I had said that!" Again, communication is the act of sending and receiving messages.

Painfully Clear Communication: I heard about a wife who painfully but clearly communicated with her husband. They were riding mules down into the Grand Canyon, when all of the sudden, the wife's mule stumbled on the steep trail. The man's wife calmly said, "That's one." As they continued on down the winding trail, the mule stumbled again. She calmly said, "That's two." They went a little further, and the mule stumbled a third time. The man's wife calmly said, "That's three," promptly pulled out a .44, and shot the mule in the head. Her husband was shocked, and he said, "What in the world did you do that for? Are you crazy? Have you lost your mind?" His wife put the gun back in her bag, looked up at her husband and calmly said, "That's one!" I'll bet he kept his mouth shut the rest of the trip, Amen?

Dangerous to Safest Communication: I received an email titled "Hormone Hostage." Every hormone hostage knows there are days in the month when all a man has to do is open his mouth and he takes his life in his hands. This is a handy guide that should be as common as a driver's license in the wallet of every husband:

DANGEROUS: What's for dinner?
SAFER: Can I help you with dinner?
SAFEST: Where would you like to go for dinner?

DANGEROUS: What did you DO all day?
SAFER: I hope you didn't overdo it today.
SAFEST: You know, I've always loved you in that robe.

DANGEROUS: Why are you eating ice cream out of the carton?
SAFER: Have you had a bad day?
SAFEST: Can I bring you some hot fudge? Oreos?

STATS, STORIES, AND MORE—*Continued*

DANGEROUS: What are you so worked up about?
SAFER: Could we be just a tad bit overreacting?
SAFEST: Here's my Gold Card.

Learn to Listen: A man waited impatiently at a phone booth for 30 minutes because there was another man in there. He was standing in there, holding the phone to his ear, standing like a stone statue, and never said a word. Finally, the man that was waiting couldn't stand it anymore, tapped the guy on the shoulder and said, "Friend, I'm in a hurry, you've had that phone to your ear for half an hour and you haven't said a word!" He covered the phone and said, "Please excuse me, I'm talking with my wife." Women just talk more than men. A husband said, "My wife and I had words last night . . . unfortunately I didn't get a chance to use mine."

Communicate Clearly: Mrs. Jones noticed that the husband next door was very attentive to his wife, always bringing her flowers and candies and gifts. Mrs. Jones saw him bringing in a big bouquet of flowers and was finally fed up, so she said to her husband, "Why don't you do that?" He said, "I hardly know that woman." Sometimes you have to make it really clear.

SUGGESTED ORDER OF WORSHIP

Prelude—Instrumental
   Days of Elijah

Prelude—Instrumental Group
   Come, Now Is the Time to Worship

Call to Worship
   CH 42/43 *All Hail the Power of Jesus' Name*

Welcome—Pastoral Staff

Song of Welcome—Congregation (meet and greet)
   CH 601 *I'll Say, Yes, Lord Yes*

Video Testimony (2-minute testimony on video about the
   faithfulness of God)

Song of Testimony—Solo with Praise Team
   CH *I Need Thee Every Hour*

Worship Prayer—Pastoral Staff

Worship and Praise
  God's Faithfulness from Tapestry of Praise Book:
  What a Mighty God
  The Steadfast Love of the Lord
  In Moments Like These
  Great Is Thy Faithfulness

Offertory Prayer—Pastoral Staff

Offertory Praise

Message—Pastor

Hymn of Response/Invitation—Congregation
  CH *Only Believe*

Hymn of Benediction—Congregation
  CH 107 *Lord, I Lift Your Name on High*

Postlude—Instrumental
  We Bring a Sacrifice of Praise

Additional Sermons and Lesson Ideas

SERIES: FAITH IS THE VICTORY

Focus on Faith
Date preached:

By Dr. Denis Lyle

Scripture: 1 Thessalonians 3:1–13

Introduction: It was Charles Spurgeon who said, "A little faith will bring your soul to heaven, but a great faith will bring heaven to your soul." Paul teaches us to focus on faith:

1. **Our faith needs to grow (vv. 1, 2).**
2. **Our faith needs to know (vv. 3–5).**
3. **Our faith needs to show (vv. 6–13).**

Conclusion: Is your faith growing in the Lord? Do you know how to react to trials and temptations? Is your faith showing?

SERIES: HOW TO PRAY FOR THE PRESIDENT

Praying for the President, Part 2
Date preached:

By Dr. Kent Spann

Scripture: 1 Timothy 2:1–4

Introduction: Thomas Jefferson, our third president, knew his need for prayer. He once said,

> I shall need, too, the favor of that Being in whose hands we are, who led our fathers, as Israel of old, from their native land and planted them in a country flowing with all the necessaries and comforts of life; who has covered our infancy with His providence and our riper years with His wisdom and power, and to whose goodness I ask you to join in supplications with me that He will so enlighten the minds of your servants, guide their councils, and prosper their measures that whatsoever they do shall result in your good, and shall secure to you the peace, friendship, and approbation of all nations.

How can we pray for our president?

1. Pray for his protection (Ps. 20:9; 91:1–16). The world we live in is dangerous as it faces threats from multiple enemies. As the leader of our nation, the president becomes a major target.
2. Pray for his family.
   A. Pray for the wife of the president.
      i. She would live a virtuous life (Prov. 12:4; 31:10–31).
      ii. She would show respect toward her husband (Eph. 5:33).

    B. Pray for the children of the president.
       i They would honor their parents (Eph. 6:1–3).
       ii. They would live wisely (Prov. 15:20).
    C. Pray for his marriage.
       i. He would remain faithful to his wife (2 Sam. 11; Prov. 5:15–
         20). He faces many temptations because of his position and
         power. He must remain true to his wife.
       ii. He would love his wife (Eph. 5:25, 28).
  3. Pray that he would govern with wisdom (1 Kin. 3:9–12; Prov. 3:13;
    4:5).
  4. Ask that God would keep him humble (Is. 66:1, 2; James 4:6–10).

Conclusion: Next week we will look at the last six ways to pray for the president.

JULY 4, 2010

SUGGESTED SERMON

Christian Citizenship Sunday: Maximum Patriotic Impact

Date preached:

By Dr. Kenyn M. Cureton

Scripture: Matthew 22:15–21, "Give to Caesar what is Caesar's . . ."

Introduction: On July 4, 1776, our Founding Fathers signed a document declaring our independence from British tyranny. Yet when we declared our *independence* from Great Britain, we just as strongly declared our *dependence* upon Almighty God. In fact, four times they appealed to God and expressed their reliance upon Him. *Reliance* means dependence. Consequently, our Founding Fathers did not believe in the separation of God from government, rather that it all depends upon Him!

Jesus set forth the proper relationship of His followers to government in Matthew 22:21. All citizens, including His followers, are obligated to support their government. America's government "of the people, by the people, and for the people" requires our active participation. Here are five ways to have maximum patriotic impact as we celebrate America's birthday:

Seek God for your government. Pray for our leaders that they would seek God's wisdom as they lead (1 Tim. 2:1–4).

Support your government.

A. *Pay taxes to your government.* Jesus commands that we are to "give to Caesar what is Caesar's" (Matt. 22:21), and He led by example (Matt. 17:24–27; cf. Rom. 13:6).

B. *Take pride in your nation.* The psalmist was patriotic (Ps. 137:5, 6). Paul admonishes us to respect and honor our government (Rom. 13:7).

Submit to your government. Government exists to keep order, and we must submit to the rule of law (See 1 Pet. 2:13, 14; cf. Rom. 13:1–5). Generally, we should respect governmental authority. While we may not have much respect for the *man* of the office, we must respect the *office* of the man.

Stand up to your government. The prophets and the apostles often had to resist unjust and unrighteous governmental authority (e.g., 1 Kin. 18, Dan. 6, Acts 4, 5, etc.). Sometimes, as Peter said, "We must obey God rather than men" (Acts 5:29). We must use our freedom to defend our freedom, or we may lose our freedom.

Select your government. There are many ways we can participate in our government, but one of the most basic ways is by voting. Voting is a simple act with a significant impact. When we vote, we help determine who will lead our nation, make our laws, and protect our freedoms (Ex. 18:21). Here are three practical steps:

Step 1: **Register to vote:** According to the U.S. Census Bureau, as many as 35% of the voting-age population are not registered and less than half of the voting-age population actually votes in a given election![1] Visit www.iVoteValues.org, a voter registration, education, and mobilization website.

Step 2: **Register a friend:** Encourage your friends to register.

Step 3: **Vote your values:** Remember, "Bad politicians are elected by good people who don't vote" (Prov. 29:2). Get informed on the issues, party platforms, candidate positions on the issues, their websites, their friends and foes. Then prayerfully consider voting for the ones who are the best match with your values. Don't just vote to be voting—vote **your** values! What should we value as Christ-followers when voting? Here are my non-negotiables:

1. **Life:** Life is precious. Miraculous. Delicate. Life is created by a loving God (Ps. 139:13–16), and is therefore a fundamental, God-given right according to the Declaration of Independence.[2] Find out where the candidates stand on protecting human life from abortion, embryo experimentation, and euthanasia, from "womb to tomb." We value life!

---

[1] See the statistics provided by the U.S. Census Bureau at http://www.census.gov/population/www/socdemo/voting.html.

[2] As found in *One Nation Under God: Our Founding Documents* (Nashville: For Faith & Family Publishing), 10: "all men are endowed by their Creator with certain unalienable rights, that among them are life, liberty and the pursuit of happiness."

2. **Family:** Family is essential. Basic. Fundamental. Family is the first institution created by God (Gen. 1:27; 2:24). Study after study shows that every child needs the influence of a father and a mother. Heterosexuality is the divine pattern; homosexuality is a deceptive perversion. Marriage is under attack by radical homosexuals and their allies who are seeking to redefine it. As goes the family, so goes the nation. Christians ought to fight for the biblical definition of marriage. We value family.

3. **Freedom:** Freedom is costly. Precious. Priceless. "It is for freedom that Christ has set us free" (Gal. 5:1). Unfortunately, our religious freedom is under fire. The U.S. Supreme Court has trashed four centuries of Judeo-Christian heritage, ignored the founders' original intent, and turned the First Amendment on its head. Find out which candidates are aligned with radical judges, the ACLU and Americans for Separation of Church and State, who seek to remove religious expression from the public arena. Find out the candidates' positions on our First Amendment right to religious freedom. We value freedom!

Conclusion: After our founding fathers approved the Declaration of Independence, there was a call to have it read publicly, to fire cannons and to ring the bells in celebration! The first bell they rang was in the hall where they approved the Declaration to summon the people to hear the first public reading of America's founding document. They rang the Liberty Bell. Where did it get its name? From the Scripture imprinted years earlier, Leviticus 25:10, which says, "Proclaim liberty throughout the land unto all the inhabitants thereof!" Proclaim liberty throughout the land. Let freedom ring![3]

---

[3]A full text version of this message may be found online: http://www.ivotevalues.org/downloads/ivv/2007CitizenshipSunday.pdf.

STATS, STORIES, AND MORE

More from Dr. Kenyn M. Cureton

Introduction: Based on their dependence upon God, the Founding Fathers were willing to pledge their lives, their fortunes, and their sacred honor. They put it all on the line. Of those fifty-six men who signed the Declaration of Independence, nine died of wounds or hardships during the war. Five were captured and imprisoned, and in each case subjected to torture. Several lost wives, children, or entire families. One lost his thirteen children. Two wives were brutalized by the British. All were at one time or another victims of manhunts and driven from their homes. Twelve signers had their homes completely burned. Seventeen lost everything they owned. Indeed these men not only pledged but gave their lives, and their fortunes, and not one went back on his sacred honor.[4] The nation they sacrificed so much to help found is still intact for us to enjoy today on this Independence Day Sunday. May God bless America even as America seeks to bless God!

Stand Up to Your Government: You can find examples throughout the Bible of believers who stood up to government leaders and spoke out about the culture.

- Moses petitioned Pharaoh for the liberty of God's people.
- Nathan confronted King David for his sinful actions as a leader.
- Elijah faced off against King Ahab, who promoted idolatry and immorality.
- Isaiah condemned moral decay in the culture.
- Amos inveighed against injustice in society.
- Daniel pronounced judgment on King Nebuchadnezzar for promoting idolatry.
- John the Baptist pointed out the adultery of King Herod.

In fact, the Hebrew midwives were blessed because of their civil disobedience to Pharaoh's edict to kill the male babies.

We need to stand up to a government funding abortion providers with our tax dollars and speak with righteous indignation: "Killing babies in a mother's womb is wrong!" We need to speak out with moral outrage to legislators promoting the gay agenda that: "Redefining marriage to include homosexuals is wrong!" We need to remind those black robed tyrants masquerading as judges about America's Judeo-Christian foundations, and with holy fury voice that: "Taking away our religious heritage is wrong!" Sometimes we must stand up to our government and say: Enough is enough!

---

[4]Summarized from Paul Harvey, *Our Lives, Our Fortunes, Our Sacred Honor* (Waco, TX: Word Books, 1976). See also, D. James Kennedy and Jerry Newcombe, *What If America Were a Christian Nation Again?* (Nashville: Thomas Nelson, 2003), 37–40.

STATS, STORIES, AND MORE—Continued

Register to Vote and Vote Your Values: I realize this is a no-brainer, but you can't vote unless you're registered. And there are a lot of eligible Americans who are not even registered to vote. According to the U.S. Census Bureau, as many as 35% of the voting-age population are not registered. That translates to as many as 65 million Americans! What's worse is that less than half of the voting-age population actually votes in a given election![5] Here are the numbers:

- In 2000, 51.3% of eligible Americans voted in the presidential election.
- In 2002, 37% of eligible Americans voted in the mid-term elections!
- In 2004, 55.1% voted in the presidential election.
- In 2006, 37.1% voted in the mid-term elections.[6]
- In 2008, 56.8% voted in the presidential election.[7]

Of self-described evangelical Christians, numbering around 60 million, the percentages are worse. In 2000, only 25% voted.[8] While nearly 50% voted in 2004,[9] the number fell back to about 33% in 2006.[10] Then the number climbed to around 50% in 2008.[11] But that is not enough. Here's

---

[5]See the statistics provided by the U.S. Census Bureau at http://www.census.gov/population/www/socdemo/voting.html.

[6]See http://www.infoplease.com/ipa/A0781453.html for the years 2000, 2002, 2004, 2006.

[7]See http://elections.gmu.edu/Turnout_2008G.html for 2008.

[8]Focus on the Family, *Citizen* magazine, September 2003, "Believers at the ballot box: Election 2000 by the numbers."

[9]A total of 125,736,000 votes were cast; twenty-three percent of voters were self-identified as "Evangelicals," thus translating into 28.9 million votes. If you say that there are 60 million evangelicals, then you get a number close to 50%. See sources at New York Times, "Religious Voting Data Show Some Shift, Observers Say," (at: http://select.nytimes.com/gst/abstract.html?res=F50F17F7355B0C7A8CDDA80994DE404482&n=Top%2fReference%2fTimes%20Topics%2fSubjects%2fE%2fEvangelical%20Movement); and U.S. Census Bureau, "Voting and Registration in the Election of November 2004" (at: http://www.census.gov/prod/2006pubs/p20-556.pdf).

[10]In the 2006 elections, a total of 85,251,089 votes were cast; twenty-four percent of voters were "Evangelicals," thus translating into 20.5 million votes. Again, if you assume 60 million evangelicals, you get basically a 1/3 voter turn out. See sources at George Mason University, "United States Elections Project: 2006 Voting-Age and Voting-Eligible Population Estimates" (at: http://elections.gmu.edu/Voter_Turnout_2006.htm); *New York Times*, "Religious Voting Data Show Some Shift, Observers Say" (at: http://select.nytimes.com/gst/abstract.html?res=F50F17F7355B0C7A8CDDA80994DE404482&n=Top%2fReference%2fTimes%20Topics%2fSubjects%2fE%2fEvangelical%20Movement).

[11]http://pewresearch.org/pubs/1022/exit-poll-analysis-religion where the evangelicals represent 23% of the electorate (132,618,580), which yields 30.5 million out of 60 or so million self-described evangelicals.

STATS, STORIES, AND MORE—*Continued*

an old proverb that is still true today: "Bad politicians are elected by good people who don't vote." Certainly, the Bible says: "When the godly are in authority, the people rejoice. But when the wicked are in power, they groan" (Prov. 29:2). And if you don't vote, you have no right to groan! Some might say: "What's the difference, my one vote doesn't really count." Yes, it does! All I need to say is "Florida recount" and you get my point.

Freedom: That is the intention of the First Amendment: "Congress shall make no law respecting an establishment of religion or prohibiting the free exercise thereof."[12] Unfortunately, the U.S. Supreme Court has trashed four centuries of America's Judeo-Christian heritage, ignored the original intent of the Founding Fathers and turned a statement in one of Jefferson's private letters on its head and therefore twisted the First Amendment by declaring a two-way "Wall of Separation" between church and state. The Result? Black robed tyrants feel compelled to remove nearly all religious influences from public institutions. The Supreme Court outlawed public prayer in the schools in 1962,[13] out went public Bible reading in 1963,[14] and in 1980, down came the Ten Commandments from school house walls![15] This agenda of radical secularization has not only been zealously prosecuted by the activist courts, but by extension, the various public entities, school boards, educators, and teachers. For example, some have declared it to be unconstitutional:

- For kindergarten students to recite, "God is great, God is good, let us thank Him for our food."[16]

- For a student to ask and for the teacher to answer whose birthday is being celebrated at Christmas.[17]

- For two middle school students to bring their Bibles to class, which were confiscated, called "garbage," and thrown into the trash can by their teacher.[18]

- For some students to pray publicly anywhere in school; an Alabama judge, Ira Dement, even assigned a taxpayer-supported "prayer monitor" in schools to ensure that students did not engage in public prayer.[19]

---

[12] *Founding Documents,* 46.

[13] *Engel v. Vitale* 370 U.S. 421 (1962).

[14] *Abingdon School District v. Schempp* 374 U.S. 203, 220–221 (1963).

[15] *Stone v. Graham* 449 U.S. 39 (1980).

[16] Frank J. Murray, "Federal Court Hears Lawsuit Over Kindergarten Christian; New York School may relent, may let tot say grace at meals," *The Washington Times,* June 12, 2002. While the child was eventually allowed to pray, the fact that her prayer was challenged by school officials demonstrates the point.

[17] *Florey v. Sioux Falls School District,* 494 F. Supp. 911 (U.S.D.C., S.D. 1979).

[18] News Release, "School Officials Trash 'Truth for Youth' Bibles and Ten Commandment Covers," Liberty Counsel, May 19, 2000.

[19] *Chandler v. Siegelman,* 230 F. 3d 1313 (11th Cir. 2000).

STATS, STORIES, AND MORE—*Continued*

- For students in nine western states to recite the Pledge of Allegiance including the words: "One Nation, Under God."[20]
- For an Honor Guardsman to say: "God bless you and this family, and may God bless this country" at the graveside of a veteran.[21]
- For a county government building exterior to display our national motto: "In God We Trust."[22]
- For a New Jersey high school coach to kneel and bow his head because the Thrid Circuit Court doesn't want his posture to be misconstrued as prayer.[23]

Hear me: If we don't use our freedom to defend our freedom, we will lose our freedom. George Washington in his Farewell Address said, "Of all the dispositions and habits which lead to political prosperity, religion and morality are indispensable supports. In vain would that man claim the tribute of patriotism, who should labor to subvert these great pillars of human happiness, these firmest props of the duties of men and citizens."[24]

---

[20] *Newdow v. United States Congress*, 292 F. 3d 597, 608 (9th Cir. 2002).

[21] David O'Reilly, "Honor Guardsman Is Fired for Blessings," *Philadelphia Inquirer*, January 22, 2003.

[22] "N.C. County Will Fight "In God We Trust" Lawsuit," The First Amendment Center, August 15, 2003; http://fac.org/news.aspx?id=11828.

[23] http://www.ca3.uscourts.gov/opinarch/063890p.pdf.

[24] Farewell Address on September 17, 1796, as found in James D. Richardson, ed., *A Compilation of the Messages and Papers of the Presidents 1789–1897*, 10 vols. (Washington, D.C.: U.S. Government Printing Office, 1897, 1899; Washington, D.C.: Bureau of National Literature and Art, 1789–1902, 11 vols., 1907, 1910), 1:213–224.

Maximum Patriotic Impact

Prelude—Instrumental Group
Americana Overture[1]

Welcome and Call to Worship—Pastoral Staff

Welcome Song—Congregation
CH 209 *This Is the Day*

Praise for Divine Guidance—Congregation
CH *God of Our Fathers* (2x)

Prayer for America—Pastor

Presentation of the Colors—Armed Forces Color Guard (Navy)

Pledge of Allegiance—Led by Worship Pastor

The National Anthem—Soloist or Congregation
The Star-Spangled Banner

Tribute to Our Armed Services
(From the Procession of the Patriots[1])
Army, Navy, Coast Guard, Air Force, Marines

Salute to Our Fallen Heroes[2]

Offertory Prayer—Guest Member of the Armed Services

Offertory Praise—Solo with Track
I Love the USA

Message—Pastor
Maximum Patriotic Impact

Hymn of Invitation—Congregation
CH *I Surrender All*

Benediction Hymn/Postlude—Congregation
God Bless America

Postlude—Instrumental Group
This Land Is Your Land, This Land Is My Land

---

[1]"Americana Overture" and "Procession of the Patriots" are written, arranged, and orchestrated by Camp Kirkland and published by Praise Gathering Music.
[2]"Salute to Our Fallen Heroes" by Randy Vadar is arranged and orchestrated Jay Rouse for Praise Gathering Music. A video track for use with solo and choir available from the publisher.

Additional Sermons and Lesson Ideas

SERIES: FAITH IS THE VICTORY

Of Whom Shall I Be Afraid

Date preached:

By Ed Dobson

Scripture: Psalm 27

Introduction: We all deal with fear, and in the time in which we are now living, fear is multiplied over and over. What's the cure for fear? The only medicine that deals with fear is faith. I would like to suggest three steps for dealing with fear and cultivating your faith:

1. Faith is a choice (vv. 1–3, especially the end of v. 3).
2. Faith is cultivated through an intimate relationship with God (vv. 4–6).
3. Faith is strengthened through prayer (vv. 7–12).

Conclusion: I began the sermon with the thesis that faith is the key to fear. I want to finish the sermon with another truth. God, who is good, is on your side (v. 13). So if you are afraid, choose to have faith. Continue in your relationship with God, continually praying, and "Wait on the LORD . . . and He shall strengthen your heart" (v. 14).

SERIES: HOW TO PRAY FOR THE PRESIDENT

Praying for the President
Part 3

Date preached:

By Dr. Kent Spann

Scripture: 1 Timothy 2:1–4

Introduction: Abraham Lincoln describing his need for divine guidance as president said,

> *"I have been driven many times to my knees by the overwhelming conviction that I had nowhere else to go. My own wisdom, and that of all about me, seemed insufficient for the day."*

We are learning how to pray for our President. In the last message we looked at the first four ways to pray for the President.

5. Pray for those advising the President.
    A. God would thwart the counsel of the unwise (2 Sam. 15:31; 16:15—17:23 key verse is 23).
    B. God would remove those who are unwise from his circle (Prov. 25:5).

    C. The President would surround himself with wise counselors (Prov. 11:14; 24:6).

    D. God would raise up a "Daniel" in his circle of influence (Dan. 2:48, 49).

6. Pray for his spiritual life.

    A. If he is not a Christian, pray for his salvation (1 Tim. 2:3, 4; 2 Pet. 3:9).

    B. If he professes to be a believer:

    He would be true to his faith. That it would not be a mere intellectual belief (James 2:19), a convenient faith to promote his career (1 Sam. 13:1–15) or a "Christless" faith (John 10:9; Acts 4:12).

    C. He would submit to Christ's Lordship.

    By listening to Christ (John 10:14–16).

    By obeying Him (Matt. 7:21–23).

    D. He would read and apply God's Word (Josh. 1:8–9; 2 Tim. 3:16, 17).

    E. He would fear God (Ps. 33:18; Prov. 9:10).

    F. He would rely upon God's strength (Ps. 27:1–3; 33:16, 17).

7. Pray that he will do what will protect the peace and well-being of our nation (1 Tim. 2:1–4; Rom. 13:3).

    A. That he will understand the nature and mindset of those who would seek to bring our nation down.

    B. That he would take the necessary steps to protect our nation from attack and danger while not diminishing the freedoms of its citizens.

8. Pray that he will stand for morality (Ps. 82:2–4; Prov. 31:8, 9; Micah 6:8).

9. Pray that he will govern with righteousness and justice (Prov. 29:4, 14).

10. Pray that he will be surrounded by love and faithfulness (Prov. 3:3, 4; 20:28).

Conclusion: It is more important now than ever that we pray for our president. Let the prayer begin.

JULY 11, 2010

SUGGESTED SERMON

How to Be a Star

Date preached:

By Dr. Timothy Beougher

Scripture: Philippians 2:14–18, especially verses 14, 15, "Do all things without complaining and disputing, that you may become blameless and harmless, children of God without fault in the midst of a crooked and perverse generation, among whom you shine as lights in the world."

Introduction: Ed McMahon was best known as Johnny Carson's sidekick, but he has more recently hosted *Star Search,* a program where aspiring actors and musicians perform before a live audience, hoping for stardom. In Philippians 2, Paul tells us how we can become stars. It has nothing to do with musical ability or acting skills, but everything to do with how we live. According to verse 15, God wants us to be lights in the world, or, as in some translations, "stars in the universe." The word "lights" refers to heavenly luminaries. How, then, do we shine as stars?

1. **Conquer Complaining (v. 14a).** Most of us tend to be negative, and some are so negative they even have negative blood! One commentator said, "I've been around Christians long enough to know that telling us not to complain is a like telling us not to breathe. It is so commonplace to grumble." Yet we're commanded to do all things without grumbling, to do everything without complaining. How can we do that?

   A. **Recognize complaining as a sin.** Grumbling/murmuring was one of the fundamental sins that kept the Israelites out of the Promised Land. It is a variety of rebellion against God (1 Cor. 10:10, 11), a questioning of His wisdom in running the universe, a doubting of His care.

   B. **Acknowledge that complaining is a problem for you.** In the words of the hymn, "It's not my brother, not my sister, but it's me, O Lord, standing in the need of prayer."

   C. **Recognize that God uses difficulties to change us.** We don't always change when we see the light, but we usually do when we feel the heat. We tend to grumble when things get difficult, but we should recognize that God uses difficulties in life to mature us (James 1:2–4).

D. Work on your heart attitude (Matt. 12:34).

2. **Avoid Arguing (v. 14b).** The word *disputing* implies a questioning mind. It suggests an arrogant attitude by those who assume they're always right. Arguing with others in the body of Christ is disruptive. That's why Paul spent the first part of chapter 2 on humility. "To dwell above, with saints we love, that will be grace and glory;/But to live below with saints we know, now that's a different story!" Why avoid arguing? Verse 15 says, "That you may become blameless and harmless, children of God without fault in the midst of a crooked and perverse generation." Over the centuries, Christians have related to the world in four ways:

A. **Total separation:** monastery; no contact.

B. **Total immersion:** lots of contact, but no impact.

C. **Split adaptation:** Sunday-only Christian; "hypocrite."

D. **Transformation:** with God's help (v. 13), it is possible to conquer complaining and avoid arguing, that we prove blameless and innocent, above reproach, in a fallen world.

3. **Recover Rejoicing (vv. 17, 18).** The "drink offering" was a libation poured out completely as part of the ritual of sacrifice. It pictures complete consecration. Observe Paul's response to suffering. He is writing from a prison cell, yet refuses to let his circumstances dictate his attitude. Joy and rejoicing ring through his book.

Conclusion: How do we have the perspective and power to do all this? Verse 16 tells us to focus on the Word! Memorize verses on problem areas. If you struggle with complaining, learn Philippians 2:14. When you begin to complain, the Holy Spirit will use that verse to help you.

Our culture is so negative that when it sees someone positive, that person shines like the North Star on a dark night. A complaining Christian is a poor witness. A disputing church is a poor witness. Rejoicing Christians and joyful churches are powerful witnesses. Jesus said they are like a city on a hill which cannot be hidden—it can be seen from great distances. A church should stand out in a community as a beacon. There are two kinds of Christians: those who "whine" and those who "shine." Are you seeking to let your light shine to others around you? Then conquer complaining. Avoid arguing. Regain rejoicing.

STATS, STORIES, AND MORE

Someone Once Said . . .

🐀 And the muttering grew to a grumbling; and the grumbling grew to a mighty rumbling; and out of the houses the rats came tumbling.
—Robert Browning in *The Pied Piper of Hamelin*

🐀 Any fool can criticize, condemn and complain—and most do.
—Dale Carnegie

Attitude

Two buckets, one an optimist and the other a pessimist, talked by the well. "There has never been a life as disappointing as mine," said the latter. "I never come away from the well full but what I return empty again." The optimistic bucket replied, "Mine is a happy life! I never come to the well empty but what I go away again full."

Illustrations from Timothy Beougher

🐀 In his book *The Total Man,* Dan Benson tells of experts who studied tape-recorded conversations from different homes over a period of time. They found ten negative comments for every one positive one. If someone recorded our conversations for a week, what would we find?

🐀 Did you hear about the husband who criticized his wife every morning? If she fixed scrambled eggs, he wanted poached; if she poached them, he wanted scrambled. One morning she scrambled one egg and poached the other. He glared at the plate and said, "Can't you do anything right? You scrambled the wrong one!"

🐀 That reminds me of the woman who was asked, "Do you ever wake up grumpy?" She replied, "No, I usually let him wake up on his own."

You've Done Nothing But Complain

A monk joined a monastery and took a vow of silence. After five years his superior called him and gave him permission to speak two words. The monk said, "Food bad." After another five years the monk again had opportunity to voice two words. This time, he said, "Bed hard." Another five years went by. When asked if he had anything to say, he responded, "I quit." "Well, you might as well," said his superior. "You've done nothing since you've been here but complain."

SUGGESTED ORDER OF WORSHIP

Theme: Chock Full of Christ

Prelude—Instrumental Group
CH 42 *All Hail the Power of Jesus' Name*/ CH 209 *This Is the Day*

Announcements and Prayer—Pastoral Staff

Welcome—Pastoral Staff

Song of Welcome (meet and greet)—Congregation
CH 195 *Bless the Name of Jesus* (3x in C)
MSPW 3 *Jesus, Your Name* (2x in C, 1x in D)

Celebrating the Wonders of the Word—Reading Team*

Worship and Praise—Congregation
CH 15 *No Other Name* (2x in D)
CH 5 *I Sing Praises* (1x in G, 1x in Ab)
CH 80 *I Stand in Awe* (verse 1x, chorus 2x in Ab)

Prayer of Worship—Worship Pastor
CH 681 *In His Time* (2x in Eb)

Offertory Prayer—Pastoral Staff

Offertory Praise—Solo or Praise Team
Hallelujah to the Lamb

Message—Pastor
Chock Full of Christ

Hymn of Response/Invitation—Congregation
CH 79 *My Jesus, I Love Thee*

Hymn of Benediction—Congregation
CH 195 *Bless the Name of Jesus* (2x in C)

Postlude—Instrumental Group
CH 195 *Bless the Name of Jesus* (2x in C)

HE IS EXALTED (Can be read by one person or as Reader's Group)

HE IS EXALTED* (Optional Reader's Group)
By Vernon M. Whaley, Ph.D.

Reader 1: God, who at various times
Reader 2: and in various ways
Reader 1: spoke in time past to the fathers by the prophets
Reader 3: has in these last days spoken to us by *His* Son,
Reader 4: [Jesus] whom He has appointed heir of all things,
Reader 1: through whom also He made the worlds;

Reader 1: *[For]* He is the image of the invisible God, the firstborn over all creation.
Reader 2: By Him all things were created that are in heaven and that are on earth,
Reader 3: Visible and invisible,
Reader 4: Whether thrones or dominions or principalities or powers.
Reader 1: All things were created through Him and for Him.
Reader 4: He is before all things, and in Him all things consist.
Reader 3: And He is the head of the body,
Reader 2: the church, who is the beginning,
Reader 3: the firstborn from the dead,
Reader 1: that in all things He may have the preeminence.
Reader 2: [For He IS] the brightness of *His* glory and the express image of His person,
Reader 3: and upholding all things by the word of His power,
Reader 4: when He had by Himself purged our sins,
Reader 1: sat down at the right hand of the Majesty on high,

Reader 2: Therefore.
Reader 3: Therefore!
Reader 4: Therefore!!
All: Therefore!!!

Reader 1: God also has highly exalted Him
All: God has exalted Him

Reader 1: and given Him the name which is above every name,
Reader 2: that at the name of Jesus every knee should bow,
Reader 3: of those in heaven, and of those on earth,

Reader 4: and of those under the earth,
Reader 1: and *that* every tongue should confess that
All: Jesus Christ *is* Lord,
Reader 1: to the glory of God the Father.
Reader 2: Amen!
Reader 4: Amen!!
Reader 3: Amen!!!
All: Amen!!!!

From Hebrews 1:1, 2; Colossians 1:15–18; Hebrews 1:3; Philippians 2:9–11 (NKJV)

1 God, who at various times and in various ways spoke in time past to the fathers by the prophets, 2 has in these last days spoken to us by *His* Son, [Jesus] whom He has appointed heir of all things, through whom also He made the worlds;

15 *[For]* He is the image of the invisible God, the firstborn over all creation. 16 For by Him all things were created that are in heaven and that are on earth, visible and invisible, whether thrones or dominions or principalities or powers. All things were created through Him and for Him. 17 And He is before all things, and in Him all things consist. 18 And He is the head of the body, the church, who is the beginning, the firstborn from the dead, that in all things He may have the preeminence.

3 [For He IS] the brightness of *His* glory and the express image of His person, and upholding all things by the word of His power, when He had by Himself purged our sins, sat down at the right hand of the Majesty on high,

9 Therefore God also has highly exalted Him and given Him the name which is above every name, 10 that at the name of Jesus every knee should bow, of those in heaven, and of those on earth, and of those under the earth, 11 and *that* every tongue should confess that Jesus Christ *is* Lord, to the glory of God the Father.

Additional Sermons and Lesson Ideas

SERIES: FAITH IS THE VICTORY

Faith in the Face of a Giant

Date preached:

By David George

Scripture: 1 Samuel 17:1–54, especially v. 45

Introduction: Don't you love the fresh-faced enthusiasm and confidence of a kid who has just joined the little league baseball team? He hasn't even played his first game but he wants to sleep in his uniform. Though inexperienced, he believes there's no ball that can get by him. David was like that. He was the youngest of his brothers, the runt, the shepherd with a few sheep, yet he was called a man after God's own heart. Against all odds, David had faith, even to face a giant. David was sent to give food to his brothers as they fought against the Philistines. As he approached the battle scene, he saw the Israelites standing opposite to the Philistines with a dried up riverbank between. The Philistine champion, Goliath, about 9 feet 9 inches tall, taunted and challenged the Israelites to send a champion to fight. How do we react to giants in our lives? We need:

1. **Simple Faith (v. 26).** There is never a thought in David's mind that this Philistine wouldn't be defeated. He only asked about what good would come to the one who killed Goliath. Where did David get this mindset? He was probably raised hearing stories of God's victory: the parting of the Red Sea, or Israel's victory at the walls of Jericho. It never occurred to David that this pagan could possibly defeat the soldiers of God. We should teach our children that God cannot be defeated. We must believe it as well.

2. **Living Faith (v. 32).** Faith matters not only at church, but when your bills are due and you have no money, when a loved one dies, or when you're persecuted at work; faith through life's circumstances is living faith. David's faith was born from defending his sheep against a lion and a bear, so David knew God would also fight Goliath through him (vv. 34–37). Without everyday use of our talents and abilities for God, we cannot face big projects or obstacles. Many of us disobey, refusing to be baptized or to tithe. We will never grow if we consistently refuse to live out our faith.

3. **Crisis Faith (vv. 45–47).** God gives us the ability to stand when no one else will during a moment of crisis. David was granted this type of faith as he faced Goliath, saying, "You come to me with a sword, with a spear, and with a javelin. But I come to you in the name of the LORD of hosts" (v. 45). "LORD of hosts" can be translated, "The Lord of our extremity." When we've reached the end of our human abilities, we come to the Lord of hosts, asking for His strength. Overcoming, overwhelming faith bears forth in the moment of crisis

from the foundation of simple, living faith. What giant are you facing? A financial giant? A hurting relationship? An addiction? Whatever it is, take these practical steps from David's example.

A. **Your encouragement cannot come from the defeated.** As David faced the Philistines, he saw the Israelites afraid (v. 24), but they were no help. If you have a drug or alcohol problem, get away from other addicts. If you have relationship problems, don't hang around divorced people who tell you how great it is. Seek encouragement from victorious Christians.

B. **Remember your past victories.** The enemy is quick to oppose us, and we tend to be quick to tremble in fear. David called on his past victories for confidence (vv. 34–37). We need to remember times when God has answered our prayers, when He has pulled us from hard situations, when He has provided.

C. **You cannot trust someone else's army.** Someone else's strategy may not work for you. Samuel tried to give David his armor. It wouldn't work. He wouldn't use spear or javelin, but preferred a simple shepherd's sling. God wants to take *your* history, *your* abilities, and *your* talents and add *His* power to accomplish *His* purposes.

D. **The threats of the enemy are just threats.** God granted David success in the face of the enemy's mockery! Greater is He that is in you than he that is in the world (1 John 4:4).

Conclusion: We must become people after God's heart through simple, living faith, faith which will not fail in crisis. Practically, we must gain encouragement from the victorious, remembering our victories, allowing God to use our genuine selves, despite circumstances or obstacles.

Chock Full of Christ
By W. H. Griffith Thomas

Date preached:

Scripture: Hebrews 1

Introduction: We know that the entire Bible serves as a sort of biography of Christ, but few passages are so "chock full of Christ" as Hebrews 1. In the preface, the writer presents Christ as:

1. **Christ the Heir (v. 2).**
2. **Christ the Creator (v. 2; see John 1:3; Col. 1:16).**
3. **Christ the Revealer (v. 3; see Col. 1:15, 16).**
4. **Christ the Sustainer (v. 3; compare Col. 1:17).**
5. **Christ the Redeemer (v. 3).**
6. **Christ the Ruler (v. 3).**
7. **Christ Supreme (v. 4).**

Conclusion: The Book of Hebrews was written to encourage Jewish believers who were in danger of fainting under pressure. Nothing strengthens us like having our thoughts fixed on Christ. If you're under pressure today, fix your eyes on Jesus (Heb. 12:2).

JULY 18, 2010

SUGGESTED SERMON

Anchors during Adversity

Date preached:

By Dr. Timothy Beougher

Scripture: Romans 5:1–11, especially verse 1, "Therefore, having been justified by faith, we have peace with God through our Lord Jesus Christ" (NKJV).

Introduction: We are all familiar with storms such as hurricanes, tornadoes, thunderstorms, and floods. These are symbolic of other types of storms we face in life: physical storms, emotional storms, spiritual storms, financial storms, and family storms. We all face storms in life. Boats have anchors to keep them steady during storms. God has given us spiritual anchors, truths that can help us to remain steady during the storms of life we face.

1. **Realizing our present position (vv. 1, 2a).** This verse begins with *therefore*, which points us back to the preceding four chapters. In Romans 1–4, we have seen the reality of human sin and depravity, and the atoning work of Christ on the Cross for sinners. In Romans 5:1, Paul then reflects on our present position. What is our present position? Those justified through faith have:

    A. **Acceptance by God.** Paul tells us we have peace with God; what a concept! Chapters 1–4 make clear that God is not at peace with sinners, but is at war with them. The word Paul uses repeatedly is *wrath* (see Rom. 1:18). He then tells how Jesus has satisfied God's wrath against sin, taking our place and our punishment on the Cross.

    B. **Access to God (v. 2a).** We have the privilege of entering God's presence at any time (cf. Heb. 10:19, 22). We can approach Him by grace. Before our justification, we stood before God as condemned criminals; now we can stand before Him as sons and daughters!

2. **Reflecting on our future hope (v. 2b).** The word *rejoice* does not indicate half-hearted smiles but a sense of jubilation. The word *hope* is not like our English word which conveys something uncertain;

biblically, *hope* means that something that has not happened yet but will certainly come to pass and is reason for praise and thanksgiving. An equivalent English word is *confidence*. We have hope and confidence in the glory of God (cf. Rom. 8:18).

3. **Recognizing God's purposes (vv. 3, 4).** How many of you like to suffer? How many of you wish you could suffer more? None of us likes to suffer. An anchor during adversity is the recognition of God's purpose. These verses refer to the knowledge we have during adversity. What knowledge? It is the knowledge that all things work together for our good (Rom. 8:28). But how can this be? God doesn't always tell us but in Romans 5:3–5, God does give us at least a glimpse into one part of the answer. This passage doesn't attempt to explain everything we might want to know about suffering, but it does highlight the fact that sufferings work together to promote spiritual growth. A little poem beautifully illustrates this principle:

> I walked a mile with pleasure, she chatted all the way
> But left me none the wiser, with all she had to say.
> I walked a mile with sorrow, and never a word said she,
> But, oh, the things I learned from her, when sorrow walked with me.

Can we really have confidence in God through the worst of suffering? Verse 5 tells us, "Hope does not disappoint, because the love of God has been poured out in our hearts by the Holy Spirit who was given to us."

4. **Recalling God's amazing love (vv. 6–8).** We might be willing to die for a friend or family member, but for an enemy? Are you kidding? Humans without Christ are described as without strength, ungodly, sinners, and enemies (vv. 6, 8, 10). God's love was not motivated by anything in us. Because this love is unmerited and is not dependent on us, it will never change! God's love is the permanent possession of the child of God.

5. **Rejoicing in God's person (vv. 9, 10).** Salvation involves justification: we have been saved from the penalty of sin. It involves sanctification: we are being saved from the power of sin. It involves glorification: we will be saved from the presence of sin. God has already pronounced His verdict!

Conclusion: All our anchors during adversity revolve around the truth given to us in verse 11: We can rejoice in the reconciled relationship we have with God through Jesus Christ. The storms of life are going to come. When they do, we can turn to the spiritual anchors that God has provided for us.

STATS, STORIES, AND MORE

More from Dr. Timothy Beougher
God accomplishes certain things in our lives through suffering that He could not accomplish any other way!

God's love is unconditional. It's also invincible.

A Christian who was suffering under Communists once said, "We are like nails: the harder you hit us the deeper you drive us."

We have an anchor that keeps the soul/Steadfast and sure while the billows roll./Fastened to the Rock which cannot move,/Grounded firm and deep in the Savior's love. —Priscilla Owens

These Strange Anchors
The late Dr. Thomas Lambie, missionary to Ethiopia, had to ford many streams and rivers during his years in Africa. The danger in swollen waters was great, for one can easily be swept off one's feet and carried down the stream to greater depths or hurled to death against hidden rocks. Dr. Lambie learned from the nationals the best way to make such a hazardous crossing. A local person would find a large stone, the heavier the better, lift it onto his shoulder, and carry it across the stream as "ballast." The extra weight of the stone kept his feet solid on the bed of the stream allowing him to cross safely without being swept away. Dr. Lambie said, "While crossing the dangerous stream of life, enemies constantly seek to overthrow us and rush us down to ruin. We need the ballast of burden bearing, a load of affliction, to keep us from being swept off our feet."

The Gospel According to You

Prelude—Instrumental Group
  Shout to the Lord

Song of Praise—CH 21 *O for a Thousand Tongues to Sing* (v 1, 2, 3, Ab, mod, v 5 in A)

Prayer of Worship—Pastoral Staff

Welcome—Pastoral Staff

Song of Welcome—Congregation (meet and greet)
  CH 171 *Come into His Presence*

Worship and Praise—Congregation
  CH 128 *I Sing the Mighty Power*
  CH 10 *Majesty*
  CH 9 *Glorify Thy Name*
  Shout to the Lord (from *God for Us*)

Offertory Prayer—Pastoral Staff

Offertory Praise—Soloist and Praise Team or Solo
  with Congregation
  Lamb of God

Message—Pastor
The Gospel According to You—I Thess. 2:1–12

Hymn of Response/Invitation—Congregation
  CH *Just As I Am*

Hymn of Benediction—CH 439 *Song of the Nation* (1x in Ab, 1x in A)

Postlude—Instrumental Group
  CH 171 *Come into His Presence*

Additional Sermons and Lesson Ideas

SERIES: FAITH IS THE VICTORY

Feeble Faith Meets Strong Savior
Date preached:

Adapted from a sermon by Charles Haddon Spurgeon

Scripture: Mark 9:14–29, especially verses 23–27

Introduction: *U.S. News and World Report* said in a recent issue, "In the United States, 27 million adults and 7.5 million children have a diagnosable mental disorder—more than the combined number of people with cancer, heart disease, and lung disorders." For many, that mental disorder is anxiety, worry, a fretful heart. The man in today's story was in the grips of an understandable anxiety attack, for his son was in crisis. Our greatest worries are often over those we love the most. Perhaps the only good thing we can say about worry is that it sometimes drives us to the Lord. In our story today, it brought this father to Jesus, but once there, his unbelief threatened his receiving of the Lord's help. While worry may sometimes drive us to the Lord, it can so dominate our prayers that we have trouble claiming God's answers by faith. Perhaps this father's case may help us understand our own. Let us note the case carefully and observe . . .

1. **The Suspected Difficulty**
   The father may have thought . . .
   A. **The disciples were incompetent.** Despite their bravado, they seemed unable to help. Sometimes other people, despite good intentions, can't relieve our need. Sometimes even our Christian friends in the church appear to be powerless to help.
   B. **The problem was hopeless.** The boy's disease was fitful, mysterious, and terribly violent. We sometimes forget that the Lord delights to work impossibilities.
   C. **The Savior was powerless.** The man half hinted at this when he said, "Master, if you can do anything." The people of Isaiah's day grew discouraged in their exile, wondering if God saw their problems or cared about their cause (Is. 40:25). Anxiety whispers demonically in our ear, "God doesn't care. The Savior is powerless."

2. **The Tearful Discovery**
   "He said with tears . . ."
   A. His small faith discovered his unbelief. Sometimes we have just enough faith to realize how weak our belief really is. That isn't a great faith, but it's enough to start with. If we have just enough faith to recognize its own weakness, we have a place to start. God has a foothold in our hearts. Sometimes in rock climbing, all you need is the smallest crevice for a foothold or a tiny crack for inserting a finger.
   B. He was distressed at the sight of his own unbelief. Worry and anxiety is tantamount to unbelief, and unbelief is a great sin. It

kept the children of Israel out of the Promised Land for 40 years. Unbelief doubts:

- The power of omnipotence.
- The value of biblical promises.
- The efficacy of Christ's blood.
- The prevalence of Christ's pleas on our behalf.
- The very truth of Scripture.

C. He turned his thoughts in that direction, no longer saying, "Lord, help my child!" but, "Lord, help my unbelief!"

3. **The Intelligent Appeal**

The poor father cried to Jesus . . .

A. **On the basis of faith.** "Lord, I believe." Can you come to Christ today with even a small amount of faith? Isaiah 42:3 says, "A bruised reed shall he not break, and the smoking flax shall he not quench."

B. **With confession of sin.** "My unbelief." Chronic anxiety represents the sin of unbelief, a serious sin needing repentance.

C. **To One who knows how to help in this matter.** "Help!" And Jesus did help. And Jesus does help. And Jesus will help.

Conclusion: If you're worried about a loved one or about some other life-difficulty, come to Jesus with any case, and in every case. Come with your little faith, for in this matter He can help as no other can.

The Gospel According to You   *Date preached:*
By Dr. David Jeremiah

Scripture: 1 Thessalonians 2:1–12

Introduction: This passage gives us lessons about ministering to others, a subject on which Paul the apostle was an expert.

1. **We must be courageous as good soldiers (vv. 1, 2).** Paul was bold in his presentation of the gospel.
2. **We must be conscientious as stewards (vv. 3–5).** God has given us a sacred stewardship of the gospel, and we can never take our responsibility lightly. The gospel must be presented courageously, clearly, and convincingly.
3. **We must be cautious as gracious servants (v. 6).** Notice what this verse says about the desire, duty, and delight of a servant.
4. **We must be comforting as a godly mother (vv. 7, 8).**
5. **We must be careful as a good example (vv. 9, 10).**
6. **We must be concerned as a father (vv. 11, 12).**

Conclusion: Our goal is to bring people to a place where they walk in a godly lifestyle. That isn't just the responsibility of pulpit and preacher; it's the responsibility of us all.

JULY 25, 2010

SUGGESTED SERMON

The Forgotten Secret
of Happiness

Date preached:

By Michael Easley

Scripture: Psalm 32, especially verse 1, "Blessed is he whose transgression is forgiven, whose sin is covered."

Introduction: Some suffering in life is hard to explain, but much of it is self-inflicted. Could your misery be due to poor choices? Due to apathy or indifference? Could our suffering be due to sin? Psalm 32 shows God's blessings for those who are forgiven. This psalm gives us the forgotten secret of happiness, telling us that sin brings sorrow, but confession brings forgiveness and forgiveness brings joy.

1. **The joy of forgiveness (vv. 1, 2).** "Blessed" is one of those religious words that's hard to translate into practical terms. Perhaps the closest we can come is "happiness." The psalmist says that the blessed person is the one who understands forgiveness. We can't understand the reality of forgiveness if we don't understand the concept of sin, so David uses three words to describe sin:

   - Transgression—Rebellion against God.
   - Sin—Missing the mark or falling short of a standard.
   - Iniquity—Treachery, deceit.

   The psalmist was happy that . . .

   - His transgression was forgiven (lifted, carried away).
   - His sin was covered (hidden, concealed by removal).

   The Lord does not impute iniquity. This is an accounting term, as in reckoning to an account; it is not counted against us. A rough illustration is when you get pulled over for speeding and the kind officer tells you it will not go on your record. Now taken together, we have the comprehensive nature of our sins and the comprehensive nature of God's forgiveness. This is reason for joy!

2. **The misery of unconfessed sin (vv. 3, 4).** Notice the shift to a personal pronoun. David is giving us a personal illustration about the power of unconfessed sin. When I kept silent, he said, unwilling to confess sin, my body wasted away and God dealt with me so severely that my vitality was drained like a man suffering in the summer heat. Do you recall a time when the summer's heat was so oppressive you found it difficult to even breathe? Unconfessed sin hunts us down, oppresses us, keeps us awake at night.

3. **Confession and repentance (v. 5).** In this verse, David used the same three words he used in verses 1–2, saying that he had learned to acknowledge his sin, to expose his iniquity to the Lord, and to confess his transgressions.

4. **Instruction (vv. 6, 7).** Now the psalmist is going to pass along the lesson he learned. He calls on us to turn to God as he did, and to find in Him relief, release, and protection. He depicts God's protection in three ways:

   A. A hiding place.
   B. Preservation from trouble.
   C. Surrounded by songs of deliverance.

5. **The wisdom of God (vv. 8–10).** Now Psalm 32 shifts gears, warning the reader not to be like a horse or mule that requires a bit and bridle. Those who do not want God, who do not care about God, choose the hard way, the way of sin.

6. **The glad response (v. 11).** The one who groaned under the weight of sin (vv. 3, 4) now rejoices and shouts for joy.

Lessons:

We have a deficient view of repentance. Repentance isn't penance, reparation, or self-punishment. It isn't morbid introversion. True repentance involves contrition, sorrow, remorse, guilt, grief, and regret. But it is primarily a turning, a changing, a choice.

Forgiveness does not necessarily mean God removes the *consequences* of our sins.

The believer has assurance that God forgives sin. Forgiveness is the removal of sin. It is lifted. The debt is canceled. All the debt of sin—impossible for us to pay off—is forgiven in Christ's work on the Cross. We can have full assurance of that.

When we understand forgiveness, we're thankful. This psalm has a thankful message. There is great joy in forgiveness.

The only real happiness is forgiveness from sin. Apart from forgiveness, there's no real joy. To live in sin is to live in grief. To live in sin is to lose joy. The only real happiness is being forgiven. Everything else is an artificial attempt to dull the pain.

Conclusion: Sin brings sorrow, confession brings forgiveness, and forgiveness brings joy. How many struggles in our lives are due to sin! Why not confess it? Why not admit to God what He already knows? Why not ask Him this minute? Why not come to the Cross of Jesus Christ?

STATS, STORIES, AND MORE

John Stott wrote about Marghanita Laski, one of England's best-known secular humanists and novelists. Just before she died in 1988, she said in a television interview, "What I envy most about you Christians is your forgiveness; I have nobody to forgive me."

In his book *Healing for Damaged Emotions,* David Seamands writes about a young minister who once came to see him. He was having a lot of problems getting along with other people, especially his wife and family. He was continually criticizing her. He was sarcastic and demanding, and he was destroying their marriage. His attitude was also harsh toward members of his church.

Finally in desperation, he came to see Dr. Seamands, and after a while, the painful root of the matter came to light. Seamands wrote:

"While he was in the armed forces in Korea, he had spent two weeks of R & R in Japan. During that leave, walking the streets of Tokyo, feeling empty, lonely, and terribly homesick, he fell into temptation and went three or four times to a prostitute.

"He had never been able to forgive himself. He had sought God's forgiveness, and with his head, believed he had it. But the guilt still plagued him and he hated himself. Every time he looked in the mirror, he couldn't stand what he was seeing.

"When he returned home to marry his fiancée, who had faithfully waited for him all those years, his emotional conflicts increased because he still could not accept complete forgiveness. . . . He felt he had no right to be happy.

"As A. W. Tozer put it, the young minister was living in 'the perpetual penance of regret.' "

SUGGESTED ORDER OF WORSHIP

Prelude—Instrumental Group
Evermore

Announcements—Pastoral Staff

Song of Praise—Congregation
CH 35 *He Is Exalted* (2x with tag in F)
CH 153 *Worthy of Worship* (verse 1, 2, 3 in F)

Prayer of Worship—Pastoral Staff

Welcome—Pastoral Staff

Song of Welcome—Congregation
CH *Yes, Lord Yes* (2x in Eb)

Worship and Praise—Congregation
CH 339 *By His Grace* (2x in Eb)
CH 344 *Grace Greater Than All Our Sin* (chorus, v. 1, v. 2 chorus in G)
MSPW 2 100 *Grace Alone* (2x in C)

Offertory Prayer—Pastoral Staff

Offertory Praise—Solo and Praise Team
Song for the Nations

Message—Pastor
Amazing Grace—Titus 2:11–15

Hymn of Response/Invitation—Congregation
CH 506 *I'd Rather Have Jesus*

Hymn of Benediction—CH 195 *Bless the Name of Jesus* (2x in C)

Postlude—Instrumental Group
He Is Exalted (2x in F)

Additional Sermons and Lesson Ideas

SERIES: FAITH IS THE VICTORY

Is Your Faith Genuine?

Date preached:

By Dr. Timothy Beougher

Scripture: James 2:14–20, especially verse 17

Introduction: Kent Hughes writes about a cartoon in *The New Yorker* that showed a large sign out in front of a church which read: "The Lite Church: 24% Fewer Commitments, Home of the 7.5% tithe, fifteen-minute sermons, forty-five-minute worship services. We have only eight commandments—your choice. We use just three spiritual laws. Everything you've wanted in a church . . . and less!" Unfortunately that cartoon paints an accurate picture. Many people today are looking for a "lite church," a "lite faith," and a "lite commitment." In the passage we're studying today, James asks each of us a question, "Is your faith genuine?" How can we know if we have real faith or "lite faith"?

1. **The Argument Stated (v. 14).** In verse 14, James writes, "If someone says he has faith." James doesn't say this individual actually does have faith, but simply that this person claims to have faith. The verb translated here "to claim," or "to say" is in the present tense, which suggests this person is continually asserting his faith, constantly saying, "I have faith. I have faith," but his words are hollow. No outward evidence supports his claim. So James is referring to the profession of faith, not to the possession of faith. The faith that James denounces is a mere creedal confession, not a faith that entails wholehearted acceptance. James has nothing against faith. In fact, throughout his letter he shows us he is a great supporter of faith (1:3, 6; 2:1, 5), but he wants it to be genuine, wholehearted faith. James would agree with those who say that we aren't saved by faith plus works, but we are saved by a faith that works. It must have follow-through. If there is a root, it will eventually bear fruit; no fruit means no root. Where works do not exist, neither does faith (see v. 18).

2. **The Principle Illustrated (vv. 15, 16, 19).** James goes on to illustrate the logical absurdity of faith without works. The "brother" or "sister" is probably a believer, maybe a needy person in the congregation. James attacks those who only speak kind words to this needy soul. Isn't it enough to be kind? No! The needy person's body is still cold; his stomach is still empty. To make it personal, there are those in this community needing our help. The test for us is how we react to them. Do we simply smile and say, "I hope it gets better," or do we cook them dinner, keep their children, or help them move into their new apartment? Genuine conversion leads to genuine compassion. James gives a further example of false faith in verse 19. His reference to the demons makes a graphic point. No demon is an

atheist. They believe in God, they exercise "faith," yet we know they are spiritually dead; we know they are not saved nor have the kind of faith God requires. A kind of belief exists which is not true faith. The man in verse 14 had intellectual faith. Demons not only have this, but they are in full agreement emotionally with the truth of who God is. But they lack the type of faith that "trusts in" or "relies upon" God. Saving faith involves all three components: knowledge, agreement, and trust. That is, the mind, emotions, and will. A belief that does not work is no better than that which the demons have.

3. **The Conclusion Drawn (vv. 17, 20).** What is James' conclusion? Faith that does not evidence itself outwardly is not genuine faith. Faith, by itself, is dead. If it produces no works, it is lifeless and ineffective to justification. Faith alone without works is as dead as a body without breath. If you put a monitor on someone who professes to have faith but displays no outward evidence, the monitor will show a flat line. That person can talk all they want, but they do not have genuine faith. Without the outward evidence of deeds, a mere profession of faith is simply that: a profession without possession, an impostor posing as a believer. Could that be you?

Conclusion: A line from a Rich Mullins song says, "Faith without works is like a screen door on a submarine." It's worthless and it sinks. Do you claim to have faith? Does your life really show it? A workless faith is a worthless faith. We must ask ourselves, "If I were arrested for being a Christian, would there be enough evidence to convict me?"

A Mood–altering Prayer
By Robert Morgan

Date preached:

Scripture: 1 Samuel 1

Introduction: Too many of us are victims of our moods. We suffer from low spirits, anger, depression, or anxiety, often brought on by difficult circumstances. We need to practice "mood-altering" prayers. One of the Bible's best examples is Hannah, the mother of Samuel.

1. Difficult Conditions (vv. 1–7).
2. Depressed Spirits (v. 8). According to David Hazard, 43 percent of Americans suffer adverse health effects due to stress. One million Americans miss work each day due to stress, and 75–90 percent of doctor visits are stress-related complaints.
3. Earnest Prayer (vv. 9–16).
4. Shared Burden (v. 17). Eli's response helped Hannah realize that God was sharing her burden.

5. Changed Attitude (v. 18). Hannah's circumstances had not changed, but her frame of mind was completely different.
6. Heaven's Answer (vv. 19, 20).

Conclusion: Cast your burden on the Lord, and He will sustain your spirits.

AUGUST 1, 2010

SERIES: GOD-FOCUSED LEADERSHIP   SUGGESTED SERMON

Leading by God's Plan

Date preached:

By Rev. Steve Hopkins

Scripture: Jeremiah 29:11–14

Introduction: *"God loves you and has a wonderful plan for your life."* Sounds great when we like the plan. But what happens when things are not going our way, when the job doesn't work out, the test results are not good, and home is not so sweet? Jeremiah 29:11 is often quoted as a great verse of encouragement, but seldom is the context taken into consideration. Jeremiah 28 contains the debate between Hananiah and Jeremiah. Hananiah says the captivity is only going to last two years. Jeremiah writes to the captives telling them to build houses, plant gardens, marry, have children, seek the peace, and pray for Babylon because they will be there for not two, but seventy years! (Jer. 29:1–10) But in the midst of the bad news, there is good news.

1. **God's Plan (Jer. 29:11)**

   God says, "I know the plans *I* have." The words refer to plans already made by God. They are His plans, on His timetable. Blanchard, Hybels and Hodges write, "If you want to make God laugh, tell Him *your* plans."[1] Sometimes when we pray, we expect God to say, "Well Steve, I never thought of that!" How foolish! We think we are going to come up with a plan that impresses God.

   We are God's creation: "Created in Christ Jesus for good works, which God prepared ahead of time so that we should walk in them" (Eph. 2:10). We are to discover His plan, not invent our own (Prov. 3:5, 6). Alignment with His plans is the issue, not my agenda. The business world often refers to the principle: Every organization is in perfect alignment for the results they are currently getting. If we do not like the results, we must examine the alignment that is producing those results. The challenge: I love *my* plans and agenda. The question: Who follows whom? Jesus chose to only do what He saw the Father doing (John 5:19, 20, 30), how much more should we operate by that principle!

---

[1] Ken Blanchard, Bill Hybels and Phil Hodges, *Leadership by the Book* (Morrow, 1999), 77.

2. God's People (Jer. 29:11)

"I know the plans I have for *you.*" Jeremiah reminded them that God's love for us never changes (Jer. 31:3). Romans 8:38, 39 reminds us nothing "will have the power to separate us from the love of God that is in Christ Jesus our Lord!"

Two of the greatest truths of all time: God is there, and God is there for you!

3. God's Purpose (Jer. 29:11)

"Plans for a *future* and a *hope.*" God's purpose never changes (Is. 14:24). My plans often change because 1.) I don't have perspective, foresight, to know everything that is going to happen, and 2.) I don't have power to implement the plan, or the time, money, energy, etc. God doesn't have those limitations. He does not have a Plan B. I am always on God's Plan A (Rom. 8:28).

Response:

Jeremiah continues in verses 13 and 14 with our response to God's plan. "Call to Me and come and pray to Me, and I will listen . . . seek Me . . . search for Me with all your heart." Our response is to call upon Him, and see what He has planned (Jer. 33:3). The *who* is much more important than the *what* or the *how.* We must learn to trust Him, not a plan, not a method, not a program.

Illustrations:

We often say, "My car is out of alignment." However, it is in alignment—alignment to pull left. What we need to do is have it aligned to go straight. Often we wrestle the wheel of our life, trying to keep it going straight, when it would be much better to stop and get our life in alignment. We tear up a lot of tires, tie rods, etc., trying to wrestle an out-of-alignment life, when adjusting to be in alignment with the Father would make life so much easier.

Most of us want a "trip tik," with every turn marked clearly. But then we would trust the trip tik, and not Him. Jesus used terms like "take up My yoke and learn from Me" and "abide in Me" to describe seeking alignment with Him (Matt. 11:25–30; John 15). When life is about the Father and His work, it isn't about me. It is all about living for the Audience of One rather than the applause of the crowd. It is focused on His name, not our own.

"God has kingdom work to do on earth, and He is looking for

believers through whom He can do His work. We're looking for better methods; God is looking for better men and women. When it comes to serving God, total dependence is better than talent and determination. Our best efforts will always come short of what God could do through our lives if we would learn to trust Him."[2]

A Hurt Only God Can Heal

Postlude—Instrumental Group
Evermore

Welcome—Pastoral Staff

Song of Welcome—Congregation (meet and greet)
CH 212/213 *We Bring the Sacrifice* (2x in D)
CH 214 *He Has Made Me Glad* (1x in D, 1x in Eb)

Songs of Praise and Worship
CH 86 *Jesus, Name Above All Names* (1x in Eb, 1x in F)
CH 102/103 *All Hail King Jesus* (1x in Ab)
CH 146 *I Worship You, Almighty God* (1x in Ab, 1x in Bb)
WH 4 *How Great Thou Art* (1x in Bb, 1x in C)

Offertory Prayer—Pastoral Staff

Offertory Praise—Solo with Praise Team
CH 490 *Lord, I'm Coming Home*

Message—Pastor
A Hurt Only God Can Heal

Hymn of Response/Invitation—Congregation
CH *I Surrender All*

Benediction Hymn—Congregation
CH 5 *I Sing Praises* (1x in G, 1x in Ab)

Postlude—Instrumental Group
CH 5 *I Sing Praises*

---

[2]Henry Blackaby and Melvin Blackaby, *Experiencing the Spirit* (Multnomah, 2009), 56.

Additional Sermons and Lesson Ideas

Conditions of Revival
Outline by W. Graham Scroggie

Date preached:

Scripture: Various

Introduction: The blessing of revival is conditional. God has made promises, but He has also given precepts that we must obey to receive the blessings. Let's look at some of these conditions:

1. There must be a consciousness of the need of revival (Rev. 3:14–18).
2. There must be a firm belief in the possibility of revival (Matt. 21:22).
3. There must be a true recognition that god wills our revival (Is. 48:18; Ps. 81:13, 16; Hosea 11:7–8; 14:4).
4. There must be a strong sense of the urgency of revival (Rev. 3:19, 20).
5. There must be an earnest desire for revival (Ps. 103:5; Acts 1:7, 12–14).
6. There must be a genuine willingness to pay for revival (Matt. 10:17–23).
7. There must be a determined pursuit of revival (Acts 1:12–26).

Conclusion: O Lord, help us to desire, understand, and pursue revival among Your people!

A Hurt Only God Can Heal
By Robert Morgan

Date preached:

Scripture: 1 Samuel 2:1–10

Introduction: The prophet Samuel, a man of prayer, learned the art of prayer from his mother. Out of the 37 verses about Hannah in the Bible, 23 describe her at prayer. In chapter 1, she took a hurt only God could heal and turned it into a prayer only God could hear. In chapter 2, she offered praise only God deserved.

1. **God satisfies the soul (v. 1).** Contrast with her story in chapter 1. When everything seems against us, we find God alone satisfies our souls.
2. **God rectifies the score (vv. 2–5).** Hannah left her enemies with the Lord.
3. **God fortifies the saved (vv. 6–9a).** In prayer, we gain new strength.
4. **God glories the son (vv. 9b, 10).** This is a prophecy about Christ, and it's the first time in Scripture He's given the title Messiah. The virgin Mary later used this prayer as a basis for her own Magnificat.

Conclusion: Learn to turn hurts only God can heal into prayers only He can hear.

AUGUST 8, 2010

SUGGESTED SERMON

Leading by Revelation or Resolution?

Date preached:

By Rev. Steve Hopkins

Scripture: Joshua 1:1–9

Introduction: How do you face new challenges? What do you do with an uncertain future? A familiar verse is often quoted, Proverbs 29:18, "Where there is no vision, the people perish." Most modern translations will translate "vision" as "revelation": "Where there is no revelation, the people cast off restraint; but happy is he who keeps the law" (NKJV); "Without revelation people run wild" (HCSB). We are tempted to face challenges based on resolution, and we see what we can do for God. We must learn to face challenges based on "revelation," and see what God can do through us. The key: to hear a clear word from God and allow Him to direct our paths. Proverbs 3:5–7 says, "Trust in the Lord with all your heart, and lean not on your own understanding; In all your ways acknowledge Him, and He shall direct your paths. Do not be wise in your own eyes."

Joshua was standing on the banks of a new adventure and heard a word from God, a revelation on which he could face his challenge.

1. **The Reason for Revelation (Josh. 1:1, 2).** The times were desperate times. Their great leader, Moses, was dead. Joshua had only been an assistant. Three reasons Joshua needed a word of revelation: he faced a God-sized task to be done in God's timing, and he was to take God's people with him.

   A. **God-sized task:** Joshua had big shoes to fill (Deut. 34:10–12). Can you imagine trying to follow a legendary leader like Moses?

   B. **God's timing:** "Now . . . cross over the Jordan." According to Joshua 3:15, the river was flooded. The temptation would be to delay until the flood dissipated, and then figure out a way to cross, using our best engineers to get the job done.

C. **God's people:** Joshua was commanded to go: "You and all the people." A lot of people, stubborn, disobedient people at that, who had been grumbling all the way through the wilderness. God never sends us across the river alone.

2. **The Reality of Revelation (Josh. 1:3, 4)**

Notice the tense in verse 3, "I have given you." It is past tense. It is already done; not might, not maybe. His confidence is not in what Joshua can do, but what God has done. Throughout all the book of Joshua you will find evidence that the battle is the Lord's: "The Lord fought for Israel" is a favorite refrain. When we live life based on revelation the promise of verse 5 is realized, "I will be with you." Joshua's hope was in the *Who*, not the *what* or the *how*.

We often need to be reminded that He will not leave us or forsake us. He knows our address geographically, physically, emotionally, financially, relationally, and spiritually.

3. **The Response to Revelation (Josh. 1:6–9)**

Three times God says to Joshua, "Be strong and of good courage." Ever wonder why three times? Could it have been Joshua was not very strong and not very courageous? That gives us hope when we don't feel very strong or courageous.

How do we grow in strength and courage? By doing God's word! Jesus issued the same challenge in the invitation of the Sermon on the Mount. "Everyone who hears these words of mine and puts them into practice is like a wise man who built his house on the rock" (Matt. 7:24). What is the foundation on which you are building your life? Satan's temptation always begins with doubting God's word, "Did God really say" (Gen. 3:1).

If anyone ever had an excuse for not doing a daily quiet time, it would have been Joshua. For the next seven years he was going to be the military leader, the spiritual leader, and the political leader of a nation behind enemy lines! But God instructed him in verse 8 to spend time in His word *"day and night . . . for then you will prosper and succeed in whatever you do."*

Do you believe everything you read in the newspaper, see on TV, view on the internet? What about what is written in God's word? Then why do we spend more time reading the newspaper, watching TV, and surfing on the internet than reading the Bible? To do the word of God we must know the word of God! "So faith comes by hearing, and hearing by the word of God" (Rom. 10:17).

Response: Notice the beginning of verse 9, "Have I not commanded you?" God is saying to Joshua, when I send you across the river, you can go across the river. Where God guides, God provides. Philippians 4:13 reminds us we can do what God commands us to do in His strength.

Mary faced the greatest challenge of her life, giving birth to the Christ child. She heard the angel say, "For nothing will be impossible with God." Her response was what our response must be today, "Let it be to me according to Your word" (Luke 1:37, 38).

SUGGESTED ORDER OF WORSHIP

The World Is a Dangerous Place

Prelude—Instrumentalist
Shout to the Lord

Call to Prayer—Pastoral Staff

Worship and Praise—Congregation
CH 102/103 *All Hail King Jesus* (1x in Eb, 1x in F)
CH 104 *O Worship the King* (vv. 1, 2 in G, v. 4 in Ab)

Baptismal Celebration—Pastoral Staff

Welcome—Pastoral Staff

Song of Welcome—Congregation (meet and greet)
CH 757 *Soon and Very Soon* (4x in F)

Worship and Praise—Congregation
MSPW 12 *The Name of the Lord* (4x in F)
SPW 220 *You Are My All in All* (As written F/G with tag)
SPW *Praise You* (1x in A, 1x in Bb)

Prayer of Worship and Praise—Worship Pastor
CH 139 *Great Is Thy Faithfulness* (v. 1, chorus, v. 2, chorus in D, chorus in Eb)

Offertory Prayer

Offertory Praise—Soloist and Praise Team
Show Me Your Ways

Message—Pastor
The World Is a Dangerous Place

Hymn of Response/Invitation—Congregation
CH 488 *Just As I Am*

Benediction Hymn—Congregation
MSPW 12 *The Name of the Lord* (2x in F)

Postlude—Instrumental Group
MSPW 54 *As for Me and My House*

Additional Sermons and Lesson Ideas

SERIES: THE WAY OF THE DISCIPLE

Remain in Me!
By Rev. Mark Hollis

Date preached:

Scripture: John 15:1–8

Introduction: As Jesus and His disciples walked from the upper room to the Mount of Olives, they must have passed many grape arbors. Perhaps it was at one of those that Jesus stopped and—pointing at the vines—offered the words of John 15:1–8.

1. The Analogy (v. 1).
   A. Jesus is the vine.
   B. We are the branches.
   C. The Father is the gardener.
2. The Teaching (vv. 2–4).
   A. The unfruitful are cut off.
   B. The fruitful are pruned.
   C. The pruning is through God's Word.
   D. The fruit comes as we remain connected to the vine.
3. The Warning (vv. 5, 6).
   A. Those who remain connected to Jesus will bear much fruit.
   B. Those who do not remain connected to Jesus will be thrown away, wither, and burn.
4. The Promise (vv. 7, 8).

Conclusion: How is God at work pruning me? Have I become unfruitful? Have I become disconnected? How might I revitalize my relationship?

The World Is a Dangerous Place
By Kevin Riggs

Date preached:

Scripture: Psalm 3

Introduction: Dates like June 7, 1941, and September 11, 2001, remind us that the world is full of evil. To survive in this dangerous world, Psalm 3 tells us we should:

1. Look to God for Protection (vv. 3, 4). Ultimately, the source of all our protection is the hand of God, our shield.
2. Look to God for Security (vv. 5, 6). God watches over us as we sleep, and wakes us up each morning.
3. Look to God for Deliverance (vv. 7, 8). David compared his enemies to wild animals whom God disarms, rendering them harmless.

Conclusion: The world may be a dangerous place to live, but it is also a beautiful place, and a perfect place for the exercise of faith.

AUGUST 15, 2010

SERIES: GOD-FOCUSED LEADERSHIP   SUGGESTED SERMON

Leading: The Cost Has Been Counted

Date preached:

By Rev. Steve Hopkins

Scripture: Luke 14:25–31

Introduction: Our commandment as the church is to "make disciples" (Matt. 28:18–20). "Disciple" is the most common word in the New Testament for followers of Christ, used 264 times in the Gospels and Acts. In Luke 14:25–33, three times Jesus uses the phrase "cannot be My disciple." Until this point in the gospel, multitudes were following Him. This becomes the watershed passage. Jesus was interested in making disciples, not increasing attendance.

1. **Commandment to be kept (Luke 14:25, 26)**
   Jesus' words sound harsh. Is He negating the fifth commandment? (Ex. 20:12). Is He contradicting the word on loving wife and children? (Eph. 5:25; 1 Tim. 5:8). A good commentary on the verse is Matthew 10:37, where He says we are not to love anyone "more than Me." The point is my love for God is the upper most limit on my love for anyone or anything else. The first of the Ten Commandments is that we have no other gods before Him. If I want to love my wife or children more than I love God, there are going to be problems. The key is, the more I love Him, the more I can love my wife and children.

   We often try to fulfill the Great Commission without first fulfilling the Great Commandment (Matt. 22:37–40). Jesus' question to Peter after the Resurrection was, "Do you love me?" (John 21:15–19). How often has Jesus said, "Follow Me," and we have answered, "But first . . ." (Luke 9:57–62).

2. **Cross to be carried (Luke 14:27)**
   Salvation is through coming to the Cross; discipleship is through carrying the Cross. When do I take up the Cross? Jesus gives us a great example in the Garden of Gethsemane (Luke 22:41–42). When my will *crosses* God's will, I have a decision to make. If I cease to

make self the object of my life and actions, when I deny my own agenda, and seek His kingdom, not mine, I have taken up the cross. Paul wrote, "I did not set aside the grace of God," not to be crucified with Christ is to treat Christ's death as meaningless (Gal. 2:20, 21). Jesus commanded those who would follow Him to take up the cross *daily* (Luke 9:23). It is not just a one-time experience. It is a *cross*, not a *thorn* (2 Cor. 12:7). Crosses are voluntary, a decision—thorns are not. It is not something that irritates us, but a way of life. All four Gospels mention the cross to be carried (Matt. 16:24–25; Mark 8:34–37; Luke 9:23–25; 14:27; John 12:24–26).

3. Cost that has been counted (Luke 14:28–33)

This passage is often viewed from the perspective that we must count the cost. Consider this: Jesus is the builder (Matt. 16:18) and the King (Rev. 19:16). He has counted the cost; He knows what it will take to build His kingdom. There is no math for us to calculate; here is the bottom line: "Every one of you who does not say good-bye to all his possessions cannot be my disciple" (Luke 14:33). We must have the attitude that "I don't have to survive." That attitude is seen in all those God has used to build His kingdom. Think on these examples: Abraham (Gen. 12:4); Hebrew boys (Dan. 3:17–18); Daniel (Dan. 6); Esther (Esth. 4:16); the widow (Mark 12:41–44); Stephen (Acts 7); Paul (Acts 20:24); the heroes of the faith (Heb. 11:35–39); Jesus (Phil. 2:5–13).

Response: There is one question which determines if I am a disciple, "Have I given up everything for Christ?" It could also be asked, "Am I in control, or is He in control?" The issue is one of surrender.

STATS, STORIES, AND MORE

More Illustrations from Rev. Steve Hopkins

First Things First

"When I have learned to love God better than my earthly dearest, I shall love my earthly dearest better than I do now. In so far as I learn to love my earthly dearest at the expense of God and instead of God, I shall be moving towards the state in which I shall not love my earthly dearest at all. When first things are put first, second things are not suppressed but increased."   —C. S. Lewis

Surrender vs. Commitment

"Josef T'son was being harassed by the Communist thugs in Romania. This was under the brutal dictatorship of Ceausescu. Government officials warned, "Josef, if you don't get in line and register with the Communist government and let us control your ministry you know what we can do to you." Josef answered, "I know what you can do. Your chief weapon is killing, but let me tell you what my chief weapon is. My chief weapon is dying. And I want to warn you, if you use yours, I will be forced to use mine." When Josef was asked what he meant by using dying as a weapon he said, "If you kill me, you sprinkle every book that I have written, every sermon that I have preached with my blood. People will know that I believed enough in what I preached to die for it. So if you use your weapon, I will be forced to use mine," Adrian Rogers, *The Incredible Power of Kingdom Authority* (Broadman and Holman, 2002, 59).

"I had the privilege to preach in Romania shortly after God brought spiritual revival to this nation that had been liberated from a cruel Communist government. One of the leaders in that revival was a man named Josef T'son. Part of what made this man a mighty servant of the Lord was his exercise of Kingdom Authority in his life. Suffering at the hands of the Communists with brutal beatings, imprisonments, and death threats, he learned victory that comes so sweetly in surrendering to the Savior.

"As Josef and I rode along in his car, I said, 'Josef, tell me about American Christianity.'

"He said, 'Adrian, I had rather not.'

"I said, 'No, I want to know.'

"He then said, 'Well, Adrian, since you have asked me, I'll tell you. The key word in American Christianity is *commitment*.'

"I said, 'That is good, isn't it, Josef?'

"He replied, 'No, it is not. As a matter of fact, the word *commitment* did not come into great usage in the English language until about the 1960s. In Romania we do not even have a word to translate the English word *commitment*. If you were to use *commitment* in your message tonight, I would not have a proper word to translate it with.'

STATS, STORIES, AND MORE—*Continued*

"Josef continued, 'When a new word comes into usage, it generally pushes an old word out. I began to study and found the old word that *commitment* replaced. Adrian, the old word that is no longer in vogue in America is the word *surrender.*'

"'Josef,' I asked, 'What is the difference between *commitment* and *surrender?*'

"He said, 'When you make a commitment, you are still in control, no matter how noble the thing you commit to. One can commit to pray, to study the Bible, to give his money, or to commit to automobile payments, or to lose weight. Whatever he chooses to do, he *commits* to. But *surrender* is different. If someone holds a gun and asks you to lift your hands in the air as a token of surrender, you don't tell that person what you are committed to. You simply surrender and do as you are told.'

"He said, 'Americans love commitment because they are still in control. But the key word is surrender. We are to be slaves of the Lord Jesus Christ.'" —Adrian Rogers, *The Incredible Power of Kingdom Authority* (Broadman and Holman, 2002, 60–61)

❧ Your Sword First

"After a great naval battle, the French admiral came aboard Admiral Nelson's British ship to surrender with his hand outstretched. But Nelson said, "Your sword first, sir." Before we embrace the Lord Jesus, we have to lay down our swords. We have to put away our agendas. We have to pry our fingers from the things we clench. Jesus is Lord of all them now."
—Adrian Rogers, *The Incredible Power of Kingdom Authority* (Broadman and Holman, 2002, 106)

❧ "The greatest enemy of hunger for God is not poison but apple pie. It is not the banquet of the wicked that dulls our appetite for heaven, but endless nibbling at the table of the world. It is not the X-rated video, but the prime-time dribble of triviality we drink in every night. For all the ill that Satan can do, when God describes what keeps us from the banquet table of his love, it is a piece of land, yoke of oxen, and a wife (Luke 14:18–20). The greatest adversary of love to God is not his enemies but his gifts. And the most deadly appetites are not for the poison of evil, but for the simple pleasures of earth. For when these replace an appetite for God himself, the idolatry is scarcely recognizable, and almost incurable." —John Piper, *Hunger for God* (Crossway, 1997, 14)

The Way of the Disciple: Dead Center

Prelude—Instrumentalist
We Bring the Sacrifice of Praise

Worship and Praise—Congregation
CH *'Tis So Sweet to Trust in Jesus* (3x in F)

Prayer of Worship—Pastoral Staff (keyboard continue to play during prayer)
CH *I Love You, Lord* (2x in F)

Welcome—Pastoral Staff

Song of Welcome—Congregation (meet and greet)
SPW 87 *Praise the Name of Jesus* (1x in C, 1x in D)

Scripture Reading—Pastoral Staff
1 Peter 3:13—4:2

Prayer of Worship and Praise—Pastoral Staff

Worship and Praise—Congregation
CH 344 *Grace Greater Than Our Sin* (v. 1, chorus, v. 4, chorus in G)
CH 348 *My Savior's Love* (v. 1, chorus, v. 4, chorus in Ab play transition)
CH 349 *O How He Loves You and Me* (2x in Ab)

Offertory Prayer—Pastoral Staff

Offertory Praise—Solo or Praise Team
I Want to Know You More

Message—Pastor
The Way of the Disciple: Dead Center

Hymn of Response/Invitation—Congregation
CH 596 *I Surrender All*

Hymn of Benediction—
CH 5 *I Sing Praises* (1x in G, 1x in Ab)

Postlude—Instrumental Group
Shout to the Lord

Additional Sermons and Lesson Ideas

SERIES: THE WAY OF THE DISCIPLE

Dead Center
By Rev. Todd M. Kinde

Date preached:

Scripture: 1 Peter 3:13—4:2

Introduction: We all have a tendency to lose direction, wading hopelessly in a sea of activity without real purpose. Perhaps you've been searching, looking for something to keep your life from being meaningless and insignificant. Sooner or later, you'll be disappointed with whatever worldly thing is at the center of your life. The solution is submission to Christ. First Peter 3:13—4:6 describes a life with Christ at dead center. Jesus is Lord of all. As Lord, He is to be the center of your being. In your hearts, you are to set apart Christ as Lord. The term *to set apart* in the Bible means to take something from the periphery and put it in the center.

1. **When Christ is the center of our being, we are people of hope (3:13–17).** Peter reminds us that we who have trusted the Lord Jesus Christ as Savior from our sin and as Lord of our life are blessed. It is true that suffering may accompany the Christian life. Suffering here and now is temporal and should be understood as such. Blessing is eternal and so are our lives in Christ. So, we can function—even amid suffering—with joy. Our hope is in Christ. We need not fear the wrath of God, for we have trusted in His Word. Death and destruction are nothing to us, for the God we serve is able to bring life out of death. Since Christ is central to our being, we will be ready and willing to share of the hope we have in Christ Jesus our Lord, always being ready to give an answer to everyone who asks us about it. Timidity and shyness are pushed away as the hope of Christ comes rushing through our beings and out of our lives. But this will always be done in the character of Christ's submissive spirit—with gentleness and respect. We will speak the truth with love. When Christ is central, we will give the reason for the hope we have in Christ, the hope of eternity with God.

2. **When Christ is the center of our being, we are dead to sin (3:18–22).** Some of our attitudes need to change. Fear and pride must be eradicated. Because of our sinfulness, the only way to do away with fear and pride is to die to sin and to self. To do this we must identify with the death of Jesus our Lord. Christ suffered in His body. His suffering was to pay what we owed God for our sin and to satisfy the anger of God over our sin. Jesus was without sin, a perfect person, indeed, God in the flesh. It is only a perfect person who could pay the penalty: the righteous for the unrighteous. Christ suffered and died once for all. It cannot be repeated ever again, nor does it need

to be. God the Father raised the Son to life anew by the power of the Spirit. The Spirit gives life.

Jesus said, "as it was in the days of Noah, so it will be also in the days of the Son of Man" (Luke 17:26; Matt. 24:37 NKJV). Peter here says that the gospel was preached to the world in the days of Noah before the flood. God waited patiently 120 years while Noah built the ark. During that time, Noah preached with a hammer in his hand (2 Pet. 2:5; Heb. 11:7). This brief statement recalls everything that is in Genesis 6. One hundred and twenty years of preaching resulted in rejection of the message. Eight souls, however, were saved through the floodwater, Noah's family. What about your family? Have you testified of God's salvation to your family?

Peter says this floodwater is a symbol of baptism. It is a baptism not merely of water that washes dirt off your body, but a baptism with Christ. Christ refers to His death as a baptism (Mark 10:32–45; Luke 12:50). When we are converted, we are baptized into Christ's death. We die to sin and self. The ordinance of water baptism is a symbol of that inner regeneration that took place. Paul states in Romans, "How shall we who died to sin live any longer in it? Or do you not know that as many of us as were baptized into Christ Jesus were baptized into His death? Therefore we were buried with Him through baptism into death, that just as Christ was raised from the dead by the glory of the Father, even so we also should walk in newness of life. For if we have been united together in the likeness of His death, certainly we also shall be in the likeness of His resurrection" (Rom. 6:2–5 NKJV).

3. **When Christ is the center of our being, we are alive to God's will (4:1, 2).** Baptism also symbolizes our new life, the power and presence of the Holy Spirit to live that new life through us for the will of God. No longer do the passions of the flesh defeat you. You will not participate in the satisfying of baser desires. Your satisfaction is found in the ultimate desire, the desire for God—the hunger for God. Water baptism testifies to your desire and commitment of exclusive loyalty to the will of God.

Conclusion: Water baptism is not an option in the Christian life. It is a necessary part of our testimony. When Christ is central to our being, we will have hope, we will die to sin and self, and we will be alive to the will of God. Baptism symbolizes this reality of being dead center with Christ. Will you consider participating in this rite of water baptism? Will you publicly testify that you have died to sin and live for Christ?

Boast in the Cross

By W. Graham Scroggie

Date preached:

Scripture: Galatians 6:14

Introduction: What are you most proud of? Is it your children, your sports ability, your mind? Paul turns our attention to what we should glory in above all, the Cross of Jesus Christ.

1. A historical fact is announced: the Cross of Christ.
2. A spiritual experience is affirmed: the world has been crucified to us, and we to the world.
3. A personal attitude is assumed: God forbid that we should boast in anything but the Cross.

Conclusion: The attitude we should have is expressed in the hymn "Rock of Ages," "Nothing in my hand I bring, simply to the cross I cling."

AUGUST 22, 2010

SERIES: GOD FOCUSED LEADERSHIP   SUGGESTED SERMON

Leading: Finishing Well

Date preached:

By Rev. Steve Hopkins

Scripture: Joshua 23–24

Introduction: J. Robert Clinton points to Hebrews 13:7, 8 as the "leadership mandate." We are to observe carefully those leaders who have gone before us, and imitate their faith, because "Jesus Christ is the same yesterday, today, and forever." It is all about learning to recognize the activity of Christ in their life, so we can better recognize His activity in us.[1]

Joshua finished well. His family served the Lord, his circle of influence (Israel) served the Lord, and his legacy (the elders who outlived Joshua) served the Lord (Joshua 24:15, 29, 31). We can observe his life to learn how to finish well in our leadership responsibility.

How to Finish Well . . .

1. **Perspective: Recognize what God has done.**
   There was no doubt in Joshua's heart where the credit was due. "The Lord your God did . . . it was the Lord your God who was fighting for you . . . one of you routed a thousand, because the Lord your God was fighting for you" (Josh. 23:3, 10). In Joshua 24:1–13, he referred to the Lord twenty-one times. Notice in Joshua 24:3, 12, and 13, their identity was an act of God's grace. He notes even Abraham didn't seek God, God sought him!

   Joshua repeatedly gave God the glory, the credit, for all that happened. He knew it was not about him, it was all about God. Jesus reminds us, "You did not choose Me, but I chose you" (John 15:16). Paul proclaimed, "But by the grace of God I am what I am" (1 Cor. 15:10).

   Even as Joshua began he proclaimed, "Consecrate yourselves, because the Lord will do wonders among you tomorrow" (Josh. 3:5). What an exciting way to live, constantly aware of what God wants to do in your life.

---

[1] J. Robert Clinton, *The Making of a Leader* (NavPress, 1988), 40.

2. **Purpose: Obey what God has said.**

Joshua encouraged them to "continue obeying all that is written in the book" (Josh. 23:6; see also Josh. 1:6–8). Joshua 11:15 says, "That is what Joshua did, leaving nothing undone of all that the Lord had commanded Moses." In Joshua 24:14–33, the key word is *serve*, often translated *worship*. He challenges them to "fear the Lord . . . choose . . . the one you will worship" (Josh. 24:14, 15). There can be no neutrality, a singleness of heart is required, we can't be straddling the fence. Everybody must worship something or someone. When the people declared they would serve the Lord, Joshua responds with, "You will not be able," warning them not to be superficial or careless in their commitment. God would hold them accountable (Josh. 24:19, 20). Jesus taught his disciples in Luke 14:25–33 that anyone without a commitment to complete obedience "cannot be My disciple."

3. **Passion: Love God with all your heart.**

Joshua admonishes the people to "remain faithful" or "hold fast" to the Lord. It is the same word used in Genesis 2:24 of a husband and wife cleaving to each other (Josh. 23:8). They were to "be very diligent to love the Lord your God for your own well-being." They were not to "cling to the rest of these nations" (Josh. 23:11, 12). He challenged them to "offer your hearts to the Lord" (Josh. 24:23). Love motivates us to finish well, to keep on, to never quit. When Jesus was asked, "Which is the greatest commandment?" He went immediately to the command to "love the Lord your God with all your heart" (Matt. 22:36–40).

Results of finishing well:

"After these things, the Lord's servant, Joshua . . . died" (Josh. 24:29). The designation "the Lord's servant" is rarely used in Scripture. It was used of Moses in Joshua 1:1. If Joshua would have heard that designation of him, he probably would have been embarrassed. He may have protested, "No, that was Moses." However, the baton had been successfully passed. The assistant had finished well as the leader.

In Isaiah 39:8, King Hezekiah was told the kingdom would eventually go into captivity; his response, "At least there will be peace and truth in my days." That kind of selfishness, with no concern for future generations, will never finish well.

J. Robert Clinton concludes after extensive research that less than one in three leaders finish well.[2] Our world needs to see what it looks like when a leader finishes well.

SUGGESTED ORDER OF WORSHIP

Prelude—Instrumental Group
Come, Now Is the Time to Worship

Call to Worship—Pastoral Prayer

Call to Worship—Praise Team
Jesus, Lover of My Soul

Welcome—Pastoral Staff

Song of Welcome—Congregation (meet and greet)
SPW1 *We Bring a Sacrifice of Praise* (1x in C, 1x in Db)

Worship and Praise—Congregation
CH 214 *I Will Enter His Gates* (1x in Db, 1x D)
MSPW 1 *Ancient of Days* (2x in D)
MSPW 52 *Sanctuary* (1x in D, 1x in E)
We Sing Worthy (Geron Davis–Integrity Mu) (1x in E, 1x in F, 1x in G)
SPW 123 *Because He Lives* (chorus only) (1x in G, 1x in Ab)

Offertory Prayer—Pastoral Staff

Offertory Praise—Praise Team
All of the Glory (Geron Davis–Benson-Brentwood Pub)

Message—Pastor

Hymn of Response/Invitation—Congregation
CH 596 *I Surrender All*

Hymn of Benediction—Congregation
SPW 1 *We Bring a Sacrifice of Praise*

Postlude—Instrumental Group
I Will Enter His Gates

---

[2]J. Robert Clinton, three articles *Finishing Well—Six Characteristics; Finishing Well—Six Major Barriers Identified; Finishing Well—Five Factors That Enhance It* in the *Clinton Biblical Leadership Commentary* CD 1999, 395–402. Available from www.bobbyclinton.com.

Additional Sermons and Lesson Ideas

The Upside-down Kingdom of Jesus
Date preached:
By Ed Dobson

Scripture: Mark 10:35–45

Introduction: This is our Lord's personal mission statement. If I'm to be an authentic follower of Christ, what marked His life ought to mark mine, and my personal mission statement ought to be "serving and giving." The opposite of that, of course, is to be served and to receive. I can live life with a passion to be served and to receive, or I can live with a passion to give and serve. Set your Bible down a moment and hold your hands in front of you. Clench one of your hands into a fist and leave the other open. This is the choice being a follower of Christ. Am I going to live with a clenched fist expecting others to serve me, receiving, accumulating, and getting? Or am I going to live with an open hand, giving and serving?

1. **Verse 35.** This statement is actually Christ's conclusion to a conversation with two of his disciples, which begin with a request: "Teacher, we want You to do for us whatever we ask." What an incredible request! Their view of following Jesus was not, "How can I serve Jesus?" but "What can Jesus do for me?" The root problem was selfishness.

2. **Verse 36.** Jesus responded with a question: "What do you want Me to do for you?" Matthew 20:21 adds, "in your kingdom." They believed Jesus was going to establish an earthly political kingdom, and they wanted to be Number 1 and Number 2 in that kingdom. What began as selfishness moved into pride. They wanted to be above the rest of the disciples. Where did this selfish, prideful attitude come from? You'd think that some of Jesus would have rubbed off on them. Three factors may have contributed to their attitude:
   A. They had a mother with great ambitions for her sons (see Matt. 20:20).
   B. James and John were part of the inner circle and had been privy to some incredible spiritual moments, such as in Mark 9:1–13. We have to be careful with the spiritual moments God gives us that we don't allow spiritual knowledge and experience to build pride in our lives.
   C. Their upper-class status. Mark 1:20 speaks of their owning a business and overseeing employees. There were few fishing families in Galilee with the wealth to actually hire people to fish for them. Zebedee was a cut above the rest of the fishermen.

3. **Verse 37.** "Grant that we may sit on Your right hand and on Your left." We instinctively want everyone else and everything to meet our needs.

4. **Verses 38–44.** Jesus, saying "You do not know what you ask," offers two principles in response. First, the cost of leadership: "Are you able to drink the cup that I drink?" The path to glory and greatness always takes us through suffering and difficulty. Second, the call to leadership: His is an upside-down kingdom. In the world, greatness is determined by how many people serve you. In Christ's kingdom greatness is determined by how many we serve. It's not a matter of authority and control but of humility and service.

5. **Verse 45.** Jesus concluded by saying He Himself exemplifies these principles. Obeying them is a process of becoming like Him.

Conclusion: Am I living my life expecting others to serve me? My spouse? My children? The people at work? Or do I view those around me and my circumstances as opportunities to serve both Christ and others? Am I closed-fisted or open-handed? I don't mean we will never receive and that we should never be served—there are times when that happens—but I'm talking about the passion of our life. Receiving or giving? There are also church implications. This morning many of us are in the receiving mode, but have you also come with a passion to give? To worship? To serve? Much of our culture is designed to make us feel good. The radical message of Jesus counteracts that. The greater message this morning is, "Who's in control of my life? Why am I following Christ? What am I doing for Christ?" May the Lord Jesus take our lives and let them be consecrated, Lord, to Thee.

Unbroken Cords of Friendship

Date preached:

By Drew Wilkerson

Scripture: Ecclesiastes 4:9–12

Introduction: Pepper Rogers writes, "A few years back I was in the middle of a terrible season as football coach at UCLA. It even got so bad that it upset my home life. My dog was my only friend. So I told my wife that a man needs at least two friends, and she bought me another dog." God does not want us to be lonely. Hidden within these words in Ecclesiastes we find three unifying cords necessary to build a friendship that cannot be broken.

1. Cord #1: A friend is someone dedicated to you (vv. 9–10).
2. Cord #2: A friend is someone who you can depend on (v. 11).
3. Cord #3: A friend is someone who will defend you (v. 12).

Conclusion: Two friends are invaluable, but three are priceless. To have a friend we must be a friend, and nothing can compare to the joy and strength of the unbroken cords of friendship.

AUGUST 29, 2010

SUGGESTED SERMON

How to Live in the Last Days

Date preached:

By Woodrow Kroll

Scripture: Matthew 24:32–35, especially verse 33, "So you also, when you see all these things, know that it is near—at the doors."

Introduction: Remember Chicken Little? When an acorn dropped on his head, he thought the sky was falling, and soon the whole barnyard was in an uproar. Many people feel like the sky is falling, but what does God's Word reveal about the future? Should we be in an uproar? What character should our lives take if Jesus is coming soon? Let me suggest four attitudes we ought to have:

1. **A Sense of Urgency.** If we're living in the end times, we need to have a sense that whatever we have to accomplish must be done quickly. If Jesus is coming soon, it should have a bearing on your lifestyle. There needs to be an urgency to your witness. You know that neighbor you've been thinking about witnessing to for years? This is the day. The Bible teacher F. B. Meyer asked D. L. Moody, "What's the secret of your success?" Moody replied, "For many years I have never given an address without the consciousness that the Lord may come back before I've finished."

   A. **Think of Noah in Hebrews 11:7:** "By faith Noah, being divinely warned of things not yet seen, moved with godly fear, prepared an ark for the saving of his household, by which he condemned the world and became heir of the righteousness which is according to faith." Noah had a sense of urgency, because the rain was on its way.

   B. **Think of Jonah.** When he finally got his heart straightened out and went to Nineveh, he preached an eight-word sermon: "Yet forty days, and Nineveh shall be overthrown." There was a time limit, and every passing day brought judgment closer. Jonah preached with urgency, and the city was saved.

2. **A Sense of Sinfulness.** As we draw closer to Christ's Coming, our sense of sinfulness should increase. By that, I mean we should sorrow over the sin in our own lives and seek to turn from it; and we should groan over sin in our society and warn against it.

   A. **Think of John the Baptist.** In Matthew 3, he went out proclaiming, "Repent, for the kingdom of heaven is at hand!" He believed that God was about to do something very soon, that the coming of Christ was at hand. He urgently called people to repent, to take sin seriously and to deal with it.

   B. **Think of Isaiah.** In reading Isaiah 6, you clearly see that Isaiah's sense of urgency was tied to his sense of sinfulness. The nature of our culture is increasingly sinful; and when I recognize that we are sinful people in a generation of very sinful people, then we know that Jesus' Coming can't be far off.

3. **A Sense of Longing.** For generations, people have longed for Jesus to return. Nearly 500 years ago, Martin Luther wrote, "I hope that the day is near at hand when the advent of the great God will appear, for all things are everywhere boiling, burning, moving, falling, sinking, groaning."

   A. **Think of Nicodemus.** He was a religious man with a deep longing for the Messiah. When Jesus appeared, Nicodemus recognized that if Jesus was indeed the Messiah, he had to have a relationship with Him.

   B. **Think of Zacchaeus.** He was a political man, but he so longed for the Messiah that he climbed a tree to get a glimpse of Jesus.

4. **A Sense of Exclusivity.** The world is doing its best to exclude Jesus from its future. But when Christ comes back, He will return as the only Savior and Messiah this world has ever known. We need to live exclusively for Christ, and to recognize that His is an exclusive message. We live in a world of pluralism, in which people say, "Hey, look, anybody who wants to get to God can get to Him any way they want." But that's not what the Bible says (see 1 Kin. 8:60; Is. 45:3–5; John 14:6).

Conclusion: Are we living in the end times? Yes, we probably are. It looks like we are. World events are threatening on every side, but history is *His*-story, and He shall come again soon. Are you ready to meet Him? Are you prepared for the Lord to come today?

STATS, STORIES, AND MORE

➤ "Today's world has reached a stage that if it had been described to preceding centuries, it would have called forth the cry, 'This is the apocalypse!'" —Aleksandr Solzhenitsyn

➤ "We must never speak to simple, excitable people about the Day without emphasizing again and again the utter impossibility of prediction. We must try to show them that the impossibility is an essential part of the doctrine. If you do not believe our Lord's words, then why do you believe in His return at all? And if you do not believe them, must you not put away from you utter and forever any hope of dating that return?" —C. S. Lewis

➤ "Many times when I go to bed at night I think to myself that before I awaken Christ may come." —Billy Graham

A generation ago in Great Britain there was a bishop in the church who had a deep sense of longing for the Lord. Bishop Steed would get up every morning, go to his window, raise the shade, look out, and this is what he'd say: "Perhaps today. Perhaps today, Lord. I will be busy, but I will be ready." And then at night Bishop Steed would go to the window again before retiring and he would say, "Perhaps tonight, Lord. I will be asleep, but I will be ready. I will wake up when You come."

A tourist in Switzerland visited a beautiful mansion surrounded by well-kept gardens. "How long have you been the caretaker here?" he asked the gardener. The answer was twenty years. "How often does the owner of this property come here?" The answer was only four times in the twenty years. "And to think," said the guest, "you keep this property in superb shape just as though he might come tomorrow." The caretaker replied, "No, I look after these grounds as if I expected him to come today."

SUGGESTED ORDER OF WORSHIP

Prelude—Instrumental Group
CH 209 *This Is the Day*

Prayer of Worship—Pastoral Staff

Welcome—Pastoral Staff

Welcome Song (meet and greet)—Congregation
MSPW2 *The Name of the Lord*

Worship and Praise—Congregation
MSPW2 *Jesus, Your Name*
SPW *Jesus, Name Above All Names*
SPW *I Love You, Lord*
CH 79 *My Jesus, I Love Thee*

Offertory Prayer—Pastoral Staff

Offertory Praise—Praise Team
We've Come to Worship

Message—Pastor
Grace and Glory

Hymn of Response/Invitation—Congregation
CH 488 *Just As I Am*

Benediction Hymn—Congregation
MSPW 9 *Firm Foundation* (2x in F)

Postlude—Instrumental Group
This Is the Day

Additional Sermons and Lesson Ideas

SERIES: THE WAY OF THE DISCIPLE

The Marks of Discipleship

Date preached:

Based on a Sermon by J. J. Luce

Scripture: Matthew 26:69–73; Luke 14:26, 27

Introduction: Do people at your workplace or school know that you follow Jesus? A disciple of Christ should have two main characteristics:

1. Companionship with Christ (Matt. 26:69–73). These verses are often used to show Peter's failure. They also show us his faithfulness. Even when he denied being a follower of Christ, the servant girl didn't believe him. He was with Jesus (v. 69), and even his accent gave him away (v. 73)! Do people know without a doubt that we follow Christ? Is our life so centered around following Him that our companionship with Him is unmistakable?
2. Conformity to Christ (Luke 14:26–27). Jesus made the ultimate sacrifice for us on the Cross. Our lives should be marked by sacrifice for the gospel, by giving up our sinful desires to follow Christ, and by allowing the Holy Spirit to live in us and control us completely.

Conclusion: Draw near to Jesus and allow Him to conform you into His image.

Grace and Glory

Date preached:

By Rev. Charles Haddon Spurgeon

Scripture: Psalm 84:11

Introduction: God has two packages for us to open, both gifts given freely.

1. Grace. The Lord may not give gold or gain, but He will give grace. He may send trials, but He will give grace in proportion thereto.
   A. Sustaining Grace
   B. Strengthening Grace
   C. Sanctifying Grace
   D. Satisfying Grace
2. Glory. What an *and* is in this text! We do not need glory yet, but we shall have it in due order. After we have eaten the bread of grace, we shall drink the wine of glory.

Conclusion: These words *grace* and *glory* are enough to make us dance for joy. Grace now and, in a little while, glory forever!

SEPTEMBER 5, 2010

SUGGESTED SERMON

Strategic Planning

Date preached:

By Rev. Michael Easley

Scripture: Nehemiah 2:9–20, especially verse 18, "And I told them of the hand of my God which had been good upon me, and also of the king's words that he had spoken to me. So they said, 'Let us rise up and build.' Then they set their hands to this good work" (NKJV).

Introduction: God is calling us to be spiritual leaders. Whether it is in our home, church, workplace, or anywhere else, we are called to lead our lives in such a way that others want to follow. As leaders, we are called to be strategic planners, with God as our focus. Our passage today relays the story of Nehemiah and his leadership. Through his example, we can learn how to be God-centered, prepared leaders.

1. **The Welcome (vv. 9, 10).** Nehemiah and a small band of associates traveled under military escort. The entourage wasn't as much for protection as it was to impress onlookers with the obvious credentials and backing of the king. Nehemiah was welcomed with harsh opposition from Sanballat and Tobiah. Both these men were powerful and were related to the high priest's family (Neh. 13:4ff., 28). Extra-biblical sources confirm Sanballat was governor of Samaria and Tobiah was likely governor of Ammon. They were disturbed (v. 10) that Jerusalem might be restored, so these neighboring nations were hostile toward them. Hostility is a real part of leading a godly life and leading others in His ways. Are you facing hostility? At school, do others make fun of you for being in the youth group or for holding prayer meetings? Do your fellow workers scowl when you speak of the Lord? Has the enemy interfered with your daily time with the Lord? We are all faced with opposition when we follow the Lord. How do you face opposition?

2. **The Survey (vv. 11–16).** Upon arrival, Nehemiah did not rush into action, but rested for three days. Then, he covertly inspected the situation. Nehemiah said in these verses that he did not disclose his plans to anyone, not to the enemies nor to his fellow workers, until he had accurate information. His route is traced in these

verses. If seen on a map, this trek proved to be a thorough assessment of the city's condition. How often we as Christians run blindly into ministry, as if it is random or mindless! Jesus, when speaking about ministry, said, "What king, going to make war against another king, does not sit down first and consider whether he is able with ten thousand to meet him who comes against him with twenty thousand?" (Luke 14:31 NKJV).We are to be "wise as serpents and harmless as doves" (Matt. 10:16 NKJV).

3. **The Report (vv. 17, 18).** Nehemiah exposed the negative situation: the land was desolate and the gates were burned. Then he reported the positive, "And I told them of the hand of my God which had been good upon me, and also of the king's words that he had spoken to me" (v. 18). After the reminder of God's goodness, the people responded positively. Do we as God's people get discouraged too easily? We're to focus on God's promises and believe.

4. **The Opposition (vv. 19, 20).** Now a third enemy entered the picture, Geshem. Some scholars feel he was the most powerful of all the opponents. He and his son ruled a confederacy of Arabian tribes that were in control of Moab and Edom. Surrounded with opposition, Nehemiah's answer was, "The God of heaven Himself will prosper us; therefore we His servants will arise and build" (v. 20). Notice he did not say, "King Artaxerxes will wipe you out if you mess with us." No, his faith was in the God of heaven! He continued, telling them, "You have no heritage or right or memorial in Jerusalem" (v. 20). Imagine, Jerusalem was in rubble and yet he boasted that the Lord would fulfill His promise!

Conclusion: It's been said that God never gives His people tasks they can fulfill on their own. We will find ourselves in positions to glorify the Lord in such incredible ways that we don't believe they are possible. However, these are the very plans the Lord has for us. We will encounter hostility, we will have to survey and plan, and we will have to persuade others to continue in faith. If we, like Nehemiah, have an unshakable faith and commitment to God's promises, we will see incredible fulfillment, not only rebuilding a wall or a city, but also bringing nations to faith in Jesus Christ!

STATS, STORIES, AND MORE

More from Rev. Michael Easley

Nehemiah did not believe in a one-man ministry; he challenged the leaders of the remnant to work with him (not for him) in repairing the walls. What was the motive? "That we may no longer be a reproach" (v. 17). He was concerned with the glory of God as well as the good of the nation. However, as a leader in this ministry, certainly he faced battles as we will. At least four battles face every leader:

1. Battle with self: doubt, fear, impatience, etc.
2. Battle with the mission: concerns about impossibility, timetables, cost, etc.
3. Battle with those you will lead.
4. Battle with the enemy.

I often wonder if there is a sequential connection. The better I can overcome the battle with myself and my mission, the better I'll lead others and face the enemy. Or perhaps it is reversed: the better I lead others and face the enemy, the easier it will be to overcome my insecurities or doubts about God's mission for me. In any case, we should be ready for these battles and face them with faith. As we face opposition, as did Nehemiah, there is an important principle to remember: never forget God's faithfulness in your life. Nehemiah reported the tragedy (v. 17), but he quickly informed the leaders how God had made Him successful up to that point (v. 18).

My wife has reminded me of this more vividly than anyone has. She says, "Sure, we're going to struggle. Sure, we'll have sickness. Sure, we're going to watch our kids do some things we wish they wouldn't, but we must look back and remember the good hand of God in our lives and go forward in faith."

SUGGESTED ORDER OF WORSHIP

Strategic Planning

Prelude—Instrumental Group
My Life Is in You, Lord

Prayer of Worship—Pastoral Staff

Welcome—Pastoral Staff

Song of Welcome—Congregation (meet and greet)
12[a76] *The Name of the Lord* (vv. 1, 2, chorus, v. 3, tag in F)

SUGGESTED ORDER OF WORSHIP—*Continued*

Worship and Praise—Congregation
Firm Foundation (From *God in Us* Musical) (m 69–113 tag
111–113 2x)
MSPW2 85 *The Potter's Hand* (2x in G)
MSPW2 104 *There Is None Like You* (2x in G)

Testimony of Praise (2^{1}⁄$_{2}$-minute video on God's promise and
provision)

Offertory Prayer—Pastoral Staff

Offertory Praise—Trumpet Solo
A Mighty Fortress Is Our God

Prayer for the Worker (Pastor select persons to pray for the
following)
The Farmer and Our Food
The Industrial Worker
The Professional—Doctor, Lawyer, Accountant
The Teacher
Professional Ministry Staff

Song of Praise—Praise Team
The Power of His Love

Message—Pastor
Strategic Planning

Hymn of Response/Invitation—Congregation
CH 487 *Room at the Cross* (as needed)

Benediction Hymn—Congregation
CH 195 *Bless the Name of Jesus* (2x in C)

Postlude—Instrumental Group
Evermore

Additional Sermons and Lesson Ideas

SERIES: THE WAY OF THE DISCIPLE

A Taxing Decision

By Stuart Briscoe

Date preached:

Scripture: Matthew 9:9–13, especially verse 9

Introduction: The first Gospel was written by Matthew, whose other name, Levi, indicated he had a rich and godly heritage. But he had sadly strayed far from his roots. He was a tax collector, which doesn't mean he was an upstanding employee of the Internal Revenue Service. Israel was an occupied country, and the Israelites were required to pay taxes to Rome. To collect these taxes, the occupying Romans recruited turncoat Israelis as collaborators. They were told, "You can collect any amount of money you wish, just make sure we get our official share. Anything collected over that, you can keep for yourself." So the tax collectors were not only collaborators, but extortionists. They were utterly despised. One day Matthew was sitting in his tax booth on the main road through Capernaum. Imagine his surprise when along the busy thoroughfare came Jesus. Without apology or introduction, Jesus walked up and said with compelling urgency and irresistible authority, "Follow me." Matthew got up and left his booth and his business, and followed Christ. Now, there's little likelihood that when you're sitting at your office desk tomorrow morning Jesus will walk in, tap you on the shoulder, and say, "Quit your job and follow me." Yet He still invites us to be His disciples. His final instruction to the church was to make disciples. The call to discipleship stands to this day. What does that mean?

1. **He wants us to love Him.** He wants to draw us into a loving relationship. We love Him because He first loved us. How do I know Christ loved me? I look at the Cross.

2. **He wants us to trust Him.** In His love, He made certain promises, and on the basis of His promises it is possible for us to come to a point of trusting Him. Christ promised that if I commit my future to him, He will guard it, protect it, and guarantee it. This removes an enormous amount of stress and strain about the future.

3. **He wants us to obey Him.** He has also given certain commands and instructions. There are things we must be aware of, and we must get around to doing them.

4. **He wants us to abandon our former lives.** Matthew left all and followed Christ. This is a sticking point for many who are rather attracted to the Lord Jesus. They are attracted to the idea of having their sins forgiven and to the idea of going to heaven. What they don't find attractive is giving up and walking away from certain things. But have you ever noticed that some oak trees hang on to their old, dried-up leaves no matter how much snow and rain fall? But when springtime comes, without fuss or bother these leaves drop

off. Why? Because new life has begun to flow, and as the new life begins to flow in the branches and tendrils, the old things drop off. Don't concentrate on what you have to walk away from, concentrate on the new life, and the old things begin to drop away. That's what happened to Matthew.

5. **He wants us to share Him.** Almost immediately Matthew threw a big bash and invited his friends. Now his friends were from impolite society; the banquet was to introduce them to Jesus. Then at the end of Matthew 9, we read that Jesus saw a large crowd milling around, and He sensed a lostness about them, like sheep without a shepherd. Turning to His disciples, He said, "The harvest is very plentiful, but the laborers are few." He was impressing on His disciples the enormity of human need and the fact that the Lord of the Harvest wants to send people out to meet this need in His name. In Matthew 10, Matthew explains this in further detail, and he devoted the rest of his life to sharing Christ. He even became the writer of the first Gospel.

Conclusion: Christ is the *Lord* of the Harvest, and that means He must have charge of our lives. Some years ago, there was a man who used to drive with his little boy sitting on his lap. One day while driving along, the little boy grabbed the wheel. When the little fellow turned the wheel, he turned it the way the father didn't want it to go, and a wrestling match for the wheel began. They took a zigzag course down the road. I want to suggest that the person who grabs the wheel that the Lord of the Harvest is supposed to be holding will find his life taking a zigzag course and maybe ending in a wreck. But when the Lord of the Harvest is in the driver's seat, He takes very ordinary people like you and me—and Matthew—and uses us to do extraordinary things.

A Man to Mimic

Date preached:

By Dr. David Jeremiah

Scripture: Acts 7:54—8:1

Introduction: If you want a hero to mimic, consider Stephen:

1. His Conviction (v. 54)
2. His Confidence (v. 55)
3. His Courage (vv. 56–59)
   A. His Final Testimony (v. 56)
   B. His Final Trial (vv. 57, 58)
   C. His Final Triumph (v. 59)
4. His Coronation (v. 60)
5. His Contribution (v. 1) that led to Paul's conversion

Conclusion: Sometimes God allows persecution to motivate His church to do its rightful work. Let Stephen's example be your motivation and model for ministry.

SEPTEMBER 12, 2010

SUGGESTED SERMON

Bringing a Friend to Jesus

Date preached:

By Dr. Timothy Beougher

Scripture: Mark 2:1–17, especially verse 17, "Those who are well have no need of a physician, but those who are sick. I did not come to call the righteous, but sinners, to repentance" (NKJV).

Introduction: Have you ever tried to bring a friend to Jesus? It's a difficult task. Relationships can be strained, sacrifices must be made, and the risk of feeling like a failure is a constant deterrent. Our text teaches us that, despite what it may cost, Jesus came to save sinners, and we have a great responsibility to guide them to Him.

1. **Verses 1, 2**

   Jesus entered a house in Capernaum and before too long He attracted His usual crowds. Rather than turn them away, He preached the Word to them. The crowd quickly multiplied until no room was left for anyone to squeeze by.

2. **Verses 3, 4**

   The house had an external stairway leading to a flat roof. The roof was constructed by laying beams across the tops of the walls, with smaller sticks and reeds forming a patchwork across them. This was covered with some kind of matting and hardened earth, which the men broke through to lower their paralyzed friend into the house.

3. **Verse 5**

   Jesus saw their faith and forgave the paralytic's sins. He recognized that this man's physical need was far exceeded by the sickness of his soul.

4. **Verses 6, 7**

   The scribes viewed themselves as the guardians of acceptable religious teaching. They took offense at the words of Jesus and His claim that He had the authority to speak as God. To the scribes this was blasphemy; what could be more slanderous than for a man to speak as though He has authority that clearly belongs to God alone?

5. **Verses 8–11**

Jesus challenged their unbelief. The scribes reasoned in their hearts that Jesus could not have the power to forgive sins because they were convinced Jesus was not God. Jesus exhibited His authority to forgive by healing the man. In a sense, Jesus called their bluff. He acknowledged it was easy to say something one could not verify, so Jesus manifested His authority to forgive by releasing this man from his physical bondage. What was already done in the spiritual realm was now displayed in the physical realm.

6. **Verse 12**

The people were amazed and gave glory to God!

7. **Verses 13–17**

The previous verses show us a model of bringing others to Jesus. In these verses, Jesus is the model of One who reaches out to others. Jesus sought a disciple from among the tax collectors, viewed as one of the most wretched groups of sinners in the culture of that time. Levi followed Him! As it turned out, when Levi invited his Lord to his house, many more tax collectors and sinners showed up. The scribes and Pharisees opposed Jesus' ministry to this sinful segment of society and confronted Him. His response was, "Those who are well have no need of a physician, but those who are sick. I did not come to call the righteous, but sinners, to repentance" (Mark 2:17 NKJV).

Application: These stories teach us about bringing a friend to Jesus. While not every detail in this account can be made synonymous with bringing someone to Christ today, many can be! The person who owned the house in Capernaum allowed his resources to be used; he valued people over his possessions. When we minister to others, whether in our home or in church, we will have to sacrifice. The church is to be a hospital for sinners, not a museum for saints. People matter more than things! The scribes were critical like many of us are when others are unconventional or unorthodox. The friends of the paralytic were deeply concerned about their friend. They had a sense of urgency. Don't we all have friends who need the forgiveness of Jesus? Are we urgent about it? Are we afraid of how others will react, or perhaps of how Jesus will react to our efforts? Jesus did not react harshly to their bold efforts, but compassionately. We tend to think that we must come to Jesus once we are good enough, but as we see through Levi and the other tax collectors, Jesus did not come to call those who think they are righteous, but to call sinners to repentance. What sacrifices have you made to bring others to Jesus? Are you ministering with a sense of urgency, or are you simply criticizing others like the Pharisees? Jesus gave His life to save sinners like us; what are you doing to bring others to Him?

STATS, STORIES, AND MORE

More from Dr. Timothy Beougher:
As a challenge, I'd like to read portions of a letter Jeff West wrote: "You know me. I'm the fellow that takes care of your house when you go on vacation. Sometimes we cook out together on Saturday nights and the kids play in the yard. Our wives are good friends. They drink coffee together, trade recipes, and carpool the children. We are a lot alike, you and me. We want the best for our families. We determine to stand against adversity, to try, to persevere. But sometimes you seem to have more strength than I have.

"On Sunday morning I may be in the yard watering the grass and you drive by with your family, all of you dressed in your Sunday best, and you wave at me. And I wave back knowing where you are going but not why.

"Sometimes it seems that your life is different than mine. Our wives have talked about it, but you and I are scared to mention it. There's a lot about you that I don't know. There's emptiness in my life, a void that I just can't seem to fill, no matter how hard I try. I need desperately to be answered, to be comforted, to know. And I need someone to tell me.

"But we go on; and I don't mention it because some unknown fear prevents me, and you don't mention it because some unknown power binds you. We laugh together; we joke; we share, but not the important things. I'm your neighbor, and I don't know Jesus."

Bringing a Friend to Jesus

Call to Prayer and Worship—Pastor
(All men asked to come to front of church for group prayer
for service)

Prelude—Instrumentalist
Shout to the Lord

Call to Worship—Congregation
CH 344 *Amazing Grace* (vv. 1 and 2 in G)
CH 343 *Grace Greater Than Our Sin* (chorus, vi, chorus in G)
CH 344 *Amazing Grace* (mod v. 5 in Ab)

Welcome—Pastoral Staff

Recognition of Grandparents

Welcome Hymn—Pastoral Staff (meet and greet)
CH 5 *I Sing Praises* (2x in G, 2x in Ab)

Worship and Praise—Congregation
CH 44 *Crown Him King of Kings* (1x in Ab, 1x in A)
MSPW 22 *Crown Him King of Kings* (1x in Bb)
Shout to the Lord From *God for Us* (1x in Bb, 1x in C)
CH 222 *Lord, We Praise You* (4x in C)
CH 705 *It Is Well with My Soul* (1x in C, 1x in Db)

Offertory Prayer—Pastoral Staff

Offertory Praise—Choir, Solo, or Congregation
For Our Good (from G3 Music)

Message—Pastor
Jesus Will Be Your Friend

Hymn of Response/Invitation—Congregation
CH 481 *Come Just as You Are*

Benediction Hymn/Postlude—Congregation
SPW 100 *Bless the Name of Jesus*

Additional Sermons and Lesson Ideas

SERIES: THE WAY OF THE DISCIPLE

I Pledge Allegiance to Jesus Christ

Date preached:

By Rev. Richard Sharpe

Scripture: Various, especially Matthew 10:32

Introduction: When I was in seminary, one of the students was from Russia. The one thing that surprised her the most was that we had the American flag in our churches. She said that they would never have the Russian flag in their churches. We are so used to having our flag in our churches we don't even think about what it means. We say our pledge to the American flag in our churches because we believe that we are "one nation under God." That has changed over the years. It seems that America is trying to deny its Christian heritage. Can we still confess that we are "one nation under God," or should we take the American flag out of our churches? Where is our allegiance? The word "confess" means praise, acknowledge, agree, say the same thing, promise, or admit. When we study confession, we will realize that our allegiance needs to be to Jesus Christ. We need to give Him our full attention. Let's look at some verses that will help us realize these facts.

1. **I pledge allegiance to Jesus Christ as my savior (Rom. 10:9, 10; 1 John 4:15).** The first step in our personal life with Christ is to agree that we are sinners in need of a Savior. There are many who claim to be saviors in the world, but there is only one that is presented in the Word of God. That Savior is Jesus Christ. He died on the Cross for our sins. He was buried and then raised from the dead. No other religion can claim a risen Savior; their leaders are all still dead. We need to confess or agree with God that Jesus is the only way to heaven. We have to not only say it with our mouths, but we also have to believe it in our hearts for salvation to take place. If we believe it in our hearts, then we will pledge allegiance to Jesus Christ to everyone we meet. We will tell them that Jesus is the only Son of God who died on the cross for their sins and that they need to accept Him as their personal Savior. Our allegiance belongs to Jesus as our Savior.

2. **I pledge allegiance to Jesus Christ my shepherd (Ps. 23:1; John 10:9, 11).** Once we have Christ in our hearts, we can realize that He is the Shepherd of our lives. He leads us in the direction we need to go. He gives us a guidebook called the Bible. In His Word we find all we need to live the Christian life. However, we have to go to Him in prayer to understand His guidebook. The Holy Spirit, the third Person of the Trinity, was given to us at the point of salvation to help us understand His guidebook. The Holy Spirit indwells us, baptizes us, fills us, and seals us at the point of salvation. The passage in the Gospel of John informs us that Christ's sheep hear His voice and

listen. We need to be listening to our Savior's voice on a regular basis. That can only be done through a regular, daily meditation on the Word of God. As our Shepherd, Christ is by our side in every circumstance we face. Some of the problems we have are because of our own sins, but some are trials that are sent our way to make us more Christlike in the way we live. We need to enjoy our Shepherd on a daily basis and remember that He is always with us.

3. **I pledge allegiance to Jesus Christ my high priest (Heb. 2:17, 18; 3:1, 2; 4:14–16; 1 John 1:9).** Finally, once we have accepted God's gift of salvation, once we realize that we need daily instructions on how to live the Christian life, then we will also realize that we sin even after we have Christ in our lives. What are we to do with this sin? If all our sins are forgiven when we accept Christ as our Savior, why do we have to do anything about them? At the point of salvation all our sins, including all our future sins, were covered by the blood of the Lamb. That is justification. The Father looks at us through the blood of Jesus and sees only Jesus and none of our sins. That gives us access to heaven—only because of what Christ has done for us. First John 1:9 addresses the doctrine of sanctification. Sanctification is an ongoing process that ends when we die. During this process we are growing in grace and the knowledge of the Lord Jesus Christ. During this time we sin on a daily basis because we still have a tendency to sin that is not fully removed until after we die. We have to do something with our sins after salvation, so we can have daily fellowship with Christ. Our eternal life is settled. Our daily fellowship is in need of confession. John the apostle teaches us to confess our sins and that God is faithful to forgive us when we do. Jesus has been given the responsibility of being our High Priest. The responsibility of a High Priest was to go before the Father with a sacrifice to confess the sins of the people. Christ died on the cross and brings His blood to the Father so that we can have a continual relationship with Him. The blood only needs to be brought once. Our allegiance belongs to our High Priest!

Conclusion: Who has our allegiance on a daily basis? Is it Christ? Is it our money? Is it our possessions? Is it our jobs? Is it our family? We love our nation and we're thankful for our freedom. But the Bible says that our allegiance or confession needs to start with Jesus Christ. He is the author of our salvation. He is our Shepherd. He is our High Priest. If we start each day in a right relationship with Christ, then all the other things will fall into line. If we put other things in front of Christ, then everything will fall apart. The choice is ours.

Daring Determination

Date preached:

By Dr. Timothy Beougher

Scripture: Mark 2:1–5

Introduction: How important is it to you that your friends, family, or loved ones be saved? How committed are you to bringing them to Jesus? The friends of the paralytic in our text display how daring and determined we should be!

1. **They dared to do the difficult.** These men tried to push through an incredible crowd. Their failure didn't despair them: they burst through the roof to get their friend to Jesus!
2. **They dared to do the unorthodox.** Many had pushed through the crowd, yelled, or begged Jesus to heal them, but no one had torn through a roof and lowered someone down to Him!
3. **They dared to do the costly.** When they tore through the roof, they were taking the risk of having to pay for the damage, but their friend's salvation was worth it!

Conclusion: For these friends, it didn't matter that it was difficult, or unorthodox, or costly; they were desperate to bring their friend to Jesus. Are you allowing barriers to keep you from attempting to bring another person to Jesus?

SEPTEMBER 19, 2010

SERIES: BE AN ENCOURAGER   SUGGESTED SERMON

The Barnabas Secrets

Date preached:

By Stuart Briscoe

Scripture: Acts 11:24

Introduction: If we were to ask, "What should we look for in a leader?" some would say, "Well, a leader is someone who has the ability to identify what needs to be done, the ability to communicate vision, mobilize people, and get the project done." But others would point out that leadership is more than getting projects done. It is leading people to where they need to be in the formation of their character and in the development of their lives. That's what we see in the life of Barnabas. The wonderful thing about Barnabas is that he was not a Peter and he wasn't a Paul, nor are most of us. He moved quietly in the shadows and exerted a tremendous influence, and we can all do that.

1. **He was a good man.** Acts 11:24 says that Barnabas was a "good man." One day the Lord Jesus was confronted by a young ruler asking, "Good Master, how can I have eternal life?" Jesus replied, "Why do you call me good? There is none good, but one, and that is God." In Romans, Paul quoted approvingly of what Isaiah said, "There is none good." Yet here Barnabas is called "good." Is that a contradiction? When Barnabas is described as a good man, it means he was a man of solid moral and ethical principle. When it speaks of God alone being good, the Bible is referring to perfection. When it says that Barnabas was a good man, it doesn't mean he was perfect or sinless, but that he was a moral and ethical man who lived consistently by his principles. It is possible for an ordinary fallen human being who is less than perfect to learn how to develop a moral and ethical principle, and to live consistently according to it. Now, we know that Barnabas was a Levite, which means he was thoroughly familiar with the Old Testament. So his moral and ethical principles were biblically based. They originated from God's self-revelations, from God's character. So Barnabas was a good man in the sense that his life reflected the moral and ethical principles of God.

2. **He was full of the Holy Spirit.** Verse 24 also says he was full of the Holy Spirit. Scripture gives us a very succinct statement about being filled with the Holy Spirit in Ephesians 5:18, when it tells us not to be drunk with wine, but to be filled with the Spirit. There's an obvious rhythm there. We are not to be captivated and motivated and activated by alcohol, but we are to be captivated and motivated and activated by the Holy Spirit. It's one thing to be a moral and ethical person. It is an entirely different thing to be a moral and ethical person empowered by the Holy Spirit. By implication, Barnabas exercised his spiritual gift, and he exhibited the fruit of the Spirit as described in Galatians 5:22, 23. What kind of leader, then, should you be becoming? An ethical and moral person, high-principled, exercising your gifts and attitudes in the power of the Holy Spirit.

3. **He was full of faith.** He was also full of faith. That means two things. First, his mind was fixed on certain truths he had heard, evaluated, and embraced wholeheartedly. Second, his actions were based on those beliefs. For him, it wasn't just a cognitive belief but a daily experience. He lived in conscious enjoyment of the truths his mind had embraced.

Conclusion: These qualities so impressed people that they called Barnabas the "Son of Encouragement." His name was not really Barnabas, it was Joseph. But there was a fragrance about his life. He was an upbuilder. He was an uplifter. He was a renewer. He was a refresher. When he moved through an area, people would look at each other and say, "Wasn't it good to have him around!" So his friends said, "We're not going to call you Joseph any more, but Barnabas—the Son of Encouragement." That's the kind of person God wants us to be. We may not have the limelight, but we can walk and work quietly in the shadows, uplifting and encouraging others. We may not produce many Peters here, or many Pauls. But I would love to think that this church is a breeding ground for "Barnabi."

STATS, STORIES, AND MORE

Stuart Briscoe's Encourager

On my first trip to America in my early thirties, I spoke in Grand Rapids, Michigan, and a man came up to me. I had no idea who he was. Rather brusquely, he said, "That was a good talk, young man. I want it and eleven others like it in manuscript form on my desk in three months, and we'll publish it." He thrust a card into my hands; it said, "Pat J. Zondervan, Manager-Director, Zondervan Publishing Company." In those days Pat Zondervan was called "Mr. Christian Publisher."

Years later, I got a call from Pat Zondervan, and he said, "Stuart, I'm about to retire, and I'm spending my last few weeks traveling around the country saying goodbye to the authors I've introduced to Christian publishing, and you and Jill are two of them. Can I come and have dinner with you?" Now, Pat had written to me every month in the intervening years. A very brief letter each month, three paragraphs, and in the last paragraph he would always say, "As I was reading my Bible this morning, I thought of you and this is what I prayed for you." Every month for years, I got a letter like that from Pat Zondervan.

While we were having dinner, I said, "You have the most wonderful gift of encouragement, Pat." He looked startled and said, "What did you say?" I repeated, "You have the most wonderful gift of encouragement." His eyes filled with tears and he said, "Do you really think so? I don't know. No one ever told me!" There was a man about to retire who had spent his life in public ministry, and nobody ever encouraged him, the greatest encourager I ever knew. Can you think of what it would mean in people's lives if we actually got around to encouraging them?

Someone Said . . .

❧ Everybody can be great . . . because anybody can serve. You don't have to have a college degree to serve. You don't have to make your subject and verb agree to serve. You only need a heart full of grace, a soul generated by love.　　　　　—Martin Luther King, Jr.

Sons of Encouragement

Prelude

Call to Worship—Pastor/ Congregation
WH *Joyful, Joyful, We Adore Thee*

Worship Prayer—Pastoral Staff

Welcome—Pastoral Staff

Song of Welcome—Congregation (meet and greet)
CH 757 *Soon and Very Soon* (3x)

Worship and Praise—Congregation
MSPW2 93 *Rock of Ages* (2x in A)
MSPW 56 *Come, Now Is the Time to Worship* (2x in D)
MSPW 52 *Sanctuary* (1x in D, 1x in E)
MSPW 2 109 *He Knows My Name* (2x in E)

Testimony of Praise—Pastor's Choice (prefer a 2- to 3-minute video)

Offertory Prayer—Pastoral Staff

Offertory Praise—Congregation
MSPW 2 *Who Can Satisfy?*—Praise Team on Verses, Congregation on Chorus

Message—Pastor
Sons of Encouragement

Hymn of Response/Invitation—Congregation
CH 488 *Just as I Am*

Benediction Hymn
CH *I Love You, Lord* (2x)

Postlude

Additional Sermons and Lesson Ideas

SERIES: BE AN ENCOURAGER

Sons of Encouragement
By Stuart Briscoe

Date preached:

Scripture: Acts 4:36

Introduction: Character is what God knows you are. Reputation is what people think you are. There can be an enormous gap between these two, particularly in our culture where so much emphasis is placed on "image." The great thing about Barnabas is that his character and his reputation were very much in step. We see his influence in:

1. Encouraging the Church—Acts 4:32–37. There was a generous spirit about Barnabas. It's relatively easy to be a "taker," but what a joy to find a "giver."
2. Encouraging Someone Ostracized—Acts 9:26–32 and 11:25–30. Barnabas said, "Let's reach out to this guy, Saul of Tarsus, and love him into the kingdom."
3. Encouraging Someone Who Failed—Acts 15:36–31. Barnabas gave up traveling with the great apostle Paul in order to pour his life into this wobbly kid Mark.

Conclusion: If it hadn't been for Barnabas, we wouldn't have had Mark's Gospel or Paul's Epistles. Who can you encourage this week?

SERIES: BE AN ENCOURAGER

Encouraging Others
By Dr. Timothy Beougher

Date preached:

Scripture: 1 Thessalonians 3:1–8

Introduction: Discouragement is the occupational hazard of living today. How easily we become down in the dumps, stuck in the blues, carrying the weight of the world, cast down. The wind goes out of our sails, it rains on our parade, and our bubble bursts.

1. **The Need for Encouragement (vv. 1–5).** We need encouragement because of the *trials* of life, the *temptations* of Satan, and the *turmoil* of emotions.
2. **The Focus of Encouragement (vv. 3–8).** Notice here: *Spiritual truth, spiritual fruit, and spiritual stability.*
3. **The Practice of Encouragement (Heb. 3:13; 10:25).** We encourage others by listening, praying, being transparent, expressing appreciation, challenging others, and sharing God's Word.

Conclusion: One of the best ways to overcome discouragement is to focus on others. Who can you encourage this week?

SEPTEMBER 26, 2010

SERIES: THE CHURCH IS . . . . SUGGESTED SERMON

The Church Is Christ's Body

Date preached:

By Dr. Jerry Sutton

Scripture: Ephesians 1:22, 23

The apostle Paul's letter to the Ephesians presents a theological high watermark. One of its great themes is the exalted place of the church in the economy of God. Consider four images of the church provided for us by Paul.

The Church Is Christ's Body

Ephesians records nine references to the church as the body of Christ. The concept is introduced in 1:22, 23. Consider Paul's insights and their implications.

First, notice Paul's affirmation of Christ's ultimate authority. Paul tells us that the Father, at His own initiative, put all things in subjection under Jesus' feet. This is a clear declaration of Christ's cosmic rule. He is the ultimate and final authority over all that exists.

Is this not what Christ Himself affirmed in the Great Commission when He declared, "all authority has been given to me in heaven and on earth"? And is this not what Paul was explaining in Philippians 2:9–11 when he related that the Father has highly exalted Jesus and given Him a name above every other name?

Notice that Paul tells us the Father "put all things in subjection under His feet." That word *put* means that it is an accomplished fact, which can never be reversed. He is the ultimate authority for all that exists!

Second, notice the designation of Christ's functional headship. The Father also "gave Him as head over all this to the church." Again, this decisive act of the Father cannot and will not ever be reversed. Jesus Christ is head and ruler over the church! And it is not up for debate or discussion.

Paul's point is that the Lord Jesus owns the church, leads the church, gives directions to the church, and provides the church its operational and strategic marching orders. It is not the place of the church to dictate to the head, but the head to dictate to the church! Woe to any so-called believer who assumes this truth is optional!

Third, notice the revelation of the church's exalted relationships. Paul introduces us to the concept that the church is Christ's body. He is here teaching by analogy. He is telling us that what a head is to a physical body, so Christ is to the church. We have a vital, living, exalted relationship. The next phrase, "the fullness of Him who fills all in all," tells us that we as the church are the complement of the Lord Jesus. The world sees Him by seeing us. As the head expresses itself through its body, so Christ expresses Himself in this world through His body! What a profound and sobering thought.

Now, in short, since this is reality, what are the implications of the church being Christ's body? If you are a believer in Jesus Christ, you have a vital relationship with Him (1:22, 23; 5:23).

When you took that step of faith to receive Jesus Christ as your Lord and Savior, you entered into a relationship, which will never be taken away. You now have a Savior who loves you, cares for you, desires to mature you and use you to impact this world with His reality. He knows you better than you know yourself, and loves you with an uncompromising love. Yes, you have a vital relationship with Him. Let it grow!

You have a vital relationship will all other believers (2:16; 3:6). Paul feels compelled to let the Gentile believers at Ephesus know they are not second-class citizens in the Kingdom, nor do they need to take a back seat or secondary role to their Jewish brethren. He is quick to note that we are all members of one body. The Gentile believer now stands equal with the Jewish believers. We are all "fellow-heirs of Jesus Christ, fellow-members of His body, and fellow-partners of the promises in Christ Jesus." By the way, how are your relationships? Let them be strengthened!

You should have a healthy respect for the leadership Christ gives the church (4:12). Paul relates that leadership is not elected or selected but given. Their reasonability is to equip the saints (members of the body) for the work of service and to build up the body of Christ. Any time leadership is not respected, Chris is grieved and the work of God suffers. One mark of having a vital relationship with Jesus Christ is that you have a healthy respect for the leadership God gives His church! Follow the lead!

You have vital responsibility to help build and build up the church (4:16). Paul points out that each individual part of the body has a proper function and that working together, each member can contribute to the growth of the body. Paul points out that the church is to "build up itself in love." Does this not give each of us a dual obligation? Each of us has the vital reasonability of helping to build up and strengthen the church, while at the same time helping unbelievers come to faith in Christ. After all, the church is the only organization in the world which exists for these who are not yet members. Let's reach out and build His body!

SUGGESTED ORDER OF WORSHIP

Encouraging Others

Prelude—Instrumental Ensemble
Jesus Is All the World to Me

Call to Prayer—Pastor

Song of Worship—Congregation
CH 757 *Soon and Very Soon*

Prayer of Love and Worship—Pastoral Staff

Worship and Praise
CH 517 *I Will Sing of My Redeemer* (v. 1x, chorus 2x in G)
MSPW 52 *Sanctuary* (1x in D, 1x in E)
MSPW2 109 *He Knows My Name* (2x in E)

Scripture of Encouragement—Pastoral Staff
1 Thessalonians 3:1–8

Prayer for the Encouragers—Pastoral Staff

Praise and Worship—Congregation
CH 87 *Fairest Lord Jesus* (vv. 1 and 2)
CH 88 *More Precious Than Silver* (2x in F)
CH 191 *Father, I Adore You* (2x in F)
SPW 220 *You Are My All in All* (1x in F/1x in G)

Offertory Prayer—Pastoral Staff
Praise that God Is Our Encouragement

SUGGESTED ORDER OF WORSHIP—*Continued*

Offertory Praise—Congregation
CH 497 *I Will Praise Him* (chorus, v. 1, chorus, v. 3, chorus,
v. 4, chorus in D)
CH 401 *The Church's One Foundation* (2x in D, 1x in Eb)

Message—Pastor
Encouraging Others

Hymn of Invitation/Response—Congregation
CH 505 *He Touched Me*

Postlude—Instrumental Group
No Other Name

Additional Sermons and Lesson Ideas

Some Laws of Spiritual Work
Date preached:

Based on an outline by John A. Broadus

Scripture: John 4:32–38

Introduction: Ever grow tired of doing good? Jesus was faint in John 4, so the disciples went to purchase food. When they returned, they were astonished at the change in Him. He was sitting up, face animated, eyes kindled. He told them, "I have food to eat of which you do not know." From this passage with its images, we may discover several laws of spiritual work.

1. **Spiritual work is refreshing to soul and body (v. 34).** If we love spiritual work, it will kindle our souls.
2. **There are seasons of sowing and reaping in the spiritual sphere, just as in farming (v. 35).**
3. **Spiritual work links the workers in unity (v. 36).**
4. **Spiritual work has rich rewards (vv. 36–38).**

Conclusion: God will reward all we do, and all we try to do, and all we wish to do. O blessed God! He will be our reward forever and ever.

SERIES: DROP TO YOUR KNEES

Pray!
Date preached:

By Drew Wilkerson

Scripture: 1 John 5:14–15

Introduction: Abraham Lincoln wrote, "I have been driven many times to my knees by the overwhelming conviction that I had nowhere else to go. My wisdom, and all that about me, seemed insufficient for the day." Do you feel your prayers are connecting with God? If not, put John's counsel to work.

1. Be confident when you approach God (v. 14)
2. Ask anything you want of God (v. 14)
3. Seek to know if what you're asking for is the will of God (v. 14)
4. Believe that you are heard by God (v. 14)
5. Expect that your answer will come from God (v. 15)

Conclusion: Prayer is a relationship God wants to develop with His children. It needn't become stale or boring. All we need to do is be intentional and full of assurance. As much as we need to pray, God wants to answer our prayers.

OCTOBER 3, 2010

SERIES: THE CHURCH IS . . . SUGGESTED SERMON

The Church Is Christ's Beloved   *Date preached:*

By Dr. Jerry Sutton

Scripture: Ephesians 2:1–7, especially vv. 4, 5

A second image of the church found in Ephesians is that it is Christ's beloved. The assumption here is that God the Father, God the Son, and God the Spirit work together in absolute harmony, unity, and intention.

The image of the church as Christ's "Beloved" is a direct extension of 1:23, which identifies the church as the body of Christ. In the following seven verses, we find nine personal pronouns (*you, we,* and *us*) describing the church and its relationship to the Lord.

In this passage, however, the line is found in verse 4, which tells us "but God." Everything stops and revolves around that declaration, "but God"! No circumstance, condition, problem, difficulty, or even impossibility is a matter for this simple yet profound idea, "but God"! When Noah faced the flood all would have been loss, "but God"! When Abraham stood in the precipice of losing Isaac, "but God"! When Joseph could have reaped revenge, "but God"! When Moses faced the Red Sea in front and Pharaoh's army behind, "but God"! When David the shepherd boy faced Goliath, "but God"! When the world was lost and hell-bound, "but God"! No circumstance is a model for the truth contained in that one simple declaration, "but God."

Now consider four insights that help us understand the truth that the church is Christ's beloved! Paul tells us . . .

1. Who God is (v. 4).

When Moses fell on his face at the burning bush visitation, God revealed Himself as Yahweh or Jehovah, "I am who I am." I had a professor once who made the observation that this might well be translated, "I will be who I have been." In other words, God reveals His nature by His activity. Paul is saying the same thing.

God has expressed His nature. "He is rich in mercy!" Because of God's mercy, there is hope for the hopeless, there is cleansing from sin's curse, there is deliverance from the power of the demonic, and there is an escape from the tentacles of evil! God, Paul tells us, is rich and wealthy in mercy!

Not only has God expressed His nature, He has also allowed us to see the essence of His nature "because of His great love with which He loved us." Why does God act like He acts? Because of His love! Why is God so patient? Because of His love! Why is God kind? Because of His love! Why is God faithful? Because of His love! Why is God so merciful? Because of His love! It is the driving and continual attribute of God's nature!

Paul tells us that God's love is great and that God himself loves us! This love was demonstrated in the Father's willingness to send Christ to the cross and in Christ's willingness to endure the cross! And when Jesus went to the cross, Scripture tells us "The Father laid on Him the iniquity of us all"! As Paul testifies, "He who knew no sin became sin for us that we might be made the righteousness of God in Him" (2 Cor. 5:21). Here, Paul tells us who God is. He is the one who is driven by His unconditional, uncompromising, and unwavering love! And we are its object!

2. **Paul also tells us what we were (vv. 1–3).**
This is not a pretty picture. In rapid-fire strokes of a pen, Paul lays out the brutal facts. Here is what he says:

You were dead in your trespasses and sins (v. 1); you formerly walked according to Satan's direction (v. 2); and in line with Satan's sprit, which even now controls the disobedient (v. 2). Now Paul says all of us, himself included, were locked into this sin cursed trap.

We formerly lived controlled by the lusts of our flesh (v. 3), indulged the desires of the flesh (v. 3), and the desires of a darkened mind (v. 3).

In essence, Paul writes, "we were by nature children of wrath (deserving God's wrath), even as the rest "of lost humanity"! But God! We would have stayed that way, but God acted. He demonstrated His rich mercy! Why? Because of His great love for us! In short, we are His beloved! We are the objects of His great love. That's who we were because that is who God is!

3. **Now Paul tells us what God did (vv. 5, 6).**
Even when we were dead in our trespasses and sins, He made us alive together with Christ. That is God's supernatural intervention! Paul tells us that God made us alive, raised us up, and seated us

with Christ in heavenly places in Christ Jesus. Here is the Lord Jesus in Heaven and He says, "I want you to come sit next to Me!" What a powerful thought! Friend, this Paul tells us what God's grace does at its greatest. Grace loved us, extended mercy to us, convicted us, drew us to Christ, and in its completion brought salvation!

Yet, if you are like me, you tend to see yourself in all of your shortcomings, failures, sins, habits, and mess. And you ask yourself the question, *Why would God do all that?* Why would God take a sinful people, save them, clean them up, make them brand new and bring them into His family and declare that they are His beloved?

4. **Paul tells us why God did it (v. 7).**
Paul tells us that God did all of this "in order that in the ages to come He might show the surpassing riches of His grace in kindness toward us in Christ Jesus." In short, God says, "I did all this so you will know who I am and what is in My heart." At the core of the supernatural heart that governs the entire universe is a flawless, unlimited heart of love! And this great God says, "You, church, are My beloved!"

Epaphras—The Man Who Prayed

Prelude—Instrumental Group
MSPW 41 *You're Worthy of My Praise*

Prayer

Baptismal Celebration & Prayer

Song of Worship—Congregation
MSPW2 88 *Holy Spirit, Rain Down*

Song of Worship—Solo
I Know My Redeemer Lives

Welcome

Song of Welcome—Congregation (meet and greet)
MSPW 41 *You're Worthy of My Praise*

Praise and Worship
MSPW 42 *We Sing Worthy* (2x in G, 1x in Ab)
SPW 248 *O Come, Let Us Adore Him* (1x in A with tag)

Season of Prayer for Repentance and Restoration
MSPW 19 *Shine on Us* (1x in C, 1x in F)
CH 389 *Spirit of the Living God* (1x in F)

Message—Pastor
Epaphras, the Man Who Prayed

Hymn of Repentance/Invitation—Congregation
SPW *I Love You, Lord*

Postlude—Congregation
CH 5 *I Sing Praise*

Additional Sermons and Lesson Ideas

SERIES: KINGDOM WORKERS

Kingdom Workers: Part One

Date preached:

By Dr. Timothy Beougher

Scripture: 1 Corinthians 3:5–9

Introduction: Throughout history there have been many occupations with different titles used to describe these vocations. There is one title that God has given to every single believer—"Kingdom Worker."

1. The description of kingdom workers (v. 5a).
2. The ministry of kingdom workers (v. 5b).
3. The individuality of kingdom workers (v. 5c).
4. The focus of kingdom workers (vv. 6–7, 9).
5. The unity of kingdom workers (vv. 8, 9a).
6. The reward of kingdom workers (v. 8b).

Conclusion: Are you doing your part? All believers are called to be kingdom workers, to build the kingdom of God (Eph. 2:19–22).

SERIES: DROP TO YOUR KNEES

Epaphras—The Man Who Prayed

Date preached:

By Dr. David Jeremiah

Scripture: Colossians 1:7 and 4:12

Introduction: Paul used two phrases to describe Epaphras. In Colossians 1:7 he was Paul's "dear fellow-servant," and in Colossians 4:12, he is described as "a bondservant." We can learn much from him, especially about prayer. He teaches us:

1. To be persistent in our ministry (Col. 1:7). He was faithful.
2. To be precise in our communication (Col. 1:8). Paul had never been to Colosse, yet he knew all about the church from Epaphras.
3. To be passionate in our prayer (Col. 4:12, 13). We are to pray faithfully ("always"), fiercely ("laboring"), fervently ("fervently"), factually ("that they might stand perfect and complete in the will of God").
4. To be particular about our people (Col. 4:13). He was zealous for the Colossians.

Conclusion: What would happen if we would all pray for our church as this man prayed for his?

OCTOBER 10, 2010

SERIES: THE CHURCH IS . . . .   SUGGESTED SERMON

The Church Is Christ's Building   *Date preached:*

By Dr. Jerry Sutton

Scripture: Ephesians 2:11–22, particularly vv. 19–22

How many times have you heard people refer to the church as a building? "I am going down to the church." "Look at that magnificent church." "Remember when we built the church?" All too often, people live with a misconception that the church is simply bricks and mortar. Some people are in love with their building. What is sad is that people, good people, place their loyalty and confidence in the wrong place. Interestingly enough, the church is a building, but not exactly like we tend to imagine it. Consider, again, what the apostle Paul teaches us about the church.

Never forget that the church is people, people in relationship with Jesus Christ, first, and with each other, second. To be in the church means you are connected to a family, a community of faith. Paul loves writing about the church. He never gets tired of helping believers grasp the connection between the church and the Lord. As he continues his insights into the church, consider his counsel.

1. **Remember where you were (vv. 11, 12).**
    Twice Paul uses the word "remember." In essence, he is telling us, "don't forget where you were before coming to Jesus Christ." You were "Gentiles." You were of the "uncircumcised." You were "separate from Christ." You were "excluded from the commonwealth of Israel." You were "strangers to the covenants of promise." You had "no hope because you were without God in the world"! You were an outsider, remember?

    The truth of the matter is those without Christ are in that same condition today—outsiders whom God wants to make insiders! Paul wants us to remember where we were, where we started before Christ! Next, Paul wants us to . . .

2. **Be reminded of where you are (vv. 13–18).**
    The turning point of this text is the first two words of verse 13, "But

now." Picking up on that word "formerly" (v. 11), Paul says, "But now in Christ Jesus you who formerly were far off have been brought near by the blood of Christ." Here Paul points us clearly to the cross as God's place of reconciliation. We were brought near!

Paul further tells us that because of the cross, we are now reconciled not only to God but also Jewish to Gentile believer. Paul speaks of Jesus being our peace, of Him making both groups one, of Him breaking down the barriers, of Him establishing one new man, of Him bringing peace!

Paul then reminds us that, "through Him [Jesus], we both [Jew and Gentile believer] have our access in one Spirit to the Father." That word, "access," was used to describe the solemn approach one is given into the presence of deity or royalty. It is a gift, and it is ours.

So here, Paul reminds us that we have been brought near, we have been reconciled and we have access, and it's all because of Jesus! From this urging for us to remember where we were formerly and this reminder of where we are presently, Paul now tells us to . . .

3. **Rejoice in who you are (vv. 19–22).**
Paul introduces this section with the words, "so then." This is one word in our Greek text and points to either a consequence or a conclusion. He tells the Gentile believers in Ephesus that they are "no longer strangers and aliens, but you are fellow-citizens with the saints, and are of God's household." You who were outsiders are now insiders! You who were lost are now saved! You who were not in God's family are now in God's family! What an incredible truth!

At this point, Paul shifts his language to use building metaphors. Yes, the church is a "building," but not bricks and mortar! He uses words like "built upon," "foundation," "cornerstone," "the whole building," "fitted together," "growing," "holy temple" and "the dwelling." Paul's assertion is that the church, the people in relationship with the Father on the basis of Christ's work on the cross, are a building of God. It is figurative language, but it communicates God's revelation of the church as a spiritual building. Review what Paul said in 1 Corinthians 3:16 and 6:19 and what Peter wrote in 1 Peter 2:4–8.

Consider, now the building's foundation (v. 20). Paul tells us that this spiritual building is built upon the foundation of the apostles and prophets with Christ being the cornerstone. Everything, Paul writes eventually, is built upon Jesus and his finished work at the cross! Apostles are important, and prophets are important, but Jesus the ultimate foundation is absolutely essential. Individually or collectively without the foundation of a relationship to Jesus Christ we are in a precarious position. Jesus is the foundation!

Next, Paul addresses not just the foundation, but also the building's fabrication (vv. 21, 22a). Paul tells us that in Jesus (or upon Jesus) the whole building is being "fitted together"—made to fit together just right. Every stone, every port, every person, has their appropriate place in this building! Paul continues by saying that it is growing and expanding into a holy temple in the Lord. There, he tells the Ephesian believers, "You also are being built together." Paul tells them, this is God's work to make you part of His building. You, Paul says, are being built together! Then Paul concludes by detailing.

Lastly, Paul declares the building's final destination (v.22b). "You," Paul writes, "are being built together into a dwelling of God in the Spirit." The purpose of a building is for it to be lived in. And Paul tells these Ephesian believers as he tells us today, you (individually) and you (collectively), you are the place where God dwells on earth. He lives inside and among His people. You are Christ's Building!

Drop to Your Knees

Prelude—Instrumentalist
Shout to the Lord

Call to Prayer—Pastoral Staff

Worship and Praise—Congregation
CH 510 *Heaven Came Down*
CH 508 *Love Lifted Me*

Welcome—Congregation

Song of Welcome—Congregation (meet and greet)
MSWP *Rock of Ages* (2x in D)

Worship and Praise—Congregation
MPW 51 *Step by Step* (2x in G)
CH 44 *Grace Greater Than Our Sin*
MPW2 100 *Grace Alone* (2x in C)

Offertory Prayer—Pastoral Staff

Offertory Praise—Congregation
MPW2 115 *When It's All Been Said and Done*

Message—Pastor
Praying with a Purpose

Hymn of Repentance/Invitation—Congregation
CH 583 *My All in All*

Benediction Hymn—Congregation
SPW 123 *Because He Lives* (1x in G, 1x in Ab)

Postlude—Instrumental Group
MSPW *Rock of Ages* (2x in D)

Additional Sermons and Lesson Ideas

SERIES: KINGDOM WORKERS

Kingdom Workers: Part Two

Date preached:

By Dr. Timothy Beougher

Scripture: 1 Corinthians 3:10–15

Introduction: In 1 Corinthians 3:5–9, Paul described working in the kingdom through the use of agricultural metaphors. In verses 10–15 he turned to the world of construction, as he pictured the church being built as an edifice with God as the divine Architect and with every believer working on the construction crew.

1. Recognize the foundation of kingdom ministry (vv. 10, 11).
2. Build on the foundation carefully (vv. 10b, 11–12).
3. Reflect on the testing of your labors (vv. 13–15).

Conclusion: "And behold, I am coming quickly, and My reward is with Me, to give to every one according to his work" (Rev. 22:12).

SERIES: DROP TO YOUR KNEES

Praying with a Purpose

Date preached:

By Rev. Kevin Riggs

Scripture: Philippians 1:1–11

Introduction: A person can withstand almost anything if he or she knows they are not alone. Each local church is a community of believers. We have God as our Father, and each of us as brothers and sisters. One of the best ways we can build relationships with each other is by praying for one another.

1. **Pray for love to increase (v. 9).** The word translated *abound* was also used to describe a flower going from a bud to full bloom.
2. **Pray for wisdom (v. 10).**
3. **Pray for fruit (v. 11).** The "fruit of righteousness" refers to good works, living a life that is consistent with what you say you believe.

Conclusion: Apply this message to your lives this week by partnering with another believer. As you pray, pray their love will increase, pray they will receive wisdom, and pray their lives will produce fruit.

OCTOBER 17, 2010

SERIES: THE CHURCH IS . . . . SUGGESTED SERMON

The Church Is Christ's Bride

Date preached:

By Dr. Jerry Sutton

Scripture: Ephesians 5:22–33

By the time we arrive in chapter 5 of Ephesians, we find Paul addressing practical Christian living. Yet even in his instruction on how the life is lived, the concept of church is rarely far from his mind.

In verses 15–18, Paul lays out four assignments for every Christian: Be careful how you walk (v. 15), make the most of your time (v. 16), understand God's will (v. 17) and live the Spirit-filled life (v. 18). He then points out the arenas where these assignments play out in life, how we speak to each other (v. 19), how we speak to the Lord (v. 20), and how we relate to each other (v. 21ff).

At this point, Paul focuses in on the husband-wife relationship. Yet the concept of church is never far from his conscious thought. In fact, Paul confesses in v. 32, "The mystery is great, but I am speaking with reference to Christ and the church," even as he discusses the Lord's expectations for husband-wife relationships.

Notice how six times in this passage (vv. 23–33), Paul uses the word "church," twice he refers to the church as Christ's body, and five times he uses pronouns (*she* or *her*) to refer to the church. So, in speaking of the husband-wife relationship, Paul makes thirteen references to the church. It is clear in the mind of Paul that the church is Christ's bride! This is the same concept found in Revelation 21:9, where John quotes, "Come here, I will show you the bride, the wife of the lamb." So, if the church is Christ's bride, what does Paul teach us about this relationship? Consider how Christ the bridegroom relates with His bride.

1. **Consider first Christ's identity (vv. 23, 30).**
   Paul points out that Christ as the husband or bridegroom is both the head of the church and the Savior of the body (v. 23). He then reiterates in verse 30, that we, collectively, are members of His body. As head, Jesus provides authority and gives direction. As the Savior, He is the deliver, protector and provider. Jesus is to the church what husbands are to their wives (or their brides). That's who He is!

2. **Consider second Christ's activity (vv. 25, 29).**

When we examine Paul's assessment of Jesus' role as husband, we find decisive actions. First, Paul tells us that Christ loved the church. Of course, this picks up a previous theme that the church is the object of Christ's affection. We are His beloved. But more than simply being the objects of His love, we are in a covenant relationship with Him. Christ loved the church and keeps on loving it!

Second, Paul tells us that love acted. Christ gave Himself. This, of course, refers to His sacrificial death on the cross. We can give without loving, but we cannot love without giving! And Christ expressed His love by giving Himself sacrificially and absolutely. Love held nothing back. Christ gave until he had nothing else to give.

Third, Paul tells us in verse 30 that Christ "nourishes" the church. This idea denotes the whole process of an ongoing maturing process. And finally Paul tells us that Christ "cherishes" the church. Here, Paul reminds us that Jesus Christ has a deep and tender affection for His bride! It is great to be loved!

So, here we see Christ, His love, and the resulting activity motivated by love! And at this point, Paul relates where all of this is going.

3. **Consider lastly Christ's intention (vv. 26, 27, 33).**

Four times in this passage, Paul uses what we call a purpose clause. In short, Paul is saying, this is where this leads, this is what Christ wants to accomplish, this is why Christ did what He did for His bride.

1. Christ did all this that He might *sanctify the church*. This means He worked to make her pure and clean. His desire is to remove the stain of sin, the stain of worldliness, and the stain of the flesh. Paul points out that we are cleansed "by the washing of water with the word." "Word" here is *thema*, the appropriated, obeyed Word of God.

2. Christ did all this that He might *present* to Himself the church in all her *glory* (v. 27a). In God's timetable, a day has been marked on God's eternal calendar, when the church will realize all of its fruitlessness, failures and shortcomings. All defects will be removed, and God Himself will present a glorious church, the Bride of Christ!

3. Christ did all this that the church might be *holy* and *blameless* (v. 27b). Not only has corruption been removed but now virtue is affirmed. This church is holy. And this church is blameless in the sight of Almighty God!

4. Lastly, Christ did all this that the church might respect Him (v. 33). This word is actually different from the earlier mandate that

the church should be subject to Christ (v. 24). It actually is our word for "fear." It denotes a reverent respect. This expresses itself in being submissive.

Just as it is easier for a wife to be submissive to a husband who loves her unconditionally, so too the church is to be subject to and live in reverence toward Christ because of His great love. When we consider Christ's love, its consequent activity and its ultimate intentions, certainly we can rejoice that we have been called to be the bride of Christ!

SUGGESTED ORDER OF WORSHIP

Drop to Your Knees

Prelude—Instrumentalist
We Bring a Sacrifice of Praise

Prayer of Worship—Pastoral Staff

Welcome—Pastoral Staff

Song of Welcome (meet and greet)—Congregation
CH 212/213 *We Bring the Sacrifice* (2x in D)
CH 214 *He Has Made Me Glad* (2x in D, 1x in Eb)

Reading of Scripture—*Psalm 19**—Pastoral Staff

---

*Psalm 19
For the director of music. A psalm of David.
1 The heavens declare the glory of God; the skies proclaim the work of his hands.
2 Day after day they pour forth speech; night after night they display knowledge.
3 There is no speech or language where their voice is not heard.
4 Their voice goes out into all the earth, their words to the ends of the world.
In the heavens he has pitched a tent for the sun,
5 which is like a bridegroom coming forth from his pavilion, like a champion rejoicing to run his course.
6 It rises at one end of the heavens and makes its circuit to the other; nothing is hidden from its heat.
7 The law of the Lord is perfect, reviving the soul.
The statutes of the Lord are trustworthy, making wise the simple.
8 The precepts of the Lord are right, giving joy to the heart.
The commands of the LORD are radiant, giving light to the eyes.
9 The fear of the Lord is pure, enduring forever.
The ordinances of the Lord are sure and altogether righteous.

(continued on next page)

Songs of Worship and Praise—Congregation*
  CH 53/54 *My Tribute* (2x in Bb)
  CH 55 *Bless His Holy Name* (2x in Eb)
  CH 56 *To God Be the Glory* (v. 1 and chorus in G, chorus 1x
    in Ab)

Video Testimony on Repentence and Restoration
  (http://www.wingclips.com/cart.php?target=category&
  category_id=289)

Worship and Praise—Congregation
  CH 308 *There Is a Redeemer* (3 verses and choruses)
  SPW—*Something Beautiful* (1x)
  SPW—*We Will Glorify* (2x)

Message—Pastor
  God's Prayer Requests

Hymn of Repentence/Invitation—Congregation
  CH *I Need Thee Every Hour*

Postlude—Instrumental Group
  The Heavens Declare

---

¹*Continued from previous page*
10 They are more precious than gold, than much pure gold;
they are sweeter than honey, than honey from the comb.
11 By them is your servant warned; in keeping them there is great reward.
12 Who can discern his errors? Forgive my hidden faults.
13 Keep your servant also from willful sins; may they not rule over me.
Then will I be blameless, innocent of great transgression.
14 May the words of my mouth and the meditation of my heart be pleasing in your sight,
O Lord, my Rock and my Redeemer.

Additional Sermons and Lesson Ideas

SERIES: KINGDOM WORKERS

Kingdom Workers: Part Three
By Dr. Timothy Beougher

Date preached:

Scripture: 1 Corinthians 3:16–23

Introduction: Have you ever been driving when all the sudden a sign catches your eye: "WARNING, left lane closed 500 feet ahead!" If you don't take heed, you're headed for a crash. In this section Paul gives three warnings to kingdom workers, three caution signs, three things we need to avoid.

1. **Damaging behavior (vv. 16, 17).** We are to build up, not tear down. Are you seeking to build up?
2. **Deceptive attitudes (vv. 18–20).** Are you marching to the drumbeat of this world, or are you allowing God's Word to transform your way of thinking?
3. **Misplaced devotion (vv. 21–23).** Are you rejoicing in all that you have in Jesus Christ?

Conclusion: As God's kingdom workers, we should heed His warnings and commit ourselves to His Word.

SERIES: DROP TO YOUR KNEES

Pray for Us
By Rev. Todd M. Kinde

Date preached:

Scripture: 2 Thessalonians 3:1–5

Introduction: Here is a guide for praying for one another and for our church.

1. **Pray for the propagation of the gospel (v. 1).** When we gather we are to pray that the gospel would go forth. The picture is of a runner carrying a message across a battlefield; we're to pray for rapid advance of the gospel.
2. **Pray for the protection of the church (vv. 2, 3).** Paul asked for boldness to speak the truth. Our fear in evangelism is normal, but we should pray for boldness and protection.
3. **Pray for the perseverance of the saints (vv. 4, 5).** We want to have a good start, but how important to finish well (1 Cor. 9:24)!

Conclusion: As we gather for our prayer meetings may they be characterized by these kinds of prayers.

OCTOBER 24, 2010

LORD'S SUPPER SERMON   SUGGESTED SERMON

Remembering the
Unforgettable

Date preached:

By Dr. Kent Spann

Scripture: 1 Corinthians 11:23–26

This sermon consists of two sermonettes, each preached before receiving one of the elements of the Lord's Supper.

Introduction: Have you ever forgotten something, I mean forgotten something very important? After stopping for gas in Montgomery, Alabama, a fellow by the name of Sam drove more than five hours before noticing he had left someone behind—his wife. So at the next town he asked the police to help get him in touch with her. Then Sam called his wife to tell her he was on his way back. He admitted with great embarrassment that he just hadn't noticed her absence.

If you tend to forget you are not alone. Everyone does at one time or another, according to Karen Bolla, a Johns Hopkins researcher. These are the things people most often forget:

- Names—83%
- Where something is—60%
- Telephone numbers—57%
- Words—53%
- What was said—49%
- Faces—42%
- What you just did—38%

Because we are so forgetful a whole industry has been created—Post-it notes, Franklin management materials, Day-Runners, and even a piece of string around one's finger.

The Lord knew that we are prone to forgetfulness as well, so He provided a reminder for us.

The Lord's Supper reminds us of the unforgettable.

1. **The bread, which symbolizes His body, reminds us of the unforgettable (11:23, 24).**

   The bread that we will receive today is a reminder, a reminder of his body.

   In Moscow's Red Square is a building called the Lenin Mausoleum. In that building are the remains of Lenin, the founder and first leader of the Soviet Union, who died in 1924. His body is housed in a glass coffin. The room is kept at a constant 61 degrees to preserve his remains. It serves as a reminder to all Russians of the founder of the Great Revolution. In sum it was an idol erected in memory of the founder of modern Communism and Socialism.

   Jesus didn't call His disciples to remember Him by preserving His body, and I am glad because it would become an icon, an idol men would worship. What He did do was give us a reminder of His body through the element of the bread. We don't have to go to a tomb; instead, as we receive the bread, we remember His body.

   But what are we to remember as we think of His body?

   A. The bread reminds us that Christ identified with us (John 1:14; Phil. 2:7, 8).

      (1) Christ identified with us in His incarnation.

      (2) Christ identified with us in His servanthood.

      (3) Christ identified with us in His death (Heb. 2:14–17).
         a. He didn't come to live, He came to die.
         b. He didn't come to die for Himself, but He came to die for us.

   B. The bread reminds us that Christ suffered for us (Is. 53). Why then did He suffer?

      (1) He suffered because of our sin.

      (2) He suffered because of His choice (John 10:18).

   C. The bread reminds us that He loves us (John 15:13).

Distribute and partake of the bread.

After they partook of the bread as a reminder of His incarnation, His servanthood, and His death, He then gave them another reminder.

2. **The cup, which symbolizes His blood, reminds us of the unforgettable (11:25, 26).**

A. The cup reminds us that God is holy.

The holiness of God uniquely describes Him and is the sum of all His other attributes. The holiness of God tells us that God is perfect, that He is separate from all He has created, and that there is no other remotely like Him. As Holy God he never sins, does wrong, or tolerates wrong. *He is absolutely perfect!*

Throughout the Bible, we catch glimpses of His holiness. We catch a glimpse of it when the children of Israel stood at the foot of Mount Sinai. We catch a glimpse of it in the Tabernacle that God had the people build. We catch a glimpse of it in Isaiah's encounter with the holiness of God in Isaiah 6.

But all of these pale in comparison to the glimpse we get of God's holiness in the cup. Nothing reminds us more of the holiness of God than this cup. His holiness demands that a price be paid for sin.

Hebrews 9:22 says there has to be the shedding of blood. In the Old Testament, the blood of lambs and goats was shed, but in the New Testament it was the blood of His own Son. So holy is God that it meant the death of His one and only Son to pay in full our sin debt.

B. The cup reminds us that Christ is righteous (Heb. 9:11–14).

C. The cup reminds us that Christ established a new covenant (Heb. 8:7–13; Jer. 31:31–34).

D. The cup reminds us of Christ's return (Matt. 26:29).

Distribute and partake of the cup.

Conclusion: The Lord's Supper reminds us of the unforgettable!

SUGGESTED ORDER OF WORSHIP

The Lord's Supper*

Prelude—Instrumental Group
Nothing But the Blood

Welcome and Prayer—Pastoral Staff

Praise and Worship
CH 107 *Lord, I Lift Your Name on High* (2x in G)
CH 307/308 *There Is a Redeemer* (vv. 1 and 2 in D)
MSPW *The Wonderful Cross*

Message—Pastor
The Reason for Communion

Communion

Breaking of the Bread

Scripture Reading—Pastor
*The Lord Jesus on the same night in which He was betrayed took
bread; and when He had given thanks, He broke it and said, "Take,
eat; this is My body which is broken for you; do this in remembrance
of Me."*

Song—*Broken and Spilled Out** Solo or with Congregation
on Chorus
(Deacons distribute bread during song followed by prayer)

---

*1 Corinthians 11:23–29 NKJV

23 For I received from the Lord that which I also delivered to you: that the Lord Jesus on the same night in which He was betrayed took bread; 24 and when He had given thanks, He broke it and said, "Take, eat; this is My body which is broken for you; do this in remembrance of Me." 25 In the same manner He also took the cup after supper, saying, "This cup is the new covenant in My blood. This do, as often as you drink it, in remembrance of Me." 26 For as often as you eat this bread and drink this cup, you proclaim the Lord's death till He comes. 27 Therefore whoever eats this bread or drinks this cup of the Lord in an unworthy manner will be guilty of the body and blood of the Lord. 28 But let a man examine himself, and so let him eat of the bread and drink of the cup. 29 For he who eats and drinks in an unworthy manner eats and drinks judgment to himself, not discerning the Lord's body.

*"Broken and Spilled Out" Written by Gloria Gaither and Bill George—Available through Praise Gathering Music, Alexandria, IN.

Prayer of Commitment—Deacon
    Congregation—all take the bread

Sharing of the Cup
    Scripture Reading—Pastor
The Lord Jesus on the same night in which He was betrayed also took the cup after supper, saying, "This cup is the new covenant in My blood. This do, as often as you drink it, in remembrance of Me."

    Song—Solo *Via Della Rosa* or congregation CH *Jesus Paid It All*
    (Deacons distribute element during song followed by prayer)
    Prayer of Commitment—Deacon
    Congregation: All take the cup.

    Reading by Pastor—Pastor
Jesus told his disciples, "This is my blood." This blood shed became God's new covenant poured out for all people of all generations—for the forgiveness of sins. At the conclusion of the sharing of the bread and cup, Jesus led the disciples in a hymn. Let's sing together . . .

    Song of Worship—Congregation
        CH 311 *Hallelujah, What a Savior** (vv. 1 and 4 in Bb, v. 5 in C, chorus 2x)
    Offertory Prayer—Pastoral Staff
    Offertory Praise—Congregation
        SPW—*Wonderful, Merciful Savior*** (2x)
    Hymn of Benediction—Congregation
        MPW 22 *Crown Him King of Kings* (1x in A)

    Postlude—MPW 22 *Crown Him King of Kings* (1x in A)

---

*Via Della Rosa available through Brentwood-Benson Music, Nashville, Tennessee
**Other songs appropriate for use: The Power of the Cross By Keith and Kristen Getty or In Christ Alone by Stewart Townsend and Keith Getty

Additional Sermons and Lesson Ideas

SERIES: KINGDOM WORKERS

Kingdom Workers: Part Four

Date preached:

By Dr. Timothy Beougher

Scripture: 1 Corinthians 4:1–5

Introduction: In the previous verses Paul discussed our role as workers in God's kingdom; in this section he shares three significant insights about how we are to live and minister.

    1. Our privilege: We are servants of Christ (v. 1).
    2. Our responsibility: To prove faithful (v. 2).
    3. Our evaluation: Performed by God (vv. 3–5).

Conclusion: The Lord has privileged us to be His servants here on earth, so let's take very seriously our responsibility to be faithful to what He has called us, for God Himself will evaluate every one of us.

SERIES: DROP TO YOUR KNEES

God's Prayer Requests

Date preached:

By Robert Morgan

Scripture: Various passages

Introduction: If the Lord Himself spoke audibly at one of our meetings, what prayer requests would He share? Scripture gives several, but somehow these are the requests we often neglect.

    1. "Pray for the peace of Jerusalem" (Ps. 122:6). We must pray for a resolution of the conflict in the Middle East.
    2. "For all men, for kings and all who are in authority" (1 Tim. 2:1–4). The apostles evangelized during the *Pax Romana,* a time of peace that allowed the gospel to spread quickly. Paul wanted those conditions to continue. We must pray that the gospel will be unhindered by war and conflict.
    3. "Pray for those who spitefully use you and persecute you" (Matt. 5:44). We must pray for our enemies, for those persecuting the church today.
    4. "Pray the Lord of the harvest to send out laborers into His harvest" (Matt. 9:37, 38).
    5. "Pray for one another, that you may be healed" (James 5:15).

Conclusion: God forbid that we should pray about everything except what He Himself has commanded us to remember.

OCTOBER 31, 2010

SERIES: KNOW THY ENEMY   SUGGESTED SERMON

When Satan Attacks You

(A Sermon Classic, originally titled "Satan Considering *Date preached:*
the Saints," preached April 9, 1865)

By Rev. Charles Haddon Spurgeon

Scripture: Job 1:1–12, especially verse 8

Introduction: How foolish to lay up treasures anywhere except in heaven! Job's prosperity appeared to give him much stability in life. He had around him a large household of servants. He had accumulated a kind of wealth that does not suddenly depreciate. His children were numerous enough to promise a long line of descendants. Yet beyond the clouds where no human could see, the spirit of evil stood before God, and an extraordinary conversation took place. Satan challenged God over Job, and the Lord gave permission to remove Job's supports and see whether the tower would stand in its own inherent strength. The Lord said to Satan, "Have you considered my servant Job?"

1. **How does Satan consider us?**

   A. **He considers us a marvel.** When Satan finds Christians faithful to God, he considers it a phenomenon.

   B. **He considers us to detect any flaw in us.** How he chuckles over our secret sins. Each sin born in the believer's heart cries to him, "My father! My father!" and, seeing his foul offspring, he feels something like the joy of fatherhood.

   C. **He considers us barriers to the progress of his kingdom.** He's aware that mournful Christians often dishonor the faithfulness of God by mistrusting it, and he thinks if he can worry us until we doubt the goodness of the Lord, he will have robbed God of His praise.

2. **What does Satan consider about us?** Satan isn't omniscient, but after thousands of years dealing with fallen humanity, he has acquired vast experience. He knows what the springs of human action are, and how to play on them.

A. **Satan considers our peculiar infirmities.** He looks us up and down like a horse-dealer, reckoning us heel to head, so that he will say of one, "His infirmity is lust," or of another, "She has a quick temper," or, "He is proud," or, "She is lazy."

B. **He considers our state of mind.** The devil knows when we're most vulnerable, and we're often overtaken through an unwatchful frame of mind.

C. **He considers our friends.** Among some people I can scarcely sin; among others I can scarcely remain pure. Satan knows this and tempts us accordingly.

D. **He considers our condition in the world.** He has different temptations for various people. I don't suppose the Queen's temptations ever likely annoy Mary, the kitchen-maid. On the other hand, Mary's temptations may never trouble me. Our position, capabilities, education, or standing in society may all be doors through which he attacks.

E. **He considers our objects of affection.** By blowing down the house where his children were feasting, Satan sought to derange Job's mind; he later used Job's wife.

3. **A higher consideration overrode Satan's consideration.** Satan was mining, and he intended to light the fuse to blow up God's building. All the time God was *under*mining him, planning to blow up Satan's mine before he could do any mischief. The devil is the greatest of all fools. He has more knowledge but less wisdom than any other creature. He didn't know that while he was tempting Job, he was answering God's purpose.

A. **The Lord considered exactly how far to let Satan go.** God says, "Thus far, and no farther."

B. **The Lord considered how to sustain His servant under trial.** God poured secret oil upon Job's fire of grace while the devil was throwing buckets of water on it.

C. **The Lord considered how to sanctify Job by this trial.** Job was a better man at the end of the story than at the beginning, and God gave him twice the property he had before. He made him a more famous man, whose name will ring through the ages. Instead of influencing a handful in one neighborhood, Job has touched all of history. The devil went to the forge and worked away with all his might—to make Job illustrious! Foolish devil! When he attacks us, he's piling up a pedestal on which God will set us as displays of His grace to all ages.

Conclusion: If you want to make the devil angry, throw the story of Job at him. Oh, how many saints have been comforted by this history of patience! Let us commit ourselves in faith to the care and keeping of God—come poverty, sickness, or death. Through Jesus Christ's blood we will be conquerors, and more than conquerors. May those who have not trusted Jesus be led to begin this very morning, and God shall have all the praise in us all, evermore.

STATS, STORIES, AND MORE

Quotes from Spurgeon's Actual Sermon

Where he cannot destroy, there is no doubt that Satan's object is to worry. He does not like to see God's people happy. Martin Luther used to say, "Let us sing psalms and spite the devil," and I have no doubt Martin Luther was pretty nearly right; for that lover of discord hates harmonious, joyous praise.

Oh may God grant us grace as a church to stand against the wiles of Satan and his attacks, that having done his worst he may gain no advantage over us, and after having considered, and considered again, and counted well our towers and bulwarks, he may be compelled to retire because his battering rams cannot jar so much as a stone from our ramparts, and his slings cannot slay one single soldier on the walls.

As the worker in metals knows that one metal is to be worked at such a heat, and another at a different temperature; as those who have to deal with chemicals know that at a certain heat one fluid will boil, while another reaches the boiling-point much earlier, so Satan knows exactly the temperature at which to work us to his purpose. Small pots boil directly when they are put on the fire, and so little men of quick temper are soon in a passion; larger vessels require more time and coal before they will boil, but when they do boil, it is a boil indeed, not soon forgotten or abated. The enemy, like a fisherman, watches his fish, adapts his bait to his prey; and knows in what seasons and times the fish are most likely to bite.

Satan Is OK, but Jesus Isn't

According to Charisma news service, Kaimuki High School in Honolulu has dropped a ban on clothing and accessories that promote Satanism after a protest from a member of the staff who belongs to the church of Satan. Students are now free to wear t-shirts that promote the devil. But a crucifix got Kimberly Draper in trouble in Logan County, Kentucky. She was fired for continuing to wear a cross necklace to her job at the local library, despite warnings she was violating a dress code banning religious decoration.

Baptismal Celebration

Prelude—Instrumental Group
CH 209 *This Is the Day*

Prayer of Worship—Pastoral Staff

Call to Worship—Congregation
CH 391 *Sweet, Sweet Spirit* (1x solo, 1x congregation)

Baptismal Celebration—Pastoral Staff
(Keyboard play during actual baptism service. Congregation sing chorus of "Now I Belong to Jesus" as the candidate is being brought out of the water and next candidate enters.)

Prayer of Dedication—Pastor

Welcome—Pastoral Staff

Welcome Song (meet and greet)—Congregation
SPW 1 *We Bring a Sacrifice of Praise* (1x in D, 1x in Eb)

Praise and Worship—Congregation
CH 344 *Grace Greater than Our Sin*
MSPW2 100 *Grace Alone* (2x in C)
MSPW2 106 *I Come to the Cross* (2x in F)

Prayer of Praise—Pastoral Staff
CH 340 *Turn Your Eyes Upon Jesus* (2x)

Message—Pastor

Hymn of Response/Invitation—Congregation
CH 506 *I'd Rather Have Jesus*
CH 757 *Soon and Very Soon*—Congregation

Postlude—Congregation
CH *I Will Call Upon the Lord*

Parent-Child Dedication
(This Optional Service may be an independent program or part of the previous order.)

(Pastor introduces as each set of parents, child, and any other family members and they walk in front of the church. After all family sets enter and are introduced to the congregation, the scripture is read, the charge is given, parents and friends respond, the pastor prays, and during the time families exit, the children song is sung as a solo.)

Introduction of Service—Pastor

We've met today for the purpose of presenting our children to the Lord. In I Samuel we find the story of a mother that God blessed with a little baby boy. This was a special son because God had given him to this family in direct response to Hannah's request for a child. Now, when he is approximately 3 years of age, Hannah comes to the High Priest, child in tow, and says, "The Lord answered my prayer and gave [this boy] to me. Now I give him back to the Lord. He will belong to the Lord all his life" (1 Sam. 1:27). After she gave her child back to God, she and her family stayed at the House of the Lord and worshiped.

So, today we come to give back to the Lord our children. In a few minutes, I will read a scripture from Deuteronomy 6:1–9. This command was for all the families to meet every day for the purpose of teaching God's ways diligently to their children. There were three kinds of groups here: 1) the children; for us, it is the group being dedicated; 2) the family; for us that refers to the mothers and fathers, grandparents and relatives; and, 3) the church family; yes, we too have a responsibility to teach our children, to talk of God's wonders every day, and to exhort our most cherished gifts in the ways of the Lord.

Each Family Set is introduced: parents, child, grandparents, etc.

Scripture Reading and Comments*—*Deuteronomy 6:1–9*—
Pastor

---

1 "Now this is the commandment, and these are the statutes and judgments which the LORD your God has commanded to teach you, that you may observe them in the land which you are crossing over to possess, 2 that you may fear the LORD your God, to keep all His statutes and His commandments which I command you, you and your son and your

(continued on next page)

Our promises today are taken from this passage of scripture. We will dedicate ourselves to God and renew our commitment to teach our children with diligence, dedication, and determination. We will talk of God's statutes and precepts throughout the day and share with our children the many wonders of God.

Dedication, Charge, and Commitment

Dedication Charge of Parents: *(Parents please repeat after pastor.) We hereby promise to faithfully teach and train our child in all the ways of the Lord. We promise to faithfully honor His Word and promote His Work. We promise to encourage spiritual growth through personal example of God's graces in daily living.*

Dedication Charge of Grandparents and Relatives: *(Please repeat after pastor.) We hereby promise to faithfully teach and train our child in all the ways of the Lord. We promise to faithfully honor His Word and promote His Work. We promise to encourage spiritual growth through personal example of God's graces in daily living*

Dedication and Commitment of Child: *(Parents please repeat after the pastor.) We give back to the Lord this child. We promise to encourage our child to know and love God with all their heart, soul, mind, spirit, and strength. We want God to take our child and use him/her for His Glory, Honor and Praise. We promise to love our child by being an example of His grace in our own daily living.*

(Continued from previous page)

grandson, all the days of your life, and that your days may be prolonged. *3* Therefore hear, O Israel, and be careful to observe it, that it may be well with you, and that you may multiply greatly as the LORD God of your fathers has promised you—'a land flowing with milk and honey.' *4* "Hear, O Israel: The LORD our God, the LORD is one! *5* You shall love the LORD your God with all your heart, with all your soul, and with all your strength. *6* "And these words which I command you today shall be in your heart. *7* You shall teach them diligently to your children, and shall talk of them when you sit in your house, when you walk by the way, when you lie down, and when you rise up. *8* You shall bind them as a sign on your hand, and they shall be as frontlets between your eyes. *9* You shall write them on the doorposts of your house and on your gates. *Deuteronomy 6:1–9 NKJV*

SUGGESTED ORDER OF WORSHIP—*Continued*

Commitment from the Congregation: *(Pastor turns to the congregation and says, "Please repeat after me.") As a congregation of friends, we promise to support this family. We promise to pray for them. We promise to encourage them as they seek to nurture and guide this child in all the ways of the Lord.*

Pastor says to Parents, Relatives, and Congregation: And, all God's People said, "Amen." (Everyone repeats, "Amen.")

Prayer of Dedication

Pastor—*Thank you for this moment in time. Thank you for these promises and commitments. We do give this child back to you for your use in your Kingdom at your desire and for your purposes. Please bring this child to a saving knowledge of your self at an early age. May they walk with you. May they talk to you. May they remember you when they when they sit in their homes, when they lie down, when they rise up. May they think of you all throughout the day. Give us wisdom as parents, extended family and a congregation to know how to encourage, exhort and edify this child at every part of their journey with you. In Jesus' name we pray. Amen.*

Song of Dedication—Vocal Soloist
CH 261 *Away in a Manger* (Cradle Song) (vv. 2 and 3)
(Families exit during the singing of the solo)

Hymn of Benediction—Congregation
CH 583 *You Are My All in All*

Prelude—Instrumental Group
CH 588 *All for Jesus*

Additional Sermons and Lesson Ideas

SERIES: KNOW THY ENEMY

Dealing with Satan's Strategy: Part 1

By Pastor J. David Hoke

Date preached:

Scripture: Various

Introduction: Do you feel like everywhere you turn there is another temptation? Does it seem like there's always an opportunity to make a quick and sinful decision? We learn in Genesis 3 that Satan is crafty. He often makes sneak attacks rather than head-on assaults. I want to share two short messages on how to deal with his strategy as we learn from Scripture.

1. **Understand the source (James 1:13, 14).** God does not tempt us in any way.
2. **Understand the power (James 1:14).** The word in verse 14 for "enticed" is a fishing term for throwing out bait; Satan and our own evil desires "bait" the hook of sin to make it look harmless and appetizing.
3. **Understand the escape (1 Cor. 10:13).** No temptation is irresistible to the Christian. Christ in us is the way of escaping temptation!

Conclusion: God always provides a way to escape temptation in His grace. Keep your eyes fixed on Him.

SERIES: KNOW THY ENEMY

Dealing with Satan's Strategy: Part 2

By Pastor J. David Hoke

Date preached:

Scripture: Various

Introduction: We often see and feel the effects of Satan's strategy to draw us into sin through the world and through ourselves. Understanding the source, the power, and the escape of Satan's strategy, we should also look at five ways to handle temptation as given in Scripture.

1. **We must be aware of his strategy (2 Cor. 2:11).** Don't be caught off guard; Satan is crafty and will trick you any way he can.
2. **We must anticipate his attacks (1 Pet. 5:8).** Don't allow the enemy to implement a surprise attack. Guard yourself in Christ at all times.
3. **We must guard our minds (2 Cor. 11:3; 1 Peter 1:13; Rom. 12:2).**
4. **We must know our limitations (1 Cor. 1:12, 13).** Know your limitations and stay away from tempting situations.
5. **We must depend on God's resources (2 Cor. 10:3–5).**

Conclusion: The next time Satan mounts an attack against you, see it for what it is and refuse to be fooled by his trickery. Instead, take your stand against him (Eph. 6:11).

NOVEMBER 7, 2010

SERIES: COME HOLY SPIRIT SUGGESTED SERMON

Symbols of the Holy Spirit

Date preached:

By Jack W. Hayford

Scripture: Mark 1:1–11, especially verses 9 and 10

Introduction: Like a Master Teacher, the Lord uses object lessons and symbols to help us visualize the reality of His truth. When it comes to God Himself, symbols were never intended to be little artistic ideas about Him, but ways in which the reality of the invisible might penetrate the visible, helping us see and know Him better. This morning, in looking at seven biblical symbols of the Holy Spirit, the purpose is not just to study objective theology, but also to allow Him to subjectively penetrate our hearts. In other words, when we say that the Holy Spirit is like rain, the purpose isn't thinking, "Oh! The Spirit is like rain." The purpose is to get wet! The Spirit's main job is to glorify Christ—to help us see Christ more, obey better, and love Him more deeply.

1. **The Holy Spirit comes as rain.** Refreshing us where there has been dryness and barrenness (Joel 2:23–29) and restoring us where there has been loss (Is. 28:11, 12). The "pouring out" Peter refers to at Pentecost (Acts 2:17) is not an abstract use of the word; it has to do with "latter rain" that brought about the hastening of the harvest and fruitful crops. When the lawn goes through a long hot day, it dries up and needs refreshing rain. The Spirit comes to bring refreshing and restoration.

2. **The Holy Spirit comes as rivers.** Rivers are channels or conduits to places where refreshing water is needed. In John 7:37–39, Jesus promised the Holy Spirit would flow as "rivers of living water" after His Ascension. The Lord wants you to become an overflowing tributary of His Spirit's fullness to others.

3. **The Holy Spirit comes as wind.** The Spirit, coming as wind, depicts His power and guidance. When Jesus told Nicodemus about the new birth (John 3:8), He told him that the work of the Spirit in a person's life was like a gentle wisp of a breeze. You can't see where

it comes from or where it goes, but we can attest to times when God has come and dealt with us, and no human being knew how it happened.

4. **The Holy Spirit comes as oil.** The anointing, the oil of Scripture, is directly related to the Spirit's work in our life (2 Cor. 1:21, 22). The Holy Spirit's anointing makes us sensitive (1 John 2:20) and gives us wisdom in the practicals of everyday life. All the primary offices of Scripture involve anointing:

   A. **Prophets:** We are to speak the Word of the Lord, and the Spirit gives us words of comfort, exhortation, and counsel for others.

   B. **Priests:** The Lord wants to anoint us so that our worship doesn't become stale, habitual, or formal.

   C. **Kings:** It takes fresh anointing from the Spirit for the authority of His life to happen through us so we can move in confidence in ruling and managing our homes, business, and relationships. The Lord also wants to anoint us with the oil of rejoicing when we have been overcome by the spirit of mourning.

5. **The Holy Spirit comes as wine.** We are not disallowed from enjoying a number of things in life, but you can find out how much we're living the Jesus-life by how much we need the stimulants of the world. God has given the Spirit as wine (Eph. 5:18). In the Gospels, Jesus described the new work of God, conveyed by the Spirit, as new wine coming into old vessels.

6. **The Holy Spirit comes as fire.** The Holy Spirit comes as fire to probe the inner recesses of life and to refine us as gold is refined in the fire (Is. 4). He wants to enflame us with a passion for His work (Acts 2:3).

7. **The Holy Spirit comes as a dove.** The dove is gentle and a symbol of peace. The Spirit wants to rest upon you—not just sweeping throughout the world as a tidal wave of revival, but He wants to come to you personally.

Conclusion: For the next week, take one symbol of the Holy Spirit each day and invite Him to minister the richness of the Spirit to you. Ask Him to:

- Pour **rain** on you.
- Open **rivers** in you.
- Breathe **wind** in your life.
- Anoint you with **oil.**
- Fill you with holy **wine.**
- Refine and temper you with **fire.**
- Send the Holy Spirit to come to you as a **dove.**

STATS, STORIES, AND MORE

Burned Ropes
When the three Hebrew children were thrown into the furnace, not only were their lives spared, their clothes didn't burn. But the ropes holding them in bondage burned. By the "spirit of judgment"—or deliverance—"and burning" the Holy Spirit burns away the binding things that the enemy has imposed on us. —Jack Hayford

The Theology of the Spirit
The Father is made of none, neither created nor begotten. The Son is of the Father alone, not made, nor created, but begotten. The Holy Spirit is of the Father and the Son: not made, nor created, nor begotten, but proceeding. —The Athanasian Creed

God Is Light
God is light and in Him is no darkness at all. We know the Godhead consists of Three Persons: the Father, the Son, and the Holy Spirit. The Father corresponds to the chemical rays of sunlight; No man hath seen God at any time. The Son, who is the light of the world, corresponds to the light rays, the One whom we can see but not feel. The Holy Spirit corresponds to the heat rays, since He is felt in the lives of believers but never seen. —M. R. DeHaan, in *The Chemistry of the Blood*

Spotlight
In his book, *Life in the Spirit,* Robertson McQuilkin writes: "Imagine the following: the President of the United States comes to speak at your local high school auditorium. The band strikes up "Hail to the Chief" as the president strides to the microphone. The spotlight follows his every step. Suddenly the crowd, as one, rises and—what's this? They turn their backs to the stage and, pointing to the balcony, erupt in applause for the fine performance of the spotlight operator! Absurd? Of course, but it illustrates a truth about the Spirit. The Spirit glorifies—shines the spotlight on—the Son."

Holy Spirit Living

Prelude—Instrumentalists
CH 401 *The Church's One Foundation*

Announcements—Pastoral Staff

Worship in Prayer—Pastoral Staff

Worship and Praise—Congregation
PW 52 *I Will Sing of the Mercies* (2x in D)
CH 139 *Great Is Thy Faithfulness* (vv. 1 and 3 in C, D, chorus in Eb)

Welcome—Pastoral Staff

Song of Welcome—Congregation (meet and greet)
CH 107 *Lord, I Lift Your Name on High* (2x in G)

Worship and Praise—Congregation
MSPW2 88 *Holy Spirit, Rain Down* (2x in G)
MSPW2 85 *The Potter's Hand* (2x in G)
MSPW2 102 *Be Unto Your Name* (2x in C)
MSPW2 71 *The Heart of Worship* (2x in C)

Offertory Prayer—Pastoral Staff

Offertory Praise—Congregation
CH 10 *Majesty* (1x in Bb)
CH 147 *How Great Thou Art* (chorus only)

Message—Pastor
A Neglected Corner (Eph 1:13, 14; 4:30; 2 Cor 1:21, 22; 2 Cor 5:5)

Hymn of Response/Invitation—Congregation
MSPW2 109 *He Knows My Name*

Benediction Hymn—Congregation
SPW 123 *Because He Lives*

Postlude—Instrumentalists
CH 195 *Bless the Name of Jesus* (2x in C)

Additional Sermons and Lesson Ideas

SERIES: COME HOLY SPIRIT

Spirit Filled

Date preached:

By Dr. Larry Osborne

Scripture: Ephesians 5:15–20, especially verse 18

Introduction: Those of you here today who have been Christians for a long time will realize that I am not covering every detail of the Holy Spirit. Those of you who are newer Christians may feel somewhat overwhelmed. The Holy Spirit is too vast of a topic for us to cover in one sermon, so let's look at some basics of the Holy Spirit and then some practical applications.

1. **Who is the Holy Spirit and what does He do?**
   A. **He's God (Acts 5:3, 4).** This passage equates lying to the Holy Spirit with lying to God Himself. A word of advice: take this as a simple truth and don't get too hung up on trying to completely grasp the idea of the Trinity. We live in a three-dimensional world and this is a fourth-dimensional spiritual truth (Deut. 29:29).
   B. **The Spirit is the source of all spiritual knowledge and power.** Jesus, just before going to the Cross, spoke to His disciples about the Spirit whom He would send. He told them the Spirit would bring truth. The disciples were grieved that Jesus would leave them, but Jesus told them it was better that He go and the Holy Spirit come (John 14:12, 15–18; 16:5–15). When Jesus was with them, they had the Spirit *with* them. When the Spirit came at Pentecost, the Spirit was then *in* them, never to leave (Acts 1:8).
   C. **He has always been the same.** The Holy Spirit has always been the source of any act of spiritual knowledge and power in any human being. The miracles of Christ were many of the same miracles done by the Old Testament prophets (1 Kin. 17—2 Kin. 13:20). Only after His being baptized with the Holy Spirit (Matt. 3:16) did Jesus really begin His earthly public ministry.
2. **How do we get the Holy Spirit and what is it to be filled?**
   A. **We receive the Spirit when we choose to follow Jesus.** Paul taught that we were sealed with the Holy Spirit when we came to Christ (Eph. 1:13, 14). In Romans, he tells Christians that they are not controlled by the sinful nature, but by the Spirit; if we don't have the Spirit, we are not true believers (Rom. 8:9).
   B. **Filled simply means "controlled by."** For many people, being filled with the Holy Spirit means being weird: fainting "in the spirit," being manic for God, or acting outlandish. This definition is simply not scriptural. The Greek word for "being filled" means to be controlled by (Eph. 5:18; Gal. 2:20; 5:16, 22–25). Paul contrasts being filled with alcohol, which controls a person's actions

when he's drunk, with being filled with the Spirit, who controls us when we're filled! This can come through inner spiritual prompting, or simply reading and obeying a Scripture verse.

3. **How does the Spirit guide and change us from the inside out?**

 A. **Sometimes it's spectacular, most often it's subtle.** Elijah, after experiencing the spectacular work of the Spirit, is threatened by the queen. He runs away and hides in a cave, discouraged and complaining to God. God tells him to go outside the cave and that God would, in some physical way, interact with Elijah. Elijah went out and saw fire, an earthquake, and powerful wind, none of which were the interaction God spoke of. Finally, Elijah heard a still small voice, the whisper of God (1 Kin. 19:11–13). God taught Elijah that the Spirit isn't only in the big things.

 B. **We're all unique and so is our relationship with the Holy Spirit.** We do not have a special formula to follow, nor do we need to simply mimic every detail of others' relationship to the Spirit. We need to allow Him to be God and expect a unique relationship to fit our own unique personality and circumstances (see Luke 7:31–35; 1 Cor. 12:1–27; Rom. 12:3–8).

 C. **To be filled with the Spirit, we need to follow the Spirit (Eph. 5:18; Gal. 5:16–23; Prov. 4:18).** This principle is so simple, and yet the most practical. The things you know are of the Spirit, do!

 D. **To hear the Spirit, we need to stop and listen.** Why don't many Christians understand what it's like to have God guide them? We run our lives so fast, we never stop to listen (see 2 Tim. 3:16–17; Ps. 119:105; Prov. 8:34; 12:15).

Conclusion: If you're a follower, the Spirit is in you, but you've got to listen to what He says and do it!

SERIES: COME HOLY SPIRIT
A Neglected Corner
Date preached:
By Robert Morgan

Scripture: Ephesians 1:13–14; 4:30; 2 Corinthians 1:21–22; and 2 Corinthians 5:5

Introduction: The "sealing" of the Holy Spirit is a neglected corner of truth, but it is important enough to be mentioned four times in Scripture.
In antiquity people used seals to authenticate documents (Jer. 32:10), and archaeologists have discovered more than 1,200 seals from Old Testament times. In trusting Christ as Savior, we are marked with a seal, the Holy Spirit. This is:

 1. **A Mark of Ownership:** Buyers of timber in the forests of Asia Minor would select trees which would be felled, stamped them with the

buyer's seal, and floated them downstream. At the port in Ephesus, the markings would identify the logs. God stamps us with His seal, indicating ownership.

2. **An Imprint of Identity:** In biblical times, everyone's unique seal, when pressed into wax, imprinted his identity. Charles Wesley wrote in "Hark! The Herald Angels Sing": "Adam's likeness now efface; Stamp Thine image in its place."

3. **A Bond of Security:** Both Daniel's lions' den and Christ's tomb were sealed by royal decree. When we come to Christ, we are sealed with the Holy Spirit, implying security.

4. **A Deposit of Inheritance:** The Holy Spirit's presence in our heart is a down payment on the future blessings, like a child who has inherited a fortune but until he comes of age lives on an allotted amount.

Conclusion: The presence of the Holy Spirit within Christians is one of our greatest comforts and strengths.

NOVEMBER 14, 2010

SUGGESTED SERMON

Shaking Off Discouragement

Date preached:

By Stuart Briscoe

Scripture: Haggai 2, especially verse 4, "'Yet now be strong, Zerubbabel,' says the LORD; 'and be strong, Joshua, son of Jehozadak, the high priest; and be strong, all you people of the land,' says the LORD, 'and work; for I am with you,' says the LORD of hosts."

Background: Haggai appeared on the scene in Jerusalem in 520 B.C. That was a critical time in the history of Jerusalem, because approximately seventy years earlier the city had been devastated, the temple had been destroyed, and the inhabitants had been in exile. Eventually through an edict of Cyrus, the Persian king, a Jewish remnant was allowed to return to Israel, intent on re-establishing the worship of Jehovah. They started off very well, but then ran into discouraging opposition; and for eighteen years the work on restoring the temple and restoring the worship in the temple had ceased. That's when Haggai arrived. He reminded the people that whilst the temple of the Lord was being neglected, they had spent a lot of time on their own houses. He explained in chapter 1 that the hard times they were experiencing were directly related to the spiritually impoverished lives they were living. The people were very responsive, and they got to work, assured that the Lord was with them as they went about the work on His house. That is the essence of Haggai, chapter 1. Now, as we move into chapter 2, we find this dated very specifically (2:1)—October 17, 520 B.C. This is less than a month after they had set to work with a will, but their enthusiasm had drained away again, their energies had dissipated, and once again they were becoming discouraged. People *do* need an awful lot of encouragement. If we're not being continually renewed and refreshed and reminded, it's easy to slip into a low-grade attitude and to slide into a kind of spiritual depression. That's why it is so important that we constantly hear the Word of the Lord.

1. **The Debilitating Dynamic of Discouragement.** What happens to people when discouragement sets in? They become debilitated, their

energy goes, and they begin to settle for considerably less than they should be settling for. Their reasons for discouragement:

A. **Repetitive problems with the authorities (Ezra 5:1–7).**

B. **Remembrance of former glory (Hag. 2:3).**

C. **Recognition that their expectations may not be met.** The prophet Ezekiel had been talking about the future temple (Ezek. 40–48), and perhaps they realized that the temple they were going to be able to build was unlike anything Ezekiel had envisioned. Zechariah 4:10 reminded these people not to despise the day of small things. God usually begins things small and grows them.

D. **Realization that the problems are not going to be solved overnight.** It had been a time of famine. Even if God sent rains today, it would take awhile to see the results on the dinner table.

2. **The Empowering Effect of Encouragement (vv. 4, 5).** Notice the six encouragements found in these two verses:

A. **"Be strong."** Notice that three times Haggai told them to "Be strong" (v. 4).

B. **"And work."** Haggai said, in effect, "There is something to do, and the thing to do is to get on doing it." R. A. Torrey used to say, "The best way to begin is to begin."

C. **"For I am with you, says the LORD of hosts."** This is an oracle from God to be received and acted upon as unassailable truth.

D. **"According to the word that I covenanted with you when you came out of Egypt . . . "** This harkened back to Exodus 19:4–6, and reminded the workers that they were a special people with whom God has made a special covenant.

E. **"My Spirit remains among you."** The same Holy Spirit who had assisted Israel's forefathers was with them now. The same Holy Spirit who inflamed Luther, Wesley, Whitefield remains with us here today.

F. **"Do not fear."**

3. **The Positive Power of Promise (2:6–9).** Notice the repetition of the phrase, "I will . . . " God gave the people some fantastic promises

about the role of that temple in the future, and about the coming of their Messiah. God kept His promises to them, and He will keep His many promises to you.

Conclusion: What do you believe about the Lord's plan for your life? About His power? About His presence? About His promises? About the empowering that is available to you? Shake off discouragement. Be strong, and work, says the Lord, for I am with you.

STATS, STORIES, AND MORE

More from Stuart Briscoe

Shortly after Haggai started preaching, Zechariah showed up in Jerusalem, too. So they had two prophets at the same time. One probably was a Baptist, and the other was a Presbyterian, and they prophesied on opposite sides of the street, but they had more or less the same ministry. As we read Zechariah 4:10, he tells the people not to despise the day of small things. You know why some people get discouraged? Because they have grandiose ideas. They've got fantastic plans, great projects, and very rarely do things happen like that. God usually starts small and builds from that. Remember how it all started as far as the Jewish nation was concerned? It started with Abraham, one man being called out of Ur of the Chaldees. Remember how the great story of Redemption started? With a baby being born of a virgin. Remember how the church was born? It was born as a result of twelve men being discipled by the Lord Jesus, one of them turning out no good. Do you know how Elmbrook Church started? With thirteen people. Do you know how our broadcast, "Telling the Truth," started, that now literally goes around the world every day? It started down in the basement of the old church with a little tape recorder that we put on the table.

For what it's worth, discouragement overcame some of the greatest heroes of the Bible. Elijah, Moses, and Jonah all grew so discouraged in the Lord's work they prayed for death. Jeremiah spent his whole life in the throes of depression. John the Baptist asked, "Are you really the Messiah or should we look for someone else?" David said, "Why art thou cast down, O my soul, and why art thou disquieted within me?" Even the apostle Paul said that he was once so weary and worried in ministry that he couldn't preach the gospel though a great door had opened to him.

SUGGESTED ORDER OF WORSHIP

Dealing with Discouragement

Prelude—Instrumental Group
God of Wonders

Announcements

Call to Worship—Praise Team
Let the Peace of God Reign (Integrity Music)

Prayer of Worship—Pastoral Staff

Worship and Praise—Congregation
CH 737 *Like a River Glorious* (v1 chorus, v3 chorus in F)
CH 102 *All Hail King Jesus* (2x in F)
SPW 220 *You Are My All in All* (1x in F 1x in G)
MSPW 51 *Step by Step* (2x in G)

Welcome—Pastoral Staff

Song of Welcome (meet and greet)—Congregation
MSPW 12 *The Name of the Lord* (2x in F)

Testimony of Praise (2-minute video—Overcoming Depression)

Offertory Prayer—Pastoral Staff

Offertory Praise—Congregation
CH 684 *Precious Lord, Take My Hand* (2x in Ab)
SPW 248 *O Come, Let Us Adore Him* (2x in Ab, 1x in A with
    tag)

Message—Pastor
Shaking Off Discouragement—Haggai 2

Hymn of Response/Invitation—Congregation
CH 389 *Spirit of the Living God* (v 1 and v 2 in F)

Hymn of Benediction—Congregation
CH 602 *I Have Decided to Follow Jesus*

PostludeInstrumental Group
CH 431 *Shine Jesus, Shine* (2x in Ab)

Additional Sermons and Lesson Ideas

Relationships in a Model Church

Date preached:

By Dr. Timothy Beougher

Scripture: 1 Thessalonians 5:12–15

Introduction: Most of our problems in life involve other people, human relationships, getting along with those in our family, our church, our school, our work environment, our city, our world. We've had trouble getting along since the days of Cain and Abel. Much of Paul's writing dealt with relationships. Here in 1 Thessalonians 5, he speaks of . . .

1. **Relating to leaders in the church (vv. 12, 13)**. The responsibility of leaders is: hard work, leadership, and giving admonitions. Our response to leaders should be to respect them, esteem them, and live in peace with them.
2. **Relating to others in the church (vv. 14, 15)**. Our actions: 1) warn those who are idle; 2) encourage the timid; and 3) help the weak. Our attitudes: 1) patience; 2) forgiveness; 3) kindness.

Conclusion: The best way of getting along with others is with simplicity. Simply take these rules at face value and put them into practice.

Why I Am Glad I'm a Christian

Date preached:

By Dr. R. A. Torrey

Scripture: 2 Corinthians 9:5

Introduction: My heart echoes the words of Paul—thank God for His unspeakable gift. I'm glad I'm a Christian because:

1. I know my sins are forgiven (1 John 1:7, 9).
2. Jesus has set me free from sin's power (Rom. 6:14).
3. I know I'm a child of God (John 1:12).
4. I have been delivered from anxiety and fear (Phil. 4:6, 7).
5. I have found an overflowing joy (1 Pet. 1:8).
6. I know I shall live forever (1 John 2:17).
7. I have an inheritance incorruptible (1 Pet. 1:4, 5).

Conclusion: Hallelujah!

NOVEMBER 21, 2010

SUGGESTED SERMON

Thanksgiving Truths

Date preached:

By Dr. Melvin Worthington

Scripture: Psalm 100; 145 (NKJV)

Introduction: Thanksgiving is the day when we pause to reflect, remember, and respect the abundant blessings that God has bestowed upon us. Millions will use this special day, which has been appointed as Thanksgiving Day, as a day of indulgence, intemperance, and ingratitude, not respecting their Creator, conscience, or country. Thanksgiving is the act of rendering praise and thanksgiving; this praise and thanksgiving may take the form of private prayer or public proclamation as one articulates his appreciation for the blessings he enjoys. Thanksgiving is more than a day; it should be the disposition which all Christians should display every day, the attitude which should daily characterize those who are disciplined and devoted disciples of Christ.

1. **Christians thank God for His goodness (Jer. 33:11).** God's goodness leads men to repentance (Rom. 2:4). Thankfulness for God's goodness is always in order. The Psalms abound with references to God's goodness.

2. **Christians thank God for His greatness (Ps. 48:1; 145:3; 147:5).** David declared God's greatness when he said, "Great is the LORD, and greatly to be praised in the city of our God, in His holy mountain" (Ps. 48:1). In Psalm 145:3, God's greatness is described by the words "Great is the LORD, and greatly to be praised; and His greatness is unsearchable" (NKJV). Psalm 147:5 declares, "Great is our LORD, and mighty in power; His understanding is infinite" (NKJV). The greatness of God's person, power, and provisions should bring praise and thanksgiving from the heart of the Christian. Are you?

3. **Christians thank God for His grace (1 Cor. 1:4).** Grace is defined as unmerited or undeserved favor. Grace cannot be earned, but it can be experienced and enjoyed. Christians live by God's grace, learn by God's grace, labor by God's grace, look for His coming by grace, and manifest loyalty by God's grace. Believers are saved, schooled,

sanctified, secured, and satisfied by God's grace. The truth of God's grace should cause praise and thanksgiving.

4. **Christians thank God for His gospel (2 Cor. 8:18).** The gospel is God's Good News regarding the salvation provided for sinful people. In this verse, Paul gives an example of a brother whose praise is in the gospel. Paul elsewhere acknowledges preaching the gospel that is the power of God to salvation for all who believe (Rom. 1:16). He is assured of the power of the gospel to change the lives of all who believe. The gospel, which brings the news of salvation for fallen mankind, should provoke thankfulness and praise for every Christian.

5. **Christians thank God for His guidance (Ps. 67:4).** We have no reason to fret or worry, for the Lord guides the nations! The writer of Proverbs declares, "Trust in the LORD with all your heart, and lean not on your own understanding; in all your ways acknowledge Him, and He shall direct your paths" (Prov. 3:5, 6). David declared, "The steps of a good man are ordered by the LORD, and He delights in his way" (Ps. 37:23 NKJV). The Christian can be assured of and should be thankful for the Lord's personal, practical, positive, and providential guidance.

6. **Christians thank God for His government (Is. 9:6).** Jesus once said to Martha, "You are worried and troubled about many things" (Luke 10:41 NKJV). How often we are the same! We should trust rather than toil. Isaiah prophesied about Jesus, that the government would rest on His shoulders (Is. 9:6). The providence and sovereignty of God in the affairs of men are comforting truths. We can be assured "that all things work together for good to those who love God, to those who are called according to His purpose" (Rom. 8:28). The entire Book of Daniel suggests that God's hand superintends the affairs of men. The grand pillars of God's providence, which support the universe, should provoke thanksgiving and praise.

7. **Christians thank God for His gifts (2 Cor. 9:13).** Here, Paul gives thanks to God for a gift so incredible, that only He could be the true author of it. The Lord has given us salvation. He gave His Son to pay our sin debt. He has given us His Spirit. He has given us the gifts of the Spirit. The gifts that God has bestowed on His children are cause for thanksgiving and praise.

8. **Christians thank God for His gospel preachers (2 Cor. 9:13).**
Throughout the course of time, God has called individuals to declare His message. God has always had a person to do His bidding: Noah, Abraham, Moses, Daniel, Joseph, Peter, Paul, and many others, perhaps even you. Our hearts should be filled with thanksgiving and praises for those who have faithfully answered God's call to articulate God's Word.

Conclusion: Thanksgiving truths commence with God, continue with God, and consummate in God. The psalmist expressed it succinctly when he declared, "Make a joyful shout to the LORD, all you lands! Serve the LORD with gladness; come before His presence with singing. Know that the LORD, He is God; It is He who has made us, and not we ourselves; we are His people and the sheep of His pasture. Enter into His gates with thanksgiving, and into His courts with praise. Be thankful to Him, and bless His name. For the LORD is good; His mercy is everlasting, and His truth endures to all generations" (Ps. 100).

SUGGESTED ORDER OF WORSHIP

In Grateful Praise

Prelude—Instrumental Group
CH 431 *Shine Jesus, Shine* (2x in Ab)

Call to Worship—Praise Team
MSPW 1 *Ancient of Days*

Prayer of Praise and Thanksgiving—Pastoral Staff

Praise and Worship—Congregation
MSPW2 *Lord, I Lift Your Name on High* (2x in G)
MSPW3 *Jesus, Your Name* (3x in C)
MSPW3 *Knowing* You (2x in C)

Thanksgiving Video #1*—(2 minutes—*A Teen Giving Thanks for Family*)

Welcome—Pastoral Staff

---

*A short spoken testimony may be substituted for the video.

SUGGESTED ORDER OF WORSHIP—*Continued*

Song of Welcome
CH 171 *Come into His Presence* (2x in Bb)
CH 214 *I Will Enter His Gates* (2x in Eb)

Thanksgiving Video #2*—(2 minutes—*A Mother Giving Thanks for Church*)

Offertory Prayer—Pastoral Staff

Offertory Praise—Congregaton
CH 56 *To God Be the Glory* (vi chorus in G, chorus in Ab)
CH 139 *Great Is Thy Faithfulness* (2x in D, 1x in Eb)

Thanksgiving Video #3*—(2 minutes—*A Deacon Giving Thanks for Provisions*)

Worship and Praise—Congregation
CH 790 *We Gather Together* (1x in C, 1x in Db)
CH 791 *Jesus, We Just Want to Thank You* (vv 1 & 2 in D)

Message—Pastor
Thanksgiving Truths—Psalm 100; 145

Hymn of Response/Invitation—Congregation
CH 170 *Give Thanks* (2x in F)

Hymn of Benediction—Congregation
CH 795 *We Are So Blessed*—(1x in Eb)

Postlude—Instrumental Group
CH 786 *Count Your Blessings*

**A short spoken testimony may be substituted for the video.*

Additional Sermons and Lesson Ideas

Amazing Grace
By Kevin Riggs

Date preached:

Scripture: Titus 2:11–15

Introduction: After describing how Christians should live in all aspects of life (2:1–10), Paul reminded Titus of the amazing work of God's grace. God's grace is not a one-time event in our lives. Every day we become more dependent on His grace to survive. God's grace is more amazing than we could ever imagine.

1. God's grace in the past has saved us from our sins (2:11). God's grace, through faith in Jesus Christ, brought us to salvation.
2. God's grace in the present teaches us how to live (2:12). It gives us the power to break free from whatever sin is keeping us down.
3. God's grace in the future prepares us for eternity (2:13–14). God's grace assures us Jesus is returning one day. By being prepared for the future, we have purpose for the present.

Conclusion: Our motivation to live a godly life should not be guilt or fear, but love and gratitude for the grace of God. The grace that saved us, teaches us how to live and prepares us for eternity.

No Gains Without Pains
By Rev. Peter Grainger

Date preached:

Scripture: 2 Timothy 2:3–7, especially verse 3

Introduction: In his book *Holiness,* Bishop J. C. Ryle wrote: "I will never shrink from declaring my belief that there are no spiritual gains without pains. I should as soon expect a farmer to prosper in business who contented himself with sowing his fields and never looking at them till harvest, as expect a believer to attain much holiness who was not diligent about his Bible-reading, his prayers and the use of his Sundays. Our God is a God who works by means." This principle not only applies to holiness, but to Christian service. Take Paul, for example. The secret of his success was "God's grace plus hard work" (1 Cor. 15:9–10). Here in 2 Timothy, his labor was shortly to be ended by an executioner's sword, so he was entrusting the gospel work to his younger protégé, Timothy, telling him at the beginning of chapter 2 to entrust it to other faithful men who would pass it on to others as well. In the next verses Paul illustrated his point using three metaphors from the Roman Empire, each emphasizing a different aspect of the principle "no gains without pains."

1. **The Soldier, characterized by devotion (v. 4).** The Christian as a soldier is a familiar image in Paul's writings, not just because soldiers were a familiar sight in every town and outpost of the empire, but

because Paul spent years in close proximity to them. He often described the Christian life as warfare, but the emphasis here is more specific on a devotion to duty that inevitably means hardship. The Greek word implies suffering. Sharing the gospel always draws opposition from its enemies, and some of Paul's trusted "soldiers" had recently deserted him in Asia (1:15). He reminded Timothy that suffering is the badge of authenticity for genuine disciples. We must be ready for action and prepared to fight and suffer. We can't afford to be entangled in civilian affairs. There has been much discussion as to what Paul meant here by "the affairs of this life," but the key lies in the word *entangles*. It is not just sin that entangles but other things which, while legitimate, may hamper our effectiveness for Christ. A test for any activity we're considering is: Will it hamper my Christian service? Paul added that motive for this suffering is our desire to please Christ, our commanding officer.

2. **The Athlete, characterized by discipline (v. 5).** Here is another of Paul's favorite metaphors. In this instance, he emphasized the need for single-mindedness and discipline. The literal translation says that the athlete does not qualify unless he competes lawfully. In the ancient world, this word described a professional athlete. In the Greek games, the athletes had to swear on oath that they had completed a full ten months of rigorous training before they were allowed to compete in the race. So the Christian is one who is disciplined in his or her personal life and walk with God. There is no shortcut to glory, only rigorous discipline. Yet how many of us think we can get by with a minimum of effort. For some, the Christian faith is little more than a Sunday hobby, despite what they profess with their lips. Becoming good disciples means dedicated discipline over as many years as God gives us. The only alternative is to drop out of the race and become a spectator or critic—and there are plenty of those around.

3. **The Farmer, characterized by diligence (v. 6).** In the first century (and in many places today), farming was all hard, back-breaking manual labor. The word *hardworking* implies toil that produces weariness or exhaustion. The farmer doesn't just drop seed into the ground then retire to the Bahamas for a few months. He is out and about every day at all hours, tending, weeding, caring, and cultivating the precious crop. There isn't much glamour in working in the pouring rain at the end of a long day. But it's absolutely necessary if we're to reap a plentiful ingathering (Prov. 20:4; 24:30–31), and it is worth it, for we will share in the ultimate harvest.

Conclusion: There are no gains without pains, but the gains more than compensate for the pains. In the final chapter of this letter Paul writes that he has fought the good fight—he has maintained devotion, discipline, and diligence—and is ready for the crown of righteousness which has been laid up for him. May that be our experience, too, whenever He comes or calls!

NOVEMBER 28, 2010

SERIES: FIRST SUNDAY OF ADVENT   SUGGESTED SERMON

From Old, Even from Everlasting

Date preached:

By Robert Morgan

Scripture: Micah 5:1–5a, especially verse 2

Introduction: What if we could predict with confidence who would win the U.S. Presidential race two years from now? After the mess the polling organizations made in the last presidential election, we could make a fortune. But what if we could predict with certainty the name of the person to be elected President 700 years from now? The prophet Micah told us of a Messiah who would be born in a little town called Bethlehem, and he made his prediction 700 years in advance. Micah predicted:

1. **A great ruler will be preceded by national distress and divine judgment (Micah 5:1).** In verse 1, Jerusalem is told to mobilize her army and prepare for siege, for the Israelites were going be encompassed by enemies who would strike their king. That is exactly what happened. The people of Israel disregarded the Lord's prophets and disobeyed His precepts. A series of weak and wicked kings dragged the nation into a moral and military abyss until Judah fell to besieging Babylon. Later Israel experienced a series of humiliations—the tyranny of Antiochus, political confusion by the Hasmoneans, defeat by the Romans, and the despotism of half-insane Herod the Great, at which point Christ came. Sooner or later, our sins find us out (Num. 32:23; Prov. 14:24).

2. **The ruler would be born in Bethlehem (Micah 5:2a).** There were two Bethlehems in Israel in those days, one in the area of Zebulun, and the other near Jerusalem. The ancient name of the latter was Ephrathah (Gen. 35:19). Micah was being quite specific, and he especially noted the town's smallness. One of the most remarkable demographic trends of the past century has been the global shift to urbanization, but large cities have been around from antiquity. The first city to reach one million was Rome, about 130 years before Christ. You would have thought the Messiah would have been born

in Rome, Alexandria, or Jerusalem. But He came in tiny Bethlehem, and Micah was chosen to reveal that information to us, for he was a small town prophet who ministered to small towns. We think bigger is better, but the Bible tells us to despise not the day of small things. "Little is much when God is in it; / Labor not for wealth or fame. / There's a crown, and you can win it, / When you go in Jesus' name." Edward Payson, a nineteenth-century preacher in Portland, Maine, had but one hearer one stormy Sunday. Payson preached his sermon, however, as carefully as though the building had been thronged. Later his solitary listener called on him. "I was led to the Savior through that service," he said. "For whenever you talked about sin and salvation, I glanced around to see to whom you referred, but since there was no one there but me, I had no alternative but to lay every word to my own heart and conscience!"

3. **The Ruler is eternal (Micah 5:2b).** "His goings forth have been from of old, from everlasting" (KJV). Our Lord's miraculous conception in Nazareth and His birth in Bethlehem didn't mark the beginning of His existence. He once told the Jews, "Before Abraham was, I am." See John 1:1.

4. **The Messiah will be a threefold ruler.**

   A. **He is our shepherd (v. 4a).** See John 10:11–15.

   B. **He is our security.** Verse 4b in the NIV reads: "And they will live securely, for then his greatness will reach to the ends of the earth." This has millennial implications, but even now we can live securely in Him, and His greatness reaches to the ends of the earth.

   C. **He is our serenity.** Verse 5 tells us He is our peace—not just that He will establish peace, make peace, or impart peace. He *is* our peace. See Ephesians 2:14 and Isaiah 9:6.

Conclusion: Seven hundred years before His birth, the little town of Bethlehem was chosen as the town of His nativity. Still now, 2,000 years later, we celebrate the birth of Him whose goings forth have been of old, even from everlasting. And His greatness reaches to the ends of the earth. Does it reach into your heart?

> *O little town of Bethlehem, how still we see thee lie!*
> *Above thy deep and dreamless sleep the silent stars go by.*
> *Yet in thy dark streets shineth the everlasting Light;*
> *The hopes and fears of all the years are met in thee tonight.*

STATS, STORIES, AND MORE

Be Sure Your Sins Will Find You Out

The Wall Street Journal carried an article about people who accidentally jostle their cell phones and make calls unawares. One man was engaged in a very graphic, sexual conversation with his buddies when he hit a button that automatically called his mother, who overheard the whole thing. Another man accidentally called his wife while he was involved with another woman. The Bible warns that God is always listening, always watching, and that our sins will find us out.

No Man's Land

This story has been told in a variety of ways, but this is the researched version that appeared in newspapers nationwide on December 25, 1994, from the Associated Press, dateline London.

Eighty years ago, on the first Christmas Day of World War I, British and German troops put down their guns and celebrated peacefully together in the no-man's land between the trenches. The war, briefly, came to a halt.

Pvt. Oswald Tilley of the London Rifle Brigade wrote to his parents: "Just you think that while you were eating your turkey etc. I was out talking and shaking hands with the very men I had been trying to kill a few hours before!! It was astounding."

Both armies had received lots of comforts from home and felt generous and well-disposed toward their enemies in the first winter of the war, before the vast battles of attrition began in 1915, eventually claiming 10 million lives.

All along the line that Christmas Day, soldiers found their enemies were much like them and began asking why they should be trying to kill each other.

The generals were shocked. High Command diaries and statements express anxiety that if that sort of thing spread it could sap the troops' will to fight.

The soldiers in khaki and gray sang carols to each other, exchanged gifts of tobacco, jam, sausage, chocolate and liquor, traded names and addresses and played soccer between the shell holes and barbed wire. They even paid mutual trench visits.

This day is called "the most famous truce in military history" by British television producer Malcolm Brown and researcher Shirley Seaton in their book *Christmas Truce,* published in 1984.

SUGGESTED ORDER OF WORSHIP

Bless the Lord, O My Soul

Prelude—Instrumental
Days of Elijah

Call to Worship—Congregation
CH 672 *What a Mighty God* (1x in Db, 1x in D)
CH 15 *No Other Name* (2x in D)
SPW 248 *O Come, Let Us Adore Him*
CH 44 *Crown Him King of Kings* (2x in Ab)

Welcome—Pastoral Staff

Song of Welcome—Congregation (meet and greet)
CH 522 *I'm So Glad* (4x in Ab)

Scripture Reading—Congregation and Worship Pastor
CH 71 *Bless the Lord, O My Soul* (Psalm 100 NKJV)

Worship and Praise—Congregation
CH 70 *A Perfect Heart* (2x in F)
CH 62 *Blessed Be the Lord God Almighty* (1x in Bb, 1x in C)
CH 60 *Bless God* (2x in F)

Offertory Prayer—Pastoral Staff

Offertory Praise—Congregation
CH 69 *Holy, Holy, Holy*

Message—Pastor
From Old, Even from Everlasting

Hymn of Response/Invitation—Congregation
CH 47 *Jesus, Lord to Me*

Hymn of Benediction—Congregation
CH 107 *Lord, I Lift Your Name on High*

Postlude—Instrumental
We Bring a Sacrifice of Praise

Additional Sermons and Lesson Ideas

Ten Reasons for Family Devotions
By Dr. Woodrow Kroll

Date preached:

Scripture: Psalm 19:9–11, especially verse 9

Introduction: I'd like to deal with a once-popular subject that has fallen on hard times—family devotions. This old phrase simply means praying together as a family. I believe we can still find a formula for having the "family altar" if we realize how important it is. Today I'd like to share ten reasons for family devotions.

1. **Devotions provide communication with God.** They are the easiest, best way for your family to get together and talk to God (see Ps. 25:4, 5). When we have family devotions, we're communicating with God. Communication in business today is so important that 90 percent of U.S. companies provide communication skills training in the workplace. Subscribers to the *Harvard Business Review* rated the ability to communicate as more important than ambition, education, and the capacity for hard work. We teach our children how to communicate with their playmates. When do you teach them how to communicate with God? (see Ps. 119:145–152).

2. **Devotions quench spiritual thirst.** We're all thirsty for something (see Ps. 42:1, 2). Blaise Pascal, the seventeenth-century French philosopher, wrote that we all have a God-shaped vacuum that only God can fill. That's true for our children, grandchildren, and spouse. Family devotions allow the opportunity to quench our spiritual thirst (see Ps. 84:2).

3. **Devotions advance personal spiritual growth.** Yes, I know we can grow with private devotions. Praying with other members of the family helps all the family do the same (see 1 Pet. 2:2; 2 Pet. 3:18). If you're growing in God's Word but your spouse isn't, it makes for an unbalanced couple.

4. **Family devotions bring us together.** Sitting down and talking about spiritual things provides a safeguard against carnality in our homes (see 1 Cor. 3:1–3). If you want to put a hedge against worldly activity in your family, the best way is to get together each day to discuss how we relate God's Word to our lives in the world. It's a tradition your child will treasure later in life.

5. **Devotions provide insight for daily life.** Take Proverbs 10:4, for example: "Lazy hands make a man poor, but diligent hands bring wealth" (NIV). It's important for kids to know that. The Book of Proverbs gives specific advice on how to treat a mean neighbor, what to do when your wife is mad at you, how to invest properly, when to speak and when to be silent, how to know when you've angered someone, and what to do about it. And that's just one book.

6. **Family devotions prevent schizophrenic faith.** It seems to me that some Christians who believe in God and come to church also believe some of the wildest, wackiest things. They've mixed truth and error. They sing praise choruses at church, yet hold beliefs that don't square with Scripture. Family devotions counter that. Consistent time before the Lord enables us to grow.

7. **Devotions provide daily comfort and encouragement.** If I didn't have a Bible, I don't know what I'd do. If I didn't have it open, I don't know what I'd do. And if I didn't have it open every day, I don't know how I'd face life's challenges (see Ps. 119:81).

8. **Devotions prepare us to share our faith.** The more we're in God's Word, the more familiar with it we become and the more apt we are to share it (see 1 Pet. 3:15).

9. **Devotions provide daily marching orders.** When you get into Scripture, you find things that tell you what God wants you to do each day (see Deut. 5:27 and Ps. 119:105). God's will is revealed in His Word.

10. **Family devotions show respect for the author of the Bible.** The greatest compliment to pay an author is to say, "I read your book." I wonder what we'll say to God when we meet Him face to face, and He asks, "Did you read My book?" (see Ps. 119:127, 128).

Conclusion: How do you start? Well, everybody does it differently. In our family, we read a chapter every night and take a moment to discuss it. We take requests and pray, and it's a simple thing. It doesn't take long, but we never allow anything to disrupt that time. If the phone rings, we let it ring. If the doorbell rings, we don't answer it. My friend, when I'm spending time with my family, and we're spending time with God, there's nothing more vital. Having family devotions is important!

The Lord Is My . . .
By Joshua Rowe

Date preached:

Scripture: Various

Introduction: Often we view ourselves as the Lord's people, His servants, His messengers, and rightly so. I wonder how often, though, we remember what the Lord is to us.

1. The Lord is my Rock and my Fortress (2 Sam. 22:2; Ps. 18:2).
2. The Lord is my Light (Ps. 27:1).
3. The Lord is my Strength (Ex. 15:2; Ps. 28:7; 118:14).
4. The Lord is my Shield (Ps. 28:7).
5. The Lord is my Song (Ex. 15:2; Ps. 118:14).
6. The Lord is my Portion (Lam. 3:24).
7. The Lord is my Helper (Heb. 13:6).
8. The Lord is my Salvation (Ex. 15:2; Ps. 27:1).

Conclusion: May these verses encourage us to have closer intimacy with God and exhort us to daily crown Him as our Lord.

DECEMBER 5, 2010

SECOND SUNDAY OF ADVENT   SUGGESTED SERMON

A Root Out of Dry Ground

Date preached:

By Rev. Charles McGowan

Scripture: Isaiah 53:1–6, especially verse 2

Introduction: One of the amazing facts related to Christmas is that Jesus survived the efforts of Herod to kill him. More amazing yet is the impact of his life, death, and Resurrection. Isaiah spoke prophetically of this with these words: "For He shall grow up before Him as a tender plant, and as a root out of dry ground." The "dry ground" of which Isaiah spoke consisted of the humble circumstances of his birth, his growth and development, his nationality, the politics of his day, and the disciples whom he trained. Yet, the "root" sprang up and continues to spring up and thrive in the hardest and driest of soil. Reflect on the "hard soil" in which Jesus takes root and thrives.

1. **The Human Heart.** The Lord Jesus never finds the human heart to be fertile soil. It is characterized by darkness, greed, envy, and pride. In the human heart he finds not sickness, but death. This has been illustrated through the ages by the dramatic conversion of people such as Augustine, whose heart was consumed with hedonism and hardened indifference to the faith of his praying mother. Or think of Saul of Tarsus, the great persecutor of the early church whose hard and callous heart became the seedbed of the gospel. What an encouragement to someone who feels his heart is too deeply stained for God to accept him! And what an encouragement to someone whose current place in life might be characterized as dry and barren!

2. **Our Culture.** Evidence surrounds us that our culture is barren and dry. One only needs to survey the world of entertainment. Examine the ugly side of the Internet or the content of much of our culture's music. Whether it be television or the curriculum of a typical secular university, you find much barren and dry soil. The living Christ, however, takes root and thrives in the dry soil of an ungodly culture. This has always been true. Against the backdrop of the barren Middle Ages, the Reformation was born. As the Reformers planted

the rediscovered gospel of grace, the living Christ sprang up as a vibrant plant. Or think of David Wilkerson proclaiming the gospel in the barren territory of New York City gangs—only to see lives changed by the living Christ who sprang up in the most unlikely places. So we should not lose heart. The seed is planted and watered even in the hardest and driest of soils. Then, in his own time, Christ springs up and grows, changing lives and cultures.

3. **Your Place of Ministry and Service.** There are certain areas of the world where the soil is unusually hard and dry. The resistance to the gospel is strong and sometimes met with hostility. There are places where the messenger is in grave danger as he seeks to plant the seed. But, in God's time, the seed sprouts. Think of China enslaved for decades by oppressive Marxism during the twentieth century. Yet as doors began to open late in the century, it became obvious that the living Christ had taken root and flourished there. Or think of the drift of the modern church in some parts of the world toward ministries devoid of the historic gospel message. Those who remain faithful are inclined to develop an Elijah complex, assuming that all hope is lost. Yet the history of the church is replete with stories of the living Christ springing up in the midst of the sleepy, drifting church. Or think of families that appear hopeless: the husband totally consumed in patterns destructive to his marriage and family; marriages that are in disarray and on the verge of dissolution; children in rebellion. Only the eyes of faith could see the living Christ taking root in places such as these. Yet testimonies abound of the gospel doing what trained counselors could never do as the living Christ is embraced.

Conclusion: This is the message of Christmas: no circumstance, no matter how hopeless, is beyond the reach of the One who takes root in the most barren and driest places imaginable. Offer Him the soil of your barren, broken, and hopeless circumstances. Expect Him to do what He has done through the ages—grow up as a tender plant and overshadow your life and circumstance with His grace.

STATS, STORIES, AND MORE

This story has been told in a variety of ways, but this is the researched version that appeared in newspapers nationwide on December 25, 1994, from the Associated Press.

Eighty years ago, on the first Christmas Day of World War I, British and German troops put down their guns and celebrated peacefully together in the no-man's land between the trenches.

The war, briefly, came to a halt.

In some places, festivities began when German troops lit candles on Christmas trees on their parapets so the British sentries a few hundred yards away could see them.

Elsewhere, the British acted first, starting bonfires and letting off rockets.

Pvt. Oswald Tilley of the London Rifle Brigade wrote to his parents: "Just you think that while you were eating your turkey etc. I was out talking and shaking hands with the very men I had been trying to kill a few hours before!! It was astounding."

Both armies had received lots of comforts from home and felt generous and well disposed toward their enemies in the first winter of the war, before the vast battles of attrition began in 1915, eventually claiming 10 million lives.

All along the line that Christmas Day, soldiers found their enemies were much like them and began asking why they should be trying to kill each other.

The generals were shocked. High Command diaries and statements express anxiety that if that sort of thing spread it could sap the troops' will to fight.

The soldiers in khaki and gray sang carols to each other, exchanged gifts of tobacco, jam, sausage, chocolate and liquor, traded names and addresses and played soccer between the shell holes and barbed wire. They even paid mutual trench visits.

This day is called "the most famous truce in military history" by the British television producer.

Hallelujah! Jesus Has Come!

Prelude—Instrumentalists
  CH 258 *Go, Tell It on the Mountain*

Welcome and Announcements—Pastoral Staff

Worship in Prayer—Pastoral Staff

Proclaim the Word—Luke 2:16–20 NKJV

Worship and Praise—Congregation
  CH 258 *Go, Tell it on the Mountain** (2x in F)
  CH 259 *Angels from the Realms of Glory*
  CH 260 *Worthy, You Are Worthy* (3x in Eb, 1x in F)

Offertory Prayer—Pastoral Staff (Prayer of praise for provisions)

Offertory Praise—Worship Leader and Congregation
  MSPW 3 *Jesus, Your Name* (3x in C)
  CH 243 *Emmanuel* (2x in C)

Worship and Praise—Congregation
  CH 268 *Rejoice with Exceeding Great Joy* (Scripture—Luke
    2:8–14 NKJV)
  CH 269 *How Great Our Joy* (vv. 1, 2, 4 and transition)
  CH 270 *Joy to the World* (vv 1, 2, 4 and transition)
  CH 271 *Joyful, Joyful We Adore You* (2x in G)

Message—Pastor
  Worshiping God by Name

Hymn of Response/Invitation—Congregation
  MSPW2 109 *He Knows My Name*

Benediction Hymn—Congregation
  Mighty to Save

Postlude—Instrumental Group
  CH 195 *Bless the Name of Jesus* (2x in C)

---

*Meet and greet during this song of welcome.

Additional Sermons and Lesson Ideas

The Light of the World
By Rev. Peter Grainger

Date preached:

Scripture: Isaiah 9:1–7

Introduction: Have you ever seen a faithful church look like it's going under? So often, the Lord restores and revives His people despite how desperate the situation seems. In Isaiah's time, the people of Israel seemed to be "going under," but there was reason to hope; a light was coming.

> 1. **Illumination (vv. 2, 3):** *The Light Dawns.*
>   A. For the people who walked in darkness.
>   B. For those who dwelt in the land of the shadow of death.
>   C. The fulfillment (Matt. 4:12–17; 2 Cor. 4:3–6).
> 2. **Liberation (vv. 3, 4):** *The Light Shines.*
>   A. The end of oppression (see Judg. 6–7).
>   B. The end of war (v. 4; see Ps. 46:9).
>   C. The fulfillment (Luke 4:16–21; Heb. 2:14–16).
> 3. **Incarnation (vv. 6, 7):** *The Light Spreads.*
>   A. Through the government of the Son.
>   B. Through the zeal of the Lord of Hosts.
>   C. The fulfillment (1 Cor. 15:20–28; Rev. 11:15).

Conclusion: Don't be overwhelmed by the dark world around you; live in the light (1 John 1:7).

Worshiping God by Name
By Dr. David Jeremiah

Date preached:

Scripture: Psalm 23

Introduction: The Old Testament people of God knew how to celebrate Him, and they can teach us the wonderful secret of worshiping Him by name.

> 1. *Jehovah-Rohi*—The Lord My Shepherd (Ps. 23:1)
> 2. *Jehovah-Jireh*—The Lord Will Provide (Gen. 22:14)
> 3. *Jehovah-Rophe*—The Lord Who Heals (Ex. 15:26)
> 4. *Jehovah-Nissi*—The Lord Is My Banner (Ex. 17:15)
> 5. *Jehovah-Mekaddesh*—The Lord Who Sanctifies (Lev. 20:8)
> 6. *Jehovah-Shalom*—The Lord Is Peace (Judg. 6:24)
> 7. *Jehovah-Tsidkenu*—The Lord Our Righteousness (Jer. 23:6)
> 8. *Jehovah-Shammah*—The Lord Is There (Ezek. 48:35)

Conclusion: Notice how all these names of God are descriptive of the unfolding ministry the Lord provides us in Psalm 23. He meets all our needs, and He is the object of all our praise.

DECEMBER 12, 2010

Rahab: The Christmas Prostitute
The Great, Great . . . Ever So Great,
Grandmother of Jesus

Date preached:

By Dr. Calvin Miller

Scripture: Joshua 2:1–6, 8–13, 17–21; 6:22, 23; and Matthew 1:5, "Salmon begot Boaz by Rahab, Boaz begot Obed by Ruth, Obed begot Jesse."

Introduction: There is a long list of men who sired the generations that comprise Jesus' family tree. But besides the men and a single Jewish woman named Bathsheba, only two women are mentioned. Both women are Gentiles, and both are what we would now most likely call Arab women. How in this world did these Arab women become part of the lineage of Christ? Both of their names appear together in the list of generations.

Rahab, the first of the Gentile women to be mentioned, was a prostitute, and it is she who most fascinates me. Who can say why God ordained a harlot to be the "great-grandmother of Jesus"? But we can say that if God's great grace could put such a sinner in the family tree of the Christ, then surely there is hope for all of us to drink from God's cup of grace. So gracious is His chalice of life, where none is too vile to know it. These passages taken together remind us that Christmas is the time for celebrating God's grace. I for one lift my cup to Rahab, the Christmas Harlot, whose place in the kingdom of God precedes my own. Let all of us who love Christ remember we have a sister, who was saved by grace, long ago in the siege of Jericho. What made this harlot so memorable in the long, long history of Grace?

1. **Rahab was a prostitute, open to the fact that God sends those who need grace into our lives (Josh. 2:5).** A scarlet cord in Joshua leads us to celebrate the grace that is on its way to us. Here is born the unthinkable joy: Rahab could see the greatness of the moment. She sensed these spies weren't just there to measure the defenses of Jericho. They were on a mission from God and God has an agenda, not just for every nation but for every life. Rahab—though ignorant

of God—must have thought, *If God has a mission for every life, maybe He has a plan for my life. Maybe these spies aren't just here to scout out the city for a siege, maybe I can get in on the good deals of God. Maybe I can become a person of Grace. Maybe everybody doesn't have to die when the city falls under siege. Maybe someone as unworthy as I, can claim victory when the fire burns and the walls fall down flat.*

Let us never forget: nobody perishes because God hates them. Most, who never know the pleasures of eternity, are just souls who missed the Coming of God, when he passed through their neighborhood. Rahab was probably illiterate, but she could read the times. God, in the form of two Jewish spies, was in her parlor, and it would not happen twice in her lifetime. She must seize the prize while she could.

2. **She was a prostitute, on the lookout for the will of God for her world (Josh. 2:9–11).** It is sometimes hard to live in a little place—like Jericho—and see the worldwide purposes of God. Suddenly there were Israeli men in her front wall apartment that were somehow involved in a pretty big plan God held for a world that was on the way. Did she sense that if there was a brass ring on the historical merry-go-round perhaps it was to her advantage to grab it? Whether or not Rahab was that historically astute, it was still true that this Israeli God was out to claim the world, and in a way that Rahab could not guess He was going to do it—through her own great, great Grandson, a Nazarene Carpenter.

I think what I like most about Jesus and the whole Hebrew Christian movement is that God was not a parochial God. No, never! He is the God of the ages with an ages-wide agenda. And He uses the most ordinary people to be the major actors in His theater of Grace. I have always said of Jesus, Rahab's Grandson, that one thing I admire about Jesus is that He could take a bunch of fishers and prostitutes and so infuse them with the wideness of God's global dream that they—who have grasped his worldwide vision—would each die a thousand miles from their rural homelands in the service of their Lord.

3. **So here you have it. A scarlet cord! (Josh. 2:18)** There it is, the scarlet cord, hanging here not just in a harlot's window but in the very center of Jewish history. But what does it say about this wise and hopeful prostitute? It says that God who could care this much about

a fallen woman is quite a God! What it really says is that if Rahab is to be seated at the great Marriage Supper of the Lamb, just about anybody can get into the Kingdom of Heaven. Grace, Grace, Grace! The generosity we don't deserve! Grace is a wondrous song none of us deserve to sing.

What is notable is that the Israelites are receiving a salvation they didn't deserve. And the spies are saving a woman who didn't deserve it. None deserved it, but on the day the walls came down, they were all looking up to God and clutching the scarlet cord. And which of us would have the gall to stand and brag we were worthy of all that God did? None of us! We shall live lives that outlast the stars for only one reason, we are clinging to the scarlet cord of Grace.

4. **She counted on the promises that God would rescue her on the day of siege (Josh. 6:22, 23).** Are the promises of God faithful? In but a brief four chapters of Joshua, we see Rahab and her entire family coming unto safety. She would become a person of grace. It is amazing what happens to us when we give up our self will and decide to become persons of grace. Christmas is a time of struggle and hurried living and it's pretty much, for most people, a time of selfishness. But here and there we can elect to become people of grace.

John D. Rockefeller became a millionaire at twenty-three years of age. He became the world's first billionaire at fifty-three years of age. But when he was fifty-four, he was in such poor health that he was eaten alive with ulcers and so sick that he couldn't eat anything but crackers and milk. He could literally afford any meal he wanted to buy, and if the meal wasn't right he could buy any restaurant and order them to cook it. But his motor-driven life was all but over, and he knew it.

His doctors affirmed his diagnosis: he was dying! In fact, they prophesied that he would be dead within a year. In preparing to die he decided how to spend some of the money in his billionaire's bank account. He formed the Rockefeller Foundation, and he began to give away vast sums of his money. He became Mr. Charity and turned his vast wealth into redeeming humanity in a myriad of good causes. That very year, his ulcers began to heal and the more money he gave away, the better his health became. He finally lived to do the world a lot of good and died when he was 97 years old.

What happened to him? He made the conscious decision to become a person of grace. He hung the scarlet cord of grace in the middle of his "What's in it for me?" life.

5. **Thirty generations later, the tax collector, Matthew, told us of Rahab's relationship to Christ (Matt. 1:5).** Rahab holds the center of my esteem. Why? She just didn't deserve to be there—smack-dab in the middle of Jesus' family tree. And what was God thinking, putting an Arab harlot in the lineage of the Messiah? It's a grace thing and can only be understood by the undeserving, who, because of Jesus, always get so much more than they deserve. But there are other people of grace in this family tree. Then, of course, there's Salmon, her husband. What did he get besides a harlot for his wife? He might have been a Jew but probably the gossips of Israel all said he couldn't have been much of a religious man, marrying a harlot like he did.

There was no question that Salmon married Rahab after she had been at her business for a while. It's possible that at one time she had been one of his one-night stands. But he did marry her and here's the marriage that brought the smile of God: a child resulted from their union, little baby Boaz, another of Jesus' ancestors. It was all a great family affair that spelled grace for the entire kingdom of God. But then that's what should have happened. After all, that's what the Incarnation is about. God becoming man through the lowest of human agency.

Conclusion: It is Christmas, and Christmas is more than a mere winter festival. It is a vast story of the length God reaches to hand grace right in the center of your life. How much does God love you? So much that He sent Jesus, and Jesus came holding out to you the scarlet cord of your salvation. Here's the cost of God's good grace. It is free for you, but it cost God everything. Long ago Alphonsus Maria de Liguori wrote the story of your salvation in these words:

"The Son of God, seeing man thus lost and wishing to save him from death, offered to take upon Himself our human nature and to suffer death Himself, condemned as a criminal on a cross."

"But my Son," we might imagine the eternal Father saying to Him, "think of what a life of humiliation and suffering Thou wilt have to lead on earth. Thou wilt have to be born in a cold stable and laid in a manger, the feeding trough of beasts. While still an infant, Thou wilt have to flee into Egypt, to escape the hands of Herod. At Thy return Thou wilt have to live and work in a shop as a lowly servant, poor and despised. And finally, worn out with suffering, Thou wilt have to give up Thy life on a cross, put to shame and abandoned by everyone."

"Father," replies the Son, "all this matters not. I will gladly bear it all, if only I can save man."[1]

So this is the story of life, perhaps the story of your life. No one has to perish, there is a Scarlet Cord in the window, and life eternal is yours. Merry Christmas!

SUGGESTED ORDER OF WORSHIP

Christmas Baptismal Service

Prelude—Instrumental Group
   CH 275 *Sing We Now of Christmas*

Announcements—Pastoral Staff

Call to Worship—Congregation
   CH 260 *Worthy, You Are Worthy* (vv. 1, 2 in Eb, v. 3 in F)
   CH 278 *Angels We Have Heard on High*

Baptismal Celebration—Pastor

Prayer of Worship—Pastor

Worship and Praise—Congregation
   CH 271 *Joyful, Joyful, We Adore You* (2x in G)
   CH 284 *The Birthday of a King* (2x in G)
   CH 285 *O Holy Night* (3x in C)

Offertory Prayer—Pastoral Staff

Offertory Praise—Congregation
   CH 253 *Silent Night! Holy Night*
   CH 254 *Isn't He?* (1x in G)

---

[1]Alphonsus de Liguori, *Book of the Novenas* (New York: John J. Crowley and Co., 1956), pp. 2–4.

Christmas Scripture Reading*—Gal. 4:3–7
CH 249 *O Come, All Ye Faithful* (1x in G, 1x in Ab)

Message—Pastor
A Humble Holiday

Hymn of Response/Invitation—Congregation
CH 389 *Spirit of the Living God*

Hymn of Benediction—Congregation
CH 296 *Hosanna* (2x in G)

Postlude—Instrumental Group
CH 431 *Shine, Jesus, Shine* (2x in Ab)

***Christmas Scripture:**
When we were children, were in bondage under the elements of the world. **4** But when the fullness of the time had come, God sent forth His Son, born of a woman, born under the law, **5** to redeem those who were under the law, that we might receive the adoption as sons. **6** And because you are sons, God has sent forth the Spirit of His Son into your hearts, crying out, "Abba, Father!" **7** Therefore you are no longer a slave but a son, and if a son, then an heir of God through Christ.

Additional Sermons and Lesson Ideas

A Humble Holiday

Date preached:

By Robert Morgan

Scripture: Luke 1:39–54

Introduction: You wouldn't think it by taking a shopping trip to our affluent malls, but Christmas began as a very humble event, an event that exhibited the greatest humility the world has ever seen—the God of glory being laid in a cattle trough. We see:

1. **Humility exhibited in Mary's situation.** Everything about Mary was humble—her hometown, her poverty, her hardships, her displacement in Bethlehem, her setting.
2. **Humility expressed in Mary's song.** In her *Magnificat,* she spoke of how God resists the proud but exalts the lowly.
3. **Humility exemplified in Mary's Son.** Jesus came: "Out of the Ivory Palaces, into a world of woe."

Conclusion: We take pride in birth and rank, but He was a carpenter's son. We take pride in possessions, but He had nowhere to lay His head. Is there any way in which we can observe Christmas with the personal humility that reflects our Savior? God opposes the proud but gives grace to the humble.

Celebrating Christmas

Date preached:

By Dr. Timothy Beougher

Scripture: Luke 2:17–20

Introduction: We can look back to the first Christmas celebration to gain insight on how we as twenty-first-century believers can and should celebrate Christmas.

1. **We celebrate Christmas by telling others about Christ.** Verse 17 says: "When they had seen Him, they made widely known the saying which was told them concerning this Child."
2. **We celebrate Christmas by reflecting on its wonderful meaning.** Verses 18 and 19 tell us that everyone who heard about the birth of Christ marveled, and Mary pondered these things in her heart.
3. **We celebrate Christmas by offering praise and glory to God.** Verse 20 tells us the shepherds glorified and praised God for all they had heard and seen.

Conclusion: Put Christ back into your Christmas. Tell others about Him and invite them to our church Christmas services. Make time to ponder Him in your heart, and take every opportunity of praising the Christ of Bethlehem.

DECEMBER 19, 2010

FOURTH SUNDAY IN ADVENT   SUGGESTED SERMON

Who Is He in Yonder Stall?   *Date preached:*

By Morris Proctor

Scripture: Matthew 1:18–25, especially verse 21

Introduction: An old hymn asks, "Who is He in yonder stall at whose feet the shepherds fall?" That question and its answer are critical. If we answer incorrectly, we miss our Messiah. We can be mistaken about many things and still enter heaven, but we mustn't be wrong about the Baby in the manger. He is the God-Man, both human and divine, two complete natures combining in one Person. Let's investigate Jesus' deity as discussed in Matthew's account of the Christmas story. Matthew would make a good Sgt. Joe Friday of *Dragnet* because he gives "just the facts" without a lot of commentary (v. 18).

1. **The virgin birth reveals Jesus' deity (v. 18).** Matthew states that Mary and Joseph were betrothed. In the ancient culture, parents arranged marriages for their children. When the "engaged" children reached mid-teens, they entered a betrothal period, and it was during this time that Mary became pregnant. There were only two options: either she was a virgin or she was not. Let's assume she was not a virgin. Now we have two more options. Either she had relations with Joseph or with some other man. Nothing we know of Mary indicates unfaithfulness to Joseph, and nothing we know of Joseph indicates he would disclaim responsibility if it were his. If Mary had not been with a man, then she was, in fact, a virgin. How is that possible? When Mary asked that question Luke 1:34, the angel said: "The Holy Spirit will come upon you, and the power of the Highest will overshadow you; therefore, also, that Holy One who is to be born will be called the Son of God." *Son of God* is a Hebrew idiom meaning possessing the nature of God. Without His deity there is no explanation for the virgin conception and birth.

2. **The angel's words announce Jesus' deity (vv. 19, 20).** On learning of Mary's pregnancy, Joseph was crushed. But an angel appeared to him saying, "That which is conceived in her is of the Holy

Spirit." Literally, it is "out of the Holy Spirit," implying source and substance. The substance or essence of this child is God Himself.

3. **Jesus' mission demands His deity (v. 21).** The angel continued, "You shall call His name Jesus, for He will save His people from their sins." The name *Jesus* means "God saves." Jesus' name and mission reveal His deity. Do you recall from algebra class a formula that states, "If A = B and B = C, then A = C"? God saves. Jesus saves. Hence, Jesus is God. Why must Jesus be God in order to save us? Sin created a penalty—"the penalty of eternal destruction, away from the presence of the Lord and from the glory of His power" (2 Thess. 1:9 NASB). The penalty for sin is an eternal penalty. If our Savior were a mere man, how long would he be paying the penalty? Forever. We'd never be saved because the penalty would never be paid. If we're to be saved, we have to have a Savior who can pay an eternal penalty without taking eternity to do it. Only God Himself can do that (see Is. 43:11).

4. **Isaiah predicts Jesus' deity (vv. 22, 23).** Matthew refers to Isaiah 7:14, in which armies attacked the kingdom of Judah led by King Ahaz. Fear gripped Ahaz, and God instructed Isaiah to calm him by allowing him to ask for a sign. When Ahaz refused, Isaiah said, "The Lord Himself will give you a sign. Behold, the virgin shall conceive and bear a Son, and shall call His name Immanuel." God's promise was that a young woman who currently hadn't known a man would bear a son. Before the boy was old enough to know the difference between good and evil, God would rid Judah of these invaders. The promise was, "Ahaz, when you're afraid, relax and look at the boy, Immanuel. He is a sign that God is with you." Matthew explained that the ultimate fulfillment of Isaiah 7:14 is Jesus Himself. He is a sign God will deliver His people. He is "God with us."

5. **Joseph's faith embraced Jesus' deity (vv. 24, 25).** Hearing the angel, Joseph awakened and obeyed. What faith! It overcame crushed emotions and public ridicule. It overcame physical desire, keeping Mary a virgin until after Christ was born. What could fuel such faith? The fact that this was no ordinary conception. This was miraculous. This was God Himself.

Conclusion: How should we respond to Matthew's Christmas story? Just as Joseph did. In this day of political correctness where Jesus is not to be mentioned, let alone declared to be God, we are ready to declare our Savior's name. Who is that in yonder stall? He is Jesus, Immanuel, God with Us. My God is in yonder stall.

STATS, STORIES, AND MORE

"I do not think of Christ as God alone, or man alone, but both together. For I know He was hungry, and I know that with five loaves He fed five thousand. I know He was thirsty, and I know that He turned the water into wine. I know he was carried in a ship, and I know that He walked on the sea. I know that He died, and I know that He raised the dead. I know that He was set before Pilate, and I know that He sits with the Father on His throne. I know that He was worshipped by angels, and I know that He was stoned by the Jews. And truly some of these I ascribe to the human, and others to the divine nature. For by reason of this He is said to have been both God and man." —Attributed to John Chrysostom (ca. A.D. 347–407), Bishop of Constantinople

---

SUGGESTED ORDER OF WORSHIP

Who Is He in Yonder Stall?

Prelude—Instrumental Group
Mighty to Save

Call to Worship—Praise Team
MSPW 4 *God of Wonders*

Announcements—Pastoral Staff

Prayer of Praise—Pastoral Staff

Praise and Worship—Congregation
MSPW2 *Lord, I Lift Your Name on High* (2x in G)
CH 247 *Let's Worship and Adore Him* (1x in G, 1x in Ab)
WH 168 *Who Is He?* (vv. 1–5 in Ab)
CH 248/249 *O Come, All Ye Faithful* (2x in Ab)

Welcome—Pastoral Staff

SUGGESTED ORDER OF WORSHIP—*Continued*

Welcome Song—Congregation
CH 244 *Come, Thou Long-Expected Jesus* (2x in F)

Offertory Prayer—Pastoral Staff

Offertory Praise—Congregation
CH 261 *Away in a Manger* (1x in F)
CH 262 *Away in a Manger* (v. 2 in F)
CH 261 *Away in a Manger* (1x in F)
CH 253 *Silent Night* (vv. 1, 2, 4 in Bb)
CH 254 *Isn't He* (1x in G)

Message—Pastor
Who Is He in Yonder Stall?

Hymn of Response/Invitation—Congregation
CH 243 *Emmanuel* (2x in C)

Hymn of Benediction—Congregation
CH 795 *We Are So Blessed* (1x in Eb)

Postlude—Instrumental Group
MSPW2 *Lord, I Lift Your Name on High*

Additional Sermons and Lesson Ideas

Why Did He Come?   *Date preached:*
By Dr. Timothy Beougher

Scripture: Hebrews 2:14–18

Introduction: Jesus did not enter the world just to be here; He had a mission to fulfill.

1. He came to deliver us from the fear of death (vv. 14, 15). George Bernard Shaw said, "The ultimate statistic is this: 1 out of 1 dies." Jesus came to deliver us from death and its terrors.
2. He came to deliver us from the fury of judgment (vv. 16, 17). He has made propitiation for our sins.
3. He came to deliver us from the force of temptation (v. 18). This remarkable verse tells us that Christ identifies with our temptation; He can overcome.

Conclusion: He has come for us; now He invites us to come to Him.

Christmas Eve Service
The Greatest Gift of All   *Date preached:*
By Dr. Kent Spann

Scripture: 2 Corinthians 9:15, "Thanks be to God for His indescribable gift!"

The Best Christmas Gift
No doubt the tree is surrounded by gifts of all kinds tonight. If you have kids or grandkids, I am sure by now they are excited about waking up tomorrow to find the gifts around the tree.

What is the best Christmas gift you have ever received?

Tonight I want us to consider the greatest gift of all.

The Greatest Gift of All
Paul since chapter 8 has been talking about giving of our resources. He has pointed out the generosity of the Macedonians and encouraged the Corinthians to be generous as they gave to the special Jerusalem offering.

As he concludes his teaching on giving, like always his thoughts take him to Christ which leads to an outburst of excitement and praise.

"Thanks be to God for His indescribable gift!" (2 Cor. 9:15)

I can see Paul contemplating the great truth of the indescribable gift given in Christ. He is a little more than enthusiastic; he is jumping up and down. Maybe he throws his hands up and shouts as he writes this.

Paul says that God's gift is indescribable. This particular word is found only here in the New Testament. Paul reaches for a word to describe, and the only word he can come up with is "indescribable." Have you ever tried to describe something about which you were so excited, you couldn't find the words to describe it? It is the greatest gift of all.

1. **The greatest gift of all is mysterious.** What do you think of when you hear the term "mysterious gift"? Perhaps you think of a white elephant gift that you got at a party. It may bring to mind that gift which Aunt Susie sent you one year which you have never figured out. If you travel a lot, you may think about a strange package that has been left in a corner.

   When I speak about a gift being mysterious, I am speaking of a gift that causes a person to be filled with awe and wonder. It is a gift that eludes comprehension or explanation.

   When you consider the gift of the Incarnation, the coming of the Christ into the world, the feeling should be of awe and wonder. Sadly, the story of the Incarnation has become so commonplace, it has been stripped of the mysterious.

   In this poem written some fifteen centuries ago, Augustine tried to capture the mystery of the Incarnation:

   > *Maker of the sun,*
   > *He is made under the sun.*
   > *In the Father he remains,*
   > *From his mother he goes forth.*
   > *Creator of heaven and earth,*
   > *He was born on earth under heaven.*
   > *Unspeakably wise,*
   > *He is wisely speechless.*
   > *Filling the world,*
   > *He lies in a manger.*
   > *Ruler of the stars,*
   > *He nurses at his mother's bosom.*
   > *He is both great in the nature of God,*
   > *and small in the form of a servant.*

   I would invite you to rekindle the mystery of Christ. Let your heart be filled with wonder and awe of what God did that first Christmas. Let the wonder of Mary the mother of Jesus fill your heart:

   "But Mary kept all these things and pondered them in her heart." (Luke 2:19)

2. **The greatest gift of all is miraculous.**
   Miracles have fallen into disrepute. In our secular culture where we can come up with a logical answer for every happening, there is little room for the miraculous. Yet according to a 2008 study by the Pew Forum, 79 percent of Americans believe in miracles.

There is no miracle greater than the Incarnation. Think of all the miraculous things that happened that first Christmas.

A. The Old Testament prophecies were fulfilled:

"But you, Bethlehem Ephrathah, Though you are little among the thousands of Judah, Yet out of you shall come forth to Me The One to be Ruler in Israel, Whose goings forth are from of old, From everlasting." (Micah 5:2)

B. Angels visited Mary and Joseph on separate occasions

C. An angelic choir appeared to a group of lowly shepherds

D. A star unlike any other appeared in the sky and led the Magi to the Christ child

E. There were vision and dreams

F. The mother was a virgin

G. But none is bigger than this, this child was Immanuel:

"'Behold, the virgin shall be with child, and bear a Son, and they shall call His name Immanuel,' which is translated, 'God with us.'" (Matt. 1:23)

This child was the infinite God-man. There is no logical human explanation, try as you may, to explain Immanuel. It is a miracle.

3. **The greatest gift of all is magnificent.**

A. This gift is magnificent because it provides peace with God.

B. This gift is magnificent because it promises forgiveness of all your sin.

C. This gift is magnificent because it brings eternal joy.

D. This gift is magnificent because it meets your deepest needs and longings.

E. This gift is magnificent because it sets you free from bondage and slavery.

F. This gift is magnificent because it catapults us into the love of God.

G. This gift is magnificent because it brings us into the presence of God.

H. This gift is magnificent because it keeps giving for all of eternity.

4. **The greatest gift of all is matchless.**

There is no gift that compares with the gift of the Christ. The best Christmas gift that you have ever received pales in comparison to the gift God gave that first Christmas to you and me.

5. **The greatest gift of all is measureless.**

During the Christmas season stores will run special sales with this little disclaimer, "While supplies last." What they are offering is in limited supply.

That is not the case with the greatest gift of all. There is no disclaimer, "while supplies last." This gift is measureless. All who ask for this gift will receive it.

Conclusion: The gift of Christ is the greatest gift of all. Have you received this gift?

DECEMBER 26, 2010

SUGGESTED SERMON

What Do We Do Now That Christmas Is Over?

Date preached:

By Dr. Kent Spann

Scripture: Matthew 2:1–12

Twas the day after Christmas, and all through the house,
Every creature was hurtin' even the mouse.
The toys were all broken, their batteries dead;
Santa passed out, with some ice on his head.

Wrapping and ribbons just covered the floor,
While upstairs the family continued to snore.
And I in my T-shirt, new Reeboks and jeans,
I went into the kitchen and started to clean.

When out on the lawn there arose such a clatter,
I sprang from the sink to see what was the matter.
Away to the window I flew like a flash,
Tore open the curtains, and threw up the sash.

When what to my wondering eyes should appear,
But a little white truck, with an oversized mirror.
The driver was smiling, so lively and grand;
The patch on his jacket said "U.S. POSTMAN."

With a handful of bills, he grinned like a fox.
Then quickly he stuffed them into our mailbox.

Bill after bill, after bill, they still came.
Whistling and shouting he called them by name:
"Now Dillard's, now Broadway's, now Penny's and Sears
Here's Robinson's, Levitz's and Target's and Mervyn's.
To the tip or your limit, every store, every mall,
Now chargeaway-chargeaway-chargeaway all!"

He whooped and he whistled as he finished his work.
He filled up the box, and then turned with a jerk.

He sprang to his truck and he drove down the road,
Driving much faster with just half a load.

Then I heard him exclaim with great holiday cheer,
"ENJOY WHAT YOU BOUGHT . . . .
YOU'LL BE PAYING ALL YEAR!"

After Christmas Syndrome

The gifts have been unwrapped and your trash can is full. All the friends and family are on their way home from the holidays. The tree is ready to be taken down along with all the other decorations. Another Christmas has come and gone leaving with you with the post-holiday blues.

What do Christians do, now that Christmas is over? Do we simply settle back into the old routine? Do we become blue? Do we pack away the Christmas spirit? Do we put it up until next year? A family was driving by the church a few days after Christmas when the little boy noticed that the nativity scene had been taken down. He said, innocently enough, "I see they've put Jesus away for another year." Unfortunately, all too often that is what happens. Jesus gets put away with all the wrappings, nativity scenes, lights, ornaments, etc.

What do we do now that Christmas is over? Well, there are some people who can show us what to do now that Christmas is over. Their story is found in Matthew 2:1–12. It is the account of the Wise Men, or the Magi.

The Magi

Who were these Magi? According to the ancient historian Herodotus, the Magi were a tribe of people within the larger people called the Medes. They were a hereditary priesthood tribe, somewhat like the Levites in Israel. They functioned as the priests in their pagan rituals. From the time of the Babylonian Empire to the Roman Empire, they maintained a place of tremendous prominence and significance in the Orient.

Is it strange that God chose them to show us what we should do now that Christmas is over? There are two things the Magi did that we can do all throughout the year:

1. **We can seek Christ throughout the year (2:1, 2).** The text makes it clear they were on a mission. They were seeking the King of the Jews. These men sought the Christ long after the miracle of the birth took place.

   A. **When we genuinely seek Christ, it will require some things of us.** They choose to seek the Christ, but it required some things of them. The same is true for us. When we seek Christ, it will require some things of us.

      *It takes **effort** to seek Christ.* They had to make a long journey and overcome some great obstacles. On top of that, they had to deal with some difficult people such as the religious leaders and the self-absorbed and dangerous King Herod.

It takes **time** *to seek Christ.* It took a lot of the Magi's time. Seeking Christ is not a one-time experience. Seeking Christ is not something that can be rushed. It requires that we spend time with Him.

It takes **sacrifice** *to seek Christ.* These Magi made great sacrifices to find the Christ. Seeking Christ will require sacrifices on your part. Paul certainly was willing to make those sacrifices (Phil. 3:1–11).

B. When we genuinely seek Christ, we will find Him.

"And you will seek Me and find Me, when you search for Me with all your heart." (Jer. 29:13)

C. When we genuinely seek Christ, we will be richly blessed.

We will be richly blessed as we experience His presence (2:11).

We will be richly blessed as we experience His joy (2:10).

"You will show me the path of life; In Your presence is fullness of joy; At Your right hand are pleasures forevermore." (Ps. 16:11)

How do we seek Him? Here are a few things we can do.

- Pray
- Spend time daily in God's Word
- Maintain a daily quiet time
- Attend church regularly

2. **We can worship Christ throughout the year (2:11).** Worship is the most important work of the church. Worship is the lifeblood of the church. Worship is the most important service of the believer; therefore, it should be the highest priority of the believer.

How do we worship Christ? We can learn some things from these Magi.

A. We make Him the focus of our worship as the Magi did when they immediately focused on the Christ child.

B. We submit our life to Him as the Magi did when they bowed before Christ.

C. We give our all to Him as the Magi did when they gave their expensive gifts to Christ.

Conclusion: What do we do now that Christmas is over? We seek and worship Christ. We worship Him year-round. We seek Him every day!

A man was sitting in his living room in the middle of January when he heard a thin, piping voice singing "O Come, All Ye Faithful." He went to his front door and opened it, and there was a little boy singing Christmas carols.

He said to the boy, "What are you doing?"

The child replied, "I'm singing Christmas carols."

The man said, "Why, son, it's the middle of January."

The little boy said, "I know, but I had the measles during Christmas, and I'm just now getting around to doing my caroling."

Let's not just do it at Christmas but year-round!

SUGGESTED ORDER OF WORSHIP

Prelude—Instrumental Group
   CH 129 *Great and Mighty*

Call to Worship—Congregation
   MSPW *Open the Eyes of My Heart* (2x in G)

Prayer of Worship—Pastoral Staff

Welcome—Pastoral Staff

Worship Song—Congregation (meet and greet)
   CH 107 *Lord, I Lift Your Name on High* (2x in G)
   CH 90 *Joyful, Joyful* (1x in G)

Testimony of Praise (2-minute video, *Giving Praise for God's Faithfulness in 2010*)
   CH 139 *Great Is Thy Faithfulness* (vv. 1, 2 in D, chorus in Eb)
   MSPW2 109 *He Knows My Name* (2x in E)
   MSPW 24 *Jesus, We Crown You With Praise* (2x in E)

Offertory Prayer—Pastoral Staff

Offertory Praise—Congregation
   CH 213 *We Bring a Sacrifice of Praise* (slowly—a prayer of worship) (1x w/tag in D)
   CH 3 *Holy, Holy, Holy! Lord God Almighty* (vv. 1, 2 in D and v. 4 in Eb)

Message—Pastor
   What Do We Do Now That Christmas Is Over?

Hymn of Response/Invitation—Congregation
   CH 47 *Jesus, Lord to Me*

Hymn of Benediction—Congregation
   CH 107 *Lord, I Lift Your Name on High*

Postlude—Instrumental Group
   We Bring a Sacrifice of Praise (faster tempo)

Additional Sermons and Lesson Ideas

The Wonder of Christmas and New Year's Day
By Kevin Riggs

Date preached:

Scripture: Luke 2:52

Introduction: Luke 2 begins with the birth of Christ and ends by giving us a picture of His perfect humanity. We, too, should be developing in wisdom and stature, and in favor with God and man. As we prepare for a New Year, let this verse give you areas in which God wants you to grow:

1. **Intellectually, in wisdom.** Many of us quit learning the moment we finish our formal education. But we should always be challenging ourselves, stretching our minds. (See Prov. 1:7; 18:15; 24:5; 28:2.)
2. **Physically, in stature.** This involves taking care of our bodies—exercising, eating right, resting. God cares about this aspect of our lives. (See 1 Cor. 3:16–17; 6:19–20; 9:26–27.)
3. **Spiritually, in favor with God.** This defines the core value system and spiritual life. (See 1 Tim. 4:8.)
4. **Socially, in favor with man.** This involves working on relationship skills, becoming friendlier, learning to understand before being understood, reconciling, and serving. (See Rom. 12:18.)

Conclusion: Make this the year for Christlikeness!

Passing On the Timeless Message
By Rev. Peter Grainger

Date preached:

Scripture: 2 Timothy 2:1, 2

Introduction: The Christmas shepherds were the first evangelists, taking the news of Christ's birth to all they met. But they weren't the last. The transmission that propels the gospel from one generation to another is explained in 2 Timothy 2:1, 2.

1. **From Jesus to Paul.** The teachings of Jesus were entrusted to the apostles (Acts 2:42), including Paul (1 Cor. 15:1–11; Gal. 1:11, 12).
2. **From Paul to Timothy.** The message Paul preached was heard and learned by Timothy in the presence of many others (1 Tim. 6:20; 2 Tim. 1:13, 14).
3. **From Timothy to reliable men.** Men who were dependable (1 Cor. 4:1, 2).
4. **From reliable men to others.** Which includes, through the passing of time, you and me.

Conclusion: The gospel is not something we come to church to hear; it is something we go from church to tell!

FUNERAL MESSAGE FOR A BELIEVER
My First Five Minutes in Heaven
By Mark Becton

In 1940, beloved pastor Dr. A. N. Hall died suddenly of a heart attack. On the seventy-five-year-old's desk, his wife found the outline of what would have been his last sermon. The sermon he had been preparing was entitled "My First Five Minutes in Heaven."[1]

Dr. Hall had been thinking about what he would experience in his first five minutes of heaven. As believers, we often do that. (Speak of the loved one who was a believer, then share.) According to what the Bible says in Revelation 21 and other passages, let me give you an idea of (the loved one's) first five minutes in heaven.

Renewed Strength
In his (or her) first five minutes in heaven, (the loved one) experienced renewed strength of mind and body. (Read Isaiah 35:5, 6a. Then describe the loved one's condition prior to passing, and assure the family of his/her renewed strength in heaven.)

Inspiring Sights
According to Revelation 21, (the loved one) saw walls twenty stories tall made of jasper. He (or she) saw walls supported by twelve foundations. Each foundation was made of precious gems. He (or she) saw three gates on each wall. Each gate was cut from a single pearl. Stepping through a gate, he (or she) was walking on streets and looking at buildings made of transparent gold.

(Use a story or insight from the family that would give them an idea of their loved one's reaction upon seeing heaven for the first time.)

Amazing Sounds
In his (or her) first five minutes, the breathtaking sights of heaven were matched only by the sounds. God has always been a music lover. He sent His choir to sing at Jesus' birth. Over seventy times, the Psalms speak of singing to God.

The music was amazing, but so was the sound of silence. For the

---

[1]W. A. Criswell, *Standing on the Promises* (Dallas: Word Publishing, 1990), 157.

first time in his (or her) life he (or she) heard no sorrow. (Read Revelation 21:4. Then, share of the loved one's possible love for music, or if they passed after a long illness, share that they will never hear the sounds of another hospital room.)

Warm Reunions

Yet, the greatest sounds (the loved one) heard were the sounds of familiar voices—family members saying and his (or her) Lord sharing, "Welcome home." This was Jesus' promise in John 14:1–3 (Read it).

(Share about the reunion with friends and family members who were believers and the opportunity for those who are not believers to be a part of the reunion. Then, share the plan of salvation.)

(Finally, remind the family that their loved one is in heaven and is fine. They are the ones who are hurting. This would be a good time to remind them of how God was the shepherd of their loved one and that God will shepherd them through this time as well. Then, share Psalm 23.)

FUNERAL SERMON FOR UNBELIEVER

God Is . . .

By Mark Becton

A third-grade teacher asked her students to explain "God." Eight-year-old Danny Dutton wrote,

> *"One of God's main jobs is making people. He makes these to put in the place of the ones that die so there will be enough people to take care of things here on earth. He doesn't make grown-ups just babies. I think because they are smaller and easier to make. That way He doesn't have to take up His valuable time teaching them to talk and walk. He can just leave that up to the mothers and fathers. I think it works out pretty good."* (Evangelical Press News Service)

It seems everyone at every age has an opinion of God. And at a moment like this, I believe your opinion of God determines whether or not you feel His comfort.

(Mention the loved one and his or her relationship with all who are there. He or she was their parent, grandparent, sibling, friend, etc. God knows their hurt over the loss and offers His comfort.)

Countless throughout history have hurt the way you are hurting right now and have experienced God's comfort. According to Psalm 46, you can, too, when you stop and realize all that God is. (Read Psalm 46:1, 2)

God Is . . . Home Base

Verse 1 literally states that God is our refuge and strength in "tight places." (The Hebrew word for *trouble* means "tight places.") Each of us knows what it's like to be in a tight place. We felt it as children playing "Hide and Seek." When the one who was "IT" drew closer, we felt the pressure and ran as hard as we could to find home base.

You feel something like that when you lose a loved one. It's a "tight place." Here, God says, "Run to me, hold on to me and let me be your home base."

God Is . . . Big Enough!

When you run to God as your home base, you will find Him to be big enough for whatever you face—even for something as hard as losing a loved one. Sally learned this. Sitting in her daddy's lap, Sally asked him, "Daddy, how big is God?" Though he could have talked about the vastness of the universe, he wisely said, "Honey, God will always be a little bigger than you need."

Psalm 46:8, 9 reminds you how big God is. (Read the verses. Then, talk of how the loved one may have seemed bigger than life to them. Then, say that it's time to let God be there for them. He will always be bigger than they need.)

God Is . . . In the Stillness!
A natural question to ask is, "How can I find God as my home base, and how will I know that He is big enough to help me?" Psalm 46:10 provides the answers (Read verse 10).

Times like the loss of a loved one force us to be still. We change schedules and cancel plans to be together and be still. These times also cause us to evaluate our lives. We ask ourselves, "Do I have a relationship with God so that He will always be my home base and will always be bigger than I need?" If God's not, He can. (Share the plan of salvation.)

My prayer is that you have experienced God's comfort today and that you will have His comfort for the rest of your life . . . because you have established Him forever as your home base.

FUNERAL MESSAGE FOR A BELIEVER

Living Well; Dying Well

By Dr. Kent Spann

Scripture: Philippians 1:20, 21

It is not a secret that our society is enamored with living well. The Baby Boomers definitely have been consumed with living well. People want to know how to live well physically, that is, staying in good shape as long as they can. People want to know how to live well financially, that is, being financially secure and ready to retire. People also want to know how to live well relationally, thus the popularity of Dr. Phil and Oprah Winfrey.

How do we live well? If you Google the phrase "live well" it will come up with over 3 million hits. Some of the advice is good, but some of it is pure nonsense. So, how do we live well? It is an important question and one worthy of every person's consideration. Benjamin Franklin said, "Wish not so much to live long as to live well."

In the midst of this obsession with living well, there is another question that needs to be asked. "How do we die well?" People want to know how to live well, but they don't really want to think about how to die well. Art Buchwald once said, "Dying is easy. Parking is hard." Of course that comes from someone who wasn't dying.

How do we die well? Epicurus, the Greek philosopher (341 B.C.– 270 B.C.) made a very wise statement when he said, "The art of living well and the art of dying well are one." He realized they go hand in hand.

Today, I want us to ponder the question, "How do we live and die well?" I want to speak to those who are living. We have considered the life of the person whom we are gathered to remember. They lived their life. The question today is "How can those of us gathered here today live and die well?"

The answer is found in the Bible.

> *According to my earnest expectation and hope that in nothing I shall be ashamed, but with all boldness, as always, so now also Christ will be magnified in my body, whether by life or by death. For to me, to live is Christ, and to die is gain. (Phil. 1:20, 21)*

Paul knew how to live well and he knew how to die well. When he wrote it, he was in a prison waiting for what he was sure would be a death sentence by the cruel Nero. His advice is very simple.

1. **If we want to live well, we must live for Christ.** We all live for something. Film actor Johnny Depp, after the birth in May 1999 of his daughter Lily-Rose Melody, said in *The London Daily Telegraph* (Jan. 6, 2000):

   > *My little girl is not just the greatest thing that's ever happened to me— she's the only thing that has ever happened to me. I've been floating and haven't touched the ground ever since she was born. It's the only reason to live. It's the only reason to wake up in the morning. It's the only reason to draw breath.*

   For Johnny, living is his little girl. For some, it is career advancement. For another, it is a relationship. While for others, it is getting a certain position. For Paul, living was *all* about Christ.

   How do we live for Christ? I want to let God's Word answer that question for us today.

   A. **We believe in Him (Rom. 10:9, 10).** It begins with believing Christ as your Savior.

   B. **We know Him (Phil. 3:7, 8).**

   C. **We obey Him (Phil. 1:21).**

   D. **We serve Him (1 Tim. 1:12).**

   E. **We proclaim Him (Phil. 1:18).** For Paul it was all about living for Christ.

   > *I have been crucified with Christ; it is no longer I who live, but Christ lives in me; and the life which I now live in the flesh I live by faith in the Son of God, who loved me and gave Himself for me. (Gal. 2:20)*

   So if we want to live well, we must live for Christ.

2. **If we want to die well, we must die in Christ.** Paul says that for him death is a gain. The word *gain* was a financial word indicating a profit.

   How can Paul say that to die is gain? Because he was in Christ. Consider just three things that happen when we die in Christ according to the Bible.

A. We get set free from this earthly body (23b). The word "depart" is a nautical term indicating loosing the anchor or the moorings of a ship in order to sail out of port. When the believer dies, he is loosed from this body of sin and given a new body.

Listen to 2 Corinthians 5:1.

B. We get to be with Christ forever (23b). Jesus promised in John 14:1–3 that where He is the believer will be.

C. We get to live in a better place called heaven (23b). There is no place like home, and for the believer Heaven *is* home (Phil. 3:20, 21).

Conclusion: The secret to living well is dying well, while the secret to dying well is living well, and the key to both is Christ. Are you living well, that is, living for Christ? Will you die well, that is, die in Christ? Now is the time to do a thorough examination of your life and make sure.

Parent–Child Dedication

(Pastor introduces as each set of parents, child, and any other family members and they walk in front of the church. After all family sets enter and are introduced to the congregation, the scripture is read, the charge is given, parents and friends respond, the pastor prays, and during the time families exit, the *Cradle Song* is sung as a solo.)

Introduction of Service—Pastor
We've met today for the purpose of presenting our children to the Lord. In I Samuel we find the story of a mother that God blessed with a little baby boy. This was a special son because God had given him to this family in direct response to Hannah's request for a child. Now, at approximately 3 years of age, Hannah comes to the High Priest, child in tow, and says, "The Lord answered my prayer and gave [this boy] to me. Now I give him back to the Lord. He will belong to the Lord all his life" (1 Sam. 1:27). After she gave her child back to God, she and her family stayed at the House of the Lord and worshiped.

So, today we come to give back to the Lord our children. In a few minutes, I will read a scripture from Deuteronomy 6:1–9. This command was for all the families to meet every day for the purpose of teaching God's ways diligently to their children. There were three kinds of groups here: 1) the children; for us, it is the group being dedicated; 2) the family; for us that refers to the mothers and fathers, grandparents and relatives; and, 3) the church family; yes, we too have a responsibility to teach our children, to talk of God's wonders every day, and to exhort our most cherished gifts in the ways of the Lord.

Introduction of Parents and Children
Each Family Set is introduced: parents, child, grandparents, etc.

Scripture Reading and Comments—Deuteronomy 6:1–9—Pastor
1 "Now this is the commandment, and these are the statutes and judgments which the LORD your God has commanded to teach you, that you may observe them in the land which you days of your life, and that your days may be prolonged.

3 Therefore hear, O Israel, and be careful to observe it, that it may be well with you, and that you may multiply greatly as the LORD *God of your fathers has promised you—'a land flowing with milk and honey.' 4 "Hear, O Israel: The* LORD *our God, the* LORD *is one! 5 You shall love the* LORD *your God with all your heart, with all your soul, and with all your strength. 6 "And these words which I command you today shall be in your heart. 7 You shall teach them diligently to your children, and shall talk of them when you sit in your house, when you walk by the way, when you lie down, and when you rise up. 8 You shall bind them as a sign on your hand, and they shall be as frontlets between your eyes. 9 You shall write them on the doorposts of your house and on your gates. Deuteronomy 6:1–9* NKJV

Our promises today are taken from this passage of scripture. We will dedicate ourselves to God and renew our commitment to teach our children with diligence, dedication, and determination. We will talk of God's statutes and precepts throughout the day and share with our children the many wonders of God.

Dedication, Charge and Commitment

Dedication Charge of Parents: *(Parents please repeat after pastor.) We hereby promise to faithfully teach and train our child in all the ways of the Lord. We promise to faithfully honor His Word and promote His Work. We promise to encourage spiritual growth through personal example of God's graces in daily living.*

Dedication Charge of Grandparents and Relatives: *(Please repeat after pastor.) We hereby promise to faithfully teach and train our child in all the ways of the Lord. We promise to faithfully honor His Word and promote His Work. We promise to encourage spiritual growth through personal example of God's graces in daily living.*

Dedication and Commitment of Child: *(Parents please repeat after the pastor.) We give back to the Lord this child.*

> We promise to encourage our child to know and love God with all their heart, soul, mind, spirit, and strength. We want God to take our child and use him/her for His Glory, Honor and Praise. We promise to love our child by being an example of His grace in our own daily living.

> **Commitment from the Congregation:** *(Pastor turns to the congregation and says, "Please repeat after me.") As a congregation of friends, we promise to support this family. We promise to pray for them. We promise to encourage them as they seek to nurture and guide this child in all the ways of the Lord.*

Pastor says to Parents, Relatives, and Congregation: *And, all God's People said, "Amen." (Everyone repeats, "Amen.")*

Prayer of Dedication

Pastor—*Thank You for this moment in time. Thank You for these promises and commitments. We do give this child back to You for Your use in Your Kingdom at Your desire and for Your purposes. Please bring this child to a saving knowledge of Your self at an early age. May they walk with You. May they talk to You. May they remember You when they when they sit in their homes, when they lie down, when they rise up. May they think of You all throughout the day. Give us wisdom as parents, extended family and a congregation to know how to encourage, exhort and edify this child at every part of their journey with You. In Jesus' Name we pray. Amen.*

Song of Dedication—Vocal Soloist
   CH 261 *Away in a Manger (Cradle Song)* (vv. 2 and 3)
   (Families exit during the singing of the solo)

Sermon by pastor if desired
   A message on children or parenting would be appropriate.

Hymn of Benediction—Congregation
   CH 583 *You Are My All in All*

Postlude—Instrumental Group
   CH 588 *All for Jesus*

Christmas Eve Candlelight Service

Prelude—Instrumental Group
CH 270 *Joy to the World* (in D)
CH 258 *Go Tell It on the Mountain* (in F)

Christmas Greeting—Pastor
O Come, O Come Emmanuel—Piano Solo
Mary Had a Baby—Vocal Solo

Scripture Reading—Deacon and Wife
Psalm 46:1–11

**Christmas Testimony (Live or by Video Approximately
2 minutes)**
I Wonder As I Wander—Vocal Solo with Guitar

Prayer of Thanksgiving—Director of Evangelism
Beautiful Baby—Ensemble or Praise Team

Scripture Reading—Young Married Couple
Is. 40:1, 3, 5, 11

Christmas Singing—Worship Leader and Congregation
CH 269 *How Great Our Joy!* (vv. 1c, 2c, 4c in C with
transition)
CH 270 *Joy to the World* (vv. 1, 2, 4 in D)

Prayer of Praise—Trustee or Sunday School Teacher

Christmas Singing—Congregation
CH 278 *Angels We Have Heard on High* (vv. 1, 3, 4 in F)

Scripture Reading—Director of Women's Ministry
Luke 2:8–14

Christmas Singing—Congregation
CH 277 *Hark, the Herald Angels Sing* (vv. 1, 2, 3 in F)

Scripture Reading—Director of Sports Ministries and Wife
Luke 1:15–20
"Infant Holy, Infant Lowly"—Solo by Child

Scripture Reading—Young Married Couple
Matthew 1:18–23
O Holy Night—Solo with Congregation singing the chorus

Offering of Praise and Worship—Pastor*
Away in a Manger—Instrumental Solo

Christmas Message—Pastor

Lighting of Candles by Congregation—Worship Leader and
Congregation
CH 147 *Silent Night, Holy Night*

Prayer of Thanksgiving—Pastor

Christmas Singing—Congregation
CH 249 *O Come All Ye Faithful* (vv. 1, 3 in F)

Postlude—Instrumental Group
CH 278 *Angels We Have Heard on High* (in F)
God Rest Ye Merry, Gentlemen

---

*Offering is highlighted by homemade manger placed at the front of the church. The pastor
invites the children to come and give a gift to the Christ Child. All proceeds go to taking
care of orphanage children.*

Christmas Eve Communion Service

Prelude

Call to Worship—Ensemble
  Hallelujah to the New Born King

Baptism—Pastoral Staff

Communion Service
  Sharing of the Bread—Pastor and Deacons
    (Music sung during the passing out of the bread)
    CH 295 *Tell Me the Story of Jesus*—Solo on verses,
      congregation on chorus
    BH 124 *Who Is He in Yonder Stall*—Solo on verses,
      congregation on chorus
  Prayer of Thanksgiving for the Bread—Pastor or Deacon
  Sharing of the Cup—Pastor and Deacons
    (Music sung during the serving of the juice)
    CH 461 *In Remembrance*—Solo with Ensemble
  Prayer of Thanksgiving for the Blood—Pastor or Deacon
    Father (from *Tapestry of Praise,* Prism Music)—Worship
      Leader with Congregation

Worship and Praise—Congregation
  CH 281 *What Child Is This?*

Offertory Prayer—Pastoral Staff

Offertory Praise—Praise Team with Congregation
  CH 280 *One Small Child*

Message—Pastor
  The Real Meaning of Christmas

Hymn of Response/Invitation—Congregation
  CH 79 *My Jesus, I Love Thee*

Benediction Hymn—Congregation
  CH 270 *Joy to the World*

Postlude—Congregation
  CH 265 *The First Noel*

Expository Preaching Plain and Simple

By Dr. Kent Spann

Big Ed goes to the revival and listens to the preacher. After a while the preacher asks anyone with needs to come forward to be prayed over. Big Ed gets in line. When it's his turn, the preacher says, "Big Ed, what do you want me to pray about?"

Big Ed says, "Preacher, I need you to pray for my hearing."

So the preacher puts one finger in Big Ed's ear and the other hand on top of his head and shouts, hollers, and prays a while.

After a few minutes, he removes his hands and says, "Big Ed, how's your hearing now?"

Big Ed says, "I don't know, Preacher, it's not until next Wednesday at the Dupage County Courthouse."

Have you ever, like Big Ed, been misunderstood by someone?

I am afraid all too often expository preaching is misunderstood. The mere mention of the term brings to mind ideas of expository preaching or preachers who define expository preaching for you. Some of you are pulling out your dictionaries to look up the phrase. Some may have a negative view of expository preaching because of what you saw as expository preaching.

I believe in this postmodern culture, it is more important than ever that we get back to expository preaching. The late Stephen Olford, speaking at The Southern Baptist Theological Seminary, made it clear that anointed expository preaching is absolutely necessary if there is going to be revival in the church. He said, *"There must be a return to anointed expository preaching of the Word of God calling for a divine verdict."* He is right on target.

What It Ain't

Sometimes the best thing to do is first clear the air before you try to explain something. There are many misconceptions about expository preaching. I want to speak to those.

1. It is not a commentary running from word to word and verse to verse without unity, outline, and pervasive drive.
2. It is not rambling comments and offhand remarks about a passage without a background of thorough exegesis and logical order.

3. It is not pure exegesis, no matter how scholarly, if it lacks a theme, thesis, outline, and development.

4. It is not a mere structural outline of a passage with a few supporting comments but without other rhetorical and sermonic elements.

5. It is not a topical homily using scattered parts of the passage but omitting discussion of other equally important parts.

6. It is not a chopped-up collection of grammatical findings and quotations from commentaries without a fusing of these elements into a smooth, flowing, interesting, and compelling message.

7. It is not a Bible reading that links a number of scattered passages treating a common theme but fails to handle any of them in a thorough, grammatical, and contextual manner.

8. It is not exclusively a Bible book study.

9. It is not preaching which explains the meaning of the text in its context without applying it to today's hearers.

10. It is not a Bible study type sermon complete with word studies and exegetical comments.

Those views or understandings of expository preaching do not properly describe expository preaching. What then is expository preaching? How do we define and describe it?

What It Is

What is expository preaching?

Some see it as a type of sermon within a classification system. Those who define it by classification usually identify three types of sermons. The classification is based on structure. The three types of sermons based on structure are textual, topical, and expository. In this system the expository sermon is one in which the preacher covers two or more verses of a particular passage.

The problem with defining expository preaching in this manner is that it "imposes too narrow a definition upon expository preaching" (Unger 1955, 48). Expository preaching should not be narrowed down to a single methodology. When properly understood, expository preaching is not a style of preaching or a method one chooses for preparing a sermon; *it is the way one deals with the biblical text.*

When properly understood, the expository sermon may take the form of a verse by verse sermon, a topical sermon, or a textual sermon. The sermon form is not the defining issue of expository preaching.

The best definition of expository preaching is found in Haddon Robinson's classic work *Biblical Preaching:*

> *Expository preaching is the communication of a biblical concept, derived from and transmitted through a historical, grammatical, and literary study of a passage in its context, which the Holy Spirit first applies to the personality and experience of the preacher, then through him to his hearers.* (p. 20)

Based on Robinson's definition, I want to draw two conclusions.

1. Expository preaching is biblically-based preaching.

In an attempt to be relevant some preachers have moved from biblically-based sermons to psychologically-based sermons. The sermon sounds more like something in a motivational or self-esteem seminar. The Scripture is used essentially to proof text what they are saying or trying to prove.

Robinson says:

> *Yet when they fail to preach the Scriptures, they abandon their authority. No longer do they confront their hearers with a word from God. That is why most modern preaching evokes little more than a wide yawn. God is not in it.* (p. 20)

When a preacher fails to preach the Scriptures, he departs from the preaching tradition of the early church. Paul, speaking of his ministry among the Ephesians:

> *"Therefore I testify to you this day that I am innocent of the blood of all men. For I have not shunned to declare to you the whole counsel of God."*

What does this mean for preaching? First, it means **the text of Scripture governs the expository sermon.** The thought and purpose of the biblical writer drives the sermon, not a person or a need.

Preachers all too often read their text, lay the Bible aside and never come back to the text. Their thoughts may be biblically based, but they are not text based. Here is an example of what I am talking about. There was a preacher who was hung up on baptism. One morning he announced his text was Genesis 3:9, which says "But the Lord God called to the man, 'Where are you?'" The preacher continued, "There are three lines we shall follow. First, where Adam was; secondly, how he got to be where he was; and thirdly and lastly, a few words about baptism." Baptism is certainly a biblical subject, but it is not the focus of the text.

Expository preaching demands we not make the text say something that is not there.

Second, it means the expository sermon is based upon sound biblical study. The expository preacher wrestles with the text to grasp the meaning the biblical writer intended. The expositor works his way back into the world of the Scriptures to understand the message as it was written. This is called the "grammatico-historical" method of study.

The expositor, based on his study, honors the meaning of the text as a matter of integrity. The expositor must practice integrity, because the preacher can twist any text to say what he wants it to say. This is what cults such as Mormonism and Jehovah's Witnesses do. They force the text to say what they want it to say.

2. Expository preaching is application-based preaching.

Expository preaching is relevant because it is applied to the life of the preacher and the listener. This is where those who are often associated with expository preaching fail. They exegete a text but never bring it home to roost. They manage to work their way back into the world of the Scriptures to understand the message, but then fail to work their way back to the world in which their audience lives.

The expository preacher, first, properly applies the Scripture to himself. Bishop William A. Quayle said:

> *Preaching is the art of making a sermon and delivering it? Why no, that is not preaching. Preaching is the art of making a preacher and delivering that!* (quoted in Robinson, p. 26)

The expositor must allow the Scripture to speak to his or her life. Only then can he properly apply the Scripture to his listeners or congregation.

Application gives expository preaching a purpose.

> *But be doers of the word, and not hearers only, deceiving yourselves. (James 1:22)*

> *But he who looks into the perfect law of liberty and continues in it, and is not a forgetful hearer but a doer of the work, this one will be blessed in what he does. (James 1:25)*

The listener is saying, "So what? What difference does this make where I live right now?" The expository preacher realizes that his audience lives at a particular address, has particular needs, as well as owns a particular mindset and system of beliefs. The expository preacher cannot ignore the world the listener lives in day to day.

Plain and Simple

In plain and simple terms, expository preaching is biblically-based, application-focused preaching. It is preaching based on the meaning of the text as it was written; and is then properly applied to the preacher's life as well as the audience's.

What is the sum of this whole article?

> *Preach the word! Be ready in season and out of season. Convince, rebuke, exhort, with all longsuffering and teaching. (2 Tim. 4:2)*

Bibliography

Robinson, Haddon. *Biblical Preaching.* Grand Rapids: Baker Publishing Company, 2007.

Unger, Merrill F. *Principles of Expository Preaching.* Grand Rapids: Zondervan Publishing House, 1955.

Planning Your Preaching

By Dr. Kent Spann

British sculptor Sir Jacob Epstein was once visited in his studio by the eminent author and fellow Briton, George Bernard Shaw. The visitor noticed a huge block of stone standing in one corner and asked what it was for.

"I don't know yet. I'm still making plans."

Shaw was astounded. "You mean you plan your work. Why, I change my mind several times a day!"

"That's all very well with a four-ounce manuscript," replied the sculptor, "but not with a four-ton block."

The preacher is dealing with something far more important than a four-ton block of stone. He is charged with the responsibility of bringing the Word of God to the people of God for the glory of God. Paul gave Timothy a very solemn charge when he said:

> I charge you therefore before God and the Lord Jesus Christ, who will judge the living and the dead at His appearing and His kingdom: Preach the word! Be ready in season and out of season. Convince, rebuke, exhort, with all longsuffering and teaching. (2 Tim. 4:1, 2)

Because we have been given so sacred a charge, good planning in preaching is absolutely essential. Alan Lakein, a world leading expert on personal time management and author of *How to Get Control of Your Time and Your Life*, said, "Failing to plan is planning to fail."

Certainly God places value on planning.

> The plans of the diligent lead surely to plenty, But those of everyone who is hasty, surely to poverty. (Prov. 21:5)

When we study the ways of God, we find that God plans.

> The counsel of the LORD stands forever, The plans of His heart to all generations. (Ps. 33:11)

A planned program of preaching is a schedule of sermons to be preached over a certain period of time. Some preachers plan out their sermons for a year, while others plan them out three months in advance.

The Value of Planning Your Preaching

There is great value in planning out your preaching.

1. It keeps your preaching fresh.

A rut, according to the dictionary, is "a fixed or established mode of procedure or course of life, usually dull or unpromising." A preacher can get in a preaching rut. Usually a congregation can tell you whether or not their pastor is in a preaching rut. It is easy to go to the same familiar themes or subjects over and over again. Someone who has a real passion for evangelism will tend to preach evangelistic messages most of the time. Some guys will go to the well of doctrine over and over again. Another preacher passionate about the family will beeline to family messages. Others are drawn to commitment type of sermons.

Vance Havner, a great preacher, once said:

Many people are in a rut and a rut is nothing but a grave—with both ends kicked out.

The preacher must guard against getting in a preaching rut. How can he do that? If you take time to seriously evaluate your previous year's preaching as you plan next year's preaching, you will avoid getting into ruts.

2. It gives you time to acquire materials.

I bought a 1997 Jeep Grand Cherokee and absolutely loved it. Until I bought my Jeep, I did not pay much attention to Jeep Grand Cherokees. Now that I have one, I notice that they are everywhere. What happened? The Grand Cherokee got on my radar screen.

Planning your series and sermons ahead allows subjects, themes, ideas, etc., to get on your radar screen. You will subconsciously look for material that falls into the subject areas you are going to preach. You will see things on television, read an article in the newspaper, or have a conversation with someone about a subject that otherwise you would not have caught. Instead of scrambling to find illustrations for your messages, you will have gathered resources in advance of your preparation.

Books are always a valuable resource to the preacher, but it takes time to get your hands on them. Planning your preaching gives you ample time to find books and get them for your future sermons.

3. **It assists you in planning worship that is meaningful.**

Today's Sunday worship event is much more complex than it used to be. It used to be that you could travel to any Baptist church in just about any place and the worship service would be the same with a few tweaks here and there. That is not the case in today's church. Worship services are much more creative with power point, video, drama, contemporary music, sophisticated audio, etc. To allow for creativity, a generous buffer of time is needed to ease the stress and pressure.

In most churches the center of the worship event is the proclamation of the Word. A good worship leader desires to plan music in coordination with the message. It is hard to do that kind of planning if the preacher does not know what he will preach in the future. A common complaint I hear from worship leaders is their pastor's lack of preaching preparation and therefore, the last-minute scramble of planning the worship service. When you are able to give your worship leader a preaching plan, it aids his planning of a meaningful worship service that connects with your preaching. He can line up soloists and music that match the theme of your sermon.

4. **It reduces the weekly anxiety of deciding what you will preach.**

I knew a preacher that determined what he would preach on a weekly basis. I also encountered a preacher that waited until Saturday night to decide what to preach. That had to be stressful, because he not only had to prepare the sermon, but he also had to decide the text and focus of that sermon. Planning your preaching eliminates that weekly stress.

5. **It frees up more of your time for actual study.**

A well-developed preaching plan facilitates your study time. You can study in advance when you have slow weeks. The big plus is you can begin studying at the beginning of the week since you have already decided what to preach.

6. **It gives you time to mediate on the passage and let God speak to you.**

Preparing one or more sermons each week is a lot of pressure. The minute Sunday morning is over, there is another Sunday coming and another sermon that needs to be prepared. Add to that all of the other duties and responsibilities you have as a preacher, and you have a full week. If you are a bi-vocational pastor, you have to add your regular job. There is not a lot of time to spare.

When you are under the gun each week, it makes meditation hard. There is not enough time to let the passage work on your heart. A preaching plan can help. You can start reflecting, memorizing and meditating on your text in advance.

7. **It results in better sermons.**
Dr. Fred B. Craddock, Bandy Distinguished Professor of Preaching and New Testament, Emeritus, in the Candler School of Theology, Emory University, says in his book *Preaching,*

> Sermons that grow and mature over a period of time are usually superior homiletically, theologically, and biblically—as well as in ease and freedom of delivery—to those "gotten up" just days or even hours prior to presentation. (Fred B. Craddock, Abingdon Press, Nashville, 1985, p. 101)

8. **It helps you maintain a balanced program of preaching.**
We all know the importance of a healthy balanced diet in our daily lives. The same is true in preaching. Our people need a healthy diet of preaching from the Old and New Testament, doctrine, stewardship, etc.

> Plan your work for today and every day, then work your plan.
> —Norman Vincent Peale

The Objections to Planning Your Preaching
Before I get into the practical aspect of planning preaching, I want to answer some of the arguments, excuses or reasons given against it.

> ❧ "I don't have time to plan my preaching."
> Donald Rumsfeld, former Secretary of Defense, said, "Think ahead. Don't let day-to-day operations drive out planning."
> If you are too busy to do some measure of planning, you are too busy. We make time for the things that are important.

> ❧ "I want to be sensitive to the Holy Spirit."
> The implication of this statement is that if you plan ahead you are not sensitive to the Holy Spirit. If you carry that argument to its logical conclusion, the preacher who is really sensitive

to the Holy Spirit will wait until he gets up on Sunday morning to preach to decide what to preach.

My response to that is, "Why can't the Holy Spirit lay on your heart in advance what you need to preach?" Doesn't God know the future? Doesn't God know what his people need even before the need arises?

Certainly the preacher who plans out his preaching must remain sensitive to the Holy Spirit, events, etc., that may change his preaching plan. I have changed my preaching plan many times because I felt led in a different direction.

It is better to plan and change than not to plan.

> "A good plan today is better than a perfect plan tomorrow."
> —General George Patton

🙠 "How can I know in advance what to preach?"

You have to trust the Holy Spirit and your pastoral instincts to guide you.

> *"A man's heart plans his way, But the LORD directs his steps." (Prov. 16:9)*

The truth of those verses has been borne out in my ministry over and over as a congregant tells me the message I preached was exactly what they needed *that day!*

The Process of Planning Your Preaching
First, determine the scope of your planning. Some like to plan three months out, while others will plan six months out. I, personally, like to plan my preaching one year in advance.

Second, determine when you are going to plan your preaching. You need to carve out a time to plan your preaching based on your ministry situation. Early on in my ministry I heard a very prominent preacher tell how he took one week a year and went off on a study retreat. That spoke to me so I began taking a study week in 1984 and have done it ever since. Not everyone can take a week off, so you might take mini-retreats for a day or two. You can even do it in chunks of time like a Saturday morning or a weekday evening.

Third, prepare for your planning time. You need to gather material, ideas, books, etc., in advance of the retreat so you are ready to get to work. Put together a preaching calendar with key dates for your church, holidays, vacation, etc.

Preach the Word

Planning a preaching calendar is hard work. Zig Ziglar says, "Success is dependent upon the glands—sweat glands."

Nothing great is ever accomplished without hard work.

The preacher of the gospel must always remember the business he is about. He is bringing the Word of God to the people of God for the glory of God.

> *Preach the word! Be ready in season and out of season. Convince, rebuke, exhort, with all longsuffering and teaching. For the time will come when they will not endure sound doctrine, but according to their own desires, because they have itching ears, they will heap up for themselves teachers; and they will turn their ears away from the truth, and be turned aside to fables. But you be watchful in all things, endure afflictions, do the work of an evangelist, fulfill your ministry. (2 Tim. 4:2–5)*

Study well!

Retelling the Old, Old Story

By Dr. Calvin Miller

Most sermons built around a biblical, narrative passage could profit from a fresh suit of clothes. I do not say this because I believe the Bible account should be ignored when we are building a story, but because generally speaking we are so used to the story as it appears in the Biblical text, that merely to repeat the tale as we know it does not often intrigue the listener much as we might wish. While the Biblical text is timeless and inspired, it also has the disadvantage of being familiar. Putting old stories in a more contemporary vernacular will often cause our listeners to hear that which they would partially ignore in its more familiar form. As an example of this, in my book *Preaching* I retell the story of Balaam's donkey recorded in Numbers 22:21–31.[1] This is how it goes in my account:

> The day was hot. Flies buzzed at the sweat that soaked the prophet's cowl that hung about his neck like a coil of rank rope. Balaam sweltered under an argument of his own making. He wanted to obey God, but Balak the King wanted him to do one simple thing: curse Israel. As Balak saw it, Israel was the curse! They were three million strong, cutting a wide swath of destruction as they passed

---

[1] 21 So Balaam rose in the morning, saddled his donkey, and went with the princes of Moab. 22 Then God's anger was aroused because he went, and the Angel of the LORD took His stand in the way as an adversary against him. And he was riding on his donkey, and his two servants *were* with him. 23 Now the donkey saw the Angel of the LORD standing in the way with His drawn sword in His hand, and the donkey turned aside out of the way and went into the field. So Balaam struck the donkey to turn her back onto the road. 24 Then the Angel of the LORD stood in a narrow path between the vineyards, *with* a wall on this side and a wall on that side. 25 And when the donkey saw the Angel of the LORD, she pushed herself against the wall and crushed Balaam's foot against the wall; so he struck her again. 26 Then the Angel of the LORD went further, and stood in a narrow place where there *was* no way to turn either to the right hand or to the left. 27 And when the donkey saw the Angel of the LORD, she lay down under Balaam; so Balaam's anger was aroused, and he struck the donkey with his staff. 28 Then the LORD opened the mouth of the donkey, and she said to Balaam, "What have I done to you, that you have struck me these three times?" 29 And Balaam said to the donkey, "Because you have abused me. I wish there were a sword in my hand, for now I would kill you!" 30 So the donkey said to Balaam, "*Am* I not your donkey on which you have ridden, ever since *I became* yours, to this day? Was I ever disposed to do this to you?" And he said, "No." 31 Then the LORD opened Balaam's eyes, and he saw the Angel of the LORD standing in the way with His drawn sword in His hand; and he bowed his head and fell flat on his face.

through his land. Balak's land was not their land. Their land was Canaan. So the King employed Balaam to curse Israel, for his curses were known far and wide to be effective.

Balaam smiled. He was good at divining things. He could split a frog gigged from the Red Sea at midnight, and from the splay of entrails, he could tell who would rule Egypt for the next one hundred years. He could predict things too. He was the wizard of wizards, and King Balak, had offered to pay him major shekels to whomp up a curse and spew it out over the advancing hordes of Hebrews. Balaam wanted the money he would make for cursing Israel, but he didn't want to tick God off by cursing his people. So he saddled up his donkey and rode in the opposite direction of God's will.

Bad Idea!

The wizard of the day turned out to be the donkey, who said, "Hey! What gives Balaam? What have I ever done to cause you to beat me these three times?'

Balaam was filled with road rage: "You have made a fool out of me. If I had a sword you'd be off to the glue factory."

"Kill me? Why? Haven't I always been a good little donkey?"

Then, poof! There stood the angel of God.

"Listen up, Balaam!" said the angel. "You may be good at divination, but you should take a short course on common sense. When a stupid man gets a chance to hear from a very bright donkey, he ought to listen. God has a plan for you, Balaam. It involves obedience. And right now it looks like your donkey is better at obedience than you are."

The angel was suddenly gone.

Balaam felt bad about having beat his little donkey. He offered the donkey a sugar cube. The donkey didn't budge.

"Isn't one enough?" asked the confused prophet.

"Make it two and I'll think about it," said the donkey.[2]

So much for the retelling of the Biblical story. What we need to see is that there are two narrative elements in this retold tale which make retelling the story a good device for getting people to hear it.

First, the old story is being told in a new way. The audience, who probably knows the Biblical account very well, has never heard it told in this particular way before. Stories creatively retold are like arranging

---

[2]Calvin Miller, *Preaching, the Art of Narrative Communication* (Baker Books: Grand Rapids, MI, 2006), pp. 156–157.

the old furniture in an old room. Suddenly the dull familiarity of things has taken on a bright aura of interest, because the arrangement of things we thought we knew so well has all been moved around and the new arrangement is fascinating. In retold tales a new brightness replaces and suffuses the old story.

Second, the drama of hyperbole has been added. Hyperbole is the art of exaggeration. When added to any story it has charm. Still, it must be clear that we are exaggerating. I often cite the late Erma Bombeck as the queen of this literary form. For instance, in one of her columns she said that she never skipped dessert. "Think of the women on the Titanic who skipped dessert," she wrote, *"and for what?"* On another occasion she confessed that she knew women who were so skinny that when they left their workout at the gym to go home at night, vultures followed them to their cars.

She is stating a kind of truth in either the Titanic reference or the skinny women metaphor. Is she lying about it? Yes, in a way, but the overstatement is clearly a fabrication. The overstatement brings the truth into sharp focus.

In the case of a prophet's donkey, the part about splitting Nile frogs and the part about the sugar cube are obvious fabrications, and yet they make the story more interesting, and such activities did, after all, belong to pagan prophets. The key is to be sure our sermonic overstatement is clearly a fictional element in our Biblical exposition.

Jesus used a hyperbole when He said that it was easier for a camel to go through the eye of a needle than for a rich man to get into heaven. Some scholars think that Jesus meant the "needle's eye" was an ancient hole in the wall, through which a camel might crawl (with great difficulty) after the city gates had been closed for the evening. Most believe the Savior was using a hyperbole to state the truth (and of course to make the truth more interesting).

Saint Paul indulged in the art in Galatians 5:12 when he says that those who preach that circumcision is necessary to salvation, might as well have themselves castrated. In this hyperbole, the apostle overstates the truth to arrive at the real meaning of truth.

Hyperbole intrigues. Try the device the next time you retell a Biblical tale in your sermon. Work on the art of storytelling. Commit yourself to the retelling of the Biblical story. With a little practice you might arrive at a place in your life in which you bless your flock with the gift of sermonic intrigue.

Compassionate Hospital Visitation

By Dr. Kent Spann

Hospital visitation is a key part of a pastor's ministry. Why is it so important? Is it because it is expected by church members? Sometimes, honestly, that is the way it feels. If we go to the Scripture, we find that it was important to Jesus. In that well-known portion of Scripture in Matthew 25 where Jesus talks about the separation of the sheep and the goats, He blesses those who visit the sick:

> *Then the King will say to those on His right hand, "Come, you blessed of My Father, inherit the kingdom prepared for you from the foundation of the world: for I was hungry and you gave Me food; I was thirsty and you gave Me drink; I was a stranger and you took Me in; I was naked and you clothed Me;* **I was sick and you visited Me;** *I was in prison and you came to Me." (Matt. 25:34–36)*

In His own personal ministry, Jesus made caring for the sick and dying a high priority:

> Then Jesus went about all the cities and villages, teaching in their synagogues, preaching the gospel of the kingdom, and healing every sickness and every disease among the people. But when He saw the multitudes, He was moved with compassion for them, because they were weary and scattered, like sheep having no shepherd. (Matt. 9:35, 36)

A careful study of the history of pastoral ministry makes it very clear that caring and visiting the sick has been an integral part of Christian compassion.

While the need for this vital ministry has not changed, the way we do it today is very different from the days of our Savior. The goal of this article is to provide some questions and tips for making a compassionate and effective hospital visit.

Preparing for a Hospital Visit

A little preparation can make the visit more effective plus save you time and embarrassment.

- What are the hospital guidelines? If you are new to the area or this is the first time to go a particular hospital, it would behoove you to call and inquire about the policies. Some hospitals require you go through a course to be approved to visit in their hospital.

- Is the patient still in the hospital? A real time waster is driving to the hospital only to find that the patient has been discharged. A quick call can save a lot of time.

- Who is the patient? What do I know about the patient? Who is their family and what is the state of the family members? Are they a member or your church or another church?

- Why are they in the hospital? This helps you know what you are going to face when you enter the room. Someone who has been diagnosed with terminal cancer requires a different kind of visit than someone who just had a baby.

- Why am I going to make this visit? Is it a social call or a ministry? Am I going with the intent of sharing the gospel with the patient?

- Does my patient want or need a visit? Sometimes you are asked by a family member, a friend, etc., to make a visit that perhaps the patient does not want.

- What are the visiting hours? Most hospitals allow the pastor to visit at any hour but don't assume that. Check with the chaplain at the hospital for guidelines.

- Are they having surgery? If yes, when and for what?

Most of the time you will know the answers to these questions without thinking about them, but it helps to have a filter to run your visit through so your visit is effective.

Entering the Patient's Room

Professional baseball player and manager Yogi Berra once made a great point, "You can see a lot just by observing." That is true in life and it is true when making a hospital visit. Here are few guidelines you need to follow.

1. Wash your hands to prevent the spread of infection to the patient.

2. Pay attention to the signs. Signs are there for a reason—your safety or the patient's well-being. If there is a sign calling for isolation, no visitors or protective garments, you should check with the nurse's station before entering.

3. If the door is closed, knock before entering. Nothing will ruin a pastoral visit like pushing the door open only to find the patient is not dressed or is in an awkward position. If there is no response, crack the door just enough to speak the patient's name. If there is still no answer, go to the nursing station before entering.

4. If the door is open, but the patient is asleep, do not awaken them. They may have been given something to sleep, or they may be just plain exhausted. Quietly leave a note that you were there with time and date.

5. If there are nurses going in and out of the room or a lot of activity, there may be a medical emergency or a procedure going on at the time. Inquire at the nurse's station before entering the room.

Visiting the Patient

When you walk into the room, take a moment to size up the situation. What is the patient doing? Are they happy or depressed? Is the patient or a family member upset? They may have just received distressing news.

Be very careful how you react to what you see. You are the pastor. The patient will note your initial response. Do not show shock at what you see.

Be sure to introduce yourself clearly and distinctly. Even a long-time member may not recognize you if they are medicated.

Let the patient lead in shaking your hand. They may have a physical condition that would prevent them from doing it. Again be sure there is no risk of infection from them to you or you to them.

Consider where you stand or sit. Notice where equipment is located, where windows are (the glare can hurt the patient's eyes), where family members are, the elevation of the patient's bed, etc. Don't sit on the patient's bed except in rare circumstances.

Let the patient lead in the conversation. They may not want to start off talking about their illness. Let them choose the course of the conversation. If they don't lead out in conversation try, "How are things going?" Avoid asking, "How do you feel?" or "What is wrong with you?"

Don't be in a hurry, but don't stay too long. If it is a stranger or someone you barely know then ten minutes or less is sufficient. If they are in intensive care, probably five or less minutes is plenty. If they are sleepy or just had company, five minutes or so is appropriate. Some visits will be longer, because you know the person or need to give more intense pastoral care.

Read Scripture and pray with the patient. This is important because in that moment you are God's representative to them. They need a word from God. (See appendix for suggested verses you can use.)

Listen to the patient and observe. Don't minimize what they say.

Be sensitive to the family members or friends. They may need ministry as well as the patient.

Leave a card with your name and phone number in case they need to contact you.

After Your Visit

Wash your hands to prevent the spread of disease or infection.

Record your visit. Keeping a record of your visit may be useful in the future.

Pray for them privately.

Do's and Don'ts of Hospital Visiting

- Do be cheerful.
- Do listen.
- Do be considerate of other patients in the room.
- Do speak to other patients in the room.
- Don't be afraid of silence.
- Do make it brief and leave.
- Don't offer false optimism.
- Don't try to second guess the doctor.
- Don't get drawn into criticism.
- Don't sit on the bed.
- Don't give them anything unless you know it is OK for them to have it. Sometimes an elderly person will beg you to give them something or do something for them.

- ❧ Don't visit if you are sick. If you cannot visit, make a phone call or send a letter or card.

- ❧ Don't discuss the sleeping patient's condition with family members in the room. They may not be sleeping. If they are in coma, they may still hear you; they just can't respond.

- ❧ When visiting on the OB floor don't speak to the mother about the baby unless you know the baby is living.

- ❧ Don't reveal anything you know about the patient. The patient may not know yet.

Scripture Passages for Those in the Hospital and Their Families

Affliction: Psalm 55:22; 2 Corinthians 4:16–18; Romans 5:3–5; Hebrews 12:10, 11

Pain, Suffering or Sickness: Job 5:6–11; Psalms 34:4, 6–8, 15, 17, 19; 41:1–3; 42:11; Jeremiah 29:11–14

Facing Surgery: Psalms 17:6–8; 27:1; 91:11; 103:1–4, 8–12; 121:1–8; Romans 8:31–39; 1 John 4:9, 10

Awaiting a Biopsy/Waiting Period: Psalm 139:1–6, 9–12, 17, 18; Isaiah 40:31; Matthew 6:30–34

Long Convalescence: Psalm 4; 43:1–15; 77:1–15; 138:1–8; John 15:1–17; Romans 12; Hebrews 11

Serious Accident: Psalm 91:1, 2, 11–16; 116:1–4: Romans 5:1–5

Little Hope for Recovery: Psalm 23; 86:1–7; Isaiah 35:10; John 10:27–28

Birth of a Child: 1 Samuel 1:19, 20, 24, 26–28; Psalm 127:1–5; Matthew 19:13–15

Permanent Injury: Psalm 57:1–3; 118:4–6; Isaiah 40:28–31; 41:10; 49:14–16; Romans 8:26–28, 39

Ministering in a Time of Death

By Mark Becton

My dad was a pastor for forty-three years. Most of what I have learned as a pastor, I learned from him . . . especially when it comes to funerals. There was one particular funeral that deeply affected Dad. It happened while he was presiding over the service of a woman he never knew. He told me,

> *Son, as I saw the family weeping I realized this was someone's mother. I thought, "What would I want the preacher to say, and how would I want him to be if he were performing my mother's funeral?" It was then I vowed to perform each funeral as though it was for someone I loved.*

This forever shaped the way Dad performed funerals, and Dad shaped me.

Dad told me that if you perform a funeral for a loved one, you would know them well. Yet still, you would also include the stories that were special to others in the family. As a pastor, you will know your members well . . . some better than others. Still, you will want to meet with the family to hear the stories that are special to them. When you allow the family to share their stories, you see God work. Hurt feelings are soothed and broken hearts are mended, all from the shared memories and laughter. That's why when you meet with the family you need to have pen and paper ready. God will use those stories to help you minister to them during the funeral.

Some pastors may struggle at helping families share stories. Here's what I do to create a story-telling atmosphere. After circling the family and having prayer together, I share,

> *Thank you for allowing me to be a part of the service. As pastor, I get to speak on your behalf. I know you wish you could share your heart, but the emotions may make it difficult. Therefore, let me ask you some questions that will help me put the service together. These questions will also enable me to get to know (____the loved one____) through your eyes.*

Here are the questions. First, "Did (____the loved one____) have scripture passages that were special to them or are there passages that are special to you?" Second, "Have you selected any songs you would like to have played or sung?" Third, "Are there any family members or friends of the family that want to speak?" Fourth, "Since I am speaking on your behalf, what memories or stories would you like me to share?"

The first three questions will help you arrange the order of the service. You will place songs, scriptures, prayer and testimonies together in a flow that will be moving. The last question will help you as you prepare the message. The stories and impressions of the family will make your message more personal.

Let's talk about the message. After you've met with the family and heard all the wonderful stories, don't be tempted to simply tell stories spiced with a few verses. God's comfort to the saved and His conviction to the lost will be stronger when you "Preach the Word" . . . particularly when you illustrate God's Word with stories from the family. (An example of this is provided in the message "My First Five Minutes in Heaven.")

You need to also remember that this is a funeral message and not a Sunday morning message. Your message should be shorter and the tone of your voice should have more empathy than energy. Yet, make no mistake. The source of any message, whether for a funeral or Sunday morning, is the same. It's God's Word.

Sharing God's Word illustrated by the life of a godly believer can be a rewarding experience for you as a pastor. At that moment, you understand why God said, "Precious in the sight of the LORD is the death of his saints" (Ps. 116:15). Yet, there will be times you are asked to perform a funeral for someone and the family is uncertain of his or her salvation. This is not the time to preach on the fires of hell, but neither can you talk about the loved one's eternity in heaven. Here, Dad wisely instructed me,

> Son, you can't change the condition of the deceased, but you can help those who are hurting over the loss. Preach about the greatness of God and His comfort for the family. This will likely provide future conversations to comfort family members who are saved or to discuss salvation with those who are lost.

(An example of this is provided in the message "God Is . . .")

You should also anticipate that not everyone attending the funeral is a believer. Thus somewhere in your message (whether the loved one was saved or not) you need to present the plan of salvation. At a funeral, people come to grips with their own mortality and want to know,

"What does the Bible say about eternity?" Their ears are more open, so you need to be more open about sharing what God says about salvation.

Finally, regarding the graveside, some pastors mistakenly see this as an opportunity to preach a second message. Actually it's an opportunity to solidify the message and experience the family had in the earlier service. All that is needed is reading a selected passage, maybe telling one more story, and a prayer. If the loved one was a believer you may choose to read John 14:1–3 or share Psalm 23.

Sharing Psalm 23 was particularly significant for my dad. If Dad knew the deceased was a believer, he shared Psalm 23 in the past tense . . . as their own confession. He said, "They would tell you, 'The Lord has been my shepherd, I've never been in want.'" Upon completing the Psalm Dad would add, "Now let One who shepherded them shepherd you."

Never underestimate the impact of being there for a family during a time of loss. If they are church members, because you were by their side when they hurt, they are more likely to be by your side as you lead. If they are lost, because you gave them time when they were hurting, they are more likely to give you time to share more about Christ. It's remarkable what will happen when you perform each funeral as though it was for one of your own loved ones.

LEADER DEVELOPMENT

Alignment Which Results in Spiritual Authority

By Steve Hopkins

There are at least three ways to lead, and leaders will find themselves using all three. First, there is *self-focused* leading which reacts to whatever happens to the leader. Reactive leading focuses on the leader and is often driven by the urgent, seldom reflecting on why things are the way they are. There is also *goal-focused* leading, focusing on an objective, a program, an event, or a task—often leaving God out of the equation. A program leader always believes he is one *program* away from a breakthrough so he travels from one program or event to another, looking for the answer. Finally, there is leading by *following, or God-focused* leading. The focus is on following the leader. The God-focused leader may not be sure where he is going, but he knows he is totally dependent on the Leader. Jesus calls us with these words: "If anyone wants to come with Me, he must deny himself, take up his cross daily, and *follow* Me" (Luke 9:23). Blanchard and Hodges write, *"God is not looking for leaders but for servants who will let Him be the leader."*[1]

Jesus illustrated this when He called the disciples in Mark 3:13–15. It is exciting to hear He "called those He wanted"—not those who needed a new assignment or those who had the most leadership potential, but those *He wanted*. His call is threefold: the call to intimacy— "to be with Him"; the call to mission—"to send them out"; and the call to spiritual authority—"to have authority." It was not a call to a spiritual to-do list—but to be with Him. The sequence intimacy— mission—authority is extremely important. Leaders often want to reverse the sequence and take activity over intimacy, and then wonder why we do not know His authority. The relationship is inseparable from mission, and mission is done in the authority created by following Him.[2]

When those early disciples met challenges, they offered Jesus. "I

---

[1]Ken Blanchard and Phil Hodges *Lead Like Jesus* (Thomas Nelson, 2005), p. 47.
[2]Gary Mayes, personal conversation, see www.aboutLEADING.com.

have neither silver nor gold, but what I have, I give to you: In the name of Jesus Christ the Nazarene, get up and walk!" (Acts 3:6) No magic tricks, fancy moves, slick curriculum, or pithy answers—but Jesus! Leaders meet people every day facing needs that if they do not meet Jesus in a fresh way, there is no other answer. We must offer them Jesus by inviting them into our journey with Him.

Leadership is often seen as a skill to master. Leaders attend workshops to gather new tools for their tool belt, wanting to become "Tim-the-Tool-Man-Taylor" of leadership. Often our tool belt is compared to someone else's to see if we measure up. Skills are important, but they must never be the primary focus. David led "them with a pure heart and guided them with his skillful hands" (Ps. 78:72).

Development as a leader is an ongoing process of responding to the Father's work in our lives, a series of adjustments to our Leader. Our responsibility is to discover how God is at work and respond to His activity.[3] J. Robert Clinton points to Hebrews 13:7–8 as the "leadership mandate." We are to observe carefully those leaders who have gone before us, and imitate their faith, because "Jesus Christ is the same yesterday, today, and forever." It is all about learning to recognize the activity of Christ in their life, so we can better recognize His activity in us.[4] Note that we are to "imitate their faith," not their results. Results are in the hand of the Father, the leader's responsibility is to faithfully follow Him.

Jesus modeled this style of leadership. In John 5:19–20 Jesus replied to those questioning Him with "The Son is not able to do anything on His own, but only what He sees the Father doing." During all those times the Scriptures record Jesus as praying He was doing more than checking off "devotions" on his to-do list. He was aligning Himself with the work of the Father.

The leader development issue then is alignment. The business world often refers to the principle: *Every organization is in perfect alignment for the results they are currently getting.* If we do not like the results, we must examine the alignment that is producing those results. When we are in alignment with the Father, there is a new power, a spiritual authority that is not based on natural ability or giftedness.[5] Jesus used

[3]Henry Blackaby and Claude King *Experiencing God: Knowing and Doing the Will of God* (LifeWay, 1990), p. 15.
[4]J. Robert Clinton, *The Making of a Leader* (NavPress, 1988), p. 40.
[5]Terry Walling, personal conversation, see www.leaderbreakthru.com.

terms like "take up My yoke and learn from Me" and "abide in Me" to describe this alignment (Matt. 11:25–30; John 15).

This has huge implications in the way we lead others. We watch for the activity of the Father in their lives, and help them learn to recognize His work and respond to Him. They become followers of the Leader, not us. So that their ". . . faith might not be based on men's wisdom, but on God's power" (1 Cor. 2:5; see also 11:1).

First Peter 5:5–10 records an amazing promise for the God-focused, following leader: "And all of you clothe yourselves with humility toward one another, because God resists the proud, but gives grace to the humble. Humble yourselves therefore under the mighty hand of God, so that He may exalt you in due time . . . Now the God of all grace, who called you to His eternal glory in Christ Jesus, will *personally* restore, establish, strengthen, and support you after you have suffered a little" (italics added). People will follow a leader who is personally restored, established, strengthened and supported by the God of all grace.

SHEPHERDING THE SHEPHERD

Your Savior, Your Spouse, and Your Specific Call

By Dr. Rich Halcombe

I've got to admit it was comical spying a three-hundred-pound fire plug scaling the foothill beside Buffalo Creek Road. He climbed it like a kid looking for buried treasure.

But he wasn't a kid, he was my dad.

As the driver home from our usual Saturday work day, I had never heard him yell halfway down the road home, "Turn it around, turn it around, turn this thing around!" Alarmed, I u-turned us to the mouth of the southeastern Ohio roadway where he leapt from the station wagon and scurried up the hill. Five and a half feet tall, his ample body cloaked the former high school athlete. But, even the size of the hill couldn't hide his love for my mother. The object of his insistence, protruding from his portly palm after coming off the hill? A flower for my mom. Not on a birthday or a Valentine's Day or a Make-Up Day for an unresolved hurt, it was an I Love You Day, just like every other day . . . because my father loved my mother. It wasn't even a great flower. That weedy stem drooped from the time it was inserted in the trifling beaker atop the television in our modest living room. But it demonstrated a great love, one that lasted as long as he did.

That video clip glimpses a man who stayed in love with his wife. Here are some ways we can:

Personality

You're last to leave the church get-together; he would rather not have gotten together. She likes the toilet paper roll hanging out from the top; it never occurred to you it could hang more than one way. She's methodical and thorough; you run out the door without the directions, and often without the keys to the car. It's a revelation to realize he's not being slow just to drive you crazy, that's the way God made him! Through counseling (where I was the counselor!), I soon recognized everybody doesn't see things the way I do. The fact that a LOT of people are like my wife was news to me. The things my wife said weren't crazy, they were common. And some of the problems wives were having with their husbands were some of the very things I was doing! Study the personality types . . . then enjoy the fact that your spouse is probably your opposite. Two good ones are Myers-Briggs[1], and Personality Profile[2]. It helps remove intent from the content. She's *not* rearranging your sock drawer just to aggravate you.

Priority

Your highest priorities are shown in two books: your checkbook (or your online banking) and your datebook. Church consultants know the true focus of a church isn't found in an elders' meeting, it's discovered in the church's budget and calendar.

Abraham Lincoln is reported to have asked, "How many legs does a dog have if you call the tail a leg?" Answering his own question, he said, "Four. Calling a tail a leg doesn't make it a leg."[3] And naming a priority does not make it one. Where a church spends money and time reveals her priorities. And what is true of the church corporately is true of us individually. As a preacher, my priorities are my Savior, my Spouse, and *then* my Specific Call. For me, it's the Master, the Mrs., and *then* the Ministry. Confusing the ministry with the master leads to misery, first for your spouse. Usually the person with misplaced priorities finds out later . . . often too late. If your spouse is truly a priority, she/he will register as a major line item in our life's budget. If you are "spent" when you get home, your spouse never showed up in the datebook. And love diminishes.

Personal Quiet Time

Ask God every day to protect your spouse and to preserve your love. No matter how many people you mention, no matter how pressing the day's events and no matter how little you slept last night, your spouse's name comes first off your lips in your daily time with the Lord. It's a daily reminder of the two most important people in your life: your savior and your sweetie.

Personal Conversations

Mention your spouse's name in conversations with the opposite sex. This sends a strong, subtle signal that your husband is your first priority. For guys, it alerts ladies to the fact that you are emotionally

---

[1]The Myers & Briggs Foundation, "My MBTI Personality Type," *http://www.myersbriggs. org/my-mbti-personality-type/*, Accessed February 28, 2009.

[2]Class Services, Inc., "Personality Profiles," *http://www.classervices.com/Online_ Store2.html*, Accessed February 28, 2009.

[3]Dog Quotations, "Abraham Lincoln Dog Quotes For You to Enjoy," *http://www. dogquotations.com/abraham-lincoln-dog-quotes.html*, Accessed February 28, 2009.

connected to one woman, and you like it that way. If you speak ill of your spouse, you are viewed as one who is looking for consolation in the wrong places.

Passwords

A cursory count revealed upwards of seventy passwords for cell phone accounts, online banking, credit union, travel sites, etc. Including your spouse's name or a word reminiscent of him/her is an encouraging reminder throughout your days who really is important to you.

Perspective

So, why would we want to stay in love with our spouses?

1. It aids outreach.
   Your marital relationship represents Christ to the world. People are more likely to believe what we say about our Messiah if our marriages are meaningful. Paul shows a close connection between the two relationships in Ephesians 5:22–33.
2. It makes you a better communicator. Both genders and all personalities hear us preach. The more we understand our partners, the more effectively we communicate God's Word to God's people. You also learn things you can use in future messages on the family and relationships. The better you treat your spouse, the better you teach His bride.
3. It honors the Lord and our love. When we follow God's prescription for relationships, He receives the glory. As we live that love, people learn from our deeds as well as our words, which is what we strive to accomplish.

So, let's climb a hill and pick a flower for that one we love!

SHEPHERDING THE SHEPHERD
Pink Elephants and Purity
By Mark fuller

The challenge for a church leader to stay pure in an increasingly polluted culture seems to grow more difficult with each passing year. Yet God's call to holiness and purity remains, "Be holy because I am holy" (Lev. 11:45b NIV). Add to this the fact that Satan strategically targets church leaders, because he knows if he can take out the shepherd he can scatter the sheep. In effect he has placed a huge "bullseye" on every spiritual leader for this reason. So what is a pastor to do? How do I keep myself morally clean amidst all the temptations and pressures that come with ministry?

The answer, like the question, is multi-faceted. And we need every resource available in God's arsenal to protect us from Satan's IEDs on the highway of holiness. One weapon I have discovered to be particularly helpful to me is a Spirit-controlled mind. Paul instructs us, "If your sinful nature controls your mind, there is death. But if the Holy Spirit controls your mind, there is life and peace" (Rom. 8:6 NLT). Instead of fixing my mind on how to overcome the temptation, whether it be for money, sex, or fame, the Holy Spirit wants me to fix my mind on what is "pure and lovely and admirable" (Phil. 4:8 NLT). When I do, those pure and lovely thoughts effectively displace the polluted and distorted thoughts from my mind.

An important component of our church's discipleship process is a class entitled "Living Life to the Max." The class is designed to help believers discover God's sanctifying grace and live a life led and controlled by the indwelling Holy Spirit. In teaching the class I illustrate the importance of a Spirit-controlled mind by asking a member of the class not to think about pink elephants. I repeatedly emphasize the importance of not thinking about pink elephants until I am practically right in his face warning, "Whatever you do, don't think about pink elephants!" Of course the one thing he is thinking about is . . . pink elephants.

The same holds true in our struggle against temptation. The more I focus on the temptation and telling myself not to fall into sin, chances are I will end up doing just that. But, if I immediately redirect those distorted thoughts in ways that honor God, I am well on the way to victory over temptation. I remember hearing Zig Ziglar apply this principle to his own life. He indicated that whenever he was tempted by lustful thoughts for another woman, he would take captive those lustful thoughts and redirect them as loving thoughts towards his wife. In this way a Spirit-controlled mind can take the very thoughts that Satan tries to use to lead us to impurity, and they in fact become a catalyst for God's holiness and purity in our lives. I love it when God takes the stick Satan tries to beat me over the head with and uses it against him!

Purity in ministry has never been more important than it is today. But purity doesn't mean you're perfect. It means being able to perfectly admit you are not. Purity starts with a humility and transparency before God and others. It requires a transformed heart and a renewed mind. The Holy Spirit is the only One who can transform a human heart. But we must cooperate with Him in this mind-renewing process. So, "Fix your thoughts on what is true and honorable and right. Think about things that are pure and lovely and admirable. Think about things that are excellent and worthy of praise" (Phil. 4:8b NLT). Then you won't have any time to worry about pink elephants.

HEROES OF THE FAITH

E. M. Bounds

By Robert Morgan

If God were blessing your church in direct proportion to your prayer life, how would it be doing? If the breadth of your preaching matched the depths of your praying, how powerful would your pulpit ministry be? Or how weak?

Edward M. Bounds, whose writings on prayer are classics, makes us face those questions every time we pick up his books. Bounds was born into a strong Christian family in Shelbyville, Missouri, on August 15, 1835. His father, a businessman and political leader, ran the local hotel and mill. But when the elder Bounds died from tuberculosis at age 44 in 1849, his family seemed emotionally lost. Young Edward, 14, along with his older brother Charles, soon joined a wagon train for the California Gold Rush of '49. The next four years tested Edward's Christian roots as he faced hardship with little to show for it amid the drunkenness, gambling, prostitution, and unrestrained atmosphere of the Wild West.

Disillusioned, Edward returned to Missouri, where he studied law in Hannibal and was licensed as the state's youngest attorney. But his heart was restless. In the late 1850s, hearing reports of revivals spreading across the nation, Edward attended a brush arbor meeting on the banks of the Mississippi River in LaGrange, Missouri, and was so moved that he resigned the law and moved to the village of Palmyra, Missouri, to attend Bible school. Two years later, on February 21, 1860, he preached before the local quarterly meeting and was appointed a Methodist circuit-rider for a rural district in Missouri. For the next year, Edward rode his horse from town to town and from farm to farm, doing pastoral work, preaching, teaching, leading Bible studies, and praying with his extended flock.

On April 12, 1861, shots were fired at Fort Sumter, sparking the War Between the States. Residents of Missouri were divided on whether to support the North or the South, and Edward became caught up in events when he was asked to preach the funeral of a 17-year-old who had been seized by Union forces and held under the frozen Grand River until he drowned.

On November 14, 1862, Edward's name appeared on a list of men to be arrested, and he was taken into custody and eventually imprisoned in Lynch's Slave Pit, amid unspeakable filth in a cold cell so crowded it was impossible to sit down. By the end of the year, he was banished from the North and on February 20, 1863, was given a pass through lines of war to secure a safe passage to the southern states. He walked over 200 miles before purchasing a mule in Arkansas and continuing southeast.

At age 28, Bounds joined the Confederate army as a chaplain, which put him in the middle of the most tragic battles of the war. He was wounded by a Union saber at the Battle of Franklin; and, when Confederate forces were routed at the Battle of Nashville, he stayed behind to care for the wounded and dying. On December 17, 1864, he was classified as captured, though not imprisoned, and was allowed to minister to wounded soldiers and to townspeople, holding Bible studies and prayer meetings. He also promoted plans for a Civil War cemetery in Franklin, which today is the only cemetery in America wholly filled with fallen Confederate soldiers.

B. F. Haynes, who was saved under Bounds' ministry and who later became president of Asbury College, recalled his impressions of E. M. Bounds during this time: "His preaching profoundly impressed me, his prayers linger until today as one of the holiest and sweetest memories of my life. His reading of hymns was simply inimitable . . . I never

---

We have emphasized sermon-preparation until we have lost sight of the important thing to be prepared—the heart.

—E. M. Bounds

---

hear these hymns today or think of them that the scene is not reenacted of the little hazel-eyed, black-haired pastor with a voice of divine love standing in the pulpit of the old Methodist church, reading one of these matchless hymns in a spirit, tone, and manner that simply poured life, hope, peace, and holy longings to my boyish heart."

When the war ended, Bounds continued preaching and pastoring in Middle Tennessee until late 1871, when, at age 36, he moved to Alabama to pastor a church, and there he began his writing ministry by contributing a column to the local paper, *The Eufaula Times*. It was also in Eufaula, while conducting a funeral, that he met Emma Elizabeth Barnette, with whom he almost instantly fell in love. When he returned to Missouri to pastor a Methodist Episcopal church in St. Louis, he kept up correspondence with Emma, and, on September 19, 1876, they were married. He was 41. The couple set up housekeeping in St. Louis, and their first child, a little girl, was born about a year later. Residents of St. Louis often saw Bounds reading and studying his Bible while riding horseback through the streets, visiting the sick and making soul-winning calls.

In 1883, Bounds was asked to become associate editor of *The St. Louis Christian Advocate,* and his writing ministry took a more serious turn. At the same time Emma's health began to fail, and, fearing the worst, Bounds gathered up his family and returned to Alabama, where her father, a medical doctor, attended her. As her condition worsened, Bounds stayed by her bedside, reading Scripture and praying. She passed away on February 18, 1886, at age 30.

Bounds' friend Dr. Luther Smith was concerned about him during this time, and a couple of months after Emma's death, he invited Edward to preach at Southern University in Greensboro, Alabama. A spirit of revival swept over the campus and more than 100 were saved. At the same time, Bounds was awarded an Honorary Doctorate of Divinity Degree. This was much against his will, for it hurt his modesty. When one lady addressed him as "Doctor," he replied with a pained expression, "Sister Hill, if you love me, call me Brother Bounds."

On her deathbed, Emma, concerned for her husband and children, had expressed a wish for Edward to marry her cousin, Harriet A. Barnett. On October 25, 1887, Emma's father performed the ceremony. From the first, Harriet called him, "Doctor," and taught the children to do the same.

The next year, Bounds resigned his position in St. Louis to move back to Nashville to become associate editor of *The Nashville Christian Advocate,* the official paper of the Methodist Episcopal Church South. He was now in his mid-fifties, preaching, writing, editing a magazine, and still fathering children. (In all, he had nine children, three from his first marriage and six from his second.)

Bounds' ministry with *The Nashville Christian Advocate* was marred by controversies in his denomination, but Bounds was chiefly concerned about the absence of power in the pulpit. He noticed that although pastors were better trained than ever and had more resources, they evidenced little spiritual unction. He addressed the issue in an article containing the following succinct words that foreshadow his later writings on prayer:

> The power of the preacher lies in his power of prayer, in his ability to pray so as to reach God, and bring great results. The power of prayer is rarely tested, its possibilities seldom understood, never

exhausted. The pulpit fixed and fired with holy desires on God, with a tireless faith, will be the pulpit of power . . . To pray over our sermons like we say grace over our meals does no good. Every step of the sermon should be born of the throes of prayer, its beginning and end should be vocal with the plea and song of prayer. Its delivery should be impassioned and driven by the power of prayer . . . Prayer that carries heaven by storm, that moves God by a relentless advocacy, these make the pulpit a throne, its deliverances like the decrees of destiny.

Bounds' articles became widely read, bringing him many speaking invitations and much respect. Still, unhealthy winds were blowing through his denomination, and it was with a foreboding spirit that he boarded a train on May 6, 1893, at Nashville's Union Station, bound for Memphis for the annual meeting of his denomination. He checked into the Peabody Hotel and started mingling with the 2,500 delegates. It proved a divisive time, and Bounds returned to Nashville troubled.

In 1894, at age 59, worn out by denominational politics, he resigned his position and moved his family into the home of his father-in-law in Washington, Georgia. Edward had no source of income, and for a time his family was dependent on his in-laws, which caused tongues to wag. Bounds hoped to return to an itinerant ministry, but he was ostracized by his denomination and few people reached out to him.

One man, however, remained faithful. Rev. C. L. Shelton, who was conducting meetings in Bounds' old stomping grounds of Franklin, Tennessee, sent for him. Soon others asked him to speak here and there, and his ministry began to flourish again. Calls started coming from across the nation.

All the while, E. M. Bounds was growing in his personal prayer habits. Each morning he would rise at 4 a.m. and pray until breakfast at seven. Every afternoon when home he would go on a prayer walk, in which he prayed for the people in the houses he passed. Often the mid-morning hours would find him in the little prayer chamber he established on the second floor of his home, and here in the atmosphere of prayer he would scratch out on little scraps of paper his thoughts about prayer. An idea for a book burned in his heart, and he began putting down his thoughts under the simple title *Preacher and Prayer*.

In the spring of 1905, while speaking at an annual Bible conference in Atlanta, Bounds met a local Atlanta pastor named Homer Hodge, who later wrote, "When I met this great saint in May 1905 he was seventy years old. He was then writing his *Preacher and Prayer* . . . He coaxed us to rise with him at 4:00 a.m. and wrestle for a lost world and for money to publish his books."

In 1907, at the urging of Dr. G. Campbell Morgan, Bounds traveled to London to present his manuscript to the editors of Marshall Brothers, who agreed to publish it.

For several years, E. M. Bounds enjoyed his work, praying, preaching, and setting forth his thoughts about prayer. In late 1912 and early 1913, Bounds continued meeting with Dr. Hodge about his books, and

> *What the Church needs today is not more machinery or better, not new organizations or more and novel methods, but men whom the Holy Ghost can use—men of prayer, men mighty in prayer.*
>
> —E. M. Bounds

Hodge became the primary force behind getting his manuscripts into printed form. Bounds himself was growing weaker. When he died on August 24, 1913, at age 78 in his home in Washington, Georgia, he was not particularly well-known or outwardly successful. But he had left behind in manuscript form and on miscellaneous scraps of paper some of history's richest ideas about the life of prayer.

Dr. Homer Hodge assumed responsibility for crafting these writings into books. Hodge once said, "I have been among many ministers and slept in the same room with them for several years. They prayed, but I was never impressed with any special praying among them until one day a small man with gray hair and an eye like an eagle came along. We had a ten-day convention. We had some fine preachers around the home, and one of them was assigned to my room. I was surprised early next morning to see a man bathing himself before day and then see him get down and begin to pray. I said to myself, 'He will not disturb us, but will soon finish,' and he kept on softly for hours, interceding and weeping softly, for me and my indifference, and for all the ministers of God. He spoke the next day on prayer. I became interested for I was young in the ministry, and had often desired to meet with a man of God that prayed like the saints of the Apostolic age. Next morning he was up praying again, and for ten days he was up early praying for hours. I became intensely interested and thanked God for sending him. 'At last,' I said, 'I have found a man that really prays. I shall never let him go.' He drew me to him with hooks of steel."

Largely due to Homer Hodge, E. M. Bounds is now remembered as one of Christianity's most prolific and eloquent writers on the subject of prayer. His books became classics long after his body was deposited in the old Methodist graveyard in Washington, Georgia.

His initial book, *Preacher and Prayer,* was later re-titled *Power Through Prayer,* but it is still addressed primarily to those in ministry. I have an old copy under the original title which I keep on the bookshelf over my desk with a bookmark at the place where I left off at the last reading. I frequently pick it up and read a few paragraphs or a page or two, carefully underlining the best sentences in pencil. Apart from the Bible, it provides more motivation for a solid, daily prayer life than anything else. Here is how it begins:

> We are constantly on a stretch, if not on a strain, to devise new methods, new plans, new organizations to advance the church and secure enlargement and efficiency for the gospel. This trend of the day has a tendency to lose sight of the man or sink the man in the plan or organization. God's plan is to make much of the man, far more of him than of anything else. Men are God's method. The church is looking for better methods; God is looking for better men. "There was a man sent from God whose name was John." The dispensation that heralded and prepared the way for Christ was bound up in that man John. "Unto us a child is born, unto us a son is given." The world's salvation comes out of that cradled Son. When Paul appeals to the personal character of the men who rooted the gospel in the world, he solves the mystery of their success. The glory and efficiency of the gospel is staked on the men who proclaim it. When God declares that "the eyes of the Lord run to and fro throughout the whole earth, to show himself strong in the behalf of them whose heart is perfect toward him," he declares the necessity of men and his dependence on them as a channel through which to exert his power upon the world. This vital, urgent truth is one that this age of machinery is apt to forget. The forgetting of it is as baneful on the work of God as would be the striking of the sun from his sphere. Darkness, confusion, and death would ensue.
>
> What the church needs today is not more machinery or better, not new organizations or more and novel methods, but men whom

the Holy Ghost can use—men of prayer, men mighty in prayer. The Holy Ghost does not flow through methods, but through men. He does not come on machinery, but on men. He does not anoint plans, but men—men of prayer.

HEROES OF THE FAITH

Mordecai Ham

By Ruth Schenk

When sin-hating, soul-winning Kentucky evangelist Mordecai Ham sailed into Charlotte, North Carolina, for a revival in 1934, it was a citywide event few wanted to miss. Night after night, thousands packed the sprawling, ramshackle tent on the edge of town for the meetings. Some attended because they were curious. Ham never minced words about sin, and his bold, controversial denunciation of evil was widely reported in local newspapers.

Others attended to learn more about Christ from this preacher who knew a lot about the Bible and pounded his points home with unforgettable stories.

Still others who were skeptical attended simply to see the whole thing for themselves.

On their family dairy farm, William and Morrow Graham decided to ride into town for one of the meetings. They were devout Christians, faithful members of the Associate Reformed Presbyterian Church in Charlotte, eager to learn more about Christ.

Their eldest son, Billy Frank, wanted nothing to do with the revival.

"I told my parents I would not go to hear him," Graham said in his autobiography, *Just As I Am.*

He'd scanned newspaper articles about Ham and made up his mind.

"Everything I heard or read about him made me feel antagonistic about the whole affair. It sounded like a religious circus to me."

For some time, William and Morrow had been praying for Billy Frank.

"My father knew that I went along with the family to church every week only grudgingly, or of necessity," Billy Graham said. "I believe he sincerely wanted me to experience what he had felt a quarter-century earlier. In fact, he privately hoped and prayed that his firstborn son might someday be a preacher."

Billy Frank Graham's resolve to avoid the revival changed when Ham charged local high school students with scandalous behavior. Billy's angry classmates threatened to disrupt the meetings—even to harm Ham.

"That stirred my curiosity, and I wanted to go just to see what would happen," Billy Graham said.

But after hearing Ham's message, the 16-year-old was hooked immediately, returning to the tent night after night to hear more of Ham's preaching. One memorable evening after singing four verses of "Just As I Am" and "Almost Persuaded," Billy Frank Graham made his way down the sawdust aisle, and his life was forever changed.

In a few years, sprawling, temporary 'tabernacles' would become Billy Graham's platform. He, too, would call people to faith in Christ in revival meetings across the country.

When asked about his influence on Billy Graham, Ham said simply, "In Billy Graham's thinking at the time, his hero was Babe Ruth. Our meeting changed his hero from Babe Ruth to Jesus Christ."

Mordecai Ham was no novice when he preached in Charlotte. He'd been preaching since 1900 in revivals throughout Tennessee, Kentucky, Ohio and Texas. Though he looked more like a dignified schoolteacher than a fiery evangelist, he'd been bringing people to Christ for more than 30 years, building a solid reputation as a man of God.

During revivals, he preached five or six times a day, often speaking at area factories to reach laborers with the gospel. He believed in working closely with local churches.

Ham said God called him to preach when he was nine years old. But his road to the pulpit took a temporary detour when he dabbled in sales for a time.

"My call to the ministry was a continuous and irresistible urge," Ham said. "I fought it when I started out as a salesman, because my God had not completely whipped me, and I did not want to be a preacher until I had first made a fortune."

Ham, from Allen County, Kentucky, was named after his grandfather, who sometimes pastored six congregations in Kentucky at one time. He shepherded three churches for more than 40 years and another more than 50 years. Ham's father, Tobias Ham, started five churches, baptized 1,500 people, and performed more than 800 weddings.

Growing up, Ham said he learned about two things—hard work and spiritual sensitivity.

"My father believed in the dignity of work, and he didn't believe in labor-saving devices."

Every night in the Ham household was a mini-revival meeting.

From the time he began to preach, Ham was invited to hold meetings throughout Kentucky and became well-known as a biblical preacher.

During one of Ham's first meetings, he heard about a man in the area who didn't believe in God. Since the man refused to come near the meetings, Ham went to find him—hiding in a cornfield.

"What are you going to do?" the man asked Ham.

"Ask God to kill you," Ham matter-of-factly replied.

When the man protested, Ham said, "Why not? You don't believe there is a God, so my prayer shouldn't trouble you."

At that point, the man begged Ham not to pray that prayer.

"All right," Ham said. "I shall pray for God to save you."

The two knelt in the cornfield and the man gave his life to Christ. Before the revival concluded, the man brought his entire family to be baptized into Christ.

Ham worked with local churches whenever he held meetings. When he swept into town, Ham preached first to Christians to get their hearts right with God, and then asked them to bring family and friends to the revival meetings. It proved to be an effective strategy, as meetings were packed and many responded to the invitation to accept Christ.

As Ham traveled from church to church in the early 1900s, one of the pressing issues was prohibition. In city after city where Ham held revivals, citizens voted to outlaw liquor.

"Liquor is a lecher that feeds on communities that tolerate it," Ham said.

He was so violently opposed to liquor that sometimes he was threatened, even accosted. Local police frequently had to protect him and his family from drunken mobs.

Though Ham was ridiculed for his evangelistic efforts and public stand favoring prohibition, he continued to win the lost wherever he went. Between 1929 and 1941, Ham held 61 revivals in 15 states and saw 168,550 people won to Christ. After ending the tent meetings in 1941, when he was 64, Ham continued an extensive radio outreach and local speaking engagements until his death in December 1961.

HEROES OF THE FAITH

Richard Wurmbrand

By Ruth Schenk

> *Persecution has not, nor ever will be, foreign to the church on this earth.*
> —Richard Wurmbrand
> (1909–2001)

When Richard Wurmbrand testified before Congress in 1966, Senator Christopher Dodd asked the Romanian pastor to take off his shirt. By then, the committee had heard a few details of the 14 years the Romanian pastor spent in prison for preaching the Gospel. They knew he'd been in solitary confinement in a cell just three steps wide for three years, and they knew he'd been tortured. But knowing and seeing evidence of that torture were two different things. When Richard removed his shirt, members of Congress saw scars where he had been beaten and stabbed, evidence of broken bones that didn't heal, burns and wounds.

He could have left prison at any time—if he would have given authorities the names of Christians and agreed to stop preaching. But he wouldn't—no matter the cost.

Telling the Story

Richard and his wife Sabina were atheists with a Marxist bent when they visited a small German village and met Christian Wolfkes, a Romanian Christian carpenter, who prayed for the chance to tell someone about Jesus. Their lives changed that day as they understood sin and salvation. From then on, their one goal was telling others about Jesus.

During World War II, they reached out to German soldiers, even though Sabina's family perished in concentration camps. They preached in bomb shelters and rescued Jewish children from the ghettos.

When Soviet troops moved into Romania in 1944, the Wurmbrands began a ministry to Communist soldiers. Richard ministered to oppressed countrymen, and he shared the Gospel with Russian soldiers. When the government tried to control the church, be began an "underground" network of believers. In 1945, Romanian Communists seized power, and more than a million Russian troops occupied the country.

Every conversation about faith was risky. Anyone caught evangelizing was arrested and put in prison.

Richard was arrested on his way to church in February, 1948. For years, his family did not know if he were dead or alive. Most of the time, he was, in fact, barely alive.

Hunger took a toll as prison rations consisted of a piece of bread and dirty soup. Often prisoners had to stand day and night for weeks at a time. They were hung upside down for beatings or put in a refrigerator cell so cold that frost and ice covered inside walls. When guards saw that prisoners were close to freezing to death, they took them out of the cells and warmed them up, then put them back in the refrigerator again.

There were no Bibles, books or visits with family.

There was no violence in one of the cruelest tortures. A few times, guards told prisoners they'd see their families and allowed them to shave and get a shower. They put them in a special room to wait. They waited and waited but no one ever came. At the end of the day, guards told them no one wanted to see them, not even their wives or children.

In 1950, Sabina also was thrown in prison where the women were used as slaves to dig a canal. That left the Wurmbrands' son, nine-year-old Mihai, homeless and alone. Anyone who helped the little boy also was beaten and thrown in prison. He started working at eleven years old.

Richard said he often was too sick and weak to pray in prison.

"All I could say was, 'Jesus, I love you,'" he wrote in *Tortured for Christ*, a book that has reached millions and been translated into sixty-five languages.

The scope of suffering in Romanian prisons included hundreds of peasant boys and girls because of their faith, priests and rabbis.

Richard was released in 1956 after eight and a half years in prison with the warning never to preach again. Despite that threat and knowing what he would suffer if arrested, he began working with Christians in the underground church. Freedom lasted just three years, until a friend's betrayal in 1959 led to his arrest and sentence of another twenty-five years in prison.

Richard said the second sentence was harder than the first.

"My second imprisonment was in many ways worse than the first,"

Wurmbrand wrote. "I knew what to expect. My physical condition became very bad almost immediately. But we continued the work of the underground church wherever we could—in Communist prisons."

Preaching in prison wasn't tolerated.

"A number of us decided to pay the price for the privilege of preaching, so we accepted their terms," Richard wrote. "It was a deal: we preached and they beat us. We were happy preaching; they were happy beating us—so everyone was happy."

Richard said that many times guards burst in while one of the prisoners was preaching and hauled him down to their beating room. Later, they brought him back bloody and bruised. Slowly, he picked up his battered body, straightened his clothes and said, "Now, brethren, where did I leave off when I was interrupted?" And he continued preaching.

Prisoners who had nothing decided to tithe their meager food rations. Every tenth week, they gave their slice of bread to weaker prisoners as a tithe to Christ.

Doctors said there was no medical reason why Richard survived fourteen years in prison.

"According to our medical books, you are dead. If you are alive, then the One in whom we don't believe has kept you alive," they said.

When Wurmbrand was granted amnesty and released in 1964, friends donated funds to send him away from Romania until it was safe to return. When he left Romania, communist soldiers told Richard that they could get a gangster to kill him at any time. From exile, he supported suffering Christians around the world by telling their story and raising financial and legal aid for their families.

Since he founded Voice of the Martyrs, fourteen nations have been released and today are places where Christians are free to live their faith without fear. In forty nations, Christians still suffer. Five countries—Cuba, North Korea, China, Vietnam and Ethiopia—have been on the Voice of the Martyr's restricted-nation list for more than thirty years.

How did suffering affect the Romanian church? The Wurmbrands returned to Romania in 1989 when Nicolae Ceausescu fell from power. In twenty years of persecution, the church grew 300 percent.

To learn more about persecution around the world, go to www. persecution.com.

Special Services Registry

The forms on the following pages are designed to be duplicated and used repeatedly as needed. Most copy machines will allow you to enlarge them to fill a full page if desired.

Sermons Preached

Date	Text	Title/Subject

Sermons Preached

Date   Text   Title/Subject

Sermons Preached

Date	Text	Title/Subject

Sermons Preached

Date	Text	Title/Subject

Sermons Preached

Date	Text	Title/Subject

Marriages Log

Date	Bride	Groom

Marriages Log

Date	Bride	Groom

Funerals Log

Date	Name of Deceased	Scripture Used

Funerals Log

Date	Name of Deceased	Scripture Used

Baptisms/Confirmations

Date	Name	Notes

Baby Dedication Registration

Infant's Name: _____

Significance of Given Names: _____

Date of Birth: _____

_____

Siblings: _____

_____

_____

_____

Maternal Grandparents: _____

Paternal Grandparents: _____

Life Verse: _____

Date of Dedication: _____

Wedding Registration

Date of Wedding: _____

Location of Wedding: _____

Bride: _____

    Religious Affiliation: _____

    Bride's Parents: _____

Groom: _____

    Religious Affiliation: _____

    Groom's Parents: _____

Ceremony to Be Planned by Minister: _____ By Couple: _____

Other Minister(s) Assisting: _____

Maid/Matron of Honor: _____

Best Man: _____

Wedding Planner: _____

Date of Rehearsal: _____

Reception Open to All Wedding Guests: _____ By Invitation Only: _____

Location of Reception: _____

Wedding Photos to Be Taken: _____ During Ceremony

                                        _____ After Ceremony

Other: _____

Date of Counseling: _____

Date of Registration: _____

Funeral Registration

Name of Deceased: _____

Age: _____

Religious Affiliation: _____

Survivors: _____

    Spouse: _____

    Parents: _____

    Children: _____

    Siblings: _____

    Grandchildren: _____

Date of Death: _____

Time and Place of Visitation: _____

Date of Funeral or Memorial Service: _____

Funeral Home Responsible: _____

Location of Funeral or Memorial Service: _____

Scripture Used: _____ Hymns Used: _____

Eulogy by: _____

Other Minister(s) Assisting: _____

Pallbearers: _____

_____

Date of Interment: _____ Place of Interment: _____

Graveside Service: _____ No _____

Scripture Index